M.

F

The Social Psychology of Mental Health

The Social Psychology of Mental Health

Basic Mechanisms and Applications

Edited by
DIANE N. RUBLE
PHILIP R. COSTANZO
MARY ELLEN OLIVERI

THE GUILFORD PRESS
New York   London

© 1992 The Guilford Press
A Division of Guilford Publications, Inc.
72 Spring Street, New York, NY 10012

Printed in the United States of America

This book is printed on acid-free paper.

Last digit is print number: 9 8 7 6 5 4 3 2 1

Library of Congress Cataloging-in-Publication Data

The Social psychology of mental health: basic mechanisms
  and applications / edited by Diane N. Ruble,
Philip R. Costanzo, Mary Ellen Oliveri.
        p.   cm.
  Includes bibliographical references and index.
  ISBN 0-89862-136-4
  1. Mental health—Social aspects.   2. Mental health—Social
aspects—Research. Social psychiatry.   I. Ruble, Diane N.
II. Costanzo, Philip R.   III. Oliveri, Mary Ellen.
  [DNLM: 1. Mental Health.   2. Psychology,.
Social.   HM 251 S6795]
RA790.S6125   1992
155.9'2—dc20
DNLM/DLC
for Library of Congress   92-1540
                                                            CIP

CONTRIBUTORS

JOSHUA M. ARONSON, PhD candidate, Department of Psychology, Princeton University, Princeton, N.J.

M. ELIZABETH BENNETT, PhD, Assistant Professor, University of Pittsburgh School of Dental Medicine, University of Pittsburgh, Pa.

GARY G. BERNTSON, PhD, Professor, Department of Psychology, Ohio State University, Columbus

JOHN T. CACIOPPO, PhD, Professor, Department of Psychology, Ohio State University, Columbus

MARGARET S. CLARK, PhD, Professor, Department of Psychology, Carnegie-Mellon University, Pittsburgh, Pa.

JOEL COOPER, PhD, Professor, Department of Psychology, Princeton University, Princeton, N.J.

PHILIP R. COSTANZO, PhD, Chair and Professor, Department of Psychology, Social and Health Science, Duke University, Durham, N.C.

KAY DEAUX, PhD, Professor, Department of Psychology, City University of New York Graduate Center, New York

SUSAN GORE, PhD, Professor, Department of Sociology, University of Massachusetts, Boston

E. TORY HIGGINS, PhD, Professor, Department of Psychology, Columbia University, New York

JAMES M. JONES, PhD, Professor, Department of Psychology, University of Delaware, Newark

JOHN M. LEVINE, PhD, Professor, Department of Psychology, University of Pittsburgh, Pa.

RICHARD L. MORELAND, PhD, Professor, Department of Psychology, University of Pittsburgh, Pa.

MARY ELLEN OLIVERI, PhD, Chief, Personality and Social Processes Research Branch, Division of Basic Brain and Behavioral Sciences, National Institute of Mental Health, Rockville, Md.

DIANE N. RUBLE, PhD, Professor, Department of Psychology, New York University, New York

ERIK P. THOMPSON, PhD candidate, Department of Psychology, New York University, New York

This volume is an outgrowth of a series of workshops supported and organized by the National Institute of Mental Health (NIMH) from 1987 to 1990. Most important, it represents the culmination of the scientific efforts of an advisory panel that convened twice during 1989 and 1990, with the aim of clarifying, refining, and elaborating the contribution of basic social psychological research to the solution of major mental health problems. The panel was chaired by Diane Ruble and Philip Costanzo; in addition to the contributors to this volume, it also involved the efforts of Claude Steele of Stanford University, and Elizabeth Breckinridge and Rodney Cocking of NIMH. Stephen Koslow, director of the Division of Basic Brain and Behavioral Sciences at NIMH, was helpful in providing support for the panel's meetings. Indirectly, this effort also owes a debt to previous advisory panels, convened during 1987 and 1988, which, through their deliberations, made clear the critical place of social psychological phenomena in any comprehensive explanation of the etiology, maintenance, and cure of mental disorders.[1]

The contributions of basic social psychological research to the understanding of human behavior have been fundamental and impressive. NIMH has provided support for a significant portion of this landmark research, spanning a range of topical areas including the dynamics of interpersonal relationships, the influence of social factors on cognition, and the operation of attitudes, expectancies, prejudice, and stigma. Nonetheless, the realization has come that the potential of this field to contribute to the solution of mental health problems needs to be tapped more fully and in a more focused way. Targeted applications of knowledge from this rich and varied field of study are sorely needed in a range of critical mental health problem areas that constitute major social

[1]Participants in these previous efforts included Jonathan Baron, Marilynn Brewer, John Cacioppo, Richard Davidson, Glen Elder, John Kihlstrom, Walter Kintsch, Lewis Lipsitt, Martha McClintock, Anne Petersen, Robert Plomin, David Reiss, Arnold Sameroff, Joy Schulterbrandt, Stephen Suomi, and William Swann.

policy issues, such as homelessness, AIDS, and the unique difficulties facing economically deprived, rural, and minority
populations. The need for contributions of social psychological
perspectives, however, extends beyond these special populations
and issues. Social psychological expertise—the analysis of the behavior of individuals in the social world—must be applied to
understanding the etiology, maintenance, treatment, and prevention of a broad range of conditions (e.g., depression, conduct disturbance, anxiety disorders) that affect the entire population and
that unfold and are expressed and treated in a social context.

Accelerated progress in these important areas will best be
served by a research agenda that addresses multiple sources of
influence on behavior, ranging from biological to societal factors.
Recent findings of biological influences in mental disorder, while
illuminating, need to be complemented and elaborated by contextual approaches to both etiology and treatment. It is also critical to consider multiple directions of influence. For example, in
addition to understanding social factors involved in the development of a disorder, it is critical to assess the effects that the
severity, type, and expression of the disorder have on the immediate social context (families and other close relationships).
This latter kind of assessment contributes to understanding the
burdens that mental disorder places on families and also offers
insights into therapeutic efforts that involve families as a part of
treatment.

Since the subject matter of social psychological research concerns the interface of individuals with society, this perspective is
ideally positioned to foster broadly cross-disciplinary research.
Thus, it is hoped that one result of this volume will be an expansion of interdisciplinary efforts in both research and research
training, particularly efforts that explore the interrelationships
and interactions among social, psychological, and biological processes. Important linkages that need to be fostered, for example,
include the joining of basic social psychological perspectives with
clinical research and practice, research on educational and health
care systems, research on cultural and societal processes that
affect mental health, and the study of neurobiological and physiological contributors to mental health and disorder.

This volume has two explicit objectives. The first is to clarify
and demonstrate the significance of basic social psychological
research to major problems in mental health. This aim is not
restricted to showing the applicability of the social psychological
perspective to clinical issues such as diagnosis, treatment, or pre-

vention, although these are extremely valuable applications. More broadly, the intention is to document the substantive relevance of social psychological research to understanding the basic processes underlying mental health and disorder. Since the relationship between basic research and mental health application is seen as a two-way street, the authors of this volume intend not only to detail how basic research in this area can help elucidate mental health problems, but also to demonstrate how a mental health problem may serve as a stimulus for a basic research question, and how the conceptualization and design of basic research may be influenced and shaped by mental health issues. The second objective follows the first and is to encourage, by example, researchers in the field to heighten and solidify the significance of their own research to mental health.

The intended audience of this volume is varied: In addition to investigators in social psychology and sociology and their students, we hope that the book will capture the attention of scientific colleagues in neighboring academic disciplines, clinical investigators, and professionals in both public and private funding agencies. Clearly, the talents and efforts of professionals with a range of backgrounds and training will be needed to capitalize on the tremendous potential, for mental health, of this important and productive research field.

As this book makes clear, the possible areas of scientific reward are numerous and varied. In anticipation, consider only a few of the substantive questions that describe the unique contribution of the social psychological perspective to research in mental health:

- What are the roles of labeling and stigmatizing processes in maintaining mental illness?
- What aspects of social development and social structure underlie gender differences in the incidence of mental disorder and in treatment response?
- What are the ways in which social interaction influences and modifies information processing?
- What are the interpersonal mechanisms involved in successful therapies for mental illness?
- What are the mechanisms by which cultural variations in the incidence and nature of mental illness are mediated?
- What social-psychophysiological mechanisms underlie the relationships among stress, social support, and mental and physical health?

- What is the role in psychotherapeutic effectiveness of small-group processes such as status formation, conflict, power, coalition behavior, social influence, and group cohesion?
- What processes of self-definition and self-evaluation mediate the influence of social stigma on mental health?
- What are the roles of attributional and other social–constructive processes in influencing the outcome of a variety of stressful events and circumstances? What developmental, societal, and family differences exist in these processes and their effects?

It is hoped that these kinds of questions, plus many more, will serve as a challenge for the field of social psychology and for related disciplines, and that they will define a productive agenda for mental health research in the '90s and beyond.

Mary Ellen Oliveri
Rockville, Md.

C O N T E N T S

The Social Psychology of Mental Health

Social Psychological Foundations of Mental Health

DIANE N. RUBLE, PHILIP E. COSTANZO, and E. TORY HIGGINS

The social issues of the '90s are serious and extraordinarily complex. They include homelessness, AIDS, racism, adolescent suicide, divorce, and poverty, as well as the mental health problems that have been with us for years—anxiety disorders, alcoholism, schizophrenia, depression. The nature and intricacies of these problems require a multifaceted, interdisciplinary attack (see Cacioppo & Berntson, Chapter 11, this volume). The goal of this chapter is to describe the special nature of a social psychological analysis in solving these problems, and to examine some core social psychological processes that are central to understanding issues relevant to mental health.

THE UNIQUE CONTRIBUTION OF SOCIAL PSYCHOLOGY

The Questions Social Psychologists Ask

Contemporary social psychology is for the most part *not* explicitly concerned with practical application. By its very nature, however, social psychology addresses issues that underlie some of the most troubling questions of the day: What leads to the breakdown in social support and societal altruism that contributes to homelessness? When does education to control the spread of AIDS work and when does it fail? Why do suicide-prone adolescents continue to feel that they are inadequate even when they receive extensive feedback to the contrary?

Social psychology also focuses on a set of topics or outcomes, such as interpersonal conflict, self-esteem, and stigmatization, that seem conspicuously central to a better understanding of mental health. Many would argue, however, that what makes social psychology a crucial partner in the mental health problem-solving enterprise is its level of analysis (Pettigrew, 1988). Social psychology, as a discipline, is concerned with the processes that mediate the effects of the social environment on adaptive outcomes, such as self-esteem, often assumed to be closely linked to mental health. Other disciplines, such as sociology and much of developmental psychology, make important contributions by showing *which* environmental conditions (e.g., job strain, family environment, developmental transitions) are most closely linked to mental health outcomes (for examples, see Costanzo, Chapter 3, Gore, Chapter 2, and Ruble & Thompson, Chapter 4, this volume). Social psychology focuses on *when* and *how* these interrelations occur.[1]

Understanding why a phenomenon or interrelation occurs is crucial to problem solving because it provides a specific rationale for prevention and intervention attempts—going beyond the targeting of the problem population (e.g., divorcing couples) to say what should be done. To illustrate, we know that being embedded in social networks and perceiving that one has social support available is related to mental health (see Gore, Chapter 2, this volume). Can this knowledge be readily used by mental health practitioners in useful ways? Does it allow us to identify who will be at risk for mental health problems? Will it allow us to devise programs to prevent mental health problems? Will it allow us to devise strategies to intervene in mental health problems when they occur? Perhaps, but we argue that this knowledge alone is not sufficient. Knowing that social connections and social supports are associated with positive mental health outcomes can only lead to encouraging people to become embedded in supportive social networks. That might be good advice, but it cannot tell people how to form positive and rewarding social connections. What will draw people toward us? What contributes to making a relationship warm and supportive? What causes relationships to produce strain in one's life? What causes relationships to deteriorate? If we can answer these questions, we are in a much better position to apply our knowledge in the form of specific interventions. Here is where we believe work by social psychologists will prove especially important. Examining interpersonal processes is precisely the level at which social psychologists conduct their research (see Clark & Bennett, Chapter 6, this volume).

The effective application of social psychological theory to problems of mental health is more than mere potential (see, e.g., Fazio, 1990). It is, in fact, the basis for much of today's clinical treatment as evidenced in the success of cognitive–behavioral therapies. This approach assumes that depressed individuals have erroneous negative beliefs, such as pessimistic expectations for the future, and engage in biased information processing, such as seeking information to confirm their view of themselves as incompetent. The development of these therapies has drawn explicitly from social psychological analyses of attribution processes and social information processing (e.g., Dykman & Abramson, 1990; Hollon & Garber, 1990). For example, therapists may attempt to modify their clients' explanations for their distress in ways that are less damaging than those the clients currently use, consistent with one of Ross's (1977) three principles for changing existing beliefs (Hollon & Garber, 1990).

Another illustration involves strategies for reducing AIDS-related risk behavior. There has been considerable activity by social psychologists examining the social influence and attitudinal factors involved in the transmission of the virus (Fisher, 1988; Jones, 1988). Descriptive studies suggest that adolescents are particularly important target populations because they have high rates of other sexually transmitted diseases and are not highly knowledgeable about or motivated to take precautions (O'Keeffe, Nesselhof-Kendall, & Baum, 1990). How can their sexual attitudes and risk-relevant behaviors be changed?

Current approaches to persuasion research have identified a number of important principles that can be used to approach this question. For example, recent theories suggest that both motivation and knowledge are key to analyzing the effects of persuasive messages (Chaiken, 1980; Petty & Cacioppo, 1986). According to Chaiken's heuristic model, simple, superficial modes of processing information are likely to be used by populations low in motivation or knowledge about an issue. A particularly effective heuristic device involves the source of the information—for example, choosing one who is likable and attractive for the target population. Thus, initial attempts at persuasion directed at these groups might use popular personalities, such as Madonna, or clean-living sports figures, such as Michael Jordan, to present the messages (O'Keeffe et al., 1990). Yet, this research also suggests that attitudinal change based on heuristic processing or peripheral cues is more

susceptible to counterpersuasion than is attitudinal change based
on systematic or central route processing (Petty & Cacioppo, 1986).
Alternative or second-phase attempts at persuasion might be directed toward increasing motivation to process information about
risky sexual practices in detail.[2]

The chapters in this volume offer many other examples. More
generally, as Pettigrew (1988) notes, social psychologists' focus on
manipulable situational variables provides a particularly useful
approach to practical problems, because it is easier and more
ethical to change situations than to change people. Such interventions can take the form of either altering the actual situation or
altering the individual's perception or construction of it.

Relation to the Biological Level of Analysis

A second aspect of level of analysis concerns the distinction between social and biological levels of organization (Cacioppo &
Berntson, Chapter 11, this volume)—that is, where on the hierarchy from macro- to microlevels of analysis the primary focus lies.
The "Decade of the Brain" publicity has called attention to research on mental health and disorder and creates a belief that such
problems are solvable. But are they solvable at the biological,
behavioral, or societal level? Much of the attention so far has
focused on progress made in neuroscience and genetics, perhaps,
in part, because breakdowns in mental health are often construed
as having antecedents in bodily disease, subject largely to biomed-
ical analyses and cures. Yet, there is growing evidence that some
forms of psychotherapy are at least as effective as drugs in the
treatment of many forms of depression and anxiety disorders
(Robinson, Berman, & Neimeyer, 1990). Indeed they may even be
more resistant to recidivism (Hollon & Garber, 1990), and they
have the added benefit of cure without the side effects of drugs.

Other findings suggest how important it is that a medical
model of mental health not operate in isolation from cultural and
situational contexts. Further, it is quite difficult for researchers to
establish the primacy of biological versus functional factors in
mental health and illness. Indeed, research by Kleinman (1988)
suggests that different cultures may show quite different manifestations of the same underlying state. In his comparison of the
United States and China, for example, he found a dramatically
different frequency in the relative diagnoses of depression and
neurasthenia-chronic pain. The more affective diagnosis of depression is common in the United States but not in China, whereas the

reverse is true for diagnoses of neurasthenia-chronic pain. Klein-man's research suggests, however, that the two are really just different cultural construals of the same phenomenon. Expression of dysphoria—sadness or melancholia—is less acceptable to the self and family in China than in the United States, and thus the individual focuses on the somatic rather than the affective symptoms. A similar, though less dramatic, difference is observed in the representation of depression in the United States, with females more likely to emphasize dysphoria and males more likely to emphasize insomnia, digestive disorders, and other more behavioral or somatic complaints.

A second illustration comes from a cultural perspective on premenstrual syndrome (PMS). Depression and irritability are symptoms typically associated with menstrual distress in the Anglo culture, but less so in other cultures, such as Hispanic. It is thus quite intriguing that during the transition to junior high school, an increase in menstrual-related negative affect was reported by Anglo girls but not by Hispanic girls (Maluf & Ruble, 1992). Is this PMS or is it the usual stress reaction observed to accompany this kind of transition? If treatment is called for, should it be for PMS, depression, or school variables? In this case, it seems likely that the negative affect generated in response to a stressful transition was misattributed to a salient possible cause for Anglo girls, namely, PMS (Ruble, 1989).

Such findings illustrate why a medical model of mental health operating without an understanding of basic social psychological mechanisms can be misleading. Clinical neuroscientific research must rely to some extent on the individual's own representation of his or her affective state, and this representation depends heavily on nonbiological factors. Identical symptoms may reflect quite different underlying states, and different symptoms may reflect the same state. Such diagnostic confusion obviously complicates attempts to identify physiological precursors and treatments.

Contribution of Social Psychology as a Level of Analysis

Even among social psychologists there is a common belief that sooner or later mental health problems will be solved in the same way that physical health problems are solved—through biological or "medical" intervention. From this perspective, the value of social psychology for mental health is that the "medical" solutions for many mental health problems, especially affective and behavioral disorders, are likely to come later rather than sooner. Thus, for now "social-psychologically"-based interventions are useful and even necessary. At some point, however, a "magic pill" will make such interventions superfluous.

The notion that a "magic pill" could in the future eradicate emotional suffering is appealing, but there are numerous problems with this notion. First, an affective disorder, like any psychological object, is not a single phenomenon. Rather, there are different phenomena at different levels of analysis, and each level of analysis reveals different properties. Combining certain ingredients can produce specific "culinary" properties of a "sauce" at one level of analysis, or it can produce specific "chemical" properties of a "compound" at another level of analysis. The level of analysis appropriate to consider depends on the issue to be addressed or the problem to be solved. Water is composed of hydrogen and oxygen, but when putting out fires, it is the properties of water as a particular kind of liquid that matter rather than the properties of the molecule H_2O, never mind the properties of hydrogen or oxygen per se.

The optimum approach, then, is to find solutions for each problem identified at each level of analysis. Thus, even were a "magic pill" invented, it would only provide a solution to one problem—the problem identified at the "medical" level of analysis. The problems defined at other levels of analysis would continue to require their own solutions. To this extent, then, there will always be a need for "social" solutions to "social" problems. For example, the intergenerational perpetuation of parental abuse of children may be based on certain underlying biological similarities within families and between generations. However, the enabling social conditions and beliefs that give rise to a context of interpersonal agonism must, at the very least, be seen as potentiating biological links.

A second drawback to seeking a "magic pill" whose biochemical properties would eradicate "symptoms" is that such an approach does not appreciate the function of the symptoms themselves. The distress of an affective disorder, for example, may be required to orient and motivate a person to take the kinds of actions and make the kind of effort necessary to change the personal and interpersonal conditions responsible for the disorder. By removing the temporary symptoms and their pressure to change, the opportunity to modify the underlying maladaptive system and make long-term improvements may be lost.

More generally, a disadvantage of the "symptoms" approach is that by focusing on the more observable "costs" of an underlying regulatory system, it can overlook less apparent "benefits" of the system. There are often trade-offs to any regulatory system. For example, increasing the motivation to meet a standard of excellence increases the intensity of the negative evaluation of any failure to meet the standard, producing strong negative affect. But increasing the motivation to meet a standard also increases the likelihood that the standard will be met, producing strong positive affect. During some period an individual may be failing to meet a standard and experiencing negative affect. A "magic pill" or medical intervention that altered the regulatory system to reduce the negative affect might also alter the potential of that system to produce success and positive affect.

Third, the "magic pill" notion is limited to attempting to correct an existing problem, to removing current symptoms. But what about preventing the problem in the first place or promoting future positive outcomes? Mental health systems should enhance adaptive functioning in every way possible and not just treat constant negative outcomes. This can only be accomplished by understanding the underlying regulatory system, its changing costs and benefits over time, and its interaction with both constant and changing social contexts, including a variety of social forces (Mirowsky & Ross, 1989).

Consider the impact of the immediate context, for example. The current negative influence of a regulatory system may result from a temporary set of circumstances. What may need to be changed for the system to produce positive outcomes are the circumstances—not the underlying regulatory system. Indeed, life transitions or shifts from one stage to another might change the circumstances sufficiently for the same regulatory system to produce positive rather than negative outcomes. Intervening medically because the current outcomes are negative could reduce the likelihood of positive outcomes when the circumstances change.

Considering the role of situations raises a more fundamental point. Whether or not symptoms per se are emphasized, the medical model treats the patient as the site of both the problem and the solution. In social psychological terms, the medical model makes a "person" attribution concerning the location of the affective disorder. But affective disorders, like all complex psychological phenomena, involve multiple person–situation relations. From the intensity and persistence of the symptoms alone, it is not possible to assess the relative contribution to the disorder of person versus situation variables. It may be that the contribution of the person's specific characteristics is relatively minor in a particular case. But whether the person-specific contribution is minor, moderate, or major, the intervention will proceed as if the person contributed all of the variance. Thus, there is a potential risk of overintervention toward the person. It is like removing the wilting leaves of a plant rather than watering its soil.

The limitations and disadvantages of the medical model for intervening in complex psychological phenomena are perhaps more obvious when one considers other kinds of "social" problems, such as poor reading. The "problem" of poor reading can also be identified at multiple levels. It may be that a child cannot see the words clearly, or that many of the words are meaningless, or that the child does not want to read, or that the child has little opportunity to read. Each level of problem is best solved with an intervention at that level, such as providing glasses to children who cannot see properly, providing instruction to children for whom words are meaningless, selecting more personally relevant reading material for children who do not want to read, or providing additional reading resources to schools for children who have little opportunity to read. Although some children who read poorly do have a physical problem, most do not. For most children who read poorly a medical intervention would seem unreasonable or even bizarre. It is recognized that the problem is mostly some interaction between the cognitive–motivational characteristics of the child and the characteristics of the situation (including teachers, peers, reading material, and environment). It is not the symptoms of poor reading that are the target of intervention but the underlying person–situation characteristics that produce these symptoms.

Why not approach affective disorders like we approach poor reading? The answer seems to be that an affective disorder is considered more like a headache than a social problem. Mental health is associated with physical health, and physical health is typically approached from a biological level of analysis. The association between mental health and physical health is explicit historically in the field of psychiatry. In addition, the symptoms of mental disorders themselves include physical symptoms. Even the name "health" suggests a basic similarity. After all, one would not refer to a poor reader as an unhealthy reader. But an affective disorder is actually more like poor reading than it is like a headache. It involves a complex interaction between cognitive–motivational characteristics of the person and characteristics of the situation. In both cases it is an issue of self-regulation and social regulation, an issue of learning a complex set of skills and orientations. A social and psychological level of analysis is as useful and necessary to prevent or treat an affective disorder as to prevent or treat poor reading.

Enhancing the Relevance of Social Psychology

Why are social psychological contributions to mental health not sufficiently recognized? One reason is that the relevance of social psychological findings may not be obvious to clinicians and policymakers. Often basic social psychological research has few concrete features that suggest direct links to mental health. That is, the breakthroughs in social psychology are more abstract than in medicine and less easily conveyed. It is not possible to package innovations in the form of a pill or physical treatment as some ultimate sign of the success of the research. Moreover, social psychologists are often reluctant to move away from laboratory experiments with college students to test their theories in populations of more obvious clinical relevance. It is often very difficult to obtain appropriate samples for field studies or to deal with the numerous uncontrolled variables that accompany naturalistic or quasi-experimental designs (Argyle, 1980). Second, researchers tend not to highlight the mental health relevance of their own work. Abstracts of recent social psychology applications funded by the National Institute of Mental Health (NIMH) often do not discuss mental health relevance, even when the relevance is clear and direct. Finally, as Pettigrew (1988) notes, in the '50s a more theoretical, individually oriented wing of social psychology split from the more applied, group-oriented tradition of Kurt Lewin, and this wing later became dominant. At that point, social psychology as a field did not develop links to relevant policy networks, nor did it learn how the policy process evolves. As a consequence, social psychologists often fail to extend promising "basic mechanism" research to mental health-related populations or problems.

How could the contribution of social psychology to mental health problems be more effective? One of the most promising approaches is to foster research that involves a true integration of basic and applied concerns. This could be done in several ways: (1) promoting collaborative projects between basic researchers and clinicians or other mental health professionals; (2) providing special postdoctoral training for basic researchers in applied field or clinical settings (and vice versa); and (3) stimulating a subset of basic researchers to use prevention–intervention techniques as one means of testing their theories.

Such activities would represent a renewed, rather than a brand-new, interest in public policy. Historically, social psychology grew out of a concern about social issues and was often conducted in field settings, such as the surge of activity on applied war problems by social psychologists during World War II (Jackson, 1988). This was the position represented by the action research strategy of Lewin, who argued that our understanding of basic theoretical processes is enhanced by attempts to solve practical problems (Lewin, 1944/1951).[3]

Like Lewin, many contemporary social psychologists are recognizing and advocating the benefits for theoretical development of considering policy implications (Rodin, 1985). Collaborative efforts and new training will lead mental health professionals to a greater awareness of the potential application of theoretically driven findings. Trying to think through the implications for prevention or intervention may raise new questions or identify gaps in knowledge about how certain processes work. As Hollon and Garber (1990) note, for example, trying to understand why cognitive therapies work raises a number of basic questions (e.g., "which aspects of cognition mediate which aspects of change?" [p. 63]). Similarly, Omoto and Snyder (1990) argue that theories of relationship development may require revision as researchers attempt to understand nontraditional relationships, such as those between people with AIDS and volunteer "buddies." Attempts to address such issues could proceed simultaneously with both problem-oriented and theoretical perspectives and, in so doing, be highly informative to both theory and application. This latter point is important, because social psychology can make its greatest contribution by maintaining its basic scientific approach. Acknowledging and capitalizing on the applied significance of its basic research findings and models (as we advocate in this volume) do not render social psychology as either an applied science or a domain of "practice." Instead, the problem focus enriches social psychology by providing a new context within which to test basic theoretical issues.

Of course, not all social psychologists are likely to involve themselves directly in problem-focused collaborations. Other approaches could involve fostering communication across disciplines, so that the relevance of social psychological theory and research is more available to applied researchers and clinicians. Such approaches might take the form of mutual exchanges at annual conventions or specialized meetings—for example, NIMH-sponsored workshops on particular problems, attendance at problem-oriented meetings and conventions, or premeetings at annual conventions (see Pettigrew, 1988, for additional suggestions).

SOCIAL PSYCHOLOGICAL MECHANISMS RELEVANT TO MENTAL HEALTH

In addition to asking *how* to enhance the contribution of social psychology to mental health application, we must consider *what* areas or issues are most promising. The chapters in this volume consider this question with respect to different content areas within the discipline. In this chapter, we consider more generally how such a question might be approached, in regard to social psychological mediators or mechanisms. That is, as raised earlier, what are the specific mechanisms that link environmental context and background variables to mental health outcomes?

An illustrative model of social psychological mediation is shown in Figure 1.1. The model depicts the kinds of mechanisms that social psychologists study as mediating the impact of distal, antecedent forces, such as socialization, on direct precursors of

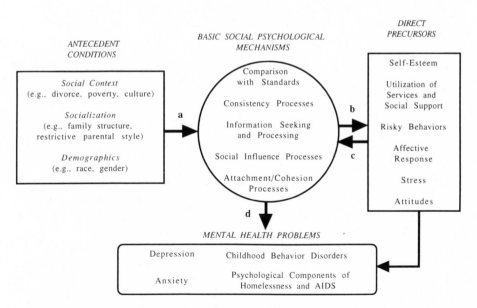

FIGURE 1.1. Mediating role of social psychological mechanisms in the study of mental health issues.

mental health outcomes, such as declines in self-esteem or the experience of stress. The mental health outcomes identified in the figure illustrate the social and mental health problems of current concern. The specific mediating processes listed (e.g., consistency processes) are those identified in the following chapters as some of the most central to understanding the link between distal forces and mental health outcomes. The particular processes represented in the figure should not be considered exhaustive but rather a list of some of the very important and pervasive processes that social psychologists have examined. (More extensive and in-depth presentations of social psychological mechanisms will be available in Higgins & Kruglanski, 1992.)

As shown in Figure 1.1, a process analysis can operate at two stages in relating antecedent forces, such as marital status, parental disciplinary styles, or gender, to mental health outcomes. At an earlier stage, social psychological mechanisms may mediate the relation between antecedent conditions, such as family structure, and direct precursors, such as self-esteem (paths a and b). At a later stage, social psychological mechanisms may mediate the relation between precursors, such as self-esteem, and mental health outcomes (paths c and d). The issues examined in the following chapters represent both of these stages, although those at the earlier stage are more common. Examples of specific questions implicit in the chapters may help illustrate such distinctions. Questions at the earlier stage include:

1. What is it about the presence of social support, group therapy, or close relationships that bolsters self-esteem or reduces subjective stress (i.e., how do they act as buffers)? The chapters by Clark and Bennett, Cooper and Aronson, Gore, Higgins, and Levine and Moreland all raise questions of this type and refer to a number of possible mechanisms that may help explain these relations, such as information seeking and processing, positive reinforcement, observational learning, consistency–dissonance, and the effects of having an audience on self-perception. For example, social support may act as a stress buffer by helping to restructure the meaning of the situation or by providing information useful for gaining a sense of confidence or control.

2. How do processes involving stigmatization, group identification, and social roles affect self-esteem; when do changing roles contribute to subjective stress? Deaux, Gore, Higgins, Jones, Levine and Moreland, and Ruble and Thompson discuss a number of possible processes relating to such questions. These

include comparison with standards (e.g., reference groups), integration of the new identity with the old, role conflict, social influence, ingroup–outgroup processes, and construct accessibility.

3. What is it about the structure of school and family environments that affects feelings of self-confidence and personal control? Cooper and Aronson, Costanzo, Levine and Moreland, and Ruble and Thompson discuss such questions in terms of processes such as attitude formation, attribution, social influence, socialization and expectancy confirmation.

Finally, questions illustrative of a process analysis at the later stage include when and how the experience of stress, such as relationship dissatisfaction, leads to depression or how feelings of closeness, trust, and warmth help foster positive mental health outcomes. Clark and Bennett's chapter, among others, discusses a number of possible mediating processes, including comparison with standards and concepts of interdependence. Other possibilities include accessibility of positive versus negative thoughts, reward–punishment processes, reduction of anxiety, and so on. As an additional example, Cooper and Aronson show how the utilization of psychotherapy services may have positive mental health benefits partly because of effort justification (consistency) mechanisms.

Thus, social psychologists are studying a large number of mechanisms that may serve as mediators of mental health outcomes. Unfortunately, the fact that so many specific mechanisms are being examined may also create certain difficulties. One general conclusion deriving from our analysis of the existing literature is that similar processes are often studied under different labels and in different contexts. To illustrate the labeling aspect, self-fulfilling prophecies and behavior confirmation are different forms of expectancy mechanisms that share a number of common features. Similarly, it is not always clear that there are meaningful distinctions among the various labels that have been applied to mastery/control processes—learned helplessness, self-efficacy, self-directedness, attributional style, and so on (see Costanzo, Chapter 3). Progress in understanding the basic operation of such mechanisms and their implications might be faster if there was better integration across differing approaches to similar problems. To illustrate with regard to context, attributional processes have been studied across a wide variety of laboratory and field settings, such as marital relationships and peer interactions in children. Social psychology might enjoy a clearer sense of progress if findings and issues from one setting were integrated into approaches and interpretations in other settings in a common attempt at theory building. Similar illustrations arise in several of the following chapters (see, e. g., Higgins's [Chapter 8, this volume] derivation of comparison with standards as a basic process underlying numerous middle-level theories).

Identifying Core Processes

Although there is widespread agreement about the importance of trying to integrate data theoretically in terms of basic social psychological processes (Jackson, 1988; Kelley, 1983; Shaw & Costanzo, 1982), the field has not tended to work this way. Certainly, identifying the features of a set of core processes or "building blocks" underlying the variety of middle-level theories in social psychology is a daunting task. Yet, there have been a few attempts (Brickman, 1980; Jackson, 1988). An especially intriguing and ambitious approach to this task was proposed by McGuire (1980; 1985).

McGuire identified 16 "guiding-idea" theories, representing four dichotomized dimensions, two of which involve forces that initiate human action and two with forces that terminate it. The two major categories of initiation theories are "need for stability" and "need for growth," in which the action is initiated to keep things at some level of equilibrium (e.g., ego defensive theories) or to achieve actualization or a higher level of complexity (e.g., stimulation theories, such as curiosity drive). Within each of these two categories, a further dichotomization involves active versus reactive instigation (i.e., initiated by forces within the person or as a reaction to outside forces). The two major categories of termination theories involve a focus on cognitive versus affective state, in which action is initiated to satisfy a cognitive need (e.g., categorization) or an affective one (e.g., need for affiliation or power). Within each of these two categories, a further dichomization is whether the goal is with respect to an external or internal relationship—that is, involving internal aspects of the person versus a relationship between the self and the external environment.

To illustrate, one such guiding-idea theory is consistency, which McGuire represents as an active need for stability on the initiation side and an external cognitive focus on the termination side. That is, consistency theories (balance, dissonance, equity, etc.) portray individuals as actively attempting to maintain cognitive stability, and as terminating activity when an equilibrium between the self and their mental representations of the external world has occurred. Another guiding-idea theory, contagion (or imitation) is represented as a need for growth theory involving reactive instigation, and terminating when a new affective relationship among elements within the self has been attained. Middle-level theories within this category include modeling, social facilitation, and social learning.

One might quibble with McGuire's specific choice of dimensions and arrangement of theory types, but attempts like his seem critical for organizing the field in ways that optimize progress and utility. The authors of the chapters in the present volume attempted a similar exercise with respect to the processes proposed in the different chapters. Although we are not proposing a system as comprehensive or elegant as McGuire's, we did identify a relatively small set of mechanisms such as those shown in Figure 1.1. Our list differs from McGuire's because we focus on similarities in the processes themselves rather than in their goals. For example, comparison processes may serve either cognitive or affective goals, but the comparison mechanism is basically the same.

An Illustration: Consistency Processes

To illustrate the possible benefits of identifying a small set of core processes, we have selected one that appears both in McGuire's analysis and in multiple chapters in the present volume: consistency. This term is most closely associated with a particular set of attitudinal theories such as balance and dissonance, (see reviews by Abelson et al., 1968; Shaw & Costanzo, 1982; Wicklund & Brehm, 1976). We are using the term somewhat more broadly to refer to any process involved in helping maintain or reestablish consistency among psychological elements, and thus include theories in the expectancy domain, such as self-fulfilling prophecy, behavioral confirmation, and self-verification (see reviews by Darley & Fazio, 1980; Jussim, 1986; Miller & Turnbull, 1986).

Such processes are invoked in almost every chapter of this volume. Consistency processes are the favored explanation for certain types of socialization influences, such as internalization of valued standards that are consistent with labels (e.g., "helpful") or with behavior that has been subtly elicited (Grusec, 1983; Lepper, 1983). Socialization agents, such as parents and schools, also influence children by eliciting behavior that is in accordance with their expectations (Costanzo, Levine & Moreland, Ruble & Thompson, Chapters 3, 5, & 4, this volume). Similarly, such "self-fulfilling prophecies" are probably involved in the negative outcomes associated with economically disadvantaged groups, minorities, and stigmatized individuals (Deaux, Jones, Chapters 10 & 7, this volume). Such processes may work to the disadvantage of the therapeutic process to the extent that therapists confirm their diagnoses or that self-verification processes act in opposition to new identities being proposed (Deaux, Higgins, Chapters 10 & 8, this volume). One might also argue that consistency processes are partly involved in the well-documented phenomenon that social support can help bolster self-esteem during times of need (Clark & Bennett, Gore, Chapters 6 & 2, this volume) in that positive expectancies by the givers of support may function as self-fulfilling prophecies. Cooper and Aronson also show how processes that *reestablish* consistency (i.e., dissonance) may work as instigators of change, including change in the context of therapy.

What might we gain by a more focused orientation toward core, underlying theories, both in theoretical development and in their application to mental health? First, this enhanced orientation may highlight questions that are basic to the process but that have remained unresolved. Eagly and Chaiken (in press), for example, in their review of consistency theories, note that the question of *why* consistency is important has received little direct attention. That is, why is inconsistency or dissonance assumed (and often shown empirically) to lead to unpleasant psychological states and an attempt to reinstate consistency? Most analyses refer to the importance of the elements being linked in some cognitive organization (Shaw & Costanzo, 1982), with the implication that creation of imbalance or inconsistency among the elements leads the system to break down and create tension. According to Heider (1958), for example, factors that influence "unit formation," such as similarity or proximity, are critical. Other explanations involve predictability and control (Newcomb, 1953)—for example, that information consistent with self-conceptions generates confidence and security, whereas inconsistent information produces fear that one does not really know oneself (Swann, 1990).

These accounts are not fully satisfying, however. The perception of imbalance or inconsistency is not inevitably negative; it sometimes leads to pleasant states, such as humor or curiosity. Moreover, it remains to be convincingly demonstrated that the negative reaction reflects something intrinsic to the inconsistency itself or to something else. Are people motivated to maintain consistency between their behavior and their perception of their own characteristics or are they motivated to match valued standards of behavior (Higgins, Strauman, & Klein, 1986)? When children labeled "generous" in one situation respond with greater generosity in other situations (Grusec & Redler, 1980), is this necessarily a reflection of consistency striving? If this were the case, one would presumably need to show similar effects for children who label themselves "stingy," but this has not been demonstrated (Rholes, Newman, & Ruble, 1990). Similarly, a number of alternatives to dissonance effects have been proposed, such as self-enhancement or a fear of rejection for violating social norms (Bramel, 1968; Steele, 1988). Analogous alternatives are relevant to understanding expectancy confirmation effects. Efforts to confirm expectations, such as stereotypes, may be due to perceptions of how oneself or another individual *should* behave, rather than a need for consistency, per se. In role theory terms, this distinction is similar to that between normative and anticipatory expectations (Secord & Backman, 1964) and between prescribed and predicted role expectations (McDavid & Harari, 1968). That is, many "consistency" effects may really be responses to norms.

Arguments that the operating process is consistency striving are based on findings showing that attempts to restore consistency occur regardless of whether the restoration results in a positively or negatively valenced outcome (Aronson, 1968; Swann, 1990). For example, receiving positive feedback when one expected negative feedback should produce a negative reaction only if the individual is driven by consistency (Aronson & Carlsmith, 1962). Such findings are rarely observed, however (Dipboye, 1977). Furthermore, the more compelling findings by Swann (1990) showing consistency strivings even when the outcome is negative may also be partially explained by processes other than the need for consistency per se. People are sometimes quite invested in their negative characteristics for functional reasons. One spouse may disavow any capability in the area of cooking or child care, whereas the other may be content with mechanical incompetence. It would be more surprising to find individuals striving to verify negative conclusions in areas in which competence was personally important, however, and, indeed, this does appear less likely (Pelham, 1991; Swann, 1990).

An orientation toward core, underlying theories may also highlight the relevance of mechanisms that have previously gone unrecognized. Consider, for example, the fact that many forms of consistency theories, notably dissonance, involve notions of arousal and tension reduction as key mediators, whereas others, such as balance restoration and expectancy confirmation, do not. Is it possible that the tension-reduction constructs might be usefully applied with respect to expectancies in certain situations? Indeed, might some of the same variables that have been shown to moderate dissonance effects, such as commitment, be informative in research on expectancies? Recent analyses of expectancy processes (Jussim, 1986; Jones, 1990) have discussed variables that are in line with this suggestion.

The basic point of the above discussion is that a joint consideration of dissonance and expectancy literatures raises fundamental questions about when consistency needs are likely to be paramount, why consistency is important, and how it functions. Some promising directions include (1) the idea that desire for consistency may vary, such that negative reactions to inconsistency may occur only for a subset of individuals (Aronson, 1968; Eisenberg, Cialdini, McCreath, & Shell, 1987); (2) analyses of contextual factors that lead to variations in consistency striving or reactions to inconsistency (Hackel & Ruble, 1992; Jussim, 1986; Swann, 1990); and (3) the idea that consistency is uniquely related to the *development* of an individuated and intrinsic identity (see Costanzo, Chapter 3, this volume). More generally, the present analysis suggests that to fully understand the operation of consistency maintenance processes and gain control over it for preventive and therapeutic interventions, accounting for the different ways the process may operate across settings, content, and time should help us bring some order to this core theoretical process.

ORGANIZATION OF THE VOLUME

The following chapters illustrate in greater detail the application of specific social psychological mechanisms to particular domains of social psychology. The arrangement of the chapters reflects roughly a direction moving from molar, structural variables (sociological analyses of stress and coping; socialization), to interpersonal processes (groups; interpersonal relations), to more individual processes (self; social cognition; attitudes). These subfields are clearly not an exhaustive representation of social psychology and its application to mental health, but rather are intended to be illustrative. The authors were asked to represent current issues and approaches within their respective subfields, to illustrate how this research does or could provide a better understanding of mental health, and finally to suggest what new directions might be taken to make greater progress in forging this link. In the final chapter, Cacioppo and Berntson discuss social psychological efforts within a broader interdisciplinary context.

George Miller (1969) argued that psychology would best grow by "giving itself away"—this is no more pertinent to any sub-discipline of psychology than social psychology which sits on the interdisciplinary bridges of many basic and applied social science efforts. Perhaps this volume will help social psychologists become "philanthropists" of their discipline—that is the hope that underlies all of our efforts in this volume.

NOTES

1. There is, of course, considerable overlap in the questions addressed and the approaches to them by individual researchers in the different disciplines; the point here is that there is a social psychological level of analysis that is unique.

2. It is also possible that strong reference group identification processes in adolescents might lead to a dual impact of (peer-aged) popular personalities—identification, as well as attractiveness—perhaps promoting both short-term and enduring change. Such issues support the general point that theoretical issues can both enrich and be enriched by attempts at extension to social policy issues.

3. Kurt Lewin's famous assertion that "there is nothing so practical as a good theory" is all too often quoted out of context to justify trivial research. In fact, Lewin went on to say that basic and applied research were synergistic, and that good theory should have application to society. Lewin himself made important contributions both to experimental approaches to behavior and to applied psychology. He was both a consummate theoretician and a longtime consultant to industry, government, and social service organizations.

REFERENCES

Abelson, R. P., Aronson, E., McGuire, W. J., Newcomb, T. M., Rosenberg, M. J., & Tannenbaum, P. H. (Eds.). (1968). *Theories of cognitive consistency: A sourcebook.* Chicago: Rand McNally.

Argyle, M. (1980). The development of applied social psychology. In R.

Gilmour & S. Duck (Eds.), *The development of social psychology* (pp. 81–106). New York: Academic Press.

Aronson, E. (1968). Dissonance theory: Progress and problems. In R. P. Abelson, E. Aaronson, W. J. McGuire, T. M. Newcombe, M. J. Rosenberg, & P. H. Tannenbaum (Eds.), *Theories of cognitive consistency: A source book* (pp. 5–27). Skokie, IL: Rand McNally.

Aronson, E., & Carlsmith, J. M. (1962). Performance expectancy as a determinant of actual performance. *Journal of Abnormal and Social Psychology, 65,* 178–182.

Bramel, D. (1968). Dissonance, expectations, and the self. In R. P. Abelson, E. Aronson, W. J. McGuire, T. M. Newcomb, M. J. Rosenbaum, & P. H. Tannenbaum (Eds.), *Theories of cognitive consistency: A sourcebook* (pp. 355–365). Chicago: Rand McNally.

Brickman, P. (1980). A social psychology of human concerns. In R. Gilmour & S. Duck (Eds.), *The development of social psychology* (pp. 5–25). New York: Academic Press.

Chaiken, S. (1980). Heuristic versus systematic information processing and the use of source versus message cues in persuasion. *Journal of Personality and Social Psychology, 39,* 752–766.

Darley, J.M., & Fazio, R. (1980). Expectancy confirmation processes arising in the social interaction sequence. *American Psychologist, 35,* 867–881.

Dipboye, R. L. (1977). A critical review of Korman's self-consistency theory of work motivation and occupational choice. *Organizational Behavior and Human Performance, 51,* 284–290.

Dykman, B., & Abramson, L. (1990). Contributions of basic research to the cognitive theories of depression. *Personality and Social Personality Bulletin, 16,* 42–57.

Eagly, A. H., & Chaiken, S. (in press). *The psychology of attitudes.* Fort Worth, TX: Harcourt Brace Jovanovich.

Eisenberg, N., Cialdini, R., McCreath, H., & Shell, R. (1987). Consistency-based compliance: When and why do children become vulnerable? *Journal of Personality and Social Psychology, 52,* 1174–1181.

Fazio, R. (1990). On the value of basic research: An overview. *Personality and Social Psychology Bulletin, 16,* 5–7.

Fisher, J. D. (1988). Possible effects of reference group-based social influence on AIDS-risk behavior and AIDS prevention. *American Psychologist, 43,* 914–920.

Grusec, J. E. (1983). The internalization of altruistic dispositions: A cognitive analysis. In E. T. Higgins, D. N. Ruble, & W. W. Hartup (Eds.), *Social cognition and social development: A sociocultural perspective.* New York: Cambridge University Press.

Grusec, J. E., & Redler, E. (1980). Attribution, reinforcement, and altruism: A developmental analysis. *Developmental Psychology, 16,* 525–534.

Hackel, L. S., & Ruble, D. N. (1992). Changes in the marital relationship after the first baby is born: Predicting the impact of expectancy disconfirmation. *Journal of Personality and Social Psychology, 62.*

Heider, F. (1958). *The psychology of interpersonal relations.* New York: Wiley.

Higgins, E.T., & Kruglanski, A. (Eds.). (1992). *Social psychology: Handbook of basic mechanisms.* Manuscript in preparation.

Higgins, E. T., Strauman, T., & Klein, R. (1986). Standards and the process of self-evaluation: Multiple affects from multiple stages. In R. M. Sorrentino & E. T. Higgins (Eds.), *Handbook of motivation and cognition: Foundations of social behavior* (Vol. 1, pp. 23–63). New York: Guilford Press.

Hollon, S. D., & Garber, J. (1990). Cognitive therapy for depression: A social cognitive perspective. *Personality and Social Psychology Bulletin, 16,* 58–73.

Jackson, J. (1988). *Social psychology, past and present.* Hillsdale, NJ: Erlbaum.

Jones, E. E. (1990). *Interpersonal perception.* New York: W. H. Freeman.

Jones, J. M. (1988). Scientific issues: Section introduction. *American Psychologist, 43,* 899.

Jussim, L. (1986). Self-fulfilling prophecies: A theoretical and integrative review. *Psychological Review, 93,* 429–445.

Kelley, H. H. (1983). The situational origins of human tendencies. *Personality and Social Psychology Bulletin, 9,* 8–30.

Kleinman, A. (1988). *The illness narratives.* New York: Basic Books.

Lepper, M. R. (1983). Social control processes and the internalization of social values: An attributional perspective. In E. T. Higgins, D. N. Ruble, & W. W. Hartup (Eds.), *Social cognition and social development: A sociocultural perspective* (pp. 294–330). New York: Cambridge University Press.

Lewin, K. (1951). *Field theory in social science* (D. Cartwright, Ed.). New York: Harper & Row. (Original work published 1944)

Maluf, J., & Ruble, D. N. (1992). *Cultural differences in adolescent girls' perceptions of menstrual symptoms.* Manuscript in preparation.

McDavid, J. W., & Harari, H. (1968). *Social psychology: Individuals, groups, societies.* New York: Harper & Row.

McGuire, W. J. (1980). The development of theory in social psychology. In R. Gilmour & S. Duck (Eds.), *The development of social psychology* (pp. 53–80). New York: Academic Press.

McGuire, W. J. (1985). Toward social psychology's second century. In S. Koch and D. E. Leary (Eds.), *A century of psychology as science* (pp. 558–590). New York: McGraw-Hill.

Miller, D. T., & Turnbull, W. (1986). Expectancies and interpersonal processes. *Annual Review of Psychology, 37,* 233–256.

Miller, G. (1969). Psychology as a means of promoting human welfare. *American Psychologist, 24,* 1063–1075.

Mirowsky, J., & Ross, C. E. (1989). *Social causes of psychological distress.* New York: Aldine de Gruyter.

Newcomb, T. M. (1953). An approach to the study of communicative acts. *Psychological Review, 60,* 393–404.

O'Keeffe, M. K., Nesselhof-Kendall, S., & Baum, A. (1990). Behavior and prevention of AIDS: Bases of research and intervention. *Personality and Social Psychology Bulletin, 16,* 166–180.

Omoto, A., & Snyder, M. (1990). Basic research in action: Volunteerism and society response to AIDS. *Personality and Social Psychology Bulletin, 16,* 152–165.

Pelham, B. (1991). On confidence and consequence: The certainty and importance of self-knowledge. *Journal of Personality and Social Psychology, 60,* 518–530.

Pettigrew, T. F. (1988). Influencing policy with social psychology. *Journal of Social Issues, 44,* 205–219.

Petty, R. E., & Cacioppo, J. T. (1986). The elaboration likelihood model of persuasion. *Advances in Experimental Social Psychology, 19,* 123–205.

Rholes, W. W., Newman, L. S., & Ruble, D. N. (1990). Understanding self and other: Developmental and motivational aspects of perceiving persons in terms of invariant dispositions. In E. T. Higgins & R. M. Sorrentino (Eds.), *Handbook of motivation and cognition: Foundations of social behavior* (Vol. 2, pp. 369–407). New York: Guilford Press.

Robinson, L. A., Berman, J. S., & Neimeyer, R. A. (1990). Psychotherapy for the treatment of depression: A comprehensive review of controlled outcome research. *Psychological Bulletin, 108,* 30–49.

Rodin, J. (1985). The application of social psychology. In G. Lindzey & E. Aronson (Eds.), *The handbook of social psychology* (3rd ed., Vol. 2, pp. 805–881). New York: Random House.

Ross, L. (1977). The intuitive psychologist and his shortcomings: Distortions in the attribution process. In L. Berkowitz (Ed.), *Advances in experimental social psychology* (Vol. 10, pp. 173–220). New York: Academic Press.

Ruble, D. N. (1989). Menarche and menstrual symptoms: Psychosocial perspectives. In B. Lerer & S. Gershon (Eds.), *New directions in affective disorders.* New York: Springer.

Secord, P. F., & Backman, C. W. (1964). *Social psychology.* New York: McGraw-Hill.

Shaw, M. E., & Costanzo, P. R. (1982). *Theories of social psychology.* New York: McGraw-Hill.

Steele, C. M. (1988). The psychology of self-affirmation: Sustaining the integrity of the self. In L. Berkowitz (Ed.), *Advances in experimental social psychology* (Vol. 21, pp. 261–346). Orlando, FL: Academic Press.

Swann, W. B. (1990). To be adored or to be known?: The interplay of self-enhancement and self-verification. In E. T. Higgins & R. M. Sorrentino (Eds.), *Handbook of motivation and cognition* (Vol. 2, pp. 408–448). New York: Guilford Press.

Wicklund, R. A., & Brehm, J. W. (1976). *Perspectives on cognitive dissonance.* Hillsdale, NJ: Erlbaum.

Social Psychological Foundations of Stress and Coping Research

SUSAN GORE

Stress is so widely discussed in American society today that some individuals have already concluded that it is a rather trivial notion. For example, in a recent conversation with the high school principal in a low-income, urban community, this man, who was deeply committed to his student body, reported that he was not convinced that much could be learned from a study of stress, since students mostly see stress as a credible excuse for not meeting responsibilities. This observation tells us two things about the public's understanding of stress: (1) it is seen as pervasive and a common scapegoat for failure and misfortune; and (2) given this popular understanding of stress, scientific study can offer little beyond confirming what everyone already knows is true. This situation suggests that the very fact that stress is not a rare disease of unknown origins places a special burden on mental health researchers to specify exactly what can be learned from the study of stress that helps us to understand the seriousness of its impact and that can contribute to and guide the public wisdom, at times contradicting it and at other times adding precision and insight. For example, under what conditions are stressors benign or even beneficial, when are the effects of stress severe, and how can intervention prevent severe stress and its ill effects from happening? What kinds of studies should be conducted to answer to these questions, what are our major findings, and why are they significant?

    This chapter considers some basic characteristics and findings from stress research that have increased our knowledge about mental illness and distress in child and adult populations. Current epidemiological reasoning about the causation of illness relies on the concept of multifactorial etiology, and accumulated evidence strongly suggests that social stressors constitute one such factor of environmental risks. In addition, stressors—which vary in nature, severity, and configuration—have been implicated in the etiology and course of a wide range of diseases, including unipolar depression, schizophrenia, alcoholism, child and adolescent conduct problems, and suicide, as well as generalized psychological distress and demoralization. This finding is consistent with the prevailing scientific view that critical social processes are not necessarily disease specific but instead interact with other environmental and biological risks in bringing about a variety of disorders. Recognizing that stress may be implicated in a number of mental health problems highlights its significance for population studies that seek to uncover general principles of prevention, as well as investigations of individuals in treatment for specific disorders. In addition, because children and adolescents are especially known to express psychological distress through a range of internalizing and externalizing mental health behaviors, how stress is implicated in varying kinds of mental health profiles is key to the broad-band approaches called for in the study of youth.

This chapter differs from others in this volume in that stress research does not advance a single line of social psychological inquiry. Rather, drawing on several of the fields discussed in this volume (such as social cognition, the self, and socialization), this chapter incorporates these ideas about complex individual–environmental transactions into the models and measurement strategies that are best suited for population studies. It then focuses on the relationships among these processes and a wide range of mental health variables. As such, stress research is an applied field of study; it uses a foundation of social psychological research to model the processes that may explain the nature and levels of distress and disorder that occur in the larger population and subgroups within it.

Since the field of stress research is expansive and represents the viewpoints of many disciplines, a unifying theme of this chapter is to characterize how sociological understandings of the processes of risk and resilience provide a point of departure for research on the stress–mental health relationship. This perspective, which argues for an explicit research focus on the processes that link societal and individual levels of behavior, also highlights the need for research on special populations.

The first part of the chapter describes a basic model for stress research in which social structural variables set in motion the stress process. This is the study of stress exposure, specifically, the characteristics of social statuses and life situations and events that make for stress and are associated with a higher probability of mental disorder. Epidemiological studies usually identify a number of risk factors each independently predictive of disorder, in partial contrast with stress research which emphasizes the interrelationships among these variables, yielding models of mediating processes (Pearlin, Lieberman, Menaghan, & Mullan, 1981). Here, mediation means several kinds of linkages: between more distal institutional structures and individual experiences, between early life experiences shaped by socialization processes and later life stresses and coping resources, and between social situation and individual characteristics and behaviors at the same point in time.

The second part of the chapter examines the ways of investigating subgroup differences in mental health responses to stress, that is, differential vulnerability or resilience to the mental health effects of stress. This builds on the first problem of stress exposure but focuses on factors that shape individual reactivity to stress. Research on coping with stress in population studies usually involves attention to group differences in interpersonal resources or social supports; in beliefs about one's self and the environment, such as self-esteem and sense of control; and in coping activities undertaken in response to various stressors. Although population studies cannot provide the detail on coping that has been gleaned from qualitative, in-depth studies of particular stressors, they are important for testing hypotheses concerning the situational factors that influence coping activity and its effectiveness, that is, the contextual processes through which personal and social variables shape stress responses.

The final section of the chapter considers areas of needed research on special populations.

SOURCES OF STRESS

Figure 2.1 depicts a model of the processes involved in the etiology of psychological distress and disorder whose broad outlines are consistent with most theories of stress and its mental health effects. The figure is roughly divided into processes of risk and resilience. In stress research, risk is understood as occurring

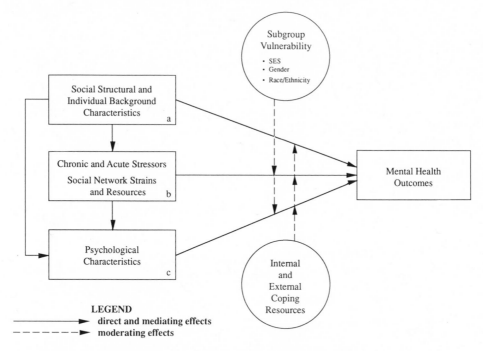

FIGURE 2.1. Social stress and mental health: risk and resilience.

through exposure to stress. The origins and dynamics of stress exposure are depicted by the set of three boxes to the left in the figure and their connecting arrows to each other and to the mental health outcomes. As noted above, the concept of resilience, or vulnerability to stress, extends this model of stress exposure to consider differential reactivity to these risks. These stress-moderating processes that account for differences in stress responses are represented in the figure by the concepts found in the circles. The dashed arrows that cut through the risk relationships in Figure 2.1 denote the idea of a stress moderating or "buffering" effect.

Turning first to the issue of stress exposure, the starting point is the set of structural positions (often called background variables) in the top box on the left, and their direct and indirect associations with indicators of mental health and well-being. Gender, socioeconomic status, race, and marital status are critical social positions that figure prominently in adult epidemiological studies. In child studies, the important background variables are components of family situation, including parents' mental and physical health history, parents' socioeconomic status, and household type (stepparent/single parent/two natural parents). In addition, a child's age (developmental status) and gender have also been the focus of considerable research. Epidemiological studies of mental disorders quite consistently indicate higher rates of stress exposure and more psychopathology among both adults and children in economically disadvantaged groups, higher rates of affective distress and depressive symptoms among women, and higher rates of deviance and distress symptoms among children in single-parent households. These associations are indicated by the arrows in Figure 2.1 that link these characteristics to the mental health variables.

Stress research has become so closely identified with the goals of psychiatric epidemiology because it emphasizes the role of social stress in explaining the higher rates of depression, distress, and other morbidity observed within subgroups of the population. Efforts to identify factors both common and distinct to various social groups that account for differences in risk for mental illness also contribute to broader behavioral sciences questions regarding the interplay between environment and person and, specifically, the problem of disentangling social causation and social selection processes.[1]

Reflecting this more structural emphasis, Figure 2.1 depicts the embeddedness of both ongoing, chronic stresses and acute life changes in broader institutional contexts, especially those involving family, gender, and the economy. Whereas static variables, such as socioeconomic status, gender, and race, represent abstract positions within the social structure and "distal" forces with respect to the immediacy of their influence on disorder, undesirable events associated with these statuses can be seen as the more proximal, mediating experiences that are formative in the etiology of illness. Research addressing how social structural conditions come to influence health and well-being was greatly facilitated by the development of life-events inventories (Holmes & Rahe, 1967). These self-report instruments assess whether any of a large number of acute life changes (e.g., marital and other relationship changes, financial and job changes) have occurred in the months prior to the interview, yielding measures of cumulative stress along one or more dimensions.[2]

An early use of life-events instruments was to explore the consistent finding in mental health research of socioeconomic differences in levels of psychological distress in community populations. Findings from a number of major studies have provided at least partial support for the idea that acute stressors and deficits in coping resources such as social support contribute significantly to social class differentials (McLeod & Kessler, 1990; Turner & Noh, 1983; Thoits, 1982). Importantly, this line of study has made considerable headway into the problem of disaggregating measures of socioeconomic status and life events to identify the dimensions of socioeconomic status and the classes of life events most important for understanding subgroup differences in vulnerability to the mental health effects of stress. Thus, innovations in stress assessment, starting with inventories of life events, have played an essential role in advancing research on the social situation and mental health of women, minorities, and low-income individuals, among many other population subgroups at risk for mental illness.

Processes of Stress Mediation

Figure 2.1 is drawn to include sets of arrows linking each of the three panels of independent variables to the mental health outcomes. These lines represent basic research findings regarding the risk factors for disorder that have been identified at the structural, situational, and individual levels. For example, public health models of risk typically focus on associations between the demographic characteristics in box (a) and mental health outcomes, such as suicidal thoughts. Similarly, early research in child psychiatry sought to establish the associations between various family characteristics such as parents' mental health status and family disruption, and indicators of child psychopathology (see review by Masten et al., 1988). Although the study of specific kinds of risk yields valuable findings regarding key associations, divergent perspectives and disciplinary concerns are not easily forged into a model of how variables at the societal, familial, interpersonal, and individual levels come to influence mental health.

The model of stress mediation in Figure 2.1 offers one such approach. The three boxes in the left-hand portion of the figure depict a set of relationships among variables at the social, interpersonal, and psychological levels, which outlines various pathways through which distal environmental structures and life situations come to influence psychological health. From a stress perspective, the prominent situational factors mediating the effects of social structural arrangements (box a) are identified in the second box (b) and include chronically stressful life situations and acute life changes, persistent strains in social relationships, and the quality of supportive ties. Experiences in these role arenas in turn influence psychological characteristics, including ideas about the self, such as self-esteem and self-worth. These psychological characteristics are noted in the last box (c). The arrows connecting panels (a) and (b) with the third panel of individual characteristics and beliefs indicate the linkages between social situation and individual-level variables—including personality, values, and beliefs—that are forged through socialization processes as well as through cumulative life experience. Thus, moving from the environmental to the individual-level variables, the vertical arrows connecting these panels indicate that the impact on mental health of the distal social status (background) variables is mediated by more proximal experiences including the social stresses and resources and individual characteristics and behaviors.

The following sections consider some of the research regarding these various interrelationships.

Social Structure and Individual Behavior

A major body of sociological research has examined the sociodemographic conditions likely to produce a number of personal beliefs and characteristics, including the sense of personal efficacy and attributions of fatalism, intellectual flexibility, and the sense of mastery. Much of the research on social structure and personal beliefs builds on the seminal sociological investigations of Kohn and Schooler (1982), who studied the conditions of work life at various socioeconomic levels and the translation of job experiences involving limited discretion into a personality trait of "learned inflexibility" that guides behavior in other life roles. This trait was seen by Kohn as a major component of the individual's "internal coping resources," with lack of flexibility functioning to limit the individual's ability to cope with life stress.

The ideas of Kohn and associates argue for linkages between social conditions and intraindividual characteristics that influence coping ability. In partial contrast, Wheaton (1980) has focused on diminished coping effort, which is also a learned response. In his conception, "fatalistic" attributions derive from the repeated failure in achieving life goals that characterizes the lower-class experience. These attributions function to limit coping effort in the face of stress because individuals come to believe that their efforts will have a low efficacy in bringing about the desired results. Wheaton's longitudinal analyses demonstrate this mediating role of fatalistic beliefs in the association between socioeconomic status and psychological distress. Similarly, in a series of analyses spanning the past decade, Mirowsky and Ross (1989) have demonstrated that perceptions of control play a significant role in mediating the mental health impact of both disadvantaged social position and undesirable life change in representative samples of the adult population. As they have also noted, there are a variety of concepts and theories that pertain to beliefs about control (e.g., sense of efficacy, mastery, hardiness, learned helplessness, and internal vs. external locus on control), and each has provided an important perspective on the linkages among social status, environmental events, and individual cognitions and beliefs.

Stress, Support, and the Self

A different literature pertains to the linkage between the social stress and social relational processes identified in the second box and the psychological characteristics in the third. Some work within the field of stress research and in studies of child and adolescent development addresses the contingent nature of self-esteem on supportive social ties and success in life roles and the role of self-esteem as a mediator of the relationship between undesirable life changes and psychological distress. Pearlin et al. (1981), for example, examined a model of social stress and mental health in which undesirable life changes such as involuntary job loss are understood to intensify role strains such as interpersonal tension and economic worries. In their view, these role strains in turn jeopardize the individuals's sense of mastery and self-esteem because, in their words, "hardships that are an enduring testimony to one's lack of success or to the inadequacy of one's efforts to avoid problems would seem to pose the most sustained affront to one's conceptions of self worth and of being in control over personal destiny" (p. 345). Their longitudinal data showed general support for this conceptualization, illustrating four significant features of the stress mediation model in Figure 2.1. First, they found that job loss, like many undesirable employment-related stressors, more often occurred to individuals in the lower socioeconomic statuses; hence, the linkage between social structure (box a) and stressors (box b). Second, there were associations between the stressors and strains identified in box (b): The occurrence of a stressor, the job loss, led to heightened role-related tensions and worries, reflecting their view that stressful life events affect mental health through creating strains in social roles. Third, the association between job loss and increases in depressive symptoms was mediated by the role strains and changes in self-esteem. Finally, an element of the model not yet discussed pertains to the effect of social support, which in Figure 2.1 is called an "external coping resource." Social support, measured as degree of emotional support and closeness to spouse and to friends and relatives, was found to indirectly affect depression through counteracting the effects of job loss on negative changes in self-esteem. In other words, changes in self-esteem seemed to be the critical mediator of stress effects, with loss of self-regard contingent upon level of perceived social support.

The complex interplay between processes of social support and self-regard has been regularly noted in research on the etiology of depression (Barnett & Gotlib, 1988; Brown & Harris, 1989). Over the past 20 years, Brown et al. (see also Brown & Harris, 1978; Brown, Andrews, Harris, Adler, & Bridge, 1986) have conducted the most intensive investigations of the precursors of clinical depression among low-income women, the subgroup of women who experience the highest rates of depression. In their general model, onset of depression is directly preceded by provoking events that involve loss of some kind and that give rise to interpretations of role failure and inadequacy. For married women, having ongoing low marital support and long-term difficulties with their husband seem to have reduced self-esteem long before the final provoking stressful event (and the long-term poor fabric of the marriage was associated with an increased chance of such events occurring). These women, in contrast with unmarried women, were more often "let down" by individuals outside the home identified as "very close" supporters. That is, the process of obtaining crisis support in the face of stressful events was less successful, and low self-esteem was most common among those who were let down. Thus, for these women, the provision of support could not interrupt the generalization of hopelessness triggered by the provoking stressful event. In contrast, having "very close" others did function to reduce the risk of depression for the unmarried women, and self-esteem and social support appeared to operate as independent protective factors.

Since Brown et al. exclusively studied lower-income women, a question arises concerning the generalizability of these findings to other populations. Although intensive interviewing procedures of this nature have not been widely used, Barnett and Gotlib (1988) have reviewed the available research on psychosocial processes and depression onset and have highlighted the same critical etiological variables and processes: triggering life stresses, especially losses, failures, and disappointments; chronic marital distress; more prolonged experience of depressive cognitions among persons with low self-esteem; and the link between difficulties in eliciting support and poor self-esteem. Thus, it seems likely that etiological processes in depression are quite similar across other groups of women, with greater exposure to economic and other stressors and higher rates of marital distress and dissatisfaction driving the larger number of depression onsets and episodes of greater duration and severity in a low-income population. To date, research on men is sparse.

Social Ties, Social Support, and Mental Health

Much of the research on the role of social factors in the etiology of mental health problems has utilized the concept of social support. Social supports are generally understood as a class of external coping resources that are made available through the larger social network in which the individual is embedded. Early epidemiological investigations were not informed by this more recent conceptualization of social support. Instead, these studies focused on indicators of social integration, including degrees of interaction in formal and informal groups, marital status, living alone, and quantities of ties; variables that are now seen as reflecting "objective" features of the social network or of support "availability." Study after study has shown these variables to be negatively related to psychological distress, data that affirm an independent, protective role of social integration in mental health and, conversely, of social isolation as a risk factor. For example, a major 9-year prospective study of the psychosocial predictors of depression (Kaplan, Roberts, Camacho, & Coyne, 1987), which was modeled after the well-known Alameda County study of mortality (Berkman & Syme, 1979), found that initial patterns of social isolation (measured as a frequency of contact with friends and relatives) independently predicted later increases in depressive symptoms. As described below, some research has begun to address the processes through which the effects of social integration on mental health are mediated. However, in many large epidemiological studies, these social integration variables (e.g., marital status, informal memberships, and amount of communication among friends and neighbors) are often averaged into a global indicator of integration versus isolation. So, a valuable first step would be to disaggregate these indices and reanalyze the data to explore the independent effects of each variable, as well as the effects of various configurations.

This positive, direct effect of social participation on mental health is depicted in Figure 2.1 by the arrow linking social network resources to mental health outcomes. It should be emphasized that an understanding of social ties as a protective factor, that is, a positive influence of mental health for all individuals, differs from the more widely discussed interactive (stress-buffering) model, in which mental health effects of social support are hypothesized as conditional on level of stress. The latter process postulates support as a vulnerability factor, one that operates to promote mental health only via its role in moderating stress effects, a line of investigation to be considered in the following section.

Some of the research examining the protective mental health effects of social membership and embeddedness has emphasized the social regulation or control functions of social ties, rather than the provision of supportive resources. For example, the married may exhibit better mental health than the unmarried in that this tie and nonsolo living place limits on deviant and risk-taking behavior. Alternatively, social psychologists have emphasized the consequences of social memberships for identity and considered how representations of the self can check the severity of negative affect associated with threatening life events. Thoits (1983), for example, studied the association between multiple social (role) identities and psychological distress, taking as her point of departure the well-documented findings that individuals who hold few role identities—the unmarried, unemployed, retired, housewives, and persons living alone—tend to report higher levels of psychological distress than their integrated counterparts. These social identities are understood to provide meaning to life activities, thus functioning as a generalized protective factor. In addition, due to the psychological importance of each such role, the disorganizing and demoralizing effects of role losses and transitions can be offset by the availability of alternative roles. Her analyses confirmed this general view and further showed that changes in numbers of identities, that is, losses and gains, were psychologically harmful and beneficial, as predicted—depending on the direction of change.

Linville (1987) has also explored the mental health benefits of multiple role memberships as indicated by their cognitive reflection in the numbers and complexity of the individual's self aspects. Her longitudinal data on change in depressive symptoms and illness reports provide support for the interpretation that people high in self-complexity suffer less severe distress responses to stress because negative affect that is activated by stressful events is limited to only a small portion of the person's total self-representation. Thus, like Thoits's more sociological data, Linville's studies provide further evidence for the significance of a differentiated social self, and the multiple ties it reflects, as a protective factor in mental health.

Taken together, the three boxes to the left in Figure 2.1, and the various direct and indirect relationships shown, offer a conceptualization of risk and protective factors that operate in an additive fashion to influence mental health and functioning. As described above, in this basic model, external coping resources such as social support act as generalized stress-resistance resources, which may counteract the effects of stress, but they are not necessarily seen as working only in conjunction with stress (i.e., the stress-buffering function or vulnerability model).

In addition, consistent with the earlier discussion, these external coping resources (i.e., social supports) are shaped by the same social structural processes and socialization experiences that have been described in relationship to stressors and psychological characteristics. For example, a considerable body of research has documented group differences in the quantity and quality of social supports and ability to mobilize social support in times of crisis. Most such research has focused on gender and social class differences in the quality of the social relational system. This is because an important sociological perspective on the social network is the effect of social stratification on power and dependency within relationships, and specifically the problem of gender inequality (Lennon, 1989).

Other research has emphasized a different consequence of stratification, namely, the social strains associated with interaction in a low-income setting. Belle (1982, 1987) has written extensively on the stresses and social networks of low-income women, noting their more intimate ties but higher "costs" of this social network involvement. These friends and associates are also low-income and similarly experience severe life problems. This network-level stress produces conflict and emotional strain on all individuals in the network and a lower availability of group resources (i.e., social support) to disperse in times of individual need. The research by Rook (1984) has established that the conflicts and strains inherent in close ties are more influential in shaping distress than positive features of relationships (i.e., supportive features); this suggests that the mental health benefits of social relationships among low-income individuals may be greatly offset by the high level of social strain characteristic of these ties. Consistent with this perspective, research by Riley and Eckenrode (1986) documents that low-income individuals are less successful than high-income individuals in mobilizing social support in times of stress, data indicating that the stress-buffering function of social ties is not evidenced to the same degree across the social class spectrum.

This emphasis on the origins or contexts of social support and coping resources is a necessary corrective in stress studies because the methods and models for studying the effects of stress on mental health have tended to omit consideration of the stress-coping resource relationship, that is, how stress depletes (or possibly enhances) coping resources and its contagion through a family or other social network. Instead, many scientists operationalize the risk-resilience paradigm as a set of risk variables, or stressors, and an orthogonal set of resilience factors. Clearly, a focus on risk and resilience in a low-income environment raises questions about the forces that shape *both* risk and resilience, and the consequences of stress for both internal and external coping resources.

In addition, in much of stress research there has been a singular focus on finding empirical evidence for stress-buffering effects of supportive transactions and individual coping behaviors. This search for statistical interactions between level of stress and level of resources has reinforced a fairly limited line of investigation that addresses whether severe mental health effects of stressful events (such as death of a spouse) can be offset through adequate provision of crisis support. As a consequence, stress research has been relatively inattentive to the role of socialization as well as cumulative social stress in shaping many processes, including continuity between early and later life course experience, vulnerability, and mental health; the quality of social support and internal coping resources; and the mode through which distress is expressed (i.e., types of affective and conduct problems).

An emerging life-course perspective in stress research, as elsewhere in the behavioral sciences, is stimulating new approaches to address these issues, such as a focus on the linkages between early and later experiences and the interpersonal and intergenerational transmission of stress (Elder & Caspi, 1988). For example, evidence indicates that risk factors early in life, such as the loss of a parent, bring about more stress, deficits in coping resources, and heightened vulnerability to stress later on (Bifulco, Brown, & Harris, 1987). Losses of this nature, and how they are "replaced," may have lasting negative effects on the formation of close ties and on the ability to elicit support and obtain comfort and other provisions from relationships, and thus, effectively cope with stress in later life. Many normative life transitions are stressful precisely because they involve a change of social contexts and disruption of relationships. Bush and Simmons (1987) have argued that the transition to junior high school is one such change, and that it more adversely affects girls than boys because girls tend to depend more on the smaller, more intimate social circles characteristic of the primary school setting. Studies such as this are illustrative of this more contextual approach to stress research, which includes attention to subgroup differences in the dynamics of stressors and social support.

Finally, the shaping of social network ties and the quality of interpersonal functioning also shed light on another issue in stress research, whether social support is a true environmental resource or an extension of personal characteristics. For some time now, researchers have been struggling with the question whether individual perceptions of support are merely the reflection of either mental health status or other psychological characteristics (Henderson, Byrne, & Duncan-Jones, 1981; Heller, 1979). If so, the argument goes, the concept of social support becomes an expendable research tool. Indeed, it may be that researchers working largely in the area of adult stress studies have relied too strongly on brief self-report measures of perceived social support that assess the perceived environment. But, this psychological perspective on social support goes too far in collapsing significant processes involving the social environment into the domain of individual characteristics, a point also made by House et al. (House, Umberson, & Landis, 1988). Although the problem of deciding where the environment leaves off and the individual begins pervades all mental health research, ecologically sensitive theory and research in child development (Sandler, Miller, Short, & Wolchik, 1989; Felner, Ginter, & Primavera, 1982) and developmental psychopathology (Werner & Smith, 1982; Sameroff, 1983) have emphasized the key role of environmental supports in shaping child health and adaptation.

RESEARCH THEMES IN RISK AND RESILIENCE

Stress Exposure and Reactivity

The discussion to this point has considered interrelationships among concepts in an additive model of risk and has emphasized the character of stress exposure as a set of experiences linking more distal social structural arrangements with individual-level psychological and behavioral responses to stress. A second means through which stress research focuses on this nexus between individual and situation is through study of processes that moderate or condition the severity of individual and subgroup responses to stress. In this interactive model of stress effects, it is hypothesized that the greatest increase in disorder will be brought about by exposure to high levels of stress in conjunction with an absence of coping resources. Consistent with this model, a strong relationship between stress exposure and disorder indicates vulnerability to the mental health effects of stress, a greater responsiveness that might be explained by an absence of coping resources or efforts. Conversely, heightened exposure to stress which fails to bring about decrements in mental health defines a situation of resilience. Social support and other coping resources are understood to shape this differential resilience through their impact on the nature, meaning, and emotional consequences of life stress.

This understanding of vulnerability to stress effects has its roots in the epidemiological studies of class and gender differential in mental health noted above. Although the study of resilience gives attention to individual-level stress moderators, such as attributions of control, the problem of differential vulnerability to the effects of stress assumes a model in which subgroup variation in mental health responses to stress is accounted for by subgroup differences in resources. Figure 2.1 depicts these interactive relationships by the dashed lines that intersect the connections between risk factors and mental health variables. They signify that the relationships between the various stress or resource variables and mental health will vary for different subgroups (the upper circle), and these conditional relationships might be explained by differences in level of internal and external resources (in the lower circle).

In the previous section, these resource variables, such as social support and cognitions of control, were discussed as protective factors, features of the environment or person that are generally associated with better mental health. The idea of differential vulnerability to the mental health effects of stress assumes a different function of these variables. Here, a resource variable, such as having a supportive spouse or reciprocal helping relationship with coworkers, may influence mental health only under conditions of high stress. Thus, subsets of the internal and external resource variables may function as vulnerability factors, that is, moderating the effects of other variables, while the effects of other resource variables will be additive. Elsewhere, I have discussed features of these models and variables in greater detail (Gore, 1985).

The work of Kessler and associates on gender differences in vulnerability to stress is illustrative of this interactive approach. Using data pooled from five major epidemiologic surveys of the general population, Kessler and McLeod (1984) examined gender differentials in exposure and vulnerability to six categories of life-event stressors: income losses, ill health, separation/divorce, other losses, deaths, and problems within the wider social network. By disaggregating cumulative stress into several theoretically relevant scales, they were able to examine whether women are more vulnerable to all classes of life stress, which would suggest that features of personality govern a pervasive vulnerability, or whether this vulnerability is specific to certain classes of stresses. Their findings indicated that women were no more reactive than men to many kinds of life stresses, and, contrary to the common belief, they were no more responsive than men to stresses within their immediate family. Women, however, were more exposed than men to the stresses of other people through their social involvements outside the nuclear family, and their greater emotional vulnerability to these network stresses accounted for the gender difference in psychological distress.

My own research (Gore, Aseltine, & Colten, 1992) on a high school–aged population similarly examined the mental health effects of exposure and vulnerability to various classes of recent stressors. In contrast with the findings above, the data did not show gender differences in vulnerability to any of the stressors identified in the friendship, family, and personal domains, and processes of stress exposure and vulnerability could not account for the observed sex difference in depressed mood. However, findings regarding the effects of socioeconomic status (SES) were striking and these varied by gender. Here, parents' SES was not strongly associated with depressive symptoms for the boys in the sample, but it was for the girls, suggesting that lower level of parental education, the indicator of SES, is a risk factor for girls but not for boys. However, this is not to say that lower parental education is not a significant influence of boys' depressed mood because boys whose parents had lower levels of education were significantly more vulnerable to the depressing effects of peer and family stresses. In other words, low SES did not operate as a source of stress exposure or directly influence boys' depressed mood; however, it was highly significant as a vulnerability factor, making these boys more reactive to stressful experiences. In partial contrast, the girls were doubly influenced by their parents' educational level, both as a vehicle for stress exposure and in enhancing their vulnerability to these stresses.

Analyses such as these provide the point of departure for investigations of coping and social support processes, that is, the responses to stress that account for variation in the mental health impact of stress. Before turning to these issues, something should be said about alternative conceptualizations of life stress and its influence on mental health.

A Note on Stress Assessment

The tradition of life-events research which informs much of the research described above has been important for establishing basic models of the processes involved in linking social experiences to mental health. The underlying theory of stress, however, is generally recognized as narrow and is currently being reexamined. At the root of the problem is that the conceptualization of stress in this framework is limited to the dimension of life change. In addition, much of this work has proceeded on the assumption that aggregate life change, rather than the character of particular events, influences mental health and that this occurs through overwhelming coping resources. We see in the studies by Kessler and myself in the previous section a movement away from this theory toward a more substantive appreciation of life events, while retaining some useful features of stress assessment.

The work of Brown and Harris (1978, 1989) has provided an important stimulus to this reorientation in that it has offered an alternative understanding of the processes linking life events to mental health as well as different research instruments. Like the life-events checklists widely used by researchers in the United States (see, e.g., Dohrenwend, Krasnoff, Askenasy, & Dohrenwend, 1978, for adult assessment, and Compas, Davis, Forsythe, & Wagner, 1987, for adolescent assessment), the Life Events and Difficulties Schedule (LEDS) yields an assessment of acute stressors, but it is unique in that it also provides data on long-term life difficulties (e.g., many chronic conditions of living related to socioeconomic status and quality of the marital relationship) and other biographical data that provide a basis for investigator ratings of "contextual threat." The latter is defined as the likely response of an average person to an event that occurs in the context of these particular life circumstances. Through this assessment procedure, the investigator rates the personal meaning of life-events in terms of their severity. This differs from the determinations of stress magnitude that are taken in conventional stress checklists. In these, either the individual provides a rating of experienced stress (or degree of life change) or the investigator may use population-derived weights to designate the severity of different events, an approach which does not take into account intraevent variations in experience.

The difference in orientation to stress assessment reflects the understanding of a "life-event" as an etiological factor. In contrast with the idea that change or disruption is the mechanism through which events affect health, Brown and associates see contextual meaning as the critical mechanism (Brown & Harris, 1989). For example, their findings indicate that threatening events alone significantly predict the onset of depression, but that predictive power increases threefold when the event can be "matched" with a prior long-term life difficulty, which for their sample typically involved children, marriage, employment, money, and housework. They give as an example a hardworking single mother who finds out that her daughter is pregnant. The event—finding out about the pregnancy—triggers the onset of depression, not because this news is disruptive and requires considerable family change or adjustment but instead because the mother interprets it as confirming her long-term belief that she has failed to adequately care for her daughter. Many of the 29 onsets in their prospective study were predicted by "failures" such as this, as well as other losses and threats to the individual's identity as a wife and mother.

On the basis of these data, replicated across studies, Brown argues that the specific cognitive–emotional quality of events defines their meanings, and that these meanings are linked with specific disorders. This idea is perhaps his most controversial; that is, that "loss" events trigger depression, "danger" events trigger anxiety, and "intrusion" events trigger schizophrenia. Brown's hypothesis regarding the link between event/meaning type and schizophrenia has received some support from recent research by Link, Dohrenwend, and Skodol (1986). They investigated differences in occupational history among individuals suffering from

schizophrenia in contrast to those having a major depressive episode and a third sample of community controls. Analyses revealed
that half of the first schizophrenic episodes were among individuals exposed to noisome job conditions just prior to the
episode, experiences fitting the criterion of "intrusive" stress identified by Brown. The other two groups were more similar to each
other in occupational history, and careful documentation of onsets
and job histories ruled out possible differences among comparison
groups due to the effects of the illness itself or other premorbid
background characteristics.

A final point regarding Brown's cognitive perspective on the
stress–disorder relationship is that the utility of this general
framework has been demonstrated by other investigators for disorders other than depression (see Brown & Harris, 1989) and
seems intriguingly consistent with the social psychological studies
by Higgins on self-guides, self-discrepancy, and emotional disorder (Higgins, 1989). Although not working within the risk and
resilience paradigm, Higgins similarly proposes that life circumstances become associated with distinct emotional states through
a self-evaluative process—Brown's idea of meaning—that points to
discrepancies between features of the actual self and various sets
of standards. Moreover, echoing Brown's linkage between the
meaning embedded in the type of event and specific expressions of
disorder, Higgins also maintains that different types of discrepancies will produce different emotional states, for example, the discrepancy between the actual self and one's own ideals should
produce dejection-related problems (as noted in Brown's description of the mother's role failure), while other discrepancies will
produce differing feeling states. These parallels between such independent lines of study demonstrate the significant potential for
cross fertilization between basic social psychological research and
population studies of distress and disorder in advancing the study
of mental illness etiology.

Coping with Stress

Social psychological research on coping with stress has concerned
itself with the types of individual coping resources and social
supports that are most effective in reducing distress responses to
stress and the mechanisms through which this occurs. Although
studies of coping with stress and those concerning the role of
support as a stress-buffering variable were initially rather distinct
lines of investigation, most recent research has emphasized a

bridging of concerns toward developing models that consider the importance both of external coping resources such as social support and internal coping resources, including cognitive styles and strategies for dealing with stress.

A first step in these efforts has been to recognize that the individual's use of personal and social resources may meet the same coping needs. For example, much research indicates that individuals who have an internal locus of control engage in more instrumental, problem-centered coping activities, thus directly altering the nature and degree of stress and reducing negative stress responses. In studies of social support, there is an entirely parallel emphasis on the importance of instrumental supports. Similarly, there are parallels between the conceptualization of "appraisal support"—the giving of information, advice, and perspective—and the cognitive strategies that individuals themselves employ to maintain self-esteem and promote benign appraisals of stress (Harter, 1986). Finally, it is important to note that perhaps the most widely researched type of social support—socioemotional—is an important social resource for the individual in the regulation of emotion (Thoits, 1984). This is why the sense of having a secure, close, and confiding social tie has been most consistently associated with positive coping outcomes, independent of any instrumental help that these significant others may offer (Wethington & Kessler, 1986). This may be especially true where the stresses themselves threaten to undermine significant social attachments.

As noted earlier in considering the interplay of social support and self-esteem, an important direction for research on coping and resilience is to understand the various ways in which the individual uses and benefits from both environmental and personal resources. For instance, there is some evidence that these resources covary, making it difficult to discern which of a number of resources is in fact the underlying resilience factor. Since research has documented that a number of individual and environmental characteristics may promote resilience in the face of stress, it may be more fruitful to investigate processes involving several such resources toward understanding their various configurations and effects. Interestingly, the research by Sandler and Lakey (1982) found that persons who were high in perceptions of internal control were also more effective in mobilizing support systems to help cope with stress than were persons who were low in perceptions of control, and that the combined effects of support and internal locus of control brought about the greatest reductions of distress associated with stress. These data give support to the notion that effective coping may involve flexible use of many coping resources.

Contextual Study of Stress and Coping: Stress and Coping across Situations and Individuals

Whereas early coping and social support research sought to identify specific variables that would account for resilience, and emphasized classifications of social support types and behaviors, recent attention is more oriented to understanding the social psychological processes that shape coping behaviors and their effects. Among the many strategies that exemplify this more contextual study of coping and support processes, two will be briefly described.

First, population studies of individuals and the situational determinants of their coping strategies offer one important approach to understanding coping behavior and its effectiveness. A point of departure for most population-centered research on the situational determinants of coping has been the work of Pearlin and Schooler (1978) who investigated the relationships among ongoing role strains in several life domains: marital, parental, work, and financial; the coping strategies utilized for dealing with these problems; and the effects of these efforts in reducing the psychological distress associated with each type of life difficulty. This study provided the first systematic data on coping variability across situations in a community cross-section and the relative effects of these efforts in counteracting the negative effects of stress on mental health. Findings revealed the importance of cognitive coping strategies such as "optimistic comparison" and "selective ignoring" in modestly reducing the stress associated with economic and occupational strains but not in coping with stress in marital and parenting roles. In this case, the most effective responses involved efforts to change the situation including negotiation and advice seeking. Interestingly, coping responses employed more often by women involved aspects of selective ignoring, coping behaviors found to exacerbate stress in the marital and parenting roles. Less educated and poor respondents reported more role strains; in addition, they less often relied on the more efficacious cognitive devices involving comparison and optimism, suggesting to the authors that their life situation would militate against these beliefs. These findings illustrates the point made earlier, that social structure shapes not only exposure to stress but the coping resources to deal with it.

Recent work has extended this line of investigation in important ways. One difficulty with the Pearlin and Schooler data is that stress is operationalized as ongoing strain within several life roles, an approach that requires a focus on role occupancy and narrows the consideration of stressors that may be experienced. Inventories of life-events provide an alternative means for investigating the various sources of stress experienced in heterogeneous populations and the situational basis for coping. Although survey research techniques have not been ideal for in-depth investigation of individual responses to particular stressors, Mattlin, Wethington, and Kessler (1990) adapted their life-events inventory to include a series of probes pertaining to the "most stressful" situation that had recently occurred, and they were able to rate such events according to severity of "loss" (involving loss of a person, object, or ideal) and "threat" (threat of future harm) and whether the event was of an acute or chronic nature. Analyses then examined associations between situation and coping behavior, and the effects of coping on reducing depression and anxiety associated with specific stress situations. These types of disaggregated analyses (by coping behavior, situation, and severity) yielded interesting findings regarding the interplay of situation and coping response. Regarding positive reappraisal, which Pearlin and Schooler identified as an important strategy, in these analyses it tended to reduce distress associated with the death of a loved one but interfered with adjustment both to low threat and practical situations, perhaps indicating that this coping response involved too much thought and too little action. As might be expected, coping was found to be generally less effective in the face of chronic difficulties, but a profile of passive coping, that is, using very few coping strategies, reduced depression associated with chronic difficulties, especially in situations high in "loss" and "threat." For example, chronic difficulties, which were defined as having begun more than 1 year before the interview, tended to cluster in the categories coded as long-term interpersonal difficulties and illness within the family. Investigator ratings of the "threat" or "loss" inherent in these situations usually pertained to a present or future possibility that some close relationship was or could be disrupted through death or disagreement. Findings that passive coping reduced the effects of these situations on depression indicate the emotional importance of resigned acceptance when the illness of a loved one is imminent and for some kinds of severe interpersonal problems. Using social support for coping was found to be effective in reducing the distress associated with illness and other high-threat events. Other analyses were similarly illustrative of the value to a situation-based study of coping in a large population study.

Research on the situational determinants of coping behavior is contextual in that it yields an understanding of coping effectiveness as a function both of the stressful situation and the coping strategy employed. The focus, however, is on stress defined as an individual problem, coping as an individual strategy, and the individual's well-being. A second contextual approach offers a more social relational perspective on coping and involves a focus on dyadic and small group processes (see Eckenrode, 1991). This is nicely illustrated in the exploratory research of Gottlieb (Gottlieb, 1991), which examined processes of dyadic marital coping with the chronic illness of a child. This research builds on an emerging line of studies on "stress contagion," which indicate that stress is an interpersonal rather than an individual affair (Eckenrode & Gore, 1990). Gottlieb's focus on the family's coping with chronic illness is interesting because evidence indicates that chronic stressors may function to undermine support systems. His qualitative data on husbands' and wives' coping with their emotions around their child's illness (cystic fybrosis and juvenile diabetes) document gender differences in responses to worries, with wives seeking to express concerns to husbands and husbands more stoic. More significantly, Gottlieb's data show that each side also copes to reduce threatening features of the other's coping style. For example, wives are more exposed through their caretaking role to upsetting medical contingencies and seek access to their husbands for reassurance, but husbands seek to insulate themselves from the threat implicit in the wives' coping behavior. These dyadic processes of coping with threat undermine the ability of each individual to offer support to the other. Thus, Gottlieb concludes that "gender and role differences are strongly implicated in creating fertile grounds for the conflict arising from the partners' shared adversity."

Research Needs: Linking Basic Studies with Social Problems

The concluding section of this chapter suggests areas for future research within the stress and coping tradition that can advance basic studies as well as inform mental health policy and programs. The following two broad topics are illustrative of the themes that can provide the integration and interdisciplinary collaboration that is needed in stress and coping research, and are clearly mental health issues for the '90s.

- Study of chronic stress and its effects on mental health and coping resources, including support systems. Relevant populations under stress include families of the chronically physically and mentally ill and low-income women.
- Study of adolescents at risk for mental health problems in the later adolescent years.

Regarding the first priority area, more basic and problem-focused studies in the area of chronic stress are needed. Wheaton (1990) has noted that the distinction between acute and chronic stress lies in the course or persistency of the stressor itself (rather than in the short- or long-term effects of stress), connoting continuing threat and excessive demands that are non–self-limiting in nature. This is a key area for study not only because research already indicates that chronic stress is a more influential etiological factor than acute stress (Avison & Turner, 1988), but also because chronic stress is likely to exert powerful negative influences on support systems. This latter process might explain why the effects of chronic stress are so great.

Recently, there has been a resurgence of interest in the concept of "family burden" which has resulted from the increasing emphasis on caring for the chronically mentally ill in the community (Benson, Fisher, & Tessler, 1991). In addition, research on intergenerational caregiving to the elderly (Gottlieb, 1989) and AIDS and Alzheimer disease caregiving (Pearlin, Mullan, Semple, & Skaff, 1990), has brought attention to the problem of caregiving as an important social relational construct. The population studies by Kessler and associates noted above as well as studies by Belle (1982) also highlight caregiving stress as an important theme for gender studies.

There has been very little controlled research on the mental health of individuals exposed to chronic stress through the caregiving burden or other processes. Important findings, however, have been reported by Breslau and Davis (1986), who followed a sample of mothers caring for a child with disabilities, contrasting them with a control group of mothers of well children with respect to depressive symptoms and onset of a diagnosed disorder. The data on the mothers' mental health subsequent to the birth of their children showed no differences between cases and controls in rates of major depression, but women in the chronic stress sample reported significantly more depressive symptoms and, if diagnosed, had an earlier age of onset and more lifetime depressive episodes. Given that these analyses considered the chronically stressed group in the aggregate, without actually measuring ongoing or acute stressful experiences, the data suggest a significant impact of caregiving burden on the mothers' mental health.

A final problem to which the study of chronic stress can be applied is the social situation and mental health of low-income women. Findings from community studies of depressive symptoms in both adult and adolescent populations tend to indicate that low-income women are the subgroup of women most at risk for elevated symptom levels. The emerging body of research on the homeless also indicates that the fastest-growing segment of this population are poor women and their children. Evidence already indicates that these children are severely developmentally delayed, although homeless women may be clinically no worse off than other low-income women (Wright & Weber, 1987). Nevertheless, there is no doubt that homelessness is the tip of the iceberg for many, and it is only one feature of a more extensive agenda for mental health research that examines the chronic adversity that characterizes the lives of low-income women.

This is not to say that the study of low-income and homeless men should be excluded from a mental health research agenda, since they also evidence high rates of mental disorder. Instead, this argument emphasizes that stress and coping perspectives have already yielded considerable understanding of women's affective disorders, from both population and clinical studies, and that the study of homeless women extends these concerns into a significant new problem area. Although intervening in the lives of the homeless and the prevention of homelessness may be regarded as something "different" in the National Institutes of Health (NIH) research agenda, the existing body of prevention research, particularly in the area of depression, has obvious linkages to this problem, notably through a common interest in the area of support systems. A continued focus on gender and the heightened risk of low-income women offers important opportunities for linking basic social psychological studies that have informed research on the mental health of women to relatively newer social problem areas such as homelessness.

A second area of needed research that could draw on the models of stress and coping processes identified in this chapter focuses on the social transitions and stresses of late adolescence. A generation of behavioral sciences research has already contributed significantly to understanding the biological, cognitive, and social transitions of early adolescence and the relationships between these normative stresses and adolescent mental health. In particular, the research by Simmons and Blyth (1987) has informed public policy regarding the structuring of the elementary school years. Similar pathbreaking research now needs to address the challenges of the later adolescent years and specifically the interplay between mental health and the transition to adulthood. This will take a considerable foundation of theory and research that must parallel the work accomplished for the early adolescent period. The transition to work roles and independent living has been studied largely from economic rather than mental health perspectives study, despite the fact that epidemiological studies document increasing rates of suicide and depression (Klerman & Weissman, 1989) among adolescents, and, in particular, high rates of distress and depressive symptoms for the low-income 18–24 age group (Holzer et al., 1986). Research must document the nature of the stresses, mental health, social relational ties, and problem-solving strategies in this age group, as well as establish what subgroups are at greatest risk and why this is the case. Among these youth, we know the least about the "forgotten half" (W. T. Grant Foundation, 1988), those who do not attend college.

In conclusion, many population subgroups at risk for mental health problems have been identified, and basic research studies have come far in describing the social psychological processes that shape well-being and functioning. Future research will emphasize the application of this knowledge to prevention and intervention in the lives of individuals who are most at risk.

NOTES

1. Considerable theoretical and methodological advances in stress research have also come from a rich tradition of clinical studies. In these, the research model is very similar, but the focus is more squarely on the stress–illness relationship and not on the social origins of stress exposure in the broader institutional forces involving economy, family/gender, race/ethnicity, and age/developmental status.

2. This conceptualization of social stress as potentiated by undesirable changes in life circumstances contrasts with other approaches that focus on the constancy of life conditions, to a large extent determined by social role occupancy, and the disorder that is brought about by normatively structured role strains. This approach is perhaps best illustrated in

the seminal research by Gove and Tudor (1973) on gender and marital status differences in treatment for psychiatric disorder and more recently in the work by Pearlin (1989). The focus on life-events stressors rapidly replaced the research emphasis on role occupancy per se since the latter was limited by its implicit rather than direct approach to stress assessment (e.g., the assumption that marriage has fewer rewards and more stress for women than for men) and, thus, the absence of a yardstick for assessing stress across widely different subgroups of individuals.

REFERENCES

Avison, W. R., & Turner, R. J. (1988). Stressful life events and depressive symptoms: Disaggregating the effects of acute stressors and chronic strains. *Journal of Health and Social Behavior, 29,* 253–264.

Barnett, P., & Gotlib, I. H. (1988). Psychosocial functioning and depression: Distinguishing among antecedents, concomitants and consequences. *Psychological Bulletin, 104,* 97–126.

Belle, D. (1982). The stress of caring: Women as providers of support. In L. Goldberger & S. Breznitz (Eds.), *Handbook of stress* (pp. 496–505). New York: Free Press.

Belle, D. (1987). Gender differences in the social moderators of stress. In R. Barnett, Biener, L., & Baruch, G. (Eds.), *Gender and stress* (pp. 257–277). New York: Free Press.

Benson, P., Fisher, G., & Tessler, R. (1991). Family responses to mental illness: Development since deinstitutionalization. In J. R. Greenley (Ed.), *Mental disorder in social context: Social problems perspectives.* (pp.   ) Greenwich, CT: JAI Press.

Berkman, L. F., & Syme, S. L. (1979). Social networks, host resistance and mortality: A 9-year follow-up study of Alameda County residents. *American Journal of Epidemiology, 109,* 186–204.

BiFulco, A. T., Brown, G. W., & Harris, T. O. (1987). Childhood loss of parent, lack of adequate parental care and adult depression: A replication. *Journal of Affective Disorders, 12,* 115–128.

Breslau, N., & Davis, G. C. (1986). Chronic stress and major depression. *Archives of General Psychiatry, 43,* 309–314.

Brown, G. W., Andrews, B., Harris, T., Adler, Z., & Bridge, L. (1986). Social support, self-esteem and depression. *Psychological Medicine, 16,* 813–831.

Brown, G. W., & Harris, T. O. (1978). *Social origins of depression: A study of psychiatric disorders in women.* New York: Free Press.

Brown, G., & Harris T. (1989). Depression. In G. Brown & T. Harris (Eds.), *Life events and illness* (pp. 49–94). New York: Guilford Press.

Brown, G. W., & Harris, T. O. (Eds.). (1989). *Life events and illness.* New York: Guilford Press.

Bush, D. M., & Simmons, R. (1987). Gender and coping with the entry into early adolescence. In R. Barnett, L. Biener, & G. Baruch (Eds.), *Gender and stress* (pp. 185–219). New York: Free Press.

Compas, B. E., Davis, G. E., Forsythe, C. J., & Wagner, B. M. (1987). Assessment of major and daily stressful events during adolescence: The adolescent perceived event scale. *Journal of Consulting and Clinical Psychology, 55*, 534–541.

Dohrenwend, B. S., Krasnoff, L., Askenasy, A. R., & Dohrenwend, B. P. (1978). Exemplification of a method for scaling life events: The PERI life events scale. *Journal of Health and Social Behavior, 19*, 205–229.

Eckenrode, J. (Ed.). (1991). *The social context of coping*. New York: Plenum Press.

Eckenrode, J., & Gore, S. (Eds.). (1990). *Stress between work and family*. New York: Plenum Press.

Elder, G. H., & Caspi, A. (1988). Human development and social change:an emerging perspective on the life course. In N. Bolger, A. Caspi, G. Downey, & M. Moorehouse (Eds.), *Persons in context: Developmental processes*. New York: Cambridge University Press.

Felner, R. D., Ginter, M., & Primavera, J. (1982). Primary prevention during school transitions: Social support and environmental structure. *American Journal of Community Psychology, 10*, 277–290.

Gore, S. (1985). Social support and styles of coping with stress. In S. Cohen & S. Syme (Eds.), *Social support and health*. New York: Academic Press.

Gore, S., Aseltine, R., Jr., & Colten, M. E. (1992). Social structure, life stress and depressive symptoms in a high school aged population. *Journal of Health and Social Behavior, 33*.

Gottlieb, B. (1989). A contextual perspective on stress in family care of the elderly. *Canadian Psychology/Psychologie Canadienne, 30*, 596–607.

Gottlieb, B., & Wagner, F. (1991). Stress and support processes in close relationships. In J. Eckenrode (Ed.), *The social context of coping* (pp. 165–188). New York: Plenum Press.

Gove, W., & Tudor, J. (1973). Adult sex roles and mental illness. *American Journal of Sociology, 78*, 812.

Harter, S. (1986). Processes underlying the construct, maintenance and enhancement of the self concept in children. In J. Suls & A. Greenwald (Eds.), *Psychological perspectives on the self* (Vol. 3). Hillsdale, NJ: Erlbaum.

Heller, K. (1979). The effects of social support: Prevention and treatment implications. In A. P. Goldstein & F. H. Kanter, (Eds.), *Maximizing treatment gains: Transfer enhancement in psychotherapy* (pp. 353–382). New York: Academic Press.

Henderson, S., Byrne, D. G., & Duncan-Jones, P. (1981). *Neurosis and the social environment*. London: Academic Press.

Higgins, E. T. (1989). Self-discrepancy theory: What patterns of self-beliefs cause people to suffer? In L. Berkowitz (Ed.), *Advances in ex-*

perimental social psychology (Vol. 22). New York: Academic Press.

Holmes, T. H., & Rahe, R. H. (1967). The social readjustment rating scale. *Journal of Psychosomatic Research, 11,* 213–218.

Holzer, C. E., Shea, B. M., Swanson, J. W., Leaf, P. J., Myers, J. K., George, L., Weissman, M. M., & Bednarski, P. (1986). The increased risk for specific psychiatric disorders among persons of low socioeconomic status. *American Journal of Social Psychiatry, VI (4),* 259–271.

House, J. S., Umberson, D., & Landis, K. K. (1988). Structures and processes of social support. *Annual Review of Sociology, 14,* 293–318.

Kaplan, G. A., Roberts, R. E., Camacho, T. C., & Coyne, J. (1987). Psychosocial predictors of depression: Prospective evidence from the human population laboratory studies. *American Journal of Epidemiology, 125 (2),* 206–220.

Kessler, R. C., & McLeod, J. D. (1984). Sex differences in vulnerability to undesirable life events. *American Sociological Review, 49,* 620–631.

Klerman, G. L., & Weissman, M. M. (1989). Increasing rates of depression. *Journal of the American Medical Association, 261(15),* 2220–2235.

Kohn, M. L., & Schooler, C. (1982). Job conditions and personality: a longitudinal assessment of their reciprocal effects. *American Journal of Sociology, 87,* 1257–1286.

Lennon, M. C. (1989). The structural contexts of stress. *Journal of Health and Social Behavior, 30,* 261–268.

Link, B. G., Dohrenwend, B. P., & Skodol, A. E. (1986). Socioeconomic status and Schizophrenia: Noisome occupational characteristics as a risk factor. *American Sociological Review, 51,* 242–258.

Linville, P. (1987). Self-complexity as a cognitive buffer against stress-related illness and depression. *Journal of Personality and Social Psychology, 52,* 663–676.

Masten, A. S., Garmezy, N., Tellegen, A., Pellegrini, D. S., Larkin, K., & Larsen, A. (1988). Competence and stress in school children: The moderating effects of individual and family qualities. *Journal of Child Psychology and Psychiatry, 29,* 745–764.

Mattlin, J. A., Wethington, E., & Kessler, R. C. (1990). Situational determinants of coping and coping effectiveness. *Journal of Health and Social Behavior, 30,* 241–256.

McLeod, J. D., & Kessler, R. C. (1990). Socioeconomic status differences in vulnerability to undesirable life events. *Journal of Health and Social Behavior, 31,* 162–172.

Mirowsky, J., & Ross, C. (1989). *Social causes of psychological distress.* Hawthorne, NY: Aldine de Gruyter.

Pearlin, L. I. (1989). The sociological study of stress. *Journal of Health and Social Behavior, 30,* 241–256.

Pearlin, L. I., Lieberman, M. A., Menaghan, E. G., & Mullan, J. T. (1981). The stress process. *Journal of Health and Social Behavior, 22,* 337–356.

Pearlin, L. I., Mullan, J. T., Semple, S. J., & Skaff, M. (1990). Caregiving and the stress process: An overview of concepts and their measures. *The Gerontologist, 30,* 583–594.

Pearlin, L. I., & Schooler, C. (1978). The structure of coping. *Journal of Health and Social Behavior, 19,* 2–21.

Riley, D., & Eckenrode, J. (1986). Social ties: Subgroup differences in costs and benefits. *Journal of Personality and Social Psychology, 52,* 770–778.

Rook, K. S. (1984). The negative side of social interaction. *Journal of Personality and Social Psychology, 46,* 1097–1108.

Sameroff, A. J. (1983). Developmental systems: contexts and evolution. In P. Mussen (Ed.), *Handbook of child psychology, Vol 1* (pp. 238–294). New York: Wiley.

Sandler, I., & Lakey, B. (1982). Locus of control as a stress moderator: The role of control perceptions and social support. *American Journal of Community Psychology, 10,* 65–80.

Sandler, I. N., Miller, P., Short, J., & Wolchik, S. (1989). Social support as a protective factor for children in stress. In D. Belle (Ed.), *Children's social networks and social support* (pp. 277–307). New York: Wiley.

Simmons, R., & Blyth, D. (1987). *Moving into Adolescence.* Hawthorne, NY: Aldine de Gruyter.

Thoits, P. A. (1982). Life stress, social support, and psychological vulnerability: Epidemiological considerations. *Journal of Community Psychology, 10,* 341–362.

Thoits, P. A. (1983). Multiple identities and psychological well-being: A reformulation and test of the social isolation hypothesis. *American Sociological Review, 48,* 174–187.

Thoits, P. A. (1984). Coping, social support and psychological outcomes: The central role of emotion. In P. Shaver (Ed.), *Review of Personality and Social Psychology* (pp. 219–238). Beverly Hills, CA: Sage.

Turner, R. J., & Noh, S. (1983). Class and psychological vulnerability among women: The significance of social support and personal control. *Journal of Health and Social Behavior, 24,* 2–15.

Wethington, E., & Kessler, R. C. (1986). Perceived support, received support, and adjustment to stressful life events. *Journal of Health and Social Behavior, 17,* 78–89.

Werner, E., & Smith, R. (1982). Vulnerable but invincible: A longitudinal study of resilient children and youth. New York: McGraw-Hill.

Wheaton, B. (1980). The sociogenesis of psychological disorder: An attributional theory. *Journal of Health and Social Behavior, 21,* 100–124.

Wheaton, B. (1990). Chronic stress. Unpublished paper. Department of Sociology University of Toronto.

William T. Grant Foundation. (1988). *The forgotten half. Pathways to success for America's youth and young families.* Washington, DC: W. T. Grant Foundation Commission on Work, Family and Citizenship.

Wright, J. D., & Weber, E. (1987). *Homelessness and Health.* New York: McGraw-Hill.

External Socialization and the Development of Adaptive Individuation and Social Connection

PHILIP R. COSTANZO

A perusal of most fine contemporary textbooks in social psychology would imply that the explicit phenomena accompanying life-course socialization are basically outside the domain of the field. Social psychologists seem to spend little time exploring the developmental origins of adult social behavior. Indeed, there are few longitudinal conceptions of social process forwarded in social psychological theory, and there is virtually no research exploring the stability and/or continuity of social–interactional behavior across life-course chronology. This past failure to substantively factor real-time socialization into social psychological research and theory is a primary "missing link" in solidifying the connections between social psychology and the understanding of mental health-related processes.

As the chapters in this book illustrate, social psychologists have developed a keen interest in studying the influences giving rise to adaptive and maladaptive processes. Several of the theoretically based models probing various domains of social behavior and thought speak directly to the issue of human adaptation. Phenomena such as depression, marital conflict, social withdrawal, self-loathing, antisocial deviance, substance abuse, anxiety, stress, and coping, and even "psychotic-like" thinking, have been modeled through the lens of social psychological theory. However the refractory characteristics of this lens "constrict" vision to the present and provide only myopic attention to the past or to developmental history. Thus, one might argue that the primary contemporary focus of the social psychology of mental health is the study of the proximal effects of situational variables on adaptation and maladaptation. This focus has more than a 40-year history in the field and is typically attributed to the Lewinian perspective (Lewin, 1943, 1946, 1951).

Lewin has been cited as urging that behavior be studied by focusing on the "behavioral field" at the moment of action (i.e., the field in the present), and for many, this has defined the purview of experimental social psychology. Yet, this derivation of Lewinian thought leaves much of his legacy to languish in the distant reaches of history. Lewin's ahistorical focus on the contemporary environment was originally accompanied by a studied attention to the historicity of the "person" term in his well known Person × Environment formula. While the "field at the moment" could indeed be proximally manipulated by experimental approaches, it also is constructed by the person on the basis of distal phenomena issuing from exposure to past fields and past social relations. As a consequence of this more complicated vision of Lewinian theory, Lewin not only was claimed by experimental social psychologists as their "father," but his works found their way to important volumes in personality (see Hall & Lindzey, 1957) and developmental psychology (see Lewin, 1946).

In many ways, then, social psychologists took away the "bath water" of Lewinian thought and left most of the baby behind. The research accomplished in the traditional experimental model has done the equivalent of varying the temperature, density, depth, and so on of the water and then viewing its effects on the baby. Usually the "water" possesses the primacy of effect and the babies who occupy it are interchangeable for each other. Although these variations in proximal dimensions have revealed important characteristics of the human adaptive response system, contemporary developments in the field signal a need to consider more elements of the baby—or Lewin's person-term. The distal determination of the person's construction of the proximal field is one important direction that has begun to emerge. In the remainder of this chapter, we consider how the interplay in distal and proximal determinants in socialization gives rise to important novel perspectives on the social psychological embeddedness of mental health, adaptation, and personal dysfunction.

EXTERNAL SOCIALIZATION: DISTAL AND PROXIMAL INFLUENCES

Socialization is an indispensable attribute of human culture and society. It refers to the interpersonal processes by which adult (or senior) members of a culture or social group affect the norm and value acquisitions of "junior" members or potential members of that culture or group. Socialization processes partly originate with a wide variety of external influence strategies of socializers and are further initiated and sustained by the internal processing of the socialized. These latter internal processes represent cognitively and affectively reconstructed sequelae of external socialization and are more completely dealt with in Ruble and Thompson, (Chapter 4, this volume). Here we largely focus on the externally directed influences that constitute the beginning of the chain of socialization effects.

Even though socialization in the classic sense of life-course transmitted internal structures (such as beliefs and values) has not been explicitly dealt with in social psychological research and theory, social influence in its proximal sense has been a primary preoccupation of social psychologists since the turn of the century (see Triplett, 1898). Socialization can be viewed as the processes by which the effects of past proximal social influence are historically conserved by the person. Given that we possess attitudes, values, beliefs, social preferences, personal styles, and relationship proclivities prior to encounters with new social influences, the collision of these conserved aspects of socialization with the immediate and present proximal influences in the environment seem to be at the heart of adaptation and maladaptation. In the main, social psychologists have evaded this "collision" by focusing on the proximal effects of contemporary influence (i.e., the bath water) and downplaying the distal or conserved effects of past idiographic experience (the "baby"). Thus, social psychology teaches us that proximal effects have many powerful effects. (Some examples of these effects are listed below.) Attitudes form and change more readily when proximal communications are credible. Conformity to current norms occurs more readily when majorities are unanimous, when stimuli are more "uncertain," and when maintaining social bonds is a compelling motive. Obedience even to deviant norms can be induced by signaling the authoritative nature of the influencer to the target. We change our preassessed attitudes when we are made to believe that our counterattitudinal behavior issues from our own choices. We like ourselves less when forced by situational contingencies to focus on inner states. We experience depressed affect when induced to perceive ourselves as incapable of controlling important events and outcomes in our life (see Cialdini, 1988, for a review of these social influence effects).

Each of these effects and myriad others are pivotal discoveries with regard to mental health relevance. Under conditions in which we randomize or equate the backgrounds and proclivities of "babies," specificable variations in the "bath water" bring about adaptive variations on a wide array of mental health-relevant affects, cognitions, behaviors, and interpersonal structures. However, real contexts are seldom as "pure" as lab-manipulated ones, and real people are seldom randomizable in their natural states. These latter facts, while compelling, do *not* seriously reduce the importance of contemporary social psychological research for an understanding of nomothetically emergent phenomena. Indeed, the rather small and error-infused effects of laboratory research do have a role to play in preventive mental health efforts. When the goals of mental illness and social distress prevention are in themselves nomothetically cast, then social psychological discoveries on the relative impact of different techniques of social influence should be quite prominently consulted. For example, when one seeks to induce mass changes in adolescent attitudes and behaviors concerning drug use, sexual choice, suicide, school dropout, etc., those dimensions of variation that ensure a more effective message impact are quite pertinent. Even if the aggregation of proximal social influence strategies into an effective package accounts for a comparatively small portion the variance in newly socialized attitudes and behaviors on a mass basis, much will be gained in the area of broad social outcomes relevant to mental health.

Proximal models of social influence effects from social psychology also bear on extreme cases of situational impact as they relate to coping and mental health-related adaptation. Coping pressures under the situational impact of "mass" stresses such as earthquakes, floods, and disasters or pervasive situational distresses like divorce, sexual violence and victimization, or death of loved ones constitute great equalizers of distally socialized differences between people. In this sense, extreme social or environmental stress tends to produce a set of conditions that mirror the independent variable manipulations of laboratory research. In essence if we raise the temperature of the "bath water" to 220°, the differential hardiness of different babies will not be a major contributor to the primary outcome. Indeed, proximal factors are adequate predictors of these kinds of primary outcomes.

Thus, social psychological research and theory, even in its proximal form, should aid mental health programmers, policymakers, and crisis intervenors in their mission. However, the bulk of everyday adaptation to life's stresses and strains is not so environmentally overdetermined as our reactivity to floods, famine, or extreme personal violence. Indeed, most proximal influences on everyday adaptation are subtle and have idiosyncratic effects. It is often difficult to define the common thread underlying everyday coping difficulties, stress inducers, and adaptive styles. The question is not whether proximal influences have effects on everyday adaptation but *what* influences affect *whom* and *why*. It is in this sense that distal socialization processes as they initiate vulnerabilities and resiliencies in a person's life courses require study. One might argue that such phenomena are in the bailiwick of "personologists" and clinical psychologists, but it is critical to recognize that the unique perspectives of social psychology (particularly the study of social influence) have much to offer the study of distal socialization effects. A long-standing theoretical interest of social psychologists relates to how the effects of proximal social influence strategies effect stable internal changes or processes in the target of influence (see Shaw & Costanzo, 1982). Social psychologists have been interested in more than momentary changes in expressed attitudes and/or behaviors. They have indeed been quite devoted to understanding how and why such momentary changes usher in stable and somewhat "permanent" alterations in attitude and belief structures. Another way of looking at this long-standing interest in the interiorization of proximal social influence is to regard it as social psychology's approach to the formation of distally determined influence. The proximal influence strategies of the past are the distal determinants of present psychological phenomena such as beliefs and behaviors by condensed representative structures (such as schemas, scripts, and "working models").

A mere sampling of the questions that have been of historical interest to social psychologists clearly reflects this focus:

1. What proximal influence phenomena result in public conformity's being transformed into private acceptance?
2. What aspects of interpersonal feedback are incorporated by its recipients into changed personal self-conceptions?
3. What factors governing behavioral "compliance" give rise to alterations in self-perceived attitude?

4. Under what conditions do others' expectations of us act as self-fulfilling prophesies that induce confirmatory long-term behavior on our part?

This restricted array of traditional social psychological queries should make the case that the field has been uniquely interested in the temporally extended effects of proximal influence. Both broad contemporary and classical theoretical perspectives on social influence exemplify this interest. Kelman's (1961) model of opinion and attitude formation depicts a course from proximal compliance through interpersonal identification to a final goal state of internalization. This model can be viewed as a clear version of social psychology's approach to socialization. That is, the degree to which socializers transform their proximal influence approach from one of coercion, to one of "symbolic following" via identification, to one enabling attitudes to be self-possessed by the socialized is a mark of "successful" socialization. How outer demands become inner rules and realities defines the socialization course.

In Cialdini's (1988) more contemporary and highly engaging approach to social influence, he goes several steps farther than Kelman. Cialdini composes social psychological mechanisms of proximal social influence into six "weapons" that he sees as triggering the automatic complicity of humans to social cue properties These weapons are reciprocation, authority, liking, social proof, scarcity, and commitment and consistency. There are copious literatures on the impact of each of these proximal cue classes on social behavior that are beyond the scope of this chapter (for a review, see Cialdini, 1988). For our purposes, it is important to note that Cialdini extends Kelman's temporal model of social influence into the distant (but unspecified) history of human social experience. From Cialdini's perspective, the socialized person not only internalizes beliefs but in the process of doing so internalizes representations of those cues that bring about belief formation and that aid in personal adaptation. For example, to the extent that past experience with authority leads to self-protective and benign outcomes, we tend to internalize representations (status, expertise, and/or credibility cues) of benign authority. When such cues occur in the context of an influence encounter, they set off a "click-whirr" kind of automatic response on the part of the target of influence. In short, from Cialdini's perspective, humans "store" symbolic cues from distal experience that operate to promote effective proximal influence. Unfortunately, despite this promising theoretical beginning, Cialdini retreats from any form of life course or developmental theorizing concerning distal socialization. Instead of developmental reasoning, he employs the sociobiological metaphor of the trigger mechanism in intraspecies automatic responding as the distal origin. This is unfortunate, because Cialdini's evocative analysis points to a conclusion that proximal influence can only be understood in terms of distal acquisition—but then backs off further specification by appealing to vaguely biological universal needs of humans. This is not a criticism of Cialdini's impressive work but rather should be used as a symptom of social psychology's uneasy encounters with life-course or developmental thinking.

In order for social psychology to truly engage the study of life-course adaptation, the study of social influence must expand to the study of socialization and its goals. Cialdini's analysis, as well as most treatises on social influence, would benefit greatly from such an expansion. In order to begin this expansion, we must ask several novel questions: What are the goals of socialization? How do these goals relate to the mediating motives important to social psychological theorizing? How does combining the intuitive inventiveness of proximal models with life-course distal considerations promote social psychological applications to mental health and adaptation? These questions take up the remaining sections of this chapter. First, we move to a broader consideration of the goals of external socialization processes than is implied in contemporary social psychology. We then use these goals to reinterpret some primary social psychological models—particularly as they apply to children. Finally, we consider approaches that factor distal life-course influence into the corpus of social psychology. My hope in all of this is that the clear gestational relevance of proximal social psychological thinking to real adaptation can give birth to a willingness of the field to venture into the distant reaches of developmental history to redirect its theoretical and empirical approaches to inquiry.

THE GOALS OF SOCIALIZATION: CONNECTING THE DISTAL WITH THE PROXIMAL

We have already noted the superordinate goal of socialization— the incorporation of young or new members of a culture into the normatively based community shared by participants in that cultural unit. Such a goal is intrinsically important to mental health and adaptation because it defines a set of bench marks for deviance and cultural conformity. Since maladaptive or "mentally ill" behavior is defined as such by the culture, subculture, or community to which one belongs (cf. Coie & Costanzo, 1981), deviance from standards of behavior set by that cultural unit becomes a quintessential aspect of mental illness labeling. In addition, internal feelings of being different, inadequate, disabled, poorly self-identified, unaccepted by peers, "crazy," and so on are also referent to exterior norms with which one is at variance or phenomenally incapable of meeting.

There is a considerable range of acceptability of norms within diverse cultures. One can be shy, retiring, modest, and easygoing, or garrulous, outgoing, ebullient, and cheerful and still "fit" within acceptable parameters of cultural identity. Usually, subcultures have narrower preferences as to the developing behavioral proclivities of its children and new entrants. Thus, in some subgroups it might be "deviant" to be laid back and unambitious; in others it might be "deviant" to be unconcerned with others, somber, and socially introverted.

Nevertheless, it is important to acknowledge that all subgroups accept a range of normatively distributed behavior among its members and that all subgroups define a set of behaviors for which deviance is critically unacceptable. This "fact" of cultural organization is critical to the emergence of two central subgoals of socialization: (1) individuation and (2) social connection. The external processes of influence giving rise to the realization of these two goals create a dynamic that ushers in the central paradox of socialization efforts. On the one hand, humans and their senior caretakers strive to establish identities that represent themselves as separate and discernible entities with a unique pattern of attitudes, preferences, styles, self-identifications, and personality attributes. On the other hand, humans and their primary socializers seek to promote a sense of belongingness, connection, and safe social placement in their reference groups. The tasks of socialization, then, are directed at two seemingly oppositional goals— personal identity, or self-perceived distinctiveness from others, and social identity, or self-perceived connectedness to others. Presumably, positive development along each dimension of self-identification should promote effective, well-modulated, and socially acceptable behavior on the part of the socialized. In addition, a balance between these two goals should promote balanced emotional responses to the challenges of adaptation embodied by everyday coping pressures.

These two primary subgoals of socialization have important culturally ordered consequences that promote sustenance of existent social structures. In this sense, there is a kind of social–evolutionary imperative directing these aspects of socialization. Social identity permits cohesion and role-based specialization in culture. It also promotes distinctive subgroupings in the larger culture that drive social organization. Distinctive personal identities drive innovation in cultures in the face of demands for normative conformity and group cohesion. This latter form of identity also promotes a sense of efficacy and self-determination of individuals in cultural units—thus increasing the potential outcomes available within a culture. In short, the emergence of personal and social identity via processes of socialization serve both the individual and the collective in meeting the demands of adaptation. While this portrayal of socialization subgoals is not a new one (see Damon, 1983), it has not often been overtly acknowledged by commentators and researchers who deal with pieces of the socialization pie. Nevertheless, some of the more prominent perspectives arising from the study of social and self-development in the life course of socialization are directly relevant to this perspective.

Harter's (1983, 1987) important work on developing self-worth in children is predicated on a similar division of identity—relevant socialization goals. Deriving her framework from the conjoint application of James's (1890) and Cooley's (1902) visions of self-worth, she explicates an interesting model bifurcating social and personal identity. On the one hand, self-worth is predicated on the individual's evaluation of his or her own success at meeting personal goals (James's ratio of success to pretension). On the other hand, the person patterns discernment of self-worth by adopting the evaluative attitude of the generalized other toward self (Cooley's "looking-glass" notion). While Harter does not focus on this implication of her model, the Jamesian vision is one that is in accord with individuation and the Cooleyian vision with social connection. Even though Harter is not terribly explicit about the external socialization processes that connect to these two emerging identities, her use of child self-report measures is quite suggestive of two accompanying processes (see Harter, 1987). On the one hand, she considers the role of the child's "intrinsic" versus "extrinsic" orientation to learning as a mark of autonomy—establishing personal identity—and self-reports of perceived social support form others as a mark of connectedness—establishing social identity. How support is conveyed and how autonomy is enabled by the socialization strategies employed by caretakers in the culture is an important missing link in this work.

Parts of this link are addressed in the work of Deci and Ryan (1985). While the implied premise of Deci and Ryan's work is that individuation as represented by intrinsic self-determination is the "mentally healthy" side of socialization outcomes, they do consider processes pertinent to emergent social identity. They describe two important "internal" consequences of socialization: (1) the internalization of extrinsic rules, norms, and motives and (2) the development of "truly" intrinsic self-directed interests and motives.

In exploring both developmental derivatives, Deci and Ryan have sought to test which forms of parent and teacher proximal influence approaches underlie each aspect of socialized self-direction. In their ongoing work, they have been able to document a number of early proximal processes that seem to "enable" the development of both internalized extrinsic norms and intrinsic motivations. Although we do not detail these preliminary findings here (see Ruble & Thompson, Chapter 4, this volume for a fuller discussion), we can generally note that individuated or intrinsic aspects of identity formation are fostered by low-control strategies while internalized "social identities" seem to be enabled by circumstances promoting identification between caretaker and child. In the future, such work should be linked to the standard proximal influence processes employed in mainstream social psychology. As we shall see in subsequent sections of this chapter, such linkages are not only possible but potentially quite productive. What is important about the work of Deci and Ryan is that it extends consideration of the dual goals of socialization to the domain of influence processes.

Deci, Ryan, and Harter are certainly not the only scholars of socialization to implicitly adopt the dual-goal model specified above. Two other sources of important work on socialization—one from social psychology; the other from developmental psychology also render prominent the dual-goal model.

Higgins's (1989) model of self-discrepancy theory addresses the adaptive consequences of two kinds of self-relevant discrepancy. The discrepancy of "actual" and ideal self-concept is directly pertinent to the dynamics involved in the individuation process, while the discrepancies between "actual" and "ought" conceptions of self relate to the emergence of social identity. Higgins is interested in the adaptive consequences of these two forms of self-discrepancy, but he is a bit less explicit about the conditions under which direct proximal influence early in development might trigger each self-referent dynamic. Yet, these processes are preliminarily explicated in his model and are also discernible from general treatises on social influence.

The critical aspect of Higgins's perspective for our purposes is his implicit recognition of the joint role of two kinds of self-standards that drive developmental identification. The first of these are comparisons between self-perceived attributes and socially mediated values (i.e., our connections to the social collective) and the second, comparisons between our self-perceived attributes and our intrinsically determined goals for self-identification (i.e., our individuated distinctiveness). This theoretical theme is compatible with the joint James–Cooley perspective noted in Harter's work and Deci's two "internalized consequences" of socialization.

A final implicit marker of the connectedness–individuation dualism in socialization issues from the literature on childrearing in developmental psychology (see Maccoby & Martin, 1983). This is a copious and rich literature extending back to the early 1950s; its main contribution to our current discussion inheres in its dualistic representation of parameters of childrearing (or socialization). On the one hand, children's personalities, social proclivities, attributes, and values are seen as mediated by parental levels of nurturance. On the other hand, those same socialization products are seen as emerging from between-parent variations in disciplinary control. To make a complex issue simple, this literature typically portrays the over and undernurtured child as developing ideologies reflecting difficulties with connectedness or social belongingness. The over or undercontrolled child, however, is typically found to develop problems of self-efficacy, differentiation, and individuation. The intersection of these two dimensions, which are presumed to be orthogonal, results in the portrayal of four broad parenting styles (loving-controlling, hostile-controlling, loving-permissive, and hostile-permissive) that partly mediate the development of personal styles in children that reflect the coaction of communal and individuated identities.

For the social psychologist, one might argue that there is no more profound arena for social influence than the family unit. It is the seat of primary compliance pressure, it pulls for commitments based on identification, and it nurtures and enables the internalization of important beliefs, values, and schemes. The processes occurring in the life-course exposure of people to their nuclear origins would seem to provide very important information for social psychology's more transitory processes of social influence. Humans influence over others can occur in a laboratory and must at times be studied in that context. But, where they are most profound is in contextually situated development of adaptive orientations, social proclivities, and beliefs about self. The primary context for such acquisitions is the family. It is curious and tantalizing that the major dimensions of social influence so necessary to the explanation of laboratory demonstrations can be characterized in the simple two-dimensional model of parenting so prominent in the childrearing literature: (1) individual control as it relates to private acceptance and internalization and (2) social support and "nurturance" as it relates to the dynamics of conformity, norm acceptance, and social integration. This overlap in perspectives on familial rearing and social influence models has not been made cogently by social or developmental psychologists. Perhaps by approaching the problems of mental health, adaptation, and life adjustment, both developmental and social psychologists will find their links to one another.

In the next two sections of this chapter we briefly address the kind of social psychological research that has greatest implications for the individuation and social connective nature of life-course acquisition. Since we focus on processes of external socialization, we adhere closely to a description of the kind of work that has existed on the borders of developmental and social psychology in our exposition. When necessary for understanding, reference to the more conventional body of adult social psychology research will be made. Our overarching goal is to illustrate that what social psychologists think about the nature of external influence plays an important role in understanding variations in mental health and adaptation. As we shall see, the trick is to extend proximal models of contemporary change to events of distal origin. Maybe by struggling with this task, we will reawaken the parts of Lewin's legacy that push toward a recognition of the *life space* as a contemporary representation of an ontogenetically constructed reality.

EXTERNAL SOCIALIZATION
AND INDIVIDUATION

Of our two primary goals of socialization, it is the attainment of individuation that has most captured the inquiring minds of American social psychologists. Indeed, it is individuation that has most typically been placed on the "psychologically healthy" side of adaptive–maladaptive continua. Resisting conformity pressures is viewed as more self-affirming than yielding to them; making choices based on internally anchored beliefs reveals more intrinsic strength than making choices based on normative convention or communal standards; linking our competence to our active agency yields psychological benefits that far exceed the linking of competence to socially enabling conditions. A good portion of social psychology is directed at demonstrating how the collusion of various social forces robs us of our deftly logical minds, our secure identities, our moral standards, or our sense of empowerment for examples.

The most dramatic and compelling social psychological studies have served to illustrate the adaptive significance of human needs for individuated identity. From Asch's (1951) conformity studies to Milgram's (1963) obedience studies to cognitive dissonance and reactance mediated effects to "bystander" studies to studies of control illusions and "depressive realism," the pivotal role of *both actual and believed* causality by self-determination and unique identity has been copiously illustrated. In each of these domains, social forces or constraints (assumed or actual) literally and figuratively keep us from acting on the basis of the things we personally believe, strongly feel, or intrinsically value. Subtle authority coercion might lead otherwise altruistic folks to hurt innocent victims; a consensual majority can push us to assert public opinions that vary from our private beliefs; the mere presence of others inhibits our "natural" tendency to help distressed persons with rapidity and purpose. In short, social psychologists have taught us that when we act under the apparent control of external forces, we are generally less effective and consistent beings than when we act on the basis of individuated attributes. Indeed, the subjective preference of humans for consistent internally driven action constitutes one of the most frequent targets of laboratory manipulations in social psychological research. Our pressing "need" for individuation and self-determination can lead us to overattribute internal determination (e.g., attitudes) for our actions when we are made to feel free in our choices or unconstrained in our behavior. In summary, autonomous and individuated "selves" are seen as the origin of the lion's share of effective and adaptive behaviors by both American social psychologists and their subjects. When this tendency or need is pushed to its limit by clever manipulations, we can as a species err in the direction of overattribution to self.

In the main, however, much of the research and theory in social psychology views autonomous self-determination as "resilience" and external determination as "vulnerability." By extension, it becomes important to explore the processes and principles by which society socializes its young to become autonomous and self-directed. In Ruble and Thompson (Chapter 4, this volume), processes that pertain to internal or self-socialization are explicitly discussed. Here we focus on the external forces that drive and initiate self-socialization and autonomous self-direction. We do this by briefly summarizing socialization principles that are conjoint derivatives of research in adult social psychology and in research from social psychology transported to childhood development.

Principle 1: *Individuated self identity flows from socialization practices that provide minimally sufficient external pressure for action.*

The initial demonstrations of the potency of this principle of socialization issued from the motivationally anchored consistency framework of '60's social psychology. Whereas this work (most prominently research on cognitive dissonance) was directed at discovering the proximal factors that produce attitude and belief change (see Cooper & Aronson, Chapter 9, this volume for a full discussion of this tradition), it became increasingly clear that the main conclusions of this work had striking implications for the distal or developmental determination of intrinsically felt beliefs, preferences, and attitudes. One of the earliest studies out of the dissonance tradition demonstrated that 3–4-year-old children were more likely to adjust their toy preferences to conform to their behavior when the constraints over their behavior were subtle and minimal (see Aronson & Carlsmith, 1963). On the other hand, when such children were "coerced" to not play with a toy they initially preferred, they did not use their behavior as a valid indicator of their preference. To put this finding in a general frame, it could be argued that external pressure from socializers undermines the tendency of children to view their actions as determined by their underlying beliefs and feelings. Lepper and his colleagues (Lepper & Greene, 1979; Lepper & Gilovich, 1981) asserted precisely this point in their exploration of the sources of children's intrinsic academic interests. In their work, it was found that self-directed interest in such activities as mathematical puzzles was more likely when past rewards for engaging these materials were less prominent. They concluded that external rewards can undermine a child's intrinsic interest in the rewarded activity. Many other investigators have explored qualifiers of these kinds of effects (e.g. Boggiano, Main, & Katz, 1988; Pittman & Heller, 1987). Nevertheless, the major principle governing these phenomena remained a rather robust one.

Although this minimal sufficiency principle has been shown to be a powerful proximal determinant of internal self-reference, our suppositions about its role in the life course of in-context socialization can at this point only be speculative. Since individuated identity and perceptions of the elements of self are so much a part of developing adaptation, it would seem important to explore the means by which the minimal sufficiency principle operates in the real circumstances of parenting and childrearing. Can such a principle be envisioned to be at the heart of distal acquisition of intrinsic beliefs about self and one's preferences and capabilities? If so, how do actual socializers implicitly and explicitly employ such a principle? How do socializer intentions to instantiate different beliefs and attitudes in their children relate to their use of subtle versus extreme socialization pressure? If children's behavior is overdetermined by external contingencies, do they develop a less secure hold on their identity or a greater susceptibility to immediate and proximal social influence effects? In short, how well does the minimal sufficiency principle describe effective distal socialization, and what does it have to do with the development of domains of vulnerability in the life course? These are questions that are pivotally important for a social psychology of mental health.

Principle II: *Individuals seek to establish agency over their outcomes and when doing so they become better able to predict and control their future behavior, affects, and choices.*

This principle of individuated socialization is pervasively represented in the field of social and personality psychology. Beginning with the seminal treatises of Heider (1958) and de Charms (1968) on personal causality, the functional significance of self-perceived agency has become a centerpiece of the social psychology of adaptation. Parallel work in personality and clinical psychology on stable individual differences in perceived agency (e.g., Rotter, 1966) buttressed social psychological perspectives. Perceiving the contingency between our own behaviors and outcomes is the first step in the reproduction of like behaviors in the future. The absence of self-perceived agency has been linked to a variety of affective and cognitive deficits. Feeling oneself as an "origin" and not a "pawn," or a person with volitional power rather than one without self-determination, is the essence of the figural definition of the self. There are numerous lines of research in social psychology that have supported both the tendency of people to seek agency and the adaptive importance of perceptions of control. Also, there are contemporary lines in research that suggest that it is a mentally healthy tendency to hold an "illusion" of agency even when it is not a reality (see Alloy & Abramson, 1988; Alloy & Ahrens, 1987).

It is not possible in the context of this chapter to review the developmental lines of evidence sustaining the importance of the "agency" principle of developing individuation, but the illustration of the work of Dweck and her colleagues brings us close to the discovery of the effects of agentic self-perception on the adaptation of children. In a variety of studies (see for example Dweck & Legget 1988; Elliot & Dweck, 1988), Dweck has demonstrated that beneficial achievement outcomes and high future expectancies for control characterize children who attribute their successful achievement outcomes to effort or agency. In this line of work, Dweck and her colleagues have also found that to the extent that children view their outcomes as changeable or incremental rather than trait determined and fixed, they are more likely to exhibit efficacy in pursuit of various outcomes. The enabling conditions that socializers create to induce developing individuals to adopt flexible, changeable, and agentic views of goal realization are important issues for subsequent study. How these socializer "techniques" are employed across the life course, and how they distally determine a pervasive sense of agentic efficacy in children, should be prominent in programs of future research.

To the extent that parents, teachers, and other socializers attend to the conditions of behavior-outcome contingency in children, one should find the emergence of self-perceived potency and "optimism." To the extent that such behavior-outcome contingencies are left to be perceived as chaotically, externally, or intractably determined, one should observe the development of pessimism, depression, and helplessness as general orientations in children. We need to know a good deal more about the distal development of agentic self-perceptions in order to understand proximal susceptibility to discouragement and depression at different points in the life course.

Principle III: *As we increasingly integrate into self-identified peer groups, we use others as bench marks for the evaluation of our own unique attributes.*

This last principle of individuation is an important addition to the agency and minimal sufficiency principles noted above. Not only do we acquire notions of a separate identity from information we glean about our cognitive capacities or our intrinsic beliefs, values, and interests, we also differentiate ourselves from others by processes of comparative evaluation. The roots of social comparison most probably derive from early family interactions with adults and siblings; they become fully realized in the context of peer groups. Part of individuating involves the process of "differencing" ourselves from others. Those with whom we compare ourselves are likely to be individuals who allow for the greatest information yield about our own attributes. The early appearance of this kind of perspective in social psychology inheres in Festinger's (1954) theory of social comparison (cf. Shaw & Costanzo, 1982). Festinger proposed that social comparison is an inevitable characteristic of individuals in human collectives. It is a part of the epistemological process of self-knowing and self-distinctiveness. The enabling proximal conditions giving rise to comparison have been the subject of a wide array of studies (see Hakmiller, 1966). Factors affecting the choice of comparison others include similarity on any number of dimensions (e.g., gender), whether a personal trait or an ability trait is the object of comparison, mood, etc. The outcome of social comparison should be a firmer fix on "who we are" and what attributes and skills define us. The most prominent researchers of social comparison in children have been Ruble and her colleagues (see Chapter 4, this volume). For our purposes, it is important to note that Ruble and her colleagues provide intriguing leads with regard to the developmental emergence of peer-based comparisons. According to this work, in the early school years (prior to third grade) children notice differences between themselves and others (e.g., in ability) and even use the recognition of comparative difference for self-evaluative purposes. However, they do not use the results of these early comparisons as bench marks of their own stable personal traits. After approximately age 9, however, children not only recognize their comparative standing but begin to experience the attributes of self derived from such comparisons as somewhat indelibly embedded as "traits." (see Ruble, Boggiano, Feldman, & Loebel, 1980).

It is noteworthy that researchers of children's conformity to peers (see Costanzo & Shaw, 1966; Costanzo, 1970) have found that peers begin to become salient sources of conformity pressure during this same post-9-year-old period. The study of social comparison in children along with other work suggesting the increasing salience of peers in middle childhood suggests that the later stages of childhood individuation are achieved in the context of peer group exchanges. That is, whereas conceptions of agency and intrinsic control may have their beginning origins in parental mediation, the playing out of separate identities may be most profoundly reflected in the comparative appraisals emergent from developing peer groups. Social psychologists have spent much time exploring the components of group structure and interaction that give rise to different outcomes, but they have not spent much research effort on mapping the developmental course of peer exchange—particularly as it effects socialization in the long run. Such inquiries are necessary to our understanding of such mental health-relevant processes as self-esteem, achievement, occupational choices, choices of partners in relationships, and the like. The principle of comparative appraisal suggests that individuated identities do not exist in a social vacuum but are continually updated by our observation of self-other comparisons. The course of change from family-based emergent self-conception to peer-mediated changes in self-conception requires careful developmental analysis.

EXTERNAL SOCIALIZATION AND SOCIAL CONNECTEDNESS

The three principles discussed above summarize how contributions from social psychology and related domains have provided suggestive evidence for the emergence of individuated identity. It is presumed that the distinct self-conceptions we develop have much to do with the affective states, adaptive responses, and interpersonal relations that either compromise or sustain mentally healthy adjustments. It is also presumed in the above treatment that careful study of the emergence of individuated identity in the life course will benefit substantially from the developmental extension of social psychology's proximal models of social influence.

Yet, the picture of the developing individual painted by principles of individuation is an incomplete one. Much of our adaptive life occurs in a socially embedded context. Although it is important to "track" ourselves by processes of difference or uniqueness establishing, it is equally important to track our developing identity as relationship partners. Who are we in the social world? Indeed, what is the social world we phenomenally confront? What external socialization processes connect us to the collective, and allow for our identity as individuals to be realized through interactive exchange?

These are daunting questions, but they constitute some of the oldest and most pervasive interests of social psychologists. Not only is the individual found in society, but society is found in the individual. And, as we implied earlier in this chapter, the dialectic dynamic that emerges between individuation and social identification drives the adaptive process in development. In order to complete our picture of developing processes ushered in by external socialization, we move to principles of the socialization of connected identity. In this discussion, we consider two broad principles derivative from the process literature on social relationships as they effect self-development. The first is the principle of socially embedded identity and the second the principle of social attachment.

Principle IV (a): *We derive a sense of "who we are" and what we can become by identifying with subgroups of individuals with whom we perceive shared fate or shared substance.*

Principle IV (b): *Once such social identities are established, they can serve to buffer us from stress, failure, depression, and other negative consequences by processes of presumed and actual social support.*

There is an entire family of proximal processes in social psychology that exemplifies each part of principle IV. From the similarity–attraction framework forwarded by Byrne (1969) to the research on ingroup identification and its effects of self-conception, there are a range of phenomena that suggest that a strong component of adaptation is mediated by our ability or opportunity to identify with others in our social worlds. These identifications of self might turn on categorical subgroupings such as ethnic and gender groups, phenotypic subgroupings as might be represented by physical characteristics (hair color) or stigmatizing conditions (e.g., obesity), or acquired categorizations (e.g., shared alma mater, fraternity, occupation, social club, or political party). What research in social psychology strongly implies is that self-placement in such reference groups has profound effects on our behavior, choices, and affects about self and other. Socialization does not only make us male or female or black or white on the outside of ourselves but also instantiates these characteristics as parts of our insides. They are the elements of society that are in the individual. These aspects of identity are anything but trivial since in history they have frequently constituted the bases for war and conflict as well as treaties and bonds. The research of social psychology is punctuated by examples of how such social identifications mediate cognition, affect, and behavior. This research also indicates that we carry these identifications with us as we approach new situations. For example, McGuire and McGuire (1988) has found that if one is the only one of a category (e.g., black) in a group, then that aspect of identity becomes a more prominent part of awareness and self-conception. The process variables that engender the effects of social identification are myriad, ranging from attitude similarity to coorientation to stimuli. What is important to explore is the degree to which these process variables have origins in the developmental context of family and peer group relationships. When (in development) does being part of a group affect the way we think, act, and feel? How does it buffer or enhance distress? How does it contribute to intrinsic self-definition across the life course? Each of these questions as well as myriad others requires extension of social psychological models to life-course development.

Principle IV (b) is similarly an important component of the social psychology of mental health. There are now numerous investigations that illustrate the potency of social support in promoting adaptation and coping (cf. Cohen & Wills, 1985; Rook, 1984). Recent work in health psychology has indicated that sharing aspects of self with others decreases stress, physical illness, and depression (cf. Pennenbaker, 1989). Such interpersonal acts of connection are enhanced by inferences of similarity, common membership, and common fate between people. Thus, connective identity is an adaptive aspect of social subgrouping. It is important to understand how it enters the system of developing self-identity and how it is sustained through adulthood.

Principle V: *In our interactions with others, we develop ideologies of social relationship that result in the repetitive enactment of self-defining and socially defining behaviors, feelings, and emotions.*

While the investigations of the proximal effects of recent social experiences in empirical social psychology provide many hints to the truth value of principle V, more recent attempts (e.g., Hazan & Shaver, 1987) to extend the study of early infant attachment to adult relationships promise a more extended life-course model of such effects. We know from many laboratory demonstrations that a prior experience of rejection or agonistic social outcome colors our subsequent interactions and social inferences. This work suggests that at least for the brief period of a laboratory encounter, we develop "working models" of anticipated social relationships from recent experience. It should be the case that the *chronic* working models we possess of social relationships should have a considerably stronger impact on our day-to-day relationships than these brief lab encounters.

Recent research and theory by both developmental and social psychologists (Hazan & Shaver, 1987; Bretherton & Waters, 1985; Main, Kaplan, & Cassidy, 1985; Putallaz, Costanzo, & Klein, 1992) has sought to explore the implications of the developmental continuity in attachment processes. For nearly two decades, the attachment framework initially introduced by Bowlby (1969) has been a fixture in the manner in which developmental psychologists understand the early emergence of relationship styles and felt security. In Bowlby's (1969, 1973, 1980) ethological–evolutionary perspective, the attachment behavioral system between infant and mother is viewed as the basis for protection from predators and safe exploration of the environment. The caregiver's sensitivity to the infant's cues and signals and availability in times of distress affect the degree of trust and security the infant develops as a consequence of the attachment relationship.

From this theory and the subsequent empirical work of Ainsworth and her colleagues, three "types" of attachment styles develop: secure, avoidant, and ambivalent attachment. It has been further presumed that these early attachment styles are interiorized as working models of all relationships and thus govern the child's (and developed adult's) approach to social others. Securely attached individuals experience pleasure in intimacy and contact, but retain a sense of security in separating from intimate others. Avoidant types experience insecurity in attachment and active indifference on rebonding. Ambivalent types experience insecurity in attachment and "cling" and "protest" in response to reunion. Each of these styles involves components of self-conception and definition of the social world. The two latter types have been linked to different forms of relationship-anchored psychopathology (e.g., Cohn, 1990).

The recent groundswell of research on personal and intimate relationships in social psychology (see Duck, 1992) has led to the emergence of similar hypotheses concerning attachment for the study of adult relationships and relationship practices. In this work, it is becoming clearer that the simple proximal effects of laboratory acceptance and/or rejection manipulations are insufficient indicators of life-course sequences of relationship development. Approaches to social connection are apparently rooted in early parental experience, and these distal events are internalized as relationship schema elicited by proximal phenomena (cf. Hazan & Shaver, 1987).

For the purposes of our analysis, it is clear that the most profound source of external socialization relating to adaptation might emerge from the conserved remnants of relationship history. Crucial aspects of our socialized identity are entangled in the history of closeness that characterizes our rearing. In order to understand why proximal social feedback has such profound short term effects, we must understand its long-term origins. Adaptation and mental health themselves are relational concepts and as such warrant careful study by social psychologists. Delving into the life-course origins of relationship proclivities should constitute a priority for the further development of a social psychology of mental health.

CONCLUSIONS

This chapter has taken a circuitous path through the garden of external socialization research and theory. Its main messages are simple to state but more difficult to implement. They are:

1. Social psychology has already yielded much in the way of knowledge concerning proximal processes of external socialization, yet it now requires an additional step in order for the promise of this work to be translated into effective models for understanding mental health-related

distress. This step involves the introduction of life-course analysis into social psychological theory.

2. In order to first engage such an analysis, we require a model that embeds social influence processes within a general model of socialization.

3. The model offered in this chapter proposes the use of a two-goal frame in which socialization as viewed as a process of (a) acquired individuation and (b) acquired social connection.

4. This requires the reconceptualization of social psychological phenomena in the form of researchable principles relating to each dimension of socialization.

Subsequent research and theory in social psychology will realize the promise of its intriguing "take" on human adaptation when it embeds itself in the confines of life trajectories. In this form, we can rediscover Lewin's legacy and reopen his path of action research so pivotal to our understanding of our own resilience and vulnerability to the pressures of social life.

REFERENCES

Alloy, L. B., & Abramson, L. Y. (1988). Depressive realism: Four theoretical perspectives. In L. B. Alloy (Ed.), *Cognitive processes in depression* (pp. 223–265). New York: Guilford Press.

Alloy, L. B., & Ahrens, A. H. (1987). Depression and pessimism for the future: Biased use of statistically relevant information in prediction for self versus others. *Journal of Personality and Social Psychology, 52*, 366–378.

Aronson, E., & Carlsmith, J. M. (1963). Effect of severity of threat on the devaluation of forbidden behavior. *Journal of Abnormal and Social Psychology, 66*, 584–588.

Asch, S. E. (1951). Effects of group pressure upon the modification and distortion of judgment. In H. Guetzkow (Ed.), *Groups, leadership, and men* (pp. 177–190). Pittsburgh, PA: Carnegie Press.

Boggiano, A. K., Main, D. S., & Katz, P. A. (1988). Children's preference for challenge: The role of perceived competence and control. *Journal of Personality and Social Psychology, 54*, 134–141.

Bowlby, J. (1969). *Attachment and loss. Vol. I. Attachment.* New York: Basic Books.

Bowlby, J. (1973). *Attachment and loss. Vol. II. Separation: Anxiety, and anger.* New York: Basic Books.

Bowlby, J. (1980). *Attachment and loss. Vol. III. Loss: Sadness and depression.* New York: Basic Books.

Bretherton, I., & Waters, E. (1985). *Growing points in attachment theory and research* (Monographs of the Society for Research in Child Development, Vol. 50, No. 1–2, Serial No. 209, pp. 3–36). Chicago: University of Chicago Press.

Byrne, D. (1969). Attitudes and attraction. In L. Berkowitz (Ed.), *Advances in experimental social psychology* (Vol. 4, pp. 35–89). New York: Academic Press.

Cialdini, R. (1988). *Influence: Science and practice.* Glenview, IL: Scott-Foresmann.

Cohen, S., & Wills, T. A. (1985). Stress, social support and the buffering hypothesis. *Psychological Bulletin, 98,* 310–357.

Cohn, D. A. (1990). Child–mother attachment at six years and social competence at school. *Child Development, 61,* 152–162.

Coie, J. D., & Costanzo, P. R. (1981). Behavioral determinants of mental illness concerns: A comparison of community subgroups. *American Journal of Community Psychology, 8,* 537–555.

Cooley, C. H. (1902). *Human nature and the social order.* New York: Scribner.

Costanzo, P. R., & Shaw, M. E. (1966). Conformity as a function of age level. *Child Development, 37,* 967–975.

Costanzo, P. R. (1970). Conformity as a function of self-blame. *Journal of Personality and Social Psychology, 14,* 266–274.

Damon, W. (1983). *Social and personality development.* New York: Horton.

de Charms, R. (1968). *Personal conversation.* New York: Academic Press.

Deci, E., & Ryan, R. (1985). *Intrinsic motivation and self-determination in human behavior.* New York: Plenum.

Duck, S. (1992). *Understanding relationship processes. Vol. 2: Learning about relationships.* New York: Sage.

Dweck, C. S., & Leggett, E. L. (1988). A social-cognitive approach to motivation and personality. *Psychological Review, 95,* 256–273.

Elliott, E. S., & Dweck, C. S. (1988). Goals: An approach to motivation and assessment. *Journal of Personality and Social Psychology, 54,* 5–12.

Festinger, L. (1954). A theory of social comparison processes. *Human Relations, 7,* 117–140.

Hakmiller, K. L. (Ed.). (1966). Social comparison [Special issue]. *Journal of Experimental Social Psychology* (Suppl. 1).

Hall, C. S., & Lindzey, G. (1957). *Theories of personality.* New York: Wiley.

Harter, S. (1983). Developmental perspectives on the self-system. In E. M. Hetherington (Ed.), *Handbook of child psychology: Socialization personality and social development* (Vol. IV, pp. 103–196). New York: Wiley.

Harter, S. (1987). Self-worth in children. In N. Eisenberg (Ed.), *Contemporary topics in child development.* New York: Wiley.

Hazan, C., & Shaver, P. (1987). Romantic love conceptualized as an attachment process. *Journal of Personality and Social Psychology, 52,* 511–524.

Heider, F. (1958). *The psychology of interpersonal relations.* New York: Wiley.

Higgins, E. T. (1989). Self-discrepancy theory: What patterns of self-beliefs cause people to suffer? In L. Berkowitz (Ed.), *Advances in experimental social psychology, 22,* 93–136. New York: Academic Press.

James, W. (1890). *Psychology.* New York: Holt.

Kelman, H. C. (1961). Processes of opinion change. *Public Opinion Quarterly, 25,* 57–58.

Lepper, M., & Gilovich, T. (1981). The multiple functions of reward: A social developmental perspective. In J. Brehm, S. Kassin, & F. Gibbons (Eds.), *Developmental social psychology* (pp. 5–31). New York: Oxford Press.

Lepper, M. R., & Greene, D. (Eds.). (1979). *The hidden costs of reward.* Hillsdale, NJ: Erlbaum.

Lewin, K. (1943). Defining the "field at a given time." *Psychological Review, 50,* 292–310.

Lewin, K. (1946). Behavior and development as a function of the total situation. In L. Carmichael (Ed.), *Manual of child psychology* (pp. 791–844). New York: Wiley.

Lewin, K. (1951). *Field theory in social science.* New York: Harper & Row.

Maccoby, E. E., & Martin, J. A. (1983). Socialization in the context of the family: Parent–child interaction. In E. M. Hetherington (Ed.), *Handbook of child psychology* (Vol. 4, pp. 1–102). New York: Wiley.

Main, M., Kaplan, N., & Cassidy, J. (1985). Security in infancy, childhood, and adulthood: A move to the level of representation. In I. Bretherton & E. Waters (Eds.), *Growing points in attachment theory and research* (Monographs of the Society for Research in Child Development, Vol. 50, No. 1–2, Serial No. 209, pp. 66–104). Chicago: University of Chicago Press.

McGuire, W. J., & McGuire, C. V. (1988). Content and process in the experience of self. In C. Berkowitz (Ed.), *Advances in experimental social psychology.* New York: Academic Press.

Milgram, S. (1963). A behavioral study of obedience. *Journal of Abnormal and Social Psychology, 67,* 371–378.

Pennebaker, J. W. (1989). Confession, inhibition, and disease. In L. Berkowitz (Ed.), *Advances in experimental social psychology* (Vol. 22, pp. 211–244). New York: Academic Press.

Pittman, T., & Heller, J. (1987). Social motivation. *Annual Review of Psychology, 38,* 461–489.

Putallaz, M., Costanzo, P. R., & Klein, T. P. (1992). Parental childhood social experiences and their effects on children's relationships. In S. Duck (Ed)., *Understanding relationship processes. Vol. 2: Learning about relationships.* New York: Sage.

Rook, K. S. (1984). The negative side of social interaction: Impact on psychological well-being. *Journal of Personality and Social Psychology, 46,* 1097–1108.

Rotter, J. B. (1966). Generalized expectancies for internal vs. external control. *Psychological Monographs, 80*(609).

Ruble, D., Boggiano, A. K., Feldman, N. S., & Loebel, J. H. (1980). A developmental analysis of the role of social comparison in self-evaluation. *Developmental Psychology, 16*, 105–115.

Shaw, M. E., & Costanzo, P. R. (1982). *Theories of social psychology.* New York: McGraw-Hill.

Triplett, N. (1898). The dynamogenic factors in pacemaking and competition. *American Journal of Psychology, 9*, 507–533.

The Implications of Research
on Social Development
for Mental Health:
An Internal Socialization Perspective

DIANE N. RUBLE and ERIK P. THOMPSON

Several million children and adolescents in the United States suffer psychological problems, and the number has increased over time. Yet children are one of the most neglected groups in mental health (Tuma, 1989), in spite of the widely held agreement that effective prevention and remediation during childhood have the greatest likelihood of long-term success. This chapter focuses on one aspect of the neglect: how basic research on social developmental processes can increase the effectiveness of prevention and remediation efforts. Curiously, clinical analyses of particular psychological problems, such as school phobia, sometimes fail to consider why such problems arise except in the most global terms, such as fear of separation from parents or particular anxieties associated with school (Last & Francis, 1988). Although a wide variety of therapeutic techniques and prevention programs are used, with indications of reasonable success (Casey & Berman, 1985; Durlak, Fuhrman, & Lampman, 1991), they are often developed and evaluated in a hit-and-miss fashion. It is acknowledged that research should be careful to specify boundary conditions—"What techniques work, for whom, and under what conditions?" (Kazdin, 1989, p. 184). But we would argue that even this is an inefficient trial-and-error approach given the level of knowledge already available in the field of social development.

Many forms of psychological impairment involve problems central to social developmental processes, either as a primary or a secondary aspect of the disorder. These include (1) interpersonal relationships and attachments, (2) self-esteem, and (3) coping and self-regulation. There is now a large body of knowledge on these processes within the field of social development (Collins & Gunnar, 1990). This knowledge could be extremely useful in the prevention–intervention enterprise, but the utilization of findings from basic social developmental research has too rarely occurred. The goals of this chapter are to (1) provide examples of how social developmental research is or could be made relevant to fostering mental health in children, (2) indicate limitations with existing knowledge in applying such findings, and (3) provide recommendations for how future research may make existing knowledge more relevant or extend the study of basic mechanisms to other relevant mental health domains.

INTERNAL SOCIALIZATION PROCESSES

The term "socialization" traditionally refers to how environmental context and socializing agents (e.g., family, social structures, culture, TV) shape a child's behavior and values. In this sense, children are socialized by processes external to them (see Chapters 2 and 3, this volume, for examples). There has been a growing awareness among developmental researchers, however, that children influence their parents as well as the reverse as part of the socialization of those children (Maccoby, 1984). In addition, developmental researchers have increasingly recognized that the impact of the external socialization context depends on what information a child seeks and how the child processes and interprets it (Ruble, Higgins, & Hartup, 1983). Such internal socialization processes are often referred to as self-socialization—that is, that children, in part, socialize themselves (Maccoby & Jacklin, 1974; Ruble, 1987) as part of their social–cognitive construction and representation processes, innate temperament and motivation, and sense of self.

In this chapter, we focus on two broad categories of internal socialization mechanisms: social cognition and intrinsic, or mastery, motivation.[1] Although these two categories do not exhaust the possibilities of internal socialization mechanisms relevant to mental health, we attempt to show that they are fundamental to understanding mental health phenomena. Moreover, these two mechanisms are featured prominently in the relevant developmental literature. The basic premise underlying research on social–cognitive processes is that the impact of the social environment on the individual cannot be predicted or understood independent of the individual's construction and interpretation of social events or conditions (e.g., Markus & Zajonc, 1985; Shantz, 1983). Thus, in order to examine psychological distress, one must consider what kinds of constructions and interpretations (about oneself and others) are maladaptive and how they are maintained. This idea is particularly important to the study of childhood and adolescence because basic cognitive processes change in ways likely to produce quite different areas of vulnerability in children at different ages.

The literature on intrinsic motivation assumes that an orientation toward mastery and effectance is a fundamental human motive (White, 1959). The basic premise is that pleasure is derived from activities that are freely engaged in and that provide a sense of progress and mastery (Deci & Ryan, 1985; Lepper & Greene, 1978). For these reasons, an intrinsic motivational orientation is believed to contribute to a sense of well-being and to have positive implications for variables related to mental health, such as self-esteem. In addition, it is assumed that a child's resilience to psychological stressors is reduced to the extent that mastery motivation and self-determination are undermined or disrupted. Thus, basic research on mechanisms maintaining or disrupting intrinsic motivation has considerable promise for identifying early precursors of mental health or distress.

Although social cognition and intrinsic motivation emphasize quite different mechanisms (cognitive constructions and interpretations vs. motivational goals and affect) and represent distinct literatures, they overlap in a number of ways as well. Mastery motivation is often represented cognitively, for example, in terms of effort attributions (Dweck, 1975). Similarly, age-related changes in social–cognitive capacities may moderate the impact of socializing forces on the ontogeny of intrinsic motivation (Pittman & Boggiano, in press; Ruble & Frey, 1991). Indeed, throughout the chapter, we attempt to highlight areas of overlap and later present a framework within which the developmental interplay of constructs from the two areas might be fully appreciated.

Social–Cognitive Processes: Illustrations of Mental Health Relevance

The literature on social cognition is concerned with how individuals construct and give meaning to their social world, how the actions of oneself and others are interpreted, how individual knowledge structures shape information seeking and information processing, and so on. Such research is widely recognized as critical to prevention and intervention efforts in the field of mental health (Alloy, 1988; Abramson, 1988; Fazio, 1990). Several recent lines of research indicate how maladaptive personal and interpersonal behaviors may emerge and be maintained by social–cognitive processes.

Information Processing and Attribution

One such line of research is concerned with biases in information processing and causal attributions concerning interpersonal events (Coie, 1990; Dodge & Feldman, 1990; Rubin, 1982). A noteworthy feature of such research is that it often focuses on at-risk samples, such as rejected or aggressive children. For example, aggressive boys have been found to expect aggression from their peers and accordingly interpret ambiguous provocations as reflecting hostile intentions rather than as neutral or accidental. In this way, they may become locked into a style of aggressiveness and rejection that is difficult to change. Some research in this area has even tested basic mechanisms by means of clinical application (e.g., Coie & Koeppl, 1990; Parke & Slaby, 1983). For example, Bierman (1986) found that successful behavioral change during social skills training with aggressive boys could be linked directly to positive changes in social–cognitive processes.

Related research in the area of self-evaluation suggests that attributional processes are critical to perceptions of success and failure as well as to affective reactions to these events (Frieze, 1981; Weiner, 1985). As with peer relations research, there are individual differences in attributional processes or styles. To illustrate, individuals who are relatively more mastery oriented and males relative to females tend to show more functional attributional styles (e.g., attributions of failure to lack of effort rather than lack of ability) (Dweck & Elliott, 1983; Forsterling, 1985; Frey & Ruble, 1987). These differential attributions are important in part because helpless responses to failure may be maintained by attributions to ability ·rather than effort. As Dweck (1975) has shown, interventions that emphasize effort attributions are effective in promoting more mastery-oriented approaches toward performance failures among school-aged children. Developmental research on processes involved in attributions for achievement has focused on age differences in children's abilities to utilize certain causal attributional principles (Ruble & Rholes, 1981; Smith, 1975). To illustrate, compensatory logic dictates that given equal performances, a person who tries harder than another person will be seen as having lower ability. Children younger than 7–9 years, however, often fail to recognize the compensatory relation between effort and ability when explaining success, and instead believe that high effort indicates high ability (Kun, 1977). Such attributional biases may partially explain young children's overly positive self-evaluations and resilience to failure experiences (Stipek & MacIver, 1989). Interestingly, then, some attributional "biases" may have positive implications for mental health. Taylor and Brown (1988) argue that positive misperceptions of oneself and one's social environment can contribute to a sense of well-being.

Finally, attributional analyses have recently been applied to parenting practices. For example, a series of studies by Eccles et al. (Eccles, Jacobs, & Harold, 1990) has shown that sex stereotypic beliefs and attributions of parents appear to contribute to girls' feelings of inadequacy in sports and science and boys sense of inadequacy in English. Dix et al. (e.g., Dix, Ruble, & Zambarano, 1989) have shown that attributional processes are linked to parents' responses to their children's misdeeds. The potential relevance of such research to mental health is suggested by recent findings that negative cognitive biases are found in parents of aggressive and abused children (Dix, 1991).

In brief, attributional biases appear to differ across individuals who show adaptive versus maladaptive interpersonal, achievement-related, and parenting behaviors. Thus, an important direction for future research is to examine factors that lead to biases and that may reduce them. Social psychological analyses show that motivational factors (such as personal relevance and accountability) often reduce information-processing biases in general (Chaiken, 1980; Erber & Fiske, 1984) and attributional biases in particular (Miller, 1976). Such analyses may provide guidance for social–cognitive research with children. Indeed, a few studies have shown that children's social information processing and behavior change when information is made personally relevant by leading children to expect future interaction with the target peers (Feldman & Ruble, 1988; Graziano, Brody, & Bernstein, 1980; Thompson, Boggiano, Costanzo, Matter, & Ruble, 1992). Such analyses cannot furnish a complete answer, however; it is highly unlikely that the attributional biases discussed above are due in any simple and direct way to low personal relevance associated with these particular contexts (interpersonal aggression, achievement, and parenting). Learning more about the etiology and maintenance of such biases may thus enrich our theories of how and when personal relevance affects information processing as well as providing knowledge potentially useful to therapeutic intervention.

Standards of Evaluation

Reactions to success or failure outcomes partly depend on which dimensions of the self are emphasized. Damon and Hart (1988) suggest that children focus on different aspects of the self at different ages, shifting, for example, from comparative features of abilities or psychological attributes during middle childhood to social skills and social "appeal" in early adolescence. The obvious mental health implication is that children are likely to be more emotionally responsive to positive and negative events that are of particular concern to their age level. Similarly, several investigators suggest that using different standards of excellence can lead to quite different emotional reactions to the same outcomes (Dweck & Elliott, 1983; Harter, 1990; Higgins, Strauman, & Klein, 1986). In a competitive classroom setting, for example, comparisons with peers may lead everyone except the highest performers to feel inadequate, whereas comparisons made with previous performance may lead most to feel successful. Even children who are very high performers may have problems with self-esteem, depending on their choice of standards (Pope, McHale, & Craighead, 1988).

Thus, suggestions that use of standards vary as a function of age (e.g., Ruble, 1983; Suls, 1986) or level of experience (Ruble & Frey, 1991) have important implications for prevention–intervention efforts. Frey and Ruble (1990), for example, suggest that different standards may differentially benefit individuals whose level of skill at a particular activity (e.g., running) is improving rather than deteriorating. Only the former are likely to feel particularly proud when they make comparisons with previous outcomes. Instead, for individuals whose performance is declining (e.g., senior runners), social comparison may prove a more adaptive standard than temporal comparison. Interestingly, a growing body of research suggests that individuals are usually extremely adept at selecting standards that enhance self-esteem, particularly when there are threats to the self (Frey & Ruble, 1990; Goethals, 1986). Further research on how and why they do this may prove fruitful in refining social–cognitive therapies for individuals who respond maladaptively to threatening circumstances.

Knowledge of Emotion Management and Coping Strategies

A third line of research is concerned with knowledge of strategies relevant to coping and emotion management. Several researchers have been examining developmental changes in children's understanding of emotions (Donaldson & Westerman, 1986; Whitesell & Harter, 1989) and in strategies for coping with negative emotions (Altshuler & Ruble, 1989; Harris, Othof, & Terwogt, 1981; Shoda, Mischel, & Peake, 1990). Such research is important, in part because emotion-relevant knowledge and self-control have been linked to effective interaction and peer acceptance (e.g., Gottman & Mettetal, 1986). In addition, prevention programs aimed at helping children cope with stressful circumstances, such as divorce or hospitalization, need to recognize that some otherwise beneficial strategies, such as cognitive distraction, may not be feasible with young children, and that other interventions (such as adult-aided distraction) may be required.

Knowledge of appropriate coping strategies is also relevant to peer interaction processes. Rejected children show less awareness of appropriate strategies for entering a peer group (Gottman, 1983; Putallaz & Wasserman, 1990), and some recent research suggests that strategic orientations more generally depend on level of development. Specifically, for children younger than 7–8 years, orientations toward peers appear to be primarily affect driven, whereas older children's orientations incorporate and may even emphasize an instrumental, strategic component (Feldman & Ruble, 1988; Graziano et al., 1980; Thompson, Ruble, Boggiano, & Pittman, 1991). One way to interpret these findings is that younger children are unable or unwilling to respond to others strategically in terms of pragmatic considerations. Effective interaction sometimes requires regulating one's behavior strategically, however, and acting differently from the way one feels. Maintaining a friendly stance in the face of initial rejection, for example, may be necessary for a newcomer to enter an existing group. Such possibilities have direct implications for promoting effective interventions. Although recent findings suggest that training in related types of strategies may be effective in reducing peer rejection problems (Coie & Koeppl, 1990), the possibility that children at different ages require different types of social skills training remains to be evaluated.

Development of Personal and Interpersonal Constructs

A fourth line of research is concerned with developmental changes in constructs relevant to adjustment or to the impact of socialization. For example, social–cognitive changes in adolescence may contribute to increasing alienation and conflict sometimes observed at this time (Powers, Hauser, & Kilner, 1989). Smetana (1988) has identified one such change—an increasing gap between parent and child perceptions of authority that appears to contribute to family conflict.

One of the most well-documented developmental changes concerns how children perceive their own characteristics (Damon & Hart, 1988; Harter, 1990; Rosenberg, 1986) and those of others (Livesley & Bromley, 1973; Rholes & Ruble, 1984). Young (under 7 years) children's conceptions emphasize concrete features (specific behaviors and physical features), whereas older children begin to view people as possessing stable, dispositional characteristics (Rholes, Newman, & Ruble, 1990; Shantz, 1983). These changes are of major mental health significance because as children become aware that there are some stabilities in the characteristics of people, such as popularity and classroom abilities, failures and interpersonal difficulties take on added significance. Children younger than 7 years of age are notably resilient in their response to failure, possibly because they believe that such an outcome is only a momentary perturbation and can easily be overcome the next time. Once children recognize the potential long-term significance of immediate behaviors, however, they become more sensitive to evaluation (Frey & Ruble, 1985) and more prone to helpless reactions to failure (Rholes, Blackwell, Jordan, & Walters, 1980; Rholes, Jones, & Wade, 1988). Similarly, children who attribute social rejection to stable, personal inadequacies are less likely to cope effectively by changing their style of interaction than those who do not (Dweck, 1991). Thus, once children begin to interpret behaviors in terms of stable constructs or events, an initial conclusion that they are not likable may lead to a maladaptive behavior pattern that maintains their rejected status.

With respect to prevention and intervention efforts, such findings suggest that teachers, parents, and relevant professionals need to be aware of such periods of developmental vulnerability associated with changing social constructs. In an achievement setting, for example, new concerns with the evaluation of one's ability may create special affiliation problems for a child low in ability. Such children may isolate themselves because of embarrassment experienced during negative social comparisons with friends. Understanding why such isolation occurs is important to designing appropriate interventions. Because ability-related comparisons are less meaningful between friends of different ages, interventions that place isolated children with younger children (Furman, Rahe, & Hartup, 1979) may be particularly appropriate. Similarly, different intervention strategies may be appropriate for children at different ages. Grusec (1983), for example, reports age differences in the effectiveness of attribution interventions. Making internal attributions for a given behavior (e.g., "What a good and helpful child you are to do that") led to a generalized change in behavior only for children older than 7 years.

Intrinsic (Mastery) Motivational Processes: Illustrations of Mental Health Relevance

The terminology and conceptualizations associated with intrinsic motivation have received considerable debate over the years (Boggiano & Hertel, 1983; Deci & Ryan, 1985; Lepper, Greene, & Nisbett, 1973; Higgins & Trope, 1990; Kruglanski, 1975; Pittman, Boggiano, & Ruble, 1986). The present discussion of "intrinsic motivation" emphasizes an orientation toward mastery, growth, and learning consistent with views describing organismic propensities toward (1) experiencing one's actions as effective in producing desirable changes in the environment (White, 1959; Deci & Ryan, 1985) and (2) personal causality—experiencing one's behavior as self-determined and freely chosen, rather than simply a set of reactions to externally initiated events (de Charms, 1968; Deci & Ryan, 1985). The present emphasis is also based on considerable support provided by recent reviews for the role of experienced competence and self-determination in the development and maintenance of intrinsic motivation (Boggiano & Pittman, in press; Deci & Ryan, 1985, 1987; Pittman & Heller, 1987). Consistent with our emphasis on propensities toward growth and mastery, intrinsically motivated behavior is seen as involving an approach toward optimal challenges (where task difficulty is moderately greater than one's current ability level), a focus on task properties rather than on task-contingent rewards or self-evaluative concerns, and with accompanying experiences of pleasure, interest, curiosity, and enjoyment. While this conceptualization does not suggest that children need to be "trained" to strive for mastery, it does hold that the physical and interpersonal context in which children's behavior is embedded can facilitate or undermine the extent to which children maintain an orientation toward intrinsic motivation throughout the course of their development.[2]

Developmental research has consistently demonstrated that children's intrinsic motivation for learning, and their concomitant perceptions of academic competence and self-worth, decline as they move through the educational system (Eccles, Midgeley, & Adler, 1984; Harter, 1981, in press; Simmons & Blythe, 1987), in part because of contextual factors of the typical educational system (drills, testing, grading on the curve, competition, emphasis on "right" and "wrong" answers, emphasis on ability vs. learning) that become increasingly prevalent in later grades. Other investigators have pointed out the potential negative impact of transitions, such as those between elementary and junior high school, on children's self-image (Simmons & Blythe, 1987), their anxiety concerning performance (Burhmester, 1980), and their preference for challenge and independent mastery (Harter, 1981). However, substantial decrements in intrinsic motivation are not inevitable for all children (Harter, 1981, Ryan & Connell, 1989), and to the extent that the maintenance of positive mastery orientations has been found to buffer children against negative experiences (Boggiano & Barrett, 1985; Harter, in press), an investment of effort to maintain and nurture children's intrinsic motivation may yield substantial mental health dividends.

Research on orientations toward mastery, competence, and self-determination has mostly focused on academic achievement in educational settings (Boggiano, Main, & Katz, 1988; Boggiano & Ruble, 1979, 1986; Deci, Schwartz, Sheinman, & Ryan, 1981; Deci, Speigel, Ryan, Koestner, & Kauffman, 1982; Harter, 1978, 1981). However, the relevance of this research to mental health issues is inherent in its implicit agenda; namely, the optimizing of both scholastic achievement *and* socioemotional well-being (Grolnick, 1990). Recent evidence suggests that these outcomes are more likely to be positively interdependent than to be incompatible (Connell & Wellborn, 1990; Grolnick & Ryan, 1989; Harter, in press; Johnson & Johnson, 1984; Ryan & Connell, 1989), both because children's self-worth is so often tied to their perceptions of academic competence (Harter, 1982) and because a positive sense of interpersonal relatedness with parents, peers, and teachers has been found to be a direct predictor of positive academic engagement and achievement (Connell & Wellborn, 1990). A number of mental health variables have been linked to children's self-perceptions of personal autonomy and effectance, including helplessness and anxiety, reactions to failure feedback (Boggiano & Barrett, 1985; Boggiano & Ruble, 1986; Dweck, 1975; Harter, in press), coping with stress (Bandura, 1990; Ryan & Connell, 1989), and self-esteem (Deci et al., 1981; Grolnick & Ryan, 1990; Harter, 1982, 1983).[3]

Mastery Motivation and Reactions to Failure: Helplessness, Anxiety, and Coping

Human reactions to failure or uncontrollable outcomes often involve effort withdrawal and feelings of dejection, a phenomenon termed "learned helplessness" (Hiroto & Seligman, 1975). Given the major role accorded to the phenomenon of learned helplessness in modern accounts of depression (Abramson, 1988; Seligman, Abramson, Semmel, & Von Baeyer, 1979), it is important to note the extent to which chronic orientations toward mastery can moderate experiences of helplessness.

Dweck (1975; Dweck & Reppucci, 1973) has found that children who have been identified as "helplessness oriented" demonstrate a maladaptive pattern of affect, cognition, and behavior following failure at an academic task, including heightened anxiety and negative self-evaluation, attributions of inadequate ability, and decreased task persistence. Mastery-oriented children, however, demonstrate a more adaptive pattern of responding to failure, including attributions to inadequate effort, plans and strategies for performance remediation, and increased task persistence. Boggiano and Barrett (1985) found that children reporting more intrinsic than extrinsic motivation for classwork persevered more after task failure than did children who reported primarily extrinsic motivation.

In a more recent, and more motivationally oriented, conceptualization, Dweck et al. (Dweck & Leggett, 1988; Elliott & Dweck, 1988) have emphasized the distinction between *performance goals*, which involve the desire to demonstrate high competence and bolster esteem, and *learning goals*, which involve the desire to increase competence and attain mastery (Leggett & Dweck, 1986). The current focus on children's goals, or motivational constructs, rather than on social–cognitive constructs alone (e.g., attributions) distinguishes this approach from those strictly emphasizing children's interpretations of failure. Since children's goals organize their affect, cognition, and action into meaningful patterns, a perspective focusing on goals allows for a systemic analysis of the full spectrum of children's responses to success and failure (Elliott & Dweck, 1988; see also Butler, 1989; Nicholls, 1984; Ryan, 1982).

Anxiety about school-related performance can have debilitating effects on children's academic and psychological functioning (Schwarzer, 1986). Ryan & Connell (1989) have presented evidence suggesting that less autonomous (i.e., "more extrinsic") forms of internalized self-regulation effectively predict children's anxiety amplification following failure, whereas more autonomous forms of self-regulation are associated with positive coping strategies, such as acting to ensure future success by determining probable causes of failure. To the extent that extrinsically motivated children are concerned with meeting externally dictated standards for performance (Harter, 1981), failure most likely will elicit affective reactions consistent with anticipated reprisals from the sources of those standards (e.g., teachers and parents). In addition, to the extent that children's motivation for performance is determined by internalized, esteem-based pressures to act (Ryan & Connell, 1989), self-induced anxiety and self-blaming are likely to accompany perceived failure. These data seem to parallel Dweck's findings regarding mastery-oriented versus helplessness-oriented children's reactions to perceived failure.

Perceived *self-efficacy*—"beliefs in one's capacities to mobilize the motivation, cognitive resources, and courses of action needed to meet given situational demands" (Bandura, Cioffi, Taylor, & Brouillard, 1988, p. 479)—is also related to anxiety and depression. Bandura (1988a) reported that low levels of perceived self-efficacy are associated with increased levels of stress and anxiety, and Bandura et al. (1988) have found that these reactions are powerful enough to activate endogenous opioid systems, which regulate stress reactions. Furthermore, Bandura (1988b) reported that perceived self-inefficacy to obtain outcomes that define one's sense of self-worth can instigate depression. Bandura's work on the relation between perceptions of self-efficacy and resilience to stressful environmental demands suggests that children high in perceived self-efficacy may cope more effectively with adverse events, such as divorce, death of a parent, school transitions, or academic failure.

Thus, a substantial literature suggests that an intrinsic motivational, or mastery, orientation may help buffer children from the negative psychological effects of the failure feedback inevitable in any child's life. Indeed, the work of independent researchers has converged on an important distinction between two fundamental patterns of cognition, affect, and behavior that may accompany negative feedback about one's progress or performance. Efforts to nurture the psychological traits (e.g., intrinsic motivation and learning goals) that moderate these patterns could be successful in reducing children's long-term vulnerability to dysphoria and depression. From an intervention perspective, then, more research is needed to address the specific factors involved in the etiology of children's orientations toward mastery, including contextual influences (Grolnick, Ryan, & Deci, 1990) and social–cognitive antecedents (Dweck & Leggett, 1988).

Self-Esteem

Several investigators have found that a child's self-esteem varies significantly as a function of variables related to intrinsic motivation, such as perceived autonomy (Deci et al., 1981; Grolnick & Ryan, 1989) and perceived competence (Harter, 1982; Harter & Connell, 1984). Deci et al. (1981) found that teachers' orientations toward supporting children's autonomy versus controlling children's behavior, and children's perceptions of the classroom climate vis-à-vis self-determination, were significantly correlated both with fourth, fifth, and sixth graders' intrinsic motivation for schoolwork as well as their general feelings of self-worth. These authors reasoned that in controlling classroom environments, where a teacher's involvement in children's learning activities is highly directive, children would feel little sense of internal impetus or initiative for learning and thus may not come to value their internal resources for learning. In contrast, in autonomy-supportive classroom environments, where teachers acknowledge the importance of children's own abilities and motivation in the enterprise of learning, children should have a greater opportunity to mobilize their own resources for, and interest in, learning and should feel better about themselves as students.

Boggiano, Barrett, and Judd (1990) corroborated these data on teachers' autonomy support in a longitudinal study controlling for children's prior achievement. In addition, Grolnick and Ryan (1989) have found that parents' support for their children's autonomy in areas such as schoolwork and household chores was a significant predictor of children's self-esteem. Others have found that more autonomous forms of self-regulation are associated with higher self-esteem in children (Ryan & Connell, 1989). The available data would indicate, then, that an important concomitant of children's orientations toward independent mastery and autonomous self-regulation is a more positive, stable sense of self-worth. High self-esteem, in turn, is an element of children's "internal resources" for coping constructively with potential insults to mental health and well-being (Grolnick, 1990).

Intrinsic Motivation and Children's Peer Relations

In the past 10 or 15 years, a great deal of systematic research has explored the development of children's peer relationships. The most consequential findings emerging from this literature are those establishing peer rejection in childhood as a risk factor for later mental illness in adolescence and young adulthood (Parker & Asher, 1987; Kupersmidt, Coie, & Dodge, 1990).

In light of these findings, efforts have been made to increase children's social skills proficiency so as to decrease the likelihood of later maladaptation (Asher & Gottman, 1981; Ladd & Mize, 1983; Coie & Koeppl, 1990; Mize & Ladd, 1990). As at least one author has noted (Boggiano, Klinger, & Main, 1986), while intervention research employing training in particular social skills has produced beneficial effects lasting up to a year (Ladd, 1981; Oden & Asher, 1977), interventions based on operant techniques (where children receive external reinforcement in exchange for performance of socially appropriate behavior) (Ladd & Mize, 1983; Mize & Ladd, 1990) produce effects that are often not maintained after treatment is terminated. The disappointing long-term effects of operantly based interventions is perhaps not surprising; the literature on intrinsic motivation and socialization suggests that positive changes in behavior are more likely to become internalized or effectively self-regulated when an internal locus of causality for behavior initiation is maintained (Deci & Ryan, 1985) and when performance of the behavior is not overjustified by external rewards or coercion (Grusec, 1983; Grusec & Redler, 1980; Lepper, 1983). Indeed, several researchers have now begun to take account of children's motivational orientations toward peer interaction and relationship development (Grusec, 1983; Ladd & Mize, 1983; Mize & Ladd, 1990; Pittman & Boggiano, in press; Pittman & Heller, 1987; Renshaw & Asher, 1982, 1983).

Several studies have suggested that environmental contingencies that promote an extrinsic motivational orientation for nonsocial activities, such as solving hidden-figures puzzles (Ryan, 1982), also can undermine intrinsic interest in social interaction. In a pioneering study, Garbarino (1975) studied fifth- and sixth-grade girls, half of whom were rewarded with movie tickets for teaching younger girls how to do a sorting task. Tutors who were promised a reward if their students learned the task successfully were more critical and demanding while tutoring and reported a more negative tone with the interaction. Pittman (1982) studied college students, half of whom were offered a small monetary reward to interact with another student (converse over an intercom). Rewarded subjects spent significantly less time talking with the other student during a subsequent "free choice" period.

Recent studies have also begun to examine the development of children's motivational orientations toward peer interaction. Promising findings by Dweck and her colleagues (Benenson & Dweck, 1986; Olshefsky, Erdley, & Dweck, 1987) extend their work on children's orientations toward mastery to the social domain. Children who approach social interactions with a goal of learning about others and forming relationships appear to be more resilient to initial peer rejection than are children who are more oriented toward affirming their likability.

Other research has examined age-related factors influencing children's peer motivation (Pittman & Boggiano, in press). Boggiano et al. (1986) reported that intrinsic interest in peer interaction was undermined by adult-administered extrinsic reasons for interaction (e.g., "because you can play with his new toys") for 9-year-olds but not for children 7 years or younger. In addition, the peer motivation of older but not younger children was enhanced by adult-administered intrinsic reasons for interacting with a particular peer (those focusing on dispositional qualities, e.g., "because he's nice"). These authors reasoned that the pattern of results stems from older children's greater appreciation of the importance of stable, internal characteristics of others, such as personality traits (Livesley & Bromley, 1973; Peevers & Secord, 1973; Rholes & Ruble, 1984), as discussed earlier.

Limitations of Existing Research for Understanding Mental Health

Although much of the research described above would appear to have direct clinical applicability, too rarely has this occurred. In this section, we identify limitations of existing research and a few possible routes to increasing our understanding of mental health processes.

Much of the research has limited the analysis to description of differences and left the critical issue of explanation open. Thus, there is a fair amount of knowledge about how problem children (e.g., aggressive, rejected, and low self-esteem) differ from children without such problems. Such research is an important step in trying to understand the nature of the psychological disturbance, and, as noted above, such research may lead to successful interventions by attempting to modify the maladaptive cognitions or motivations. There are crucial limitations to this approach, however, that constrain its usefulness to clinical application.

One problem with the descriptive studies is the difficulty of drawing causal inferences, which are useful for intervention but critical for prevention efforts. Showing that anxious or rejected children are low in mastery orientation or have maladaptive social cognitions does not necessarily imply that motivational and social–cognition processes were causally involved in the initial development of the behavior problems. Moreover, even if these processes were involved, such data do not indicate that they were a crucial or even significant cause of the initial problems. Of course, the researchers involved are well aware of such limitations in interpreting the relations they report. In order to make informed recommendations for prevention approaches, however, research aimed at pinpointing these causal issues is clearly of high priority.

Such issues suggest the need for more longitudinal research, a recommendation made recently by Gerstein, Luce, Smelser, and Sperlick (1988). Such research can indicate developmental relations among variables and suggest which are more effective at predicting subsequent problems. One recent longitudinal analysis, for example, showed that social cognitions may mediate the relation between parental abuse and later aggressive behavior in children (Dodge, Bates, & Pettit, 1990; but see Downey & Walker, 1989, for a different conclusion). Longitudinal research, too, is limited. Simply because a social–cognitive or motivational variable at time 1 predicts a behavior problem at time 2 does not necessarily imply that the two are causally related, as some third variable (such as temperament or stable parental environment) may cause both (cf. Bornstein & Tamis-LeMonda, 1989). Thus, other approaches are needed to provide converging evidence. These could include field experiments, control variables to rule out competing hypotheses, and data analytic techniques that allow causal inference.

Longitudinal designs would also help elucidate two other limitations of existing research: (1) some vagueness in explanatory mechanisms, and (2) insufficient attention to how maladaptive cognitions and motivation develop. With respect to the first limitation, even if cognitive and motivational processes can be causally linked to psychological distress, application of this knowledge requires identifying exactly which features of the link are important and how they work. The concept of intrinsic motivation, for example, includes a number of distinguishable elements—mastery goals, sense of personal control and initiative, self-confidence, and so on. Which of these are critical to maintaining self-esteem and resilience in the face of failure or other personal threats?

With respect to the second limitation, describing differences between groups may identify useful interventions, but understanding the initial development of the problems may lead to prevention efforts of greater long-term efficacy. This issue can be examined in several ways. First, basic research on social–cognitive development provides a necessary descriptive backdrop. Such studies can tell us whether there are critical points in development when children's mastery motivation is particularly vulnerable. They can also tell us when children are capable of understanding key concepts (such as intent) and of performing certain cognitive operations (such as discounting) that may be key to understanding the impact of socialization on adaptive functioning. One illustrative application of this approach concerns the study of depression. Conceptualizations of depression generally involve some notion of basic self-worth. Developmental research suggests, however, that before approximately ages 7–8, children are not likely to have concepts of self-worth relevant to depression (Harter, 1983; Higgins, 1989). What, then, is the nature of depression in younger children? Does the incidence or nature of depression increase when children achieve more mature self and social concepts? Such questions suggest that basic research on the development of self and social concepts seems likely to provide insight into several different aspects of depression: (1) it can pinpoint more precisely the role of self-worth in depression of different forms and begin to identify processes other than low self-worth that may be important, and (2) it can examine developmentally significant periods of vulnerability, when new levels of cognitive understanding may render social psychological antecedents and maintenance factors especially powerful.

Second, the development of maladaptive cognitions and motivational orientations can be examined during periods of life changes. This has been the goal of considerable research on transitions and other stressful life events—for example, divorce, entry into junior high school, and birth of a child. The research indicates that such disruptions have a variety of negative implications for mental health and has identified various external socializing factors that are important, such as social support or direct effects of pressures and conflict on arousal and negative affect. There are also important internal socialization processes that seem likely to predict how and why such events may have long-term consequences for mental health. Specifically, during times of change, individuals often construct new definitions of themselves and their life circumstances. Some research, for example, has reported that the greatest shifts in perceived competence and mastery motivation are seen at the transition to junior high school (Harter, 1981; Eccles et al., 1984). Thus, drops in self-esteem seen at this time may be viewed as a joint function of both the stress involved in change and a dismissal of previous (elementary school) self-definitions of competence and adoption of new standards (Ruble & Frey, 1991). A particularly important point about the latter process is that it may maintain mental health risk long after the immediate stress of the transition has passed.

Application of an Internal Socialization Perspective to Selected External Socialization Topics

Similar internal socialization analyses are likely to prove informative to the study of external socialization topics of known mental health relevance that, to date, have rarely incorporated this perspective. In this section, we describe three such topics as illustrations—divorce, childrearing approaches, and attachment.

The Impact of Divorce on Children

Considerable research on divorce has shown the negative effects of family conflict on the mental health of children. Although internal socialization mechanisms have not been a major focus in this area, they would seem to be significant mediating variables. First, social constructive processes may partially explain problems children experience as part of divorce. Hess and Camara (1979), for example, note that divorce requires children to change their perceptions of reality and to alter their concepts of family members and roles. Such reconstructions require time and effort that might otherwise be devoted to developing academic and social skills.

Note, as well, that children of different sexes and different ages are likely to construct different meanings about such events, potentially explaining why different short- and long-term consequences have been observed for boys and girls and for children at different age levels (e.g., Hetherington, 1979; Wallerstein & Kelly, 1980).

Second, research on attributions for negative events (Crocker & Major, 1989) suggests that children who blame themselves for their parents' marital difficulties may have more trouble adjusting to changes in the family. In addition, some investigators have found that children who have recently acquired a concept of stable dispositions (Rholes & Ruble, 1984) may focus rigidly on internal explanations for behavior (Newman, 1991). When attempting to understand their parents' separation, these children may be particularly vulnerable to drawing unfavorable conclusions about their parents' and/or their own dispositional qualities (such as aggressiveness and hostility and/or unworthiness) and may be relatively unlikely to consider potential circumstantial explanations for divorce, such as financial problems or parental incompatibility. Finally, to the extent that children retain access to the "internal resources" associated with positive mastery orientations (Grolnick, 1990), they may cope more effectively with the potential trauma of divorce.

Effects of Childrearing Techniques

Social constructive processes may also be applied to the literature on parental childrearing techniques. This literature indicates quite clearly that parental warmth is associated with child adjustment, but the impact of another key dimension—permissiveness/ restrictiveness—is more controversial. Maccoby and Martin (1983) note that the findings of the early socialization literature suggested that *less* controlling (permissive) parental styles were associated with positive child outcomes, whereas more recent findings seem to suggest the opposite—that *more* controlling (restrictive) parental styles are associated with positive outcomes.

Social–cognitive processes are potentially relevant to explaining these discrepancies, both separate from and in interaction with the motivational effects of control (see Lepper, 1983). From the child's perspective, the meaning of controlling actions by the parents, in terms of communicating interest and caring, depend on social comparison processes with the actions of parents or peers in similar circumstances. Moreover, secular trends are likely to affect the outcomes of these processes. The results of these social comparisons are likely to differ greatly from the early literature (based on studies in the '40s and '50s) to the later literature (based on studies in the '60s and '70s), because of the dramatic changes in dominant childrearing practices across these periods. That is, given the overall greater permissiveness of childrearing in the '60s and '70s as compared to the '40s and '50s, a relatively permissive style in the earlier period may be quite similar in terms of actual interactions to a relatively restrictive style in the later period. Moreover, relative permissiveness in the general context of a highly structured society (i.e., as in the '40s and '50s) might be interpreted as indicating trust, whereas relative permissiveness in a permissive society may be perceived more in terms of lack of caring or interest. Thus, it is perhaps not surprising that correlations between permissiveness/restrictiveness and child outcomes show such different patterns at the two eras. More generally, understanding the processes that mediate relations observed between childrearing practices and child outcomes should be viewed as a high priority of future research. It is quite clear that family environment is a major correlate of child adjustment (Grolnick & Ryan, 1989), but designing effective prevention and intervention efforts is unlikely until we understand more fully why these associations occur.

One particularly promising application of an analysis of parental control concerns parents' role in their children's interaction with peers. Recent research has suggested that parental involvement may facilitate the development of children's social relationships (e.g., Ladd & Golter, 1988; Parke, 1990). Research on the relevance of internal socialization mechanisms to these efforts is still in its infancy (Putallaz & Wasserman, 1990; Putallaz & Heflin, 1990) but suggests some important qualifications. To the extent that parental involvement becomes controlling or a salient cause for children's engagement in peer interaction, their interest in peers may decline rather than increase. For example, Newman and Ruble (1988) found that parental pressure for peer interaction was associated with children having less intrinsic motivation for social activities. Similarly, Fabes, Fultz, Eisenberg, May-Plumee, and Christopher (1989) found that the intrinsic prosocial motivation of children whose parents frequently used tangible rewards to control behavior was more easily undermined by similar rewards administered in a laboratory context. The available developmental data (Boggiano et al., 1986; Pittman & Dool, 1985) suggest that children's susceptibility to factors contributing to extrinsic peer orientations may be related to age and, more specifically, to their attainment of a firmly established concept of dispositional stability (Rholes et al., 1990). The implications of these data for efforts to enhance children's peer relations (and subsequent mental health) suggest that especially after age 5, intrusive parental involvement or drawing older children's attention to the extrinsic benefits of peer interaction could be counterproductive in the long run. On the other hand, drawing attention to the positive dispositional properties of a peer (e.g., "she's generous") may be a particularly effective strategy for increasing peer interest in older children.

Attachment

A related point applies to a literature that has been a major focus of much research on the origins of psychological distress in children (i.e., attachment). The pioneering ideas of Ainsworth, Blehar, Waters, and Wall (1978) and Bowlby (1971) have generated enormous excitement, voluminous research, and considerable debate (see Lamb, Thompson, Gardner, Charnov, & Estes, 1984). The construct is exciting, because it is widely believed that attachment processes during the child's first 2 years of life provide the basis for a sense of security that is essential to long-term adaptation (see Chapter 3, this volume). Recent conceptualizations of basic motivational processes have cited the importance of a sense of interpersonal relatedness, or attachment, as a determinant of constructive engagement in, and adaptation to, central life tasks in various domains across the life-span (Connell & Wellborn, 1991; Deci & Ryan, 1990; Grolnick, 1990). In fact, some researchers have even gone so far as to apply Ainsworth's basic categorization scheme for infant and toddler attachment styles to intimate adult relationships (Bartholomew & Horowitz, 1991; Hazan & Shaver, 1987; Kobak & Hazan, 1991; Mikulincer & Nachshon, 1991; Simpson, Rholes, & Nelligan, 1992).

The apparent power and impact of the construct suggests that it should be central to prevention–intervention efforts for families with young children. Unfortunately, like much of the research described above, although this line of inquiry has been enormously fruitful in generating ideas about important relations, it has remained largely descriptive and correlational in nature. As a number of compelling critiques of the literature document (e.g., Clarke-Stewart, 1989; Lamb et al., 1984), basic questions about the nature and etiology of attachment and the processes that may link it to subsequent social adjustment remain open. We do not know, for example, that attachment behavior "causes" subsequent adaptation or if, instead, both attachment and adjustment are themselves the results of other underlying processes such as temperament or stable family patterns. This latter possibility is supported by the observation that patterns of behavior in the "strange situation" paradigm have shown predictive validity only when there is stability in caretaking circumstances (Lamb et al., 1984). Even more basic, perhaps, we do not know that attachment, as operationalized by type B behavior in the "strange situation" paradigm, is necessarily desirable and adaptive in all contexts and thus worth promoting.

To illustrate such problems, consider recent findings that infants of full-time working mothers are more likely to be classified as insecurely attached than those of part-time or nonworking mothers (Belsky & Rovine, 1988; Chase-Lansdale & Owen, 1987). Do such findings imply that mothers should be discouraged from working as part of efforts to prevent behavioral problems and psychopathology in their children? There are numerous alternative interpretations, all of which highlight the need to better define the construct and mediating processes. Consistent with the above internal socialization analysis of parent–child relations, it may be argued that the manner in which a child responds to a particular situation depends, in part, on how the situation is interpreted and constructed (Clarke-Stewart, 1989). If the mother's departure from the room occurs within a family environment of frequent departures and reunions, it may be less stressful than had been assumed. Within this context, seeking proximity upon reunion is not likely to be so important, and thus differences in proximity seeking and avoidance between children who experience frequent separations are hardly surprising. That is, the same behavior may have negative implications within one family setting but positive implications (e.g., for independence and coping) within another. Findings that strange-situation classifications and correlates vary cross-culturally (Collins & Gunnar, 1990) are consistent with this interpretation.

In summary, we would argue that the encouragement of different approaches to the study of attachment is an extremely high priority to fostering understanding of mental health in children. As argued by a number of previous commentators on the field (e.g., Connell & Goldsmith, 1982; Lamb et al., 1984), a useful first step would be to identify the component processes that define attachment and link it to antecedents and consequences (Bridges, Connell, & Belsky, 1988). Moreover, attention to internal as well as external socialization mediators is needed. Some recent research has taken important steps in this direction in considering the identification (Waters, Kondo-Ikemura, Posada, & Richters, 1990) and coping/self-regulation (Connell, 1991) processes involved in attachment and its manifestations in later behavior. Moreover, further exploration of cross-cultural and subcultural variations should shed light on the adaptive significance of component behaviors, such as crying upon separation, seeking proximity upon reunion, and so on. Future research should consider as well the developmental time course involved in attachment (Maccoby, 1980) as a possible explanation of relations observed between attachment and subsequent behaviors and of cross-cultural and subcultural variations in attachment. As argued by Feinman (1984), longitudinal data on a variety of attachment behaviors and their presumed correlates assessed at multiple time points across infancy and childhood are necessary to evaluate the alternative theoretical conceptualizations of attachment and its impact.

BASIC MECHANISMS MEDIATING THE EFFECTS OF CONTEXT ON THE DEVELOPMENT OF INTRINSIC MOTIVATION: THE INTERFACE OF SOCIAL COGNITION AND INTRINSIC MOTIVATION

In our review of the potential contribution of an internal socialization perspective to efforts to understand and promote children's mental health, we have presented social–cognitive constructs, and those related to intrinsic motivation, as conceptually distinct. To illustrate, social–cognitive variables such as attributions for behavior (Dodge & Feldman, 1990) affect children's interpretation of peer's intentions, whereas motivational variables such as "interaction goals" (Olshefsky et al., 1987) determine which outcomes of peer interaction different children will find most rewarding. However, we also feel that movement toward a synthesis of these two "domains" would be a valuable step toward appreciating more fully the role of internal socialization in the ontogeny of mental health-related variables. Below we outline the initial steps toward such a synthesis by sketching a possible model of the interplay of cognitive and motivational variables in development and by identifying what may be some of the relevant variables within such a model.

The literature on the development of orientations toward

mastery has emphasized the role of contextual, environmental variables, such as support for autonomy, provision of structure, and positive interpersonal involvement (e.g., Grolnick & Ryan, 1989) in nurturing children's "internal resources"—their perceptions of self-determination, personal competence, and interpersonal relatedness. Extending this perspective, we suggest focusing on a mediating step in which children's developing social–cognitive capacities play an important role in their interpretation of environmental inputs. The acquisition of basic core concepts (such as dispositional invariance) may provide the foundation for more sophisticated social cognitions, such as multiple sufficient cause schemas and normative conceptions of ability. These middle-level concepts may further mediate children's reactions to additional environmental inputs, such as external constraint, competition and social comparison, and negative performance feedback. Finally, these reactions provide the basis for chronic orientations toward mastery or "internal resources," which have been shown to organize adaptive versus maladaptive responses to potential insults to mental health. Mastery motivation, in turn, serves to drive children's actual engagement in a particular domain (e.g., peer interactions and schoolwork), thus providing those experiences that can lead to more sophisticated cognitive structures.

The extent to which the environment is perceived as either facilitating or inhibiting to mastery attempts may take on increasing importance as children's interpretational capacities become more sophisticated and complex. While other authors have noted in a general fashion the importance of the cognitive mediation of external inputs (Deci, 1975; Deci & Ryan, 1985; Higgins, 1991), we focus on the developmental implications of specific emerging capacities. This tentative synergistic model of social–cognitive and motivational development is displayed in Figure 4.1. The starting level of mastery motivation affects the extent and nature of the child's engagement with the environment (e.g., interaction goals and interest in seeking out friends). The level of social–cognitive understanding mediates specific feedback received from the environment to influence the self-relevant implications of the feedback. To illustrate, interpersonal rejection may contribute to a growing perception of oneself as socially incompetent once children understand the stable disposition concept, but not before. This interpretation, in turn, may lead to a more negative affective reaction and may undermine the child's subsequent motivation to

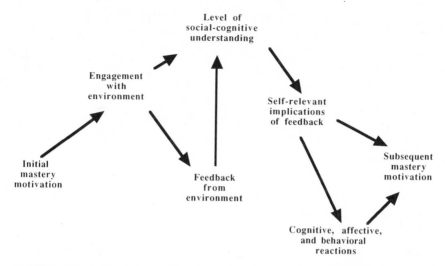

FIGURE 4.1. Synergistic model of social–cognitive and motivational development.

interact with peers. Similarly, a parent's or teacher's efforts to stimulate performance with the use of coercion may *facilitate* the child's engagement with the activity before understanding the multiple sufficient cause schema but may *undermine* it subsequently. These specific reactions, in turn, influence the child's subsequent mastery motivation for continued interaction with the environment, as well as their internal resources (e.g., feelings of self-efficacy, positive affect, persistence) for coping with potentially stressful events. This new level of mastery motivation becomes the next starting point, as the cycle begins again.

Research based on such a model could increase our understanding of the mechanisms involved in children's interpretation of information relevant to their developing motivational orientations, thereby putting us in a better position to suggest optimally effective interventions that address relevant antecedents rather than their sequelae and that are appropriate given any particular stage of development. As our aim is to focus more attention on the extent to which children's developing cognitive capacities moderate the effect of the environment on their motivational development and social–emotional well-being, we briefly offer several variables that may play such a role. These include the multiple sufficient cause schema (Kelley, 1973; Smith, 1975), a normative conception of ability (Butler, 1989, 1990;

Nicholls, 1978, 1984; Ruble, 1983), perceived ability constancy (Aboud & Ruble, 1987; Ruble & Flett, 1988), and implicit theories of ability and intelligence (Dweck & Bempechat, 1983; Dweck & Leggett, 1988; Elliott & Dweck, 1988). In reviewing the relevance of these constructs as mediators of context effects on children's intrinsic motivation, we will indicate their possible common relation to more basic social–cognitive acquisitions described earlier (e.g., Damon & Hart, 1988; Harter, 1990, Livesley & Bromley, 1973), such as the emergence of the stable dispositions concept (SDC) between 6–8 years of age (Rholes & Ruble, 1984, 1986; Ruble & Rholes, 1981).

Multiple Sufficient Cause Schema

The development of a multiple sufficient cause schema (MSCS) allows for the process of discounting, downplaying the causal potency of one possible cause (e.g., task enjoyment) because of the existence of another possible cause (e.g., prizes). The acquisition of the discounting concept may allow children to perceive their behavior as extrinsically motivated and thus may be a precursor to the development of an extrinsic motivational orientation. However, research investigating the capacity for MSCS to moderate the effects of rewards on children's actual intrinsic motivation, rather than their perceptions of intrinsic motivation in hypothetical story characters, has only recently been undertaken (Fabes et al., 1989, Morgan, 1983; Newman & Ruble, 1988; Wells & Schultz, 1980) and has produced mixed results.

Clearly, more research is needed to clarify the role of the MSCS as a moderator of children's behavioral responses to extrinsic rewards and as a potential precursor to the development of intrinsic and extrinsic motivational orientations. For example, while it is reasonable to assume that children's appreciation of multiple sufficient causes is an important and adaptive developmental advance, one might speculate that the development of a rigid tendency to overattribute causality to extrinsic sources might have deleterious consequences for the development of intrinsic motivation. Furthermore, it is important to examine how changes in person concepts are related to children's acquisition of the MSCS (Newman & Ruble, 1992; Pittman & Boggiano, in press). Children who have not yet firmly acquired a concept of dispositional stability may not distinguish between intrinsic (dispositional) and extrinsic (situational) causes (Newman, 1991).

Perceived Ability Constancy and
Normative Conceptions of Ability

Nicholls and Miller (1983) reported age differences in the extent to which children differentiate between normative and task-defined conceptions of ability. Children under the age of 6–7 years tend to define ability as determined by effortful accomplishment, whereas older children see ability as indicated by superior performance relative to others. A concept likely to be related to emerging normative concepts of ability is the extent to which they perceive ability as a constant or fixed entity, comparable to gender constancy (Slaby & Frey, 1975). This social–cognitive construct follows roughly the same developmental progression as does the normative ability concept (Ruble & Flett, 1988).

Some strongly suggestive evidence on the consequences of these social cognitions for intrinsic motivation processes has been presented in the literature. Frey and Ruble (1985) have found that an increase in children's sensitivity to public evaluation in later grades was associated with perceptions of ability as a stable, dispositional concept. As children come to perceive ability as increasingly fixed and stable, they may become more threatened by public evaluation (because of the perceived long-term implications of such evaluation), may experience more pressure to outperform other children, and may thus feel less self-determined with respect to their work. Thus, perceptions of ability constancy may introduce a readiness for children to experience the controlling properties of interpersonal evaluation that have been found to be detrimental to the maintenance of intrinsic motivation (Benware & Deci, 1984; Harackiewicz, Sansone, & Manderlink, 1985; Smith, 1974).

Another important implication of changes in children's conceptualizations of ability is the transformation of the motivational basis for social comparison. Ruble (1983) suggested that the social comparison behavior of younger children may be oriented toward learning and task mastery ("Am I doing this correctly? Are there other ways I could do it?"), whereas older children engage in social comparison primarily for reasons of self-evaluation ("Am I any good at this? Am I better at this than other kids?"). As Butler (1989, 1990) has demonstrated, social comparison that is motivated by self-evaluative concerns is detrimental to intrinsic motivation, especially in contexts that emphasize relative ability, such as competition. Presumably, self-evaluation-driven social comparison both diverts attention from intrinsically interesting task properties and also fosters a controlling state of ego-involvement antithetical to the maintenance of intrinsic interest (Butler, 1989; Nicholls, 1984; Ryan, 1982). Thus, age-related shifts to concepts of ability as stable and normatively defined can transform the implications of performance feedback, thereby affecting the development of children's intrinsic and extrinsic motivational orientations.

Children's Implicit Theories of Ability and Intelligence

Dweck and Bempechat (1983; Dweck & Leggett, 1988; Elliott & Dweck, 1988) have proposed that children who have primarily static theories of ability tend to adopt performance goals involving a desire to demonstrate high competence, whereas children with primarily malleable theories of ability tend to adopt learning goals involving a desire to increase competence (Leggett & Dweck, 1986). Thus, according to Dweck and her colleagues, the core social–cognitive construct underlying one's orientation toward mastery is one's theory of ability and intelligence as either fixed or malleable. Beliefs that ability is fixed and unchangeable could conceivably present an internal limit to children's sense of self-determination with regard to achievement. Such beliefs could also undercut the pleasure inherent in mastery of challenges, which stems from a sense of growth and development. An important direction for future research in this area is to consider the social–cognitive antecedents of the implicit theories themselves. For example, theories of ability as fixed entities may result from rigidly developed concepts of ability constancy or stable dispositions more generally. The emergence of mature concepts of dispositional regularity at around age 7–8 years may be a critical period in which children's specific experiences determine the extent to which they acquire more stable beliefs about their own and others' intelligence, abilities, and personality as fixed, static entities or as malleable, flexible capacities.

CONCLUSIONS

We have attempted to link internal socialization to mental health by means of two broad categories of psychological mechanisms: social cognition and intrinsic motivation. In doing so, we have been led to four major points. First, our literature review indicates that both mechanisms are centrally involved in the development of social skills and behaviors of direct mental health relevance (e.g., interpersonal relationships, self-esteem, and coping and self-regulation). Clinical researchers are increasingly recognizing the value of closer links to basic theoretical analyses of child functioning in order to remedy deficiencies in the conceptualization of treatment—what components are needed and how and why they relate to specific areas of dysfunction (Kazdin, 1988). The theory and research reviewed in this chapter suggest that a number of social–cognitive and motivational processes will prove useful in such efforts. Although many of the issues and data cut across these two domains, they potentially represent quite different types of mediating mechanisms. The basic social psychological processes involved in our social–cognition analyses include (1) information processing and attribution mechanisms that contribute to the construction and maintenance of core self and social orientations; (2) strategies involved in coping and emotion management; and (3) expectancy or schema-driven mechanisms that maintain concepts and conclusions previously drawn. The basic processes emphasized in our intrinsic motivation analyses concern (1) factors such as affect and goals linking motivational orientations to helpless reactions to failure, anxiety, self-esteem, and interpersonal relations; and (2) factors that maintain or undermine intrinsic motivation and self-determination (e.g., reactions to control).

Second, in spite of the usefulness of distinguishing between motivational variables (e.g., intrinsic vs. extrinsic motivational orientations and learning vs. performance goals) and social–cognitive variables (e.g., discounting, normative vs. autonomous standards for comparison and implicit theories of ability and intelligence), we have also noted the synergistic relation between motivation and cognition (Sorrentino & Higgins, 1986; Higgins & Sorrentino, 1990) and have proposed a tentative model to describe both the nature of this synergy across development and also its implications for children's mental health. Social–cognitive variables play an important role in the ontogeny of orientations toward mastery and efficacy, a process that may be conceptualized as the continual development of increasingly sophisticated, motivationally relevant cognitive structures. Throughout the course of "internal socialization," these structures direct the interpretation of contextual information relevant to self-perceptions (e.g., perceived autonomy, competence, and relatedness) that can nurture or hinder children's orientations toward mastery. Mastery motivation, in turn, facilitates the actual interaction with the environment necessary for children to acquire a more sophisticated understanding of the world, both physical and social. Mastery motivation also maintains those "internal resources" (e.g., self-esteem and positive coping strategies) that buffer children against potential mental health insults (e.g., failure in school, peer rejection and parents' divorce). To the extent that children's social cognitions (e.g., static theories of intelligence) lead to relatively extrinsic motivational orientations (e.g., performance goals), the extent and quality of active behavioral engagement may decrease and further adaptive cognitive development (e.g., acquisition of more sophisticated coping strategies) may be inhibited.

Third, we have described how an internal socialization perspective may elucidate the operation of external socialization processes of known mental health relevance—divorce, childrearing techniques, and attachment. Our emphasis on social–cognitive mediation suggests that some external influences may have different effects at different points in development. Parents, teachers, and other significant socialization agents need to be aware of the differential impact of their actions on children's intrinsic motivation and social behavior at different ages. Socialization tactics that have generally positive implications during one age period may have generally negative effects during a later age period.

Finally, we have argued that there are several unique benefits of incorporating a developmental perspective in attempts to link basic social psychological mechanisms to mental health. First, a developmental perspective allows one to examine basic processes in a different way; that is, underlying mechanisms can be examined during their natural emergence. Moreover, knowledge of natural hierarchies or developmental progressions may prove informative in understanding changes in levels of processing or in understanding cognitive developmental "regressions" that may accompany stressful experiences, especially when a new concept has been recently acquired and may not be firmly established. For example, Harris (1988) describes how negative affect may lead to a regression in children's ability to reason about emotions. Second, the development of problems in childhood often leads to adult risk. For example, considerable research suggests that early peer status is predictive of later social and emotional adjustment. Although many of the basic processes are the same (e.g., self-fulfilling prophecies) at different points in the life span, a developmental perspective introduces the notion of a critical period—that irreversible processes are set in motion at some developmental phase. Third, the nature and antecedents of basic affective problems may differ at different ages. This is relevant both to understanding the phenomenon at a given point in time (e.g., preschool) and also to understanding the multiplicity of factors involved in, for example, depression.

These developmental phenomena raise difficult but critical issues for therapeutic interventions. Maladaptive cognitions emerging at one age may be based on forms of representation that are quite different from those operable at the time of an attempted intervention. For example, poor academic performance can lead to self-esteem problems in childhood (e.g., ages 6–7 years) that persist into later years. However, once children acquire a compensatory logic for combining performance and effort information in their judgments of competence or ability, they can discount the implications of their early school performance for their academic competence (and for their low self-esteem) by claiming that since they never really tried to do well, their performance was never diagnostic of ability. Thus, at this later age, it may be difficult for someone to appreciate the fact that early failure in school can be an important antecedent of self-esteem problems. To the extent that the identification and working through of root causes is important to therapeutic outcomes, changes in developmental level can present obstacles to positive outcomes.

Acknowledgments

We are grateful to Tom Alfieri, Kay Deaux, Tory Higgins, Len Newman, Molly Oliveri, Eva Pomerantz, and Eun Rhee for many thoughtful and insightful comments on an earlier version of this chapter. Preparation of this chapter was supported by Research Grant MH 37215 and a Research Scientist Development Award MH 00484 to Diane Ruble, both from the National Institute of Mental Health.

NOTES

1. Since we, like many others, conceptualize intrinsic motivation as inherently based on organismic needs for mastery and effectance (Deci & Ryan, 1985; White, 1959; Harter, 1981), we use the terms "intrinsic motivation" and "mastery motivation" interchangeably, while noting that other conceptualizations not invoking the concept of mastery have been forwarded by some authors (see note 2).

2. Finally, we might note that several other perspectives have down-played the role of innate propensities toward mastery and effectance and have emphasized the role of cognitively mediated conditioning principles and/or the interplay of cognitive and affective variables in the acquisition of specific responses toward objects and activities (Boggiano & Hertel, 1983; Fabes, Eisenberg, Fultz, & Miller, 1988; Higgins & Trope, 1990; Pretty & Seligman, 1984). These new perspectives have the potential to extend and enrich the more traditional research on intrinsic motivation, which has focused primarily on mastery and self-determination.

3. Other research, not reviewed in this chapter, suggests that a mastery motivation perspective may be relevant to mental health disturbances arising as early as infancy. Infancy researchers have increasingly emphasized the importance of infants' perceptions of contingency, that their actions have a predictable effect on the environment (e.g., Bornstein & Tamis-LeMonda, 1989; Frodi, Bridges, & Grolnick, 1985). Indeed, a lack of mastery or effectance motivation may be one way to characterize the "failure to thrive" syndrome in infants, which is identified by nonorganic developmental delay and lack of social responsivity and relatedness. In addition, there is speculation that one factor involved in the etiology and/or maintenance of this syndrome is a lack of response-contingent social stimulation (Cicchetti, Toth, & Bush, 1988).

REFERENCES

Aboud, F. E., & Ruble, D. N. (1987). Identity constancy in children: Developmental processes and implications. In T. Honess & K. Yardley (Eds.), *Self and identity: Perspectives across the lifespan* (pp. 95–107). London: Routledge & Kegan Paul.

Abramson, L. Y. (Ed.). (1988). *Social cognition and clinical psychology: A synthesis.* New York: Guilford Press.

Ainsworth, M. D. S., Blehar, M.C., Waters, E., & Wall, S. (1978). *Patterns of attachment: A psychological study of the Strange Situation.* Hillsdale, NJ: Erlbaum.

Alloy, L. B. (Ed.). (1988). *Cognitive processes in depression.* New York: Guilford Press.

Altshuler, J. L., & Ruble, D. N. (1989). Developmental changes in children's awareness of strategies for coping with uncontrollable stress. *Child Development,* 60, 1337–1349.

Asher, S. R. & Gottman, J. M. (Eds.). (1981). *The development of children's friendships.* New York: Cambridge University Press.

Bandura, A. (1988a). Self-efficacy conception of anxiety. *Anxiety Research,* 1, 77–98.

Bandura, A. (1988b). Perceived self-efficacy: Exercise of control through self-belief. In J. P. Dauwalder, M. Perrez, & V. Hobi (Eds.), *Annual series of European research in behavior therapy* (Vol. 2, pp. 27–59). Lisse, Holland: Swets & Zeitlinger.

Bandura, A. (1990). Reflections on nonability determinants of competence. In R. J. Sternberg & J. Kolligian, Jr. (Eds.), *Competence considered* (pp. 315–362). New Haven, CT: Yale University Press.

Bandura, A., Cioffi, D., Taylor, C. B., & Brouillard, M. E. (1988). Perceived self-efficacy in coping with cognitive stressors and opioid activation. *Journal of Personality and Social Psychology, 55,* 479–488.

Bartholomew, K., & Horowitz, L. M. (1991). Attachment styles among young adults: A test of a four-category model. *Journal of Personality and Social Psychology, 61,* 226–244.

Belsky, J., & Rovine, M. J. (1988). Nonmaternal care in the first year of life and the security of infant–parent attachment. *Child Development, 59,* 157–167.

Benenson, J. F., & Dweck, C. S. (1986). The development of trait explanations and self-evaluations in the academic and social domains. *Child Development, 57,* 1179–1187.

Benware, C., & Deci, E. L. (1984). Quality of learning with an active versus passive motivational set. *American Educational Research Journal, 21,* 755–765.

Bierman, K. L. (1986). Process of change during social skills training with preadolescents and its relation to treatment outcomes. *Child Development, 57,* 151–162.

Boggiano, A. K., & Barrett, M. (1985). Performance and motivational deficits of helplessness: The role of motivational orientations. *Journal of Personality and Social Psychology, 49,* 1753–1761.

Boggiano, A. K., Barrett, M., & Judd, C. (1990). *Achievement in elementary school children: The mediating role of perceptions of control.* Unpublished manuscript, University of Colorado Boulder.

Boggiano, A. K., & Hertel, P. T. (1983). Bonuses and bribes: Mood effects in memory. *Social Cognition, 2,* 49–61.

Boggiano, A. K., Klinger, C. A., & Main, D. S. (1986). Enhancing interest in peer interaction: A developmental analysis. *Child Development, 57,* 852–861.

Boggiano, A. K., Main, D. S., & Katz, P. A. (1988). Children's preference for challenge: The role of perceived competence and control. *Journal of Personality and Social Psychology, 54,* 134–141.

Boggiano, A. K. & Pittman, T. (Eds.). (in press). *Achievement and motivation: A social-developmental perspective.* New York: Cambridge University Press.

Boggiano, A. K., &. Ruble, D. N. (1979). Competence and the overjustification effect: A developmental study. *Journal of Personality and Social Psychology, 37,* 1462–1468.

Boggiano, A. K., & Ruble, D. N. (1986). Children's responses to evaluative feedback. In R. Schwarzer (Ed.), *Self-related cognitions in anxiety and motivation* (pp. 195–228). Hillsdale, NJ: Erlbaum.

Bornstein, M. H., & Tamis-LeMonda, C. S. (1989). Maternal responsiveness and cognitive development in children. In M. H. Bornstein (Ed.), *Maternal responsiveness: Characteristics and consequences. New directions for child development* (pp. 49–61). No. 43. San Francisco: Jossey-Bass.

Bowlby, J. (1971). *Attachment and loss: Attachment* (Vol. 1). London: Pelican Books.

Bridges, L. J., Connell, J. P., & Belsky, J. (1988). Infant–mother and infant–father interaction in the strange situation: A component process analysis. *Developmental Psychology, 24*, 92–100.

Burhmester, D. (1980). *The children's concern inventory.* Unpublished manuscript, University of Denver.

Butler, R. (1989). Interest in the task and interest in peers' work in competitive and noncompetitive conditions: A developmental study. *Child Development, 60*, 562–570.

Butler, R. (1990). The effects of mastery and competitive conditions on self-assessment at different ages. *Child Development, 61*, 201–210.

Casey, R. J., & Berman, J. S. (1985). The outcome of psychotherapy with children. *Psychological Bulletin, 98*, 388–397.

Chaiken, S. (1980). Heuristic versus systematic information processing and the use of source versus message cues in persuasion. *Journal of Personality and Social Psychology, 39*, 752–766.

Chase-Lansdale, P. L., & Owen, M. T. (1987). Maternal employment in a family context: Effects on infant–mother and infant–father attachment. *Child Development, 58*, 1505–1512.

Cicchetti, D., Toth, S., & Bush, M. (1988). Developmental psychopathology and incompetence in childhood. In B. B. Lahey & A. E. Kazdin (Eds.), *Advances in clinical child psychology* (pp. 1–71). New York: Plenum Press.

Clarke-Stewart, K. A. (1989). Infant day care: Maligned or malignant? *American Psychologist, 44*, 266–273.

Coie, J. (1990). Toward a theory of peer rejection. In S. R. Asher, & J. D. Coie (Eds.), *Peer rejection in childhood* (pp. 365–402). New York: Cambridge University Press.

Coie, J., & Koeppl, G. K. (1990). Adapting intervention to the problems of aggressive and disruptive rejected children. In S. R. Asher, & J. D. Coie (Eds.), *Peer rejection in childhood* (pp. 309–337). New York: Cambridge University Press.

Collins, W. A., & Gunnar, M. R. (1990). Social and personality development. *Annual Review of Psychology, 41*, 387–416.

Connell, J. P. (1991). Context, self, and action: A motivational analysis of self-system processes across the lifespan . In D. Cicchetti, (Ed.), *The self in transition: Infancy to childhood* (pp. 213–251). Chicago: University of Chicago Press.

Connell, J. P., & Goldsmith, H. H. (1982). A structural modeling approach to the study of attachment and strange situation behaviors. In R. N.

Emde & R. J. Harmon (Eds.), *The development of attachment and affiliative systems* (pp. 213–243). New York: Plenum Press.

Connell, J. P., & Wellborn, J. G. (1991). Competence, autonomy, and relatedness: A motivational analysis of self-system processes. In M. Gunnar & L. A. Sroufe (Eds.), *Minnesota symposium on child psychology* (Vol. 23, pp. 43–78). Hillsdale, NJ: Erlbaum.

Crocker, J., & Major, B. (1989). Social stigma and self-esteem: The self-protective properties of stigma. *Psychological Review, 96,* 608–630.

Damon, W., & Hart, D. (1988). *Self-understanding in childhood and adolescence.* New York: Cambridge University Press.

de Charms, R. (1968). *Personal causation.* New York: Academic Press.

Deci, E. L. (1975). *Intrinsic motivation.* New York: Plenum Press.

Deci, E. L., & Ryan, R. M. (1985). *Intrinsic motivation and self-determination in human behavior.* New York: Plenum Press.

Deci, E. L., & Ryan, R. M. (1987). The support of autonomy and the control of behavior. *Journal of Personality and Social Psychology, 53,* 1024–1037.

Deci, E. L., & Ryan, R. M. (1990). A motivational approach to self: Integration in personality. In R. Dienstbier (Ed.), *Nebraska symposium on motivation: Vol. 38. Perspectives on motivation.* (pp. 237–288) Lincoln, NE: University of Nebraska Press.

Deci, E. L., Schwartz, A. J., Sheinman, L., & Ryan, R. M. (1981). An instrument to assess adults' orientations toward control vs. autonomy with children: Reflections on intrinsic motivation and perceived competence. *Journal of Educational Psychology, 73,* 642–650.

Deci, E. L., Speigel, N. H., Ryan, R. M., Koestner, R., & Kauffman, M. (1982). The effects of performance standards on teaching styles: The behavior of controlling teachers. *Journal of Educational Psychology, 74,* 852–859.

Dix, T. (1991). The affective organization of parenting: Adaptive and maladaptive processes. *Psychological Bulletin, 110,* 3–25.

Dix, T., Ruble, D. N., & Zambarano, R. J. (1989). Mothers' implicit theories of discipline: Child effects, parent effects, and the attribution process. *Child Development, 60,* 1373–1391.

Dodge, K. A., Bates, J. E., & Pettit, G. S. (1990). Mechanisms in the cycle of violence. *Science, 250,* 1678–1683.

Dodge, K. A., & Feldman, E. (1990). Social cognition and sociometric status. In S. R. Asher & J. D. Coie (Eds.), *Peer rejection in childhood* (pp. 119–155). New York: Cambridge University Press.

Donaldson, S. K., & Westerman, M. A. (1986). Development of children's experience of ambivalence and causal theories of emotion. *Developmental Psychology, 22,* 655–662.

Downey, G., & Walker, E. (1989). Social cognition and adjustment in children at risk for psychopathology. *Developmental Psychology, 25,* 835–845.

Durlak, J. A., Furhman, T., & Lampman, C. (1991). Effectiveness of cognitive-behavioral therapy for maladapting children: A meta-analysis. *Psychological Bulletin, 110*, 204–214.

Dweck, C. S. (1975). The role of expectations and attributions in the alleviation of learned helplessness. *Journal of Personality and Social Psychology, 31*, 674–685.

Dweck, C. S. (1991). Self-theories and goals: Their role in motivation, personality and development. In R. Dienstbier (Ed.), *Nebraska symposium on motivation: Vol. 38. Perspective on motivation* (pp. 199–235). Lincoln, NE: University of Nebraska Press.

Dweck, C. S., & Bempechat, J. (1983). Children's theories of intelligence. In S. Paris, G. Olsen, & H. Stevenson (Eds.), *Learning and motivation in the classroom* (pp. 239–256). Hillsdale, NJ: Erlbaum.

Dweck, C. S., & Elliott, E. S. (1983). Achievement motivation. In P. Mussen (Gen. Ed.) and E. M. Hetherington (Vol. Ed.), *Handbook of child psychology, Vol. 4: Social and personality development* (pp. 643–691). New York: Wiley.

Dweck, C. S., & Leggett, E. L. (1988). A social–cognitive approach to motivation and personality. *Psychological Review, 95*, 256–273.

Dweck, C. S., & Reppucci, N. D. (1973). Learned helplessness and reinforcement responsibility in children. *Journal of Personality and Social Psychology, 25*, 109–116.

Eccles, J., Jacobs, J. E., & Harold, R. D. (1990). Gender role stereotypes, expectancy effects, and parents' socialization of gender differences. *Journal of Social Issues, 46*, 183–201.

Eccles, J., Midgley, C., & Adler, T. F. (1984). Grade-related changes in the school environment: Effects on achievement motivation. In J. G. Nicholls (Ed.), *The development of achievement motivation* (pp. 283–332). Greenwich, CT: JAI Press.

Elliott, E. S., & Dweck, C. S. (1988). Goals: An approach to motivation and achievement. *Journal of Personality and Social Psychology, 54*, 5–12.

Erber, R., & Fiske, S. T. (1984). Outcome dependency and attention to inconsistent information. *Journal of Personality and Social Psychology, 47*, 709–726.

Fabes, R. A., Eisenberg, N., Fultz, J., & Miller, P. (1988). Reward, affect, and young children's motivational orientation. *Motivation and Emotion, 12*, 155–169.

Fabes, R. A., Fultz, J., Eisenberg, N., May-Plumee, T., & Christopher, F. S. (1989). Effects of rewards on children's prosocial motivation: A socialization study. *Developmental Psychology, 25*, 509–515.

Fazio, R. H. (1990). On the value of basic research: An overview. *Personality and Social Psychology Bulletin, 16*, 5–7.

Feinman, S. (1984). Correlations in search of a theory: Interpreting the predictive validity of security of attachment. *The Behavioral and Brain Sciences, 7*, 152–153.

Feldman, N. S., & Ruble, D. N. (1988). The effect of personal relevance on psychological inference: A developmental analysis. *Child Development, 59*, 1339–1352.

Forsterling, F. (1985). Attributional retraining: A review. *Psychological Bulletin, 98*, 495–512.

Frey, K. S., & Ruble, D. N. (1985). What children say when the teacher is not around: Conflicting goals in social comparison and performance assessment in the classroom. *Journal of Personality and Social Psychology, 48*, 550–562.

Frey, K. S., & Ruble, D. N. (1987). What children say about classroom performance: Sex and grade differences in perceived competence. *Child Development, 58*, 1066–1078.

Frey, K. S., & Ruble, D. N. (1990). Strategies for comparative evaluation: Maintaining a sense of competence across the lifespan. In R. J. Sternberg & J. Kolligian (Eds.), *Competence considered* (pp. 167–189). New Haven, CT: Yale University Press.

Frieze, I. H. (1981). Children's attributions for success and failure. In S. S. Brehm, S. M. Kassin, & F. X. Gibbons (Eds.), *Developmental social psychology* (pp. 51–71). New York: Oxford University Press.

Frodi, A., Bridges, L., & Grolnick, W. (1985). Correlates of mastery-related behavior: A short-term longitudinal study of infants in their second year. *Child Development, 56*, 1291–1298.

Furman, W., Rahe, D. F., & Hartup, W. W. (1979). Rehabilitation of socially withdrawn preschool children through mixed-age and same-age socialization. *Child Development, 50*, 915–922.

Garbarino, J. (1975). The impact of anticipated reward on cross-age tutoring. *Journal of Personality and Social Psychology, 32*, 421–428.

Gerstein, D. R., Luce, R. D., Smelser, N. J., & Sperlich, S. (Eds.). (1988). *The behavioral and social sciences: Achievements and opportunities* (pp. 49–81). Washington, DC: National Academy Press.

Goethals, G. R. (1986). Social comparison theory: Psychology from the lost and found. *Personality and Social Psychology Bulletin, 12*, 261–278.

Gottman, J. M. (1983). How children become friends. *Monographs of the Society for Research in Child Development, 48* (No. 3, 1–81).

Gottman, J. M., & Mettetal. (1986). Speculations about social and affective development: Friendship and acquaintanceship through adolescence. In J. M. Gottman & J. G. Parker (Eds.), *Conversations of friends: Speculations on affective development* (pp. 192–240). New York: Cambridge University Press.

Graziano, W. G., Brody, G. H., & Bernstein, S. (1980). Effects of information about future interaction and peer's motivation on peer reward allocations. *Developmental Psychology, 16*, 475–482.

Grolnick, W. S. (1990). Targeting children's motivational resources in early childhood education. *Educational Policy, 4*, 267–282.

Grolnick, W. S., & Ryan, R. M. (1989). Parent styles associated with children's self-regulation and competence in school. *Journal of Educational Psychology, 81*, 143–154.

Grolnick, W. S., & Ryan, R. M. (1990). Self-perceptions, motivation, and adjustment in children with learning disabilities: A multiple group comparison study. *Journal of Learning Disabilities, 3,* 177–184.

Grolnick, W. S., Ryan, R. M., & Deci, E. L. (1990). *The inner resources for school achievement: Motivational mediators of children's perceptions of their parents.* Unpublished manuscript, University of Rochester.

Grusec, J. E. (1983). The internalization of altruistic dispositions: A cognitive analysis. In E. T. Higgins, D. N. Ruble, & W. W. Hartup (Eds.), *Social cognition and social development: A sociocultural perspective* (pp. 275–293). Cambridge: Cambridge University Press.

Grusec, J., & Redler, E. (1980). Attribution, reinforcement, and altruism: A developmental analysis. *Developmental Psychology, 16,* 525–534.

Harackiewicz, J. M., Sansone, C., & Manderlink, G. (1985). Competence, achievement orientation, and intrinsic motivation: A process analysis. *Journal of Personality and Social Psychology, 48,* 493–508.

Harris, P. L. (1988). Children's understanding of real and apparent emotion. In J. W. Astington, P. L. Harris, & R. Olson (Eds.), *Developing theories of mind* (pp. 295–314). New York: Cambridge University Press.

Harris, P. L., Othof, T., & Terwogt, M. M. (1981). Children's knowledge of emotion. *Journal of Child Psychology and Psychiatry, 22,* 247–261.

Harter, S. (1978). Pleasure derived from challenge and the effects of receiving grades on children's difficulty level choices. *Child Development, 49,* 788–799.

Harter, S. (1981). A new self-report scale of intrinsic versus extrinsic orientation in the classroom: Motivational and informational components. *Developmental Psychology, 17,* 300–312.

Harter, S. (1982). The perceived competence scale for children. *Child Development, 53,* 87–97.

Harter, S. (1983). Developmental perspectives on the self-system. In E. M. Hetherington (Ed.) & P. H. Mussen (Series Ed.), *Handbook of child psychology. (Vol. 4): Socialization, personality, and social development* (pp. 275–386). New York: Wiley.

Harter, S. (1990). Developmental differences in the nature of self-representations: Implications for the understandng, assessment, and treatment of maladaptive behavior. *Cognitive Therapy and Research, 14,* 113–142.

Harter, S. (in press). The relationship between perceived competence, affect, and motivational orientation within the classroom: Process and patterns of change. In Boggiano, A. K., & Pittman, T. S. (Eds.), *Achievement and motivation: A social development perspective.* New York: Cambridge University Press.

Harter, S., & Connell, J. P. (1984). A model of children's achievement and related self-perceptions of competence, control, and motivational orientation. *Advances in Motivation and Achievement, 3,* 219–250.

Hazan, C., & Shaver, P. (1987). Romantic love conceptualized as an attachment process. *Journal of Personality and Social Psychology, 52,* 511–524.

Hess, R. D., & Camara, K. A. (1979). Post-divorce family relationships as mediating factors in the consequences of divorce for children. *Journal of Social Issues, 35,* 79–96.

Hetherington, E. M. (1979). Divorce: A child's perspective. *American Psychologist, 34,* 851–858.

Higgins, E. T. (1989). Continuities and discontinuities in self-regulatory and self-evaluative processes: A developmental theory relating self and affect. *Journal of Personality, 57,* 407–444.

Higgins, E. T. (1991). Development of self-regulatory and self-evaluative processes: Costs, benefits, and tradeoffs. In M. R. Gunnar & L. A. Sroufe (Eds.), *Self processes and development: The Minnesota symposium on child psychology* (Vol. 23, pp. 125–166). Hillsdale, NJ: Erlbaum.

Higgins, E. T., & Sorrentino, R. M. (Eds.). (1990). *Handbook of motivation and cognition: Foundations of social behavior* (Vol. 2). New York: Guilford Press.

Higgins, E. T., Strauman, T., & Klein, R. (1986). Standards and the process of self-evaluation: Multiple affects from multiple stages. In R. M. Sorrentino & E. T. Higgins (Eds.), *Handbook of motivation and cognition: Foundations of social behavior* (Vol. 1, pp. 23–63). New York: Guilford Press.

Higgins, E. T., & Trope, Y. (1990). Activity engagement theory: Implications of multiple identifications for intrinsic motivation. In R. M. Sorrentino, & E. T. Higgins. *Handbook of motivation and cognition: Foundations of social behavior* (Vol. 2, pp. 229–264). New York: Guilford Press.

Hiroto, D. S., & Seligman, M. E. P. (1975). Generality of learned helplessness in man. *Journal of Personality and Social Psychology, 31,* 311–327.

Johnson, D. W., & Johnson, R. T. (1984). Motivational processes in cooperative, competitive, and individualistic learning settings. In C. Ames & R. E. Ames (Eds.), *Research on motivation in education (Vol. 2): The classroom milieu* (pp. 249–286). New York: Academic Press.

Kazdin, A. E. (1988). *Child psychotherapy: Developing and identifying effective treatments.* New York: Pergamon Press.

Kazdin, A. E. (1989). Developmental psychpathology: Current research, issues, and directions. *American Psychologist, 44,* 180–189.

Kelley, H. H. (1973). The processes of causal attribution. *American Psychologist, 28,* 107–128.

Kobak, R. R., & Hazan, C. (1991). Attachment in marriage: Effects of security and accuracy of working models. *Journal of Personality and Social Psychology, 60,* 861–869.

Kruglanski, A. W. (1975). The endogenous-exogenous partition in attribution theory. *Psychological Review, 83,* 387–406.

Kun, A. (1977). Development of the magnitude-covariation and compensation schemata in ability and effort attributions of performance. *Child Development, 48,* 862–873.

Kupersmidt, J. B., Coie, J., & Dodge, K. A. (1990). The role of poor peer relationships in the development of disorder. In S. R. Asher & J. Coie (Eds.), *Peer rejection in childhood* (pp. 274–308). New York: Cambridge University Press.

Ladd, G. W. (1981). Effectiveness of a social learning method for enhancing children's social interaction and peer acceptance. *Child Development, 52,* 71–82.

Ladd, G. W., & Golter, B. S. (1988). Parents' management of their preschoolers' peer relations: Is it related to children's social competence? *Developmental Psychology, 24,* 109–117.

Ladd, G. W., & Mize, J. (1983). A cognitive–social learning model of social skill training. *Psychological Review, 90,* 127–157.

Lamb, M. E., Thompson, R. A., Gardner, W. P., Charnov, E. L., & Estes, D. (1984). Security of infantile attachment as assessed in the "strange situation": Its study and biological interpretation. *The Behavioral and Brain Sciences, 7,* 127–171.

Last, C. G., & Francis, G. (1988). School phobia. In B. B. Lahey & A. E. Kazdin (Eds.), *Advances in clinical child psychology* (Vol. 2, pp. 193–222). New York: Plenum Press.

Lepper, M. R. (1983). Social control processes and the internalization of social values: An attributional perspective. In E. T. Higgins, D. N. Ruble, & W. W. Hartup (Eds.), *Social cognition and social development: A sociocultural perspective* (pp. 294–330). Cambridge: Cambridge University Press.

Lepper, M. R., & Greene, D. (Eds.). (1978). *The hidden costs of reward: New perspectives on the psychology of human motivation.* Hillsdale, NJ: Erlbaum.

Lepper, M. R., Greene, D., & Nisbett, R. E. (1973). Undermining children's intrinsic interest with extrinsic reward: A test of the "overjustification" hypothesis. *Journal of Personality and Social Psychology, 28,* 129–137.

Livesley, W. J., & Bromley, D. B. (1973). *Person perception in childhood and adolescence.* Chichester, England: Wiley.

Maccoby, E. E. (1980). *Social development: Psychological growth and the parent–child relationship.* San Diego, CA: Harcourt, Brace, & Jovanovich.

Maccoby, E. E. (1984). Socialization and developmental change. *Child Development, 55,* 317–328.

Maccoby, E. E., & Jacklin, C. N. (1974). *The psychology of sex differences.* Palo Alto, CA: Stanford University Press.

Maccoby, E. E., & Martin, J. A. (1983). Socialization in the context of the family: Parent–child interaction. In E.M. Hetherington (Ed.), *Handbook of child psychology (Vol. 4). Socialization, personality and social development* (pp. 1–102). New York: Wiley.

Markus, H., & Zajonc, R. (1985). The cognitive perspective in social psychology. In G. Lindzey & E. Aronson (Eds.), *Handbook of social psychology* (3rd ed., Vol. 1, pp. 137–230). New York: Random House.

Mikulincer, M., & Nachshon, O. (1991). Attachment styles and patterns of self-disclosure. *Journal of Personality and Social Psychology, 61*, 321–331.

Miller, D. T. (1976). Ego-involvement and attributions for success and failure. *Journal of Personality and Social Psychology, 34*, 901–906.

Mize, J., & Ladd, G. W. (1990). Toward the development of successful social skills training for preschool children. In S. R. Asher & J. Coie (Eds.), *Peer rejection in childhood*. New York: Cambridge University Press.

Morgan, M. (1983). Decrements in intrinsic motivation among rewarded and observer subjects. *Child Development, 54*, 636–644.

Newman, L. S. (1991). Why are traits inferred spontaneously? A developmental approach. *Social Cognition, 9*, 221–253.

Newman, L. S., & Ruble, D. N. (April, 1988). *Children's friendships and the discounting principle: Age and motivational-experiential differences.* Paper presented at the meeting of the Eastern Psychological Association, Buffalo, NY.

Newman, L. S., & Ruble, D. N. (1992). *Do young children use the discounting principle?* Manuscript submitted for publication.

Nicholls, J. G. (1978). The development of the concepts of effort and ability, perception of own attainment and the understanding that difficult tasks require more ability. *Child Development, 49*, 800–814.

Nicholls, J. G. (1984). Achievement motivation: Conceptions of ability, subjective experience, task choice, and performance. *Psychological Review, 91*, 328–346.

Nicholls, J. G., & Miller, A. T. (1983). The differentiation of the concepts of difficulty and ability. *Child Development, 54*, 951–959.

Oden, S., & Asher, S. R. (1977). Coaching children in social skills for friendship making. *Child Development, 48*, 495–506.

Olshefsky, L. M., Erdley, C. A., & Dweck, C. S. (1987). *Children's theories of personality and their response to social rejection.* Unpublished raw data.

Parke, R. D. (August, 1990). *Family-peer systems: In search of linking processes.* Division 7. Presidential address delivered at the meeting of the American Psychological Association, Boston, MA.

Parke, R. D., & Slaby, R. G. (1983). The development of aggression. In E. M. Hetherington (Ed.), *Handbook of child psychology: Vol. 4. Socialization, personality, and social development* (4th ed.) (pp. 547–641). New York: Wiley.

Parker, J. G., & Asher, S. R. (1987). Peer relations and later personal adjustment: Are low-accepted children at risk? *Psychological Bulletin, 102*, 357–389.

Peevers, B. H., & Secord, P. F. (1973). Developmental changes in attribution of descriptive concepts to persons. *Journal of Personality and Social Psychology, 27*, 120–128.

Pittman, T. S. (1982). *Intrinsic and extrinsic motivational orientations toward others.* Paper presented at the meeting of the American Psychological Association, Washington, DC.

Pittman, T. S., & Boggiano, A. K. (in press). Intrinsic and extrinsic orientations in peer interactions. In Boggiano, A. K., & Pittman, T. S. (Eds.), *Achievement and motivation: A social development perspective.* New York: Cambridge University Press.

Pittman, T. S., Boggiano, A. K., & Ruble, D. N. (1986). Intrinsic and extrinsic motivational orientations: Limiting conditions on the undermining and enhancing effects of reward on intrinsic motivation. In J. Levine, & M. Wang (Eds.), *Teacher and student perceptions: Implications for learning* (pp. 319–340). Hillsdale, NJ: Erlbaum.

Pittman, T. S., & Dool, J. R. (April, 1985). *Age, source of reward, and intrinsic motivation in peer interaction.* Paper presented to the Society for Research in Child Development, Toronto.

Pittman, T. S., & Heller, J. F. (1987). Social motivation. *Annual Review of Psychology, 38,* 461–489.

Pope, A. W., McHale, S. M., & Craighead, W. E. (1988). *Self-esteem enhancement with children and adolescents.* Oxford: Pergamon Press.

Powers, S. I., Hauser, S. T., & Kilner, L. A. (1989). Adolescent mental health. *American Psychologist, 44,* 200–208.

Pretty, G. H., & Seligman, C. (1984). Affect and the overjustification effect. *Journal of Personality and Social Psychology, 46,* 1241–1253.

Putallaz, M., & Heflin, A. H. (1990). Parent-child interaction. In S. R. Asher & J. Coie (Eds.), *Peer rejection in childhood* (pp. 189–216). New York: Cambridge University Press.

Putallaz, M., & Wasserman, A. (1990). Children's entry behavior. In S. R. Asher & J. Coie (Eds.), *Peer rejection in childhood* (pp. 60–89). New York: Cambridge University Press.

Renshaw, P. D., & Asher, S. R. (1982). Social competence and peer status: The distinction between goals and strategies. In K. H. Rubin & H. S. Ross (Eds.), *Peer relationships and social skills in childhood* (pp. 375–395). New York: Springer-Verlag.

Renshaw, P. D., & Asher, S. R. (1983). Children's goals and strategies for social interaction. *Merrill-Palmer Quarterly, 29,* 353–374.

Rholes, W. S., Blackwell, J., Jordan, C., & Walters, C. (1980). A developmental study of learned helplessness. *Developmental Psychology, 16,* 616–624.

Rholes, W. S., Jones, M., & Wade, C. (1988). Children's understanding of personal dispositions and its relationship to behavior. *Journal of Experimental Child Psychology, 45,* 1–17.

Rholes, W. S., Newman, L. S., & Ruble, D. N. (1990). Understanding self and other: Developmental and motivational aspects of perceiving persons in terms of invariant dispositions. In E. T. Higgins & R. M. Sorrentino (Eds.), *Handbook of motivation and cognition: Foundations of social behavior* (Vol. 2, pp. 369–407). New York: Guilford Press.

Rholes, W. S., & Ruble, D. N. (1984). Children's understanding of dispositional characteristics of others. *Child Development, 55,* 550–560.

Rholes, W. S., & Ruble, D. N. (1986). Children's impressions of other persons: The effects of temporal separation of behavioral information. *Child Development, 57,* 872–878.

Rosenberg, M. (1986). Self-concept from middle childhood through adolescence. In J. Suls & A. G. Greenwald (Eds.), *Psychological perspectives on the self* (Vol. 3, pp. 107–135). Hillsdale, NJ: Erlbaum.

Rubin, K. H. (1982). Social and social–cognitive developmental characteristics of young isolate, normal, and sociable children. In K. H. Rubin, & H. S. Ross (Eds.), *Peer relationships and social skills in childhood* (pp. 353–374). New York: Springer-Verlag.

Ruble, D. N. (1983). The development of social comparison processes and their role in achievement-related self-socialization. In E. T. Higgins, D. N. Ruble, & W. W. Hartup (Eds.), *Social cognition and social development: A sociocultural perspective* (pp. 134–157). New York: Cambridge University Press.

Ruble, D. N. (1987). The acquisition of self-knowledge: A self-socialization perspective. In N. Eisenberg (Ed.), *Contemporary topics in developmental psychology* (pp. 243–270). New York: Wiley.

Ruble, D. N., & Flett, G. L. (1988). Conflicting goals in self-evaluative information seeking: Developmental and ability level analyses. *Child Development, 59,* 97–106.

Ruble, D. N., & Frey, K. S. (1987). Social comparison and self-evaluation in the classroom: Developmental changes in knowledge and function. In J. C. Masters & W. P. Smith (Eds.), *Social comparison and social justice: Theoretical, empirical, and policy perspectives* (pp. 81–104). Hillsdale, NJ: Erlbaum.

Ruble, D. N., & Frey, K. S. (1991). Changing patterns of comparative behavior as skills are acquired: A functional model of self-evaluation. In J. Suls, & T. A. Wills (Eds.), *Social comparison: Contemporary theory and research* (pp. 79–113). Hillsdale, NJ: Erlbaum.

Ruble, D. N., Higgins, E. T., & Hartup, W. W. (1983). What's social about social–cognitive development? In E. T. Higgins, D. N. Ruble, & W. W. Hartup (Eds.), *Social cognition and social development* (pp. 3–12). New York: Cambridge University Press.

Ruble, D. N., & Rholes, W. S. (1981). The development of children's perceptions and attributions about their social world. In J. H. Harvey, W. Ickes, & R. F. Kidd (Eds.), *New directions in attribution research* (Vol. 3, pp. 3–36). Hillsdale, NJ: Erlbaum.

Ryan, R. M. (1982). Control and information in the intrapersonal sphere: An extension of cognitive evaluation theory. *Journal of Personality and Social Psychology, 43,* 450–461.

Ryan, R. M., & Connell, J. P. (1989). Perceived locus of causality and internalization: Examining reasons for acting in two domains. *Journal of Personality and Social Psychology, 57,* 749–761.

Schwarzer, R. (1986). Self-related cognitions in anxiety and motivation: An introduction. In R. Schwarzer (Ed.), *Self-related cognitions in anxiety and motivation* (pp. 1–18). Hillsdale, NJ: Erlbaum.

Seligman, M. E. P., Abramson, L. Y., Semmel, A., & Von Baeyer, C. (1979). Depressive attributional style. *Journal of Abnormal Psychology, 88,* 242–247.

Selman, R. L. (1981). The child as a friendship philosopher. In S. R. Asher & J. M. Gottman (Eds.), *The development of children's friendships* (pp. 242–272). New York: Cambridge University Press.

Shantz, C. U. (1983). Social cognition. In J. H. Flavell & E. M. Markman (Eds.) & P. H. Mussen (Series Ed.), *Handbook of child psychology: Vol. 3. Cognitive development* (4th ed.) (pp. 495–555). New York: Wiley.

Shoda, Y., Mischel, W., & Peake, P. K. (1990). Predicting adolescent cognitive and self-regulatory competencies from preschool delay of gratification: Identifying diagnostic conditions. *Developmental Psychology, 26,* 978–986.

Simmons, R. G., & Blythe, D. A. (1987). *Moving into adolescence: The impact of pubertal change and school context.* New York: Aldine De Gruyter.

Simpson, J. A., Rholes, W. S., & Nelligan, J. S. (1992). Support-seeking and support-giving within couples in an anxiety-provoking situation: The role of attachment styles. *Journal of Personality and Social Psychology, 62,* 434–446.

Slaby, R. G., & Frey, K. S. (1975). Development of gender constancy and selective attention to same-sex models. *Child Development, 46,* 849–856.

Smetana, J. G. (1988). Adolescents' and parents' conceptions of parental authority. *Child Development, 59,* 321–335.

Smith, M. C. (1975). Children's use of the multiple sufficient cause schema in social perception. *Journal of Personality and Social Psychology, 32,* 737–747.

Sorrentino, R. M., & Higgins, E. T. (Eds.), (1986). *Handbook of motivation and cognition: Foundations of social behavior* (Vol. 1). New York: Guilford Press.

Stipek, D., & MacIver, D. (1989). Developmental change in children's assessment of intellectual competence. *Child Development, 60,* 521–538.

Suls, J. (1986). Comparison processes in relative deprivation: A life-span analysis. In J. M. Olson, C. P. Herman, & M. P. Zanna (Eds.), *Relative deprivation and social comparison: The Ontario symposium* (Vol. 4, pp. 95–116). Hillsdale, NJ: Erlbaum.

Taylor, S. E., & Brown, J. D. (1988). Illusion and well-being: A social psychological perspective on mental health. *Psychological Bulletin, 103,* 193–210.

Thompson, E. P., Boggiano, A. K., Costanzo, P. E., Matter, J. A., & Ruble, D. N. (1992). *Age-related changes in children's orientations toward strategic peer interaction: Implications for social perception and behavior.* Manuscript in preparation.

Thompson, E. P., Ruble, D. N., Boggiano, A. K., & Pittman, T. S. (April, 1991). *The development of affective versus instrumental orientations toward peer interaction.* Paper presented at the meeting of the Society for Research on Child Development, Seattle, WA.

Tuma, J. M. (1989). Mental health services for children: The state of the art. *American Psychologist, 44,* 188–199.

Wallerstein, J., & Kelly, J. (1980). *Surviving the breakup: How children and parents cope with divorce.* New York: Basic Books.

Waters, E., Kondo-Ikemura, K. Posada, G., & Richters, J. E. (1990). Learning to love: Mechanisms and milestones. In M. R. Gunnar & L. A. Sroufe (Eds.), *Minnesota symposium on child psychology: Self-processes and development* (Vol. 23, pp. 217–256). Hillsdale, NJ: Erlbaum.

Weiner, B. (1985). Attribution theory of achievement motivation and emotion. *Psychological Review, 92,* 548–573.

Wells, D., & Schultz, T. R. (1980). Developmental distinctions between behavior and judgment in the operation of the discounting principle. *Child Development, 54,* 1307–1310.

White, R. W. (1959). Motivation reconsidered: The concept of competence. *Psychological Review, 66,* 297–333.

Whitesell, N. R., & Harter, S. (1989). Children's reports of conflict between simultaneous opposite-valence emotions. *Child Development, 60,* 673–682.

Small Groups
and Mental Health

JOHN M. LEVINE and RICHARD L. MORELAND

A small group can be defined as three or more people who interact on a regular basis, have affective ties with one another, share a common frame of reference, and are behaviorally interdependent. Such groups are important because they enhance the satisfaction of several basic human needs (Forsyth, 1990; Mackie & Goethals, 1987; Moreland, 1987; Shaver & Buhrmester, 1983). In regard to survival needs, groups facilitate reproduction, childrearing, acquisition of food and shelter, and defense. In regard to psychological needs, groups allow members to satisfy their desires to affiliate with others, avoid loneliness, exercise power, and so on. In regard to informational needs, groups help members understand the world they live in, as well as their own characteristics, through the mechanisms of direct persuasion and social comparison. And, in regard to identity needs, groups allow members to view themselves as part of a positive social entity and to feel good about themselves as a result (Tajfel & Turner, 1979).

In addition to providing these benefits, however, groups also can exact certain costs. These costs include frustration of (1) survival needs (e.g., when there is competition within the group for a scarce resource, such as food), (2) psychological needs (e.g., when the group does not allow a member with high power motivation to exercise leadership), (3) informational needs (e.g., when the group isolates the member from valuable sources of information), and (4) identity needs (e.g., when the group is clearly inferior to other groups). Under certain circumstances, these costs can become quite severe and can have negative consequences for the mental health of members. Although the ubiquity of human groups suggests that the rewards of membership are typically greater than the costs, these rewards sometimes can exacerbate the costs by inhibiting members from leaving a group that is harmful to them.

Small groups play a critical role in the lives of both children and adults. At birth, we enter a family group, which exerts a profound and lasting influence on most if not all of our behavior. During childhood, adolescence, and often young adulthood, we spend substantial time in school settings, where formal and informal groups affect our social and emotional as well as intellectual development. And as adults, we spend many hours each week in work settings, where various groups influence our intangible (e.g., stress) as well as tangible (e.g., monetary) outcomes. We also participate as adults in a variety of other important groups, such as helping groups and social support networks. Because no man (or woman or child) is an island, neither adaptive nor maladaptive behavior can be adequately understood without considering the impact of membership in small groups.

CURRENT STATE OF SMALL GROUP RESEARCH

Although there is a large social psychological literature on small groups (for reviews, see Hare, 1976; McGrath, 1984; Forsyth, 1990) and excellent work in this area is currently being done by a number of social psychologists, group processes have not been a dominant research topic in our discipline for some years (Steiner, 1974, 1986). This should not be taken to mean, however, that the field of group processes is dying. Quite the contrary. After reviewing the theoretical and empirical work on small groups published since 1980, we believe that the field is quite vigorous and healthy (Levine & Moreland, 1990). It seems that, while many social psychologists have been studying the cognitive processes of individuals, investigators from other disciplines (most notably organizational psychology) have rallied to the group processes cause and are now often in the forefront of group research.

One hallmark of recent work on small groups is its multidisciplinary nature. Investigators with diverse backgrounds (e.g., social and organizational psychology, sociology, anthropology, communication) study group processes using a wide range of conceptual and methodological tools. This multidisciplinary approach is an important strength, but it has one unfortunate consequence. Because published work on small groups is scattered across journals in several different disciplines, the vitality of this

field is invisible to many of its practitioners as well as to researchers who work on other topics.

A second hallmark of current group research is an emphasis on
understanding and improving group effectiveness. Because much
of the world's work is done by small groups (e.g., families, work
crews, army squads, athletic teams, and juries), scientists and
laypersons alike want to understand the factors that influence the
ability of groups to perform effectively. This practical orientation
toward small groups has the positive consequence of encouraging
work on complex and interesting problems. It also has important
implications for the development of theory and methodology and
for the availability of research funding. Researchers are increasingly interested in developing theoretical models that can
account for complex behavior in natural groups, rather than simple behavior in laboratory groups. Laboratory experimentation is
being heavily supplemented by field research, observational techniques, archival analyses, and computer simulations. And evidence that work groups (e.g., airplane crews and military units)
often fail to function effectively is increasing corporate and military funding for research on group performance (Murphy, 1980).

RELEVANCE OF GROUP PROCESSES
TO MENTAL HEALTH

The purpose of this chapter is to discuss some linkages between
group processes and mental health and suggest some questions
that deserve further research attention. Given the large number of
potential issues that might be addressed, our discussion is illustrative rather than exhaustive. Nevertheless, we hope that it is sufficient to convince the reader of the critical role of small group
processes in producing, maintaining, ameliorating, and preventing mental health problems.

Family Contexts

The family is the most important group in human society.
McGrath (1984) argues that families "exemplify the idea of group
to an extreme degree," because they exist for a long time with a
fairly constant membership and affect a broad range of members'
activities. During some portions of a person's life, families function
as what McGrath calls "embedding systems" (i.e., total institutions), influencing all of the person's activities all of the time.

Given the importance of the family as a socializing agent, it would not be surprising if the family were implicated in the etiology and maintenance of maladaptive as well as adaptive behaviors. In fact, many classic formulations of psychosocial development and adult functioning (e.g., psychoanalytic theory) assume that families play a critical role in mental illness, and there is a large empirical literature relating family life and psychopathology (e.g., Goldstein, 1988; Jacob, 1987; Patterson, 1990).

Mothers, Fathers, and Children

Historically, analyses of familial determinants of child development focused on dyadic interactions between mothers and their children and assumed that influence within the dyad was unidirectional, from mother to child. More recently, mother–child interaction has been analyzed as a reciprocal process, in which the child also influences the mother. A good deal of evidence has accumulated about mother–child interaction; this research sheds substantial light on both normal and abnormal development (see Maccoby & Martin, 1983; Sigel, Dreyer, & McGillicuddy-DeLisi, 1984). It has been found, for example, that depressed mothers behave differently toward their children than do nondepressed mothers (e.g., Downey & Coyne, 1990; Field, 1987) and that children of depressed mothers suffer an increased risk for depression themselves (Dodge, 1990; Hops, Sherman, & Biglan, 1990). Although the mother–child dyad is clearly important, recent efforts to clarify the role of the family in development have adopted a broader perspective. In so doing, researchers have come to view the family as a complex social system, rather than simply a two-person relationship involving a mother and her child (e.g., Feinman & Lewis, 1984; Minuchin, 1988; Steinglass, 1987).

Within the last two decades, increasing attention has been given to paternal behavior. Relevant work has dealt with differences in the caregiving behaviors of fathers and mothers, the impact of individual differences among fathers on child outcomes, and system properties of the father–mother–child triad (Maccoby & Martin, 1983). This last line of work is the most interesting from a group process perspective. A number of investigators have explored the complex relationships that can occur between fathers, mothers, and their offspring (Grych & Fincham, 1990). For example, Belsky et al. (e.g., Belsky, Gilstrap, & Rovine, 1984) and Easterbrooks and Emde (1988) have investigated how parents' marital relationship affects their interaction with an infant. Downey and Coyne (1990) have proposed several alternative causal models linking marital discord, parental depression, and child problems. Hetherington and Camara (1984) have discussed the problems that divorce and remarriage pose for both parents and children. Parke, Power, and Gottman (1979) have developed a model of direct and indirect influence patterns in family triads, and Parke and Lewis (1981) have used that model to clarify how aggession may develop in three-person families. Finally, Patterson and his colleagues have done extensive work on reciprocal parental and child behaviors that elicit and maintain aggressive behavior (e.g., Patterson, 1982).

Siblings and Grandparents

Although efforts to understand interactions within father–mother–child triads represent an important extension of work on mother–child and father–child dyads, most family systems contain more than three people. And a child's development can be strongly influenced by kin besides his or her parents. In most families, the most critical nonparental socializing agents are siblings and grandparents, although others (e.g., aunts, uncles, and cousins) sometimes play an important role.

Several lines of work have been conducted on sibling relationships (Lewis, 1987). It has been found, for example, that physical aggression is quite common between siblings and that age and sex exert a strong influence on this behavior (Parke & Slaby, 1983). Other behaviors affected by sibling presence include intellectual performance (Henderson, 1981), sex typing (Huston, 1983), reactions to divorce and remarriage (Hetherington, 1988), and various psychological disorders (Martin, 1987). As in the case of father–mother–child triads, there are a number of mechanisms by which siblings can influence one another. Some of these are direct, such as one sibling delivering physical rewards and punishments to another. Others are indirect, such as the birth of an infant "dethroning" an older sibling, a younger child imitating an older sibling, and aggressive children causing stress in their parents' relationship, which in turn affects their emotional response to another child in the family (cf. Dunn, 1988; Kreppner, 1988).

Less research has been done on grandparents as socialization agents, but they are now receiving increased attention, perhaps because the high rate of maternal employment in the United States allows (or forces) grandparents to take a more active role in childrearing. Recent analyses suggest that grandparents can influence grandchildren's social and emotional development through a variety of paths (Lewis, 1987; Tinsley & Parke, 1984). These paths include serving as role models for their grandchildren, providing direct child care, and giving emotional and financial support to their adult children. The influence of grandparents is by no means simple, and a number of variables can affect their impact (e.g., the relationship between grandparents and their adult children and the ages of grandparents and grandchildren). It is important to emphasize that grandparental influence is not always beneficial to specific family members or to the family as a whole. Not only can grandparents' current behavior toward their adult children and grandchildren cause conflict, but grandparents can harm their grandchildren indirectly via their previous treatment of their own children. Work by Elder, Caspi, and Downey (1986), for example, demonstrates that unstable personalities and unstable family relations persist over generations, indicating that the sins of the fathers and mothers are visited not only on their own children, but on their grandchildren and great-grandchildren as well.

Temporal Factors in Families

The generational work by Elder and others highlights the importance of temporal factors in family interactions. Because families exist for long periods and members enter and exit at different times, Elder (1984) has suggested that three temporal dimensions must be considered simultaneously in describing each family member. One dimension (lifetime) describes the person's passage through the age structure (e.g., age = 40). A second dimension (family time) describes the person's generational status within the family (e.g., G1 = oldest generation, no surviving parent). And a third dimension (historical time) describes the person's year of birth and age cohort (e.g., birth year = 1950). This framework makes salient the importance of simultaneously considering the individual aging process, changing constellations of role demands within the family, and alterations in the social context surrounding the family. It also suggests several interesting research issues, including the impact of generational turnover on family members' status, role obligations, and self-identity (Hagestad, 1981).

A number of other analyses of family processes have also dealt with temporal issues. Gottman et al., for example, have studied how interpersonal relations between family members change over time (e.g., Gottman, 1987, 1990; Griffin & Gottman, 1990). Other researchers have focused on developmental changes in the family as a whole (Carter & McGoldrick, 1980; Duvall & Miller, 1984), and several investigators have examined families' short-term and long-term adaptations to major stressors, such as the birth of an infant, changes in parental employment, divorce and single-parenting, and the presence of handicapped children (e.g., Beckman, 1984; Eckenrode & Gore, 1990; Feiring & Lewis, 1984; Hetherington, 1988; Hoffman, 1984; Osofsky & Osofsky, 1984; Patterson & Forgatch, 1990).

Extrafamilial Influences

As the work on adaptations to stressors suggests, the family does not exist in isolation. Instead, the family's external environment exerts a profound influence on its structure and dynamics, which in turn affects the psychosocial functioning of both parents and children. Environmental influences involve a variety of interrelated factors, including the culture and subculture in which the family is embedded (Harrison, Serafica, & McAdoo, 1984; Weisner, 1984), the social class of the parents (Laosa, 1981), broad societal changes involving family employment patterns and the timing of onset of parenthood (Parke & Tinsley, 1987), and formal and informal community support systems (Parke & Lewis, 1981). Perhaps the most systematic analysis of environmental influences on families has been offered by Bronfenbrenner (1986; Bronfenbrenner, Moen, & Garbarino, 1984). He notes, for example, the importance of studying bidirectional influences between the family and other socialization settings, such as the peer group (Rubin & Sloman, 1984) and the school (Hess & Holloway, 1984), as well as children's successive transitions between and within these settings.

Directions for Future Research

Developmental and clinical psychologists are aware of the critical role that families play in psychosocial development and are making substantial contributions to our understanding of family processes and outcomes. In contrast, social psychologists interested in group processes rarely study families. Why? One reason is that, at least until recently, the dominant research paradigm in social psychology was the laboratory experiment, which is not well suited to capturing complex social interactions in natural groups. Although some promising efforts have been made to use experimental procedures for studying family dynamics (e.g., Waxler & Mishler, 1970), this approach has not been widely adopted. A second reason for social psychologists' neglect of families is related to the first—namely, ad hoc groups of college students are usually easier to recruit and study than are intact groups of family members.

If most social psychologists who study groups have paid too little attention to the family, what issues should be considered in applying findings from laboratory groups to families and in conducting new research using families? First, given our previous discussion of the importance of temporal processes in families, it is clear that developmental factors must be taken into account when analyzing family interaction patterns. These factors include the developmental level of (1) each family member, (2) the family group as a whole, and (3) the relationship between each member and the group. Moreland and Levine (1988), for example, have analyzed some of the ways in which group development (temporal changes in the group as a whole) and group socialization (temporal changes in the relationship between the group and its members) can affect one another. This analysis suggests a number of interesting research questions regarding temporal processes in families. For example, how does the developmental level of the relationship between a husband and a wife influence the techniques they use to socialize their children? And, how does the need to socialize a "difficult" child (e.g., one who is physically or mentally handicapped) affect the speed and course of family development?

Second, several differences between families and ad hoc groups need to be acknowledged (McGrath, 1984; Steinhauer, 1987; Weick, 1971). For example, family members are biologically related and have more intense affective ties than do members of ad hoc groups, which in turn produces a higher level of cohesion and commitment to the group. Families, in contrast to ad hoc groups, include people of substantially different ages and competencies, and members' similarity on these dimensions can influence several aspects of group dynamics (e.g., power and status relations and role assignments). Whereas ad hoc groups typically exist for short periods of time, families share a common history and future, which influence their flexibility in solving problems and their receptivity to new information. And, compared to ad hoc groups, families typically confront more serious problems and must solve these problems in more distracting circumstances, which affects their motivation and ability to search for optimal solutions and their affective reactions to these solutions. Clearly, families present a wide range of interesting and challenging questions for group researchers who are interested in normal as well as abnormal behavior (Walsh, 1982). It might be useful, for example, to apply social psychological theory about bargaining and negotiation, coalition formation, and majority/minority influence to the issue of conflict resolution in families.

School Contexts

Children, adolescents, and many young adults spend a large proportion of their time in school contexts, where both formal and informal groups exert a profound influence on their development. Much of the research on school effects focuses on intellectual development. Such development is relevant to mental health in that low academic achievement can have adverse effects on students' self-concept and self-esteem, social relationships, and later economic success. In addition, some research attention has been given to the social and emotional consequences of school experiences (Minuchin & Shapiro, 1983). These effects have been demonstrated at several levels of analysis. For example, some evidence indicates that both young children's aggressive behavior and older children's delinquent behavior vary as a function of the school they attend, although the specific causal mechanisms underlying these relationships are unclear (Kellam, 1990; Rutter & Garmezy, 1983). At a more molecular level, classroom grouping practices have been shown to influence students' self-perceptions and self-esteem (Madden & Slavin, 1983).

The Teacher–Student Relationship

Given the role and power disparities that exist between teachers and students in classrooms, how teachers treat students is likely to be an important determinant of children's thoughts, feelings, and behaviors. This is particularly true in the elementary grades, where students are more dependent on and fearful of authority than they are in later grades. Research indicates that teachers are quite responsive to children's personal characteristics, making attributions about problem students (Rohrkemper & Brophy, 1983) and behaving differentially toward children as function of their behavior, gender, ethnicity, and social class (Minuchin & Shapiro, 1983). Particular attention has been paid to how teachers' expectations for students' performance affect their treatment of students. Under certain conditions, teachers treat students who presumably have low ability differently than others, which in turn produces a self-fulfilling prophesy (Cooper, 1983; Harris & Rosenthal, 1986). Given that academic achievement can influence self-esteem (Harter, 1983), teacher behavior may be an important determinant of how students evaluate themselves (see also Hoge, Smit, & Hanson, 1990; Marshall & Weinstein, 1984).

Grouping Practices

Most classrooms contain students of the same chronological age, and other individual difference factors, such as ability level, are often used to group students for all or part of the school day. These grouping techniques vary on a number of dimensions (e.g., whether they apply to an entire classroom or to a subset of students within the classroom) and are labeled in several different ways (e.g., special education placement, remedial instruction, tracking). The effects of group composition on both academic and nonacademic outcomes have been extensively studied (e.g., Dar & Resh, 1986; Kulik & Kulik, 1982; Madden & Slavin, 1983; Peterson, Wilkinson, & Hallinan, 1984; Slavin, 1987; Sorensen & Hallinan, 1986). Researchers have found, for example, that assigning elementary school students to self-contained classes according to ability does not improve achievement, but that cross-grade grouping for particular subjects can be effective. In addition, children with mild academic handicaps often show greater achievement, self-esteem, and emotional adjustment when they are assigned to regular classes with some form of extra support (e.g., individualized instruction) than when they are placed in full-time special education classes. (However, handicapped children assigned to regular classes are less accepted and more rejected than their nonhandicapped classmates.) Self-contained classes may have negative effects on children with academic difficulties for several reasons, including low teacher expectations, rejection by peers in more advanced classes, and unflattering social comparisons (Madden & Slavin, 1983; Reuman, 1989; Slavin, 1987).

Peer Interaction in Formal Groups

For the most part, research on grouping practices has focused on the consequences of classroom composition and neglected the social processes that produce these effects. But other researchers have sought to clarify how specific interactions between students influence their intellectual, emotional, and social outcomes. Some of this work deals with the relationship between children's behavior in learning groups (e.g., reading and math) and their academic achievement (Peterson, Wilkinson, Spinelli, & Swing, 1984; Webb, 1982; Webb & Kenderski, 1984). It has been found, for example, that certain forms of interaction (e.g., giving explanations) are positively related to achievement, whereas other forms (e.g., receiving no explanation in response to a question) are negatively related.

Other work in this area involves peer tutoring, where students are placed into dyads and asked to provide instruction to one another (Allen, 1976, 1983; Cohen, Kulik, & Kulik, 1982; Fantuzzo, Riggio, Connelly, & Dimeff, 1989; Hartup, 1983). In most cases, the two students differ in ability and/or knowledge, so that one student plays the role of tutor and the other plays the role of tutee. Although evidence regarding the efficacy of peer tutoring is mixed, several studies suggest that this procedure can enhance learning, improve self-concept, and reduce stress for both tutors and tutees. These effects are no doubt due to multiple underlying processes, including a high level of motivation to master the academic material in the lesson, a feeling of efficacy for successfully enacting the role of tutor or tutee, and a perception of social support from the peer playing the complementary role.

In addition to being used in dyadic situations, peer tutoring is also a component of many cooperative learning programs. In these programs, students are divided into small, heterogeneous groups and expected to help one another learn academic material. Many different cooperative learning programs have been developed. These programs differ on two major dimensions (Slavin, 1983): incentive structure (group reward for individual learning, group reward for group product, and individual reward) and task structure (group study with no task specialization and task specialization). A good deal of research has been conducted on the cognitive and noncognitive consequences of participating in such programs (Ames, 1984; Bossert, 1988; Johnson & Johnson, 1983; Johnson, Johnson, & Maruyama, 1983; Madden & Slavin, 1983; Miller & Brewer, 1986; Slavin, 1983). Regarding cognitive outcomes, students seem most likely to benefit from cooperative learning programs that entail group rewards and individual accountability. In these programs, the best efforts of all members are necessary for group success, and the performance of all members is public and quantifiable. Such conditions are presumably important because they create peer norms and reward systems that encourage all members to excel. Regarding noncognitive outcomes, cooperative learning programs can have a number of positive effects, including increased helping and tutoring, attraction toward peers of different racial/ethnic groups and ability levels, capacity to take the perspective of others, and self-esteem. The most effective cooperative learning programs for promoting peer attraction are those that avoid interteam competition, focus students' attention on interpersonal processes within the group, and do not confound subgroup formation with membership in a particular racial/ethnic category.

Lest one conclude that all forms of competition in schools are bad for students, a few examples of "positive competition" might be mentioned. Most secondary schools and colleges support athletic programs in which students compete in individual and team sports. Although these programs are often criticized for reducing students' intellectual pursuits, there is a broad consensus that they have both individual and social benefits. Moreover, the positive effects of competition are not restricted to the athletic field. Social comparison on academic criteria is a ubiquitous aspect of school life (Levine, 1983; Marshall & Weinstein, 1984; Rosenholtz & Simpson, 1984; Ruble & Frey, 1987), and this comparison can have positive (as well as negative) consequences for both high and low achievers. Students who do well are likely to feel good about their performance, which may help to sustain their academic motivation. Although students who do poorly may feel bad about their performance, the assumption that they inevitably suffer low self-esteem and motivational deficits is probably incorrect. At least under certain circumstances (e.g., when students feel that they are capable of improving through effort), negative social comparisons arising from inferior performance may lead to increased motivation and higher performance (Levine, 1983; Richer, 1976). And of course, social comparison information, whether flattering or unflattering, is often helpful in setting realistic goals and deciding how to invest limited time and money. Finally, a growing body of research demonstrates that certain types of disagreement, or conflict, on academic issues can stimulate students' intellectual growth, as well as interpersonal attraction and self-esteem (Doise & Mugny, 1984; Johnson, Johnson, & Smith, 1986; Perret-Clermont, 1980).

The Role of Informal Groups

The organizational characteristics of schools and classrooms affect peer group membership (Epstein, 1983; Karweit & Hansell, 1983), which in turn exerts a profound influence on students' attitudes, values, and behaviors. According to Gecas (1981), peer groups play a critical role in three areas of socialization: the development and validation of the self, the learning of role taking and impression management skills, and the acquisition of knowledge that adults fail to transmit to children. Peer group influence may be consonant or dissonant with that exerted by other socialization agents, such as the family (Hartup, 1983), and may be mediated by several processes, including direct reinforcement, normative and comparative influence, and modeling (Hallinan & Williams, 1990; Hartup, 1983; Schunk, 1987; Singer, 1981).

The outcomes of peer relations are affected by both the quality of these relations and the nature of peer group norms. Evidence (Hartup, 1983; Parker & Asher, 1987) indicates that good peer relations are associated with several positive behaviors (e.g., sociability, regulation of aggression, and internalization of social standards), whereas poor peer relations are associated with several negative behaviors (e.g., criminality and dropping out of school). From these data, one might conclude that children and adolescents who have good peer relations are always better off than those whose relations are poor. But what if the norms of the peer group encourage undesirable behavior? In these cases, individuals who get along with their peers (and are thus receptive to group norms) are at greater risk than those who do not get along (and are thus unreceptive to group norms) (cf. Allen, 1965). Indeed, evidence indicates that peer group norms sometimes encourage positive attitudes toward marijuana use (Humphrey, O'Malley, Johnston, & Bachman, 1988), delinquent values (Jussim & Osgood, 1989), alcohol and drug use (Sutker, 1982), cigarette smoking (Krohn, Massey, & Zielinski, 1988), and aggressive behavior (Parke & Slaby, 1983).

Because most schools contain many informal groups and cliques, it is important to understand the factors that predispose students to join and/or accept influence from one group rather than another. This issue is complicated because students' membership and reference groups are not always the same and because reference groups can serve both comparative and normative functions (Singer, 1981). Two powerful determinants of informal group membership in schools have been identified—gender and race (Schofield, 1981, 1989). Racial segregation in informal groups is particularly troubling, given the strong efforts that have been made to desegregate public schools in the United States. But there is reason to hope that resegregation in schools can be reduced, though probably not eliminated entirely. Cooperative learning programs, discussed earlier, have been used to increase interpersonal attraction, as well as achievement and self-esteem, within racially and ethnically diverse classrooms. And social psychological research on intergroup relations suggests some promising avenues for reducing hostility between students of different races, such as individuating the outgroup, reducing the salience of group boundaries, and reducing identification with the ingroup (Messick & Mackie, 1989; Miller & Brewer, 1986; Stephan, 1985; Wilder, 1986).

Directions for Future Research

In order to understand how group experiences influence students' intellectual, social, and emotional development, researchers should devote more attention to role transitions in school settings (cf. Bronfenbrenner, 1986). Beginning with a young child's first day of kindergarten and ending with a young adult's final graduation ceremony, role transitions are an important aspect of school life. Students undergo several different types of role transitions during their career. These include (1) entering a social aggregate that has not yet developed a coherent group structure (e.g., starting kindergarten); (2) entering an intact group (e.g., starting sixth grade in a new school at midyear); (3) moving from one role to another within a group (e.g., becoming the leader of a clique); (4) responding to a new set of norms as part of a group making the same shift (e.g., entering first grade with classmates from kindergarten); and (5) moving into a new role either before or after other members of one's group (e.g., graduating early or late).

Regardless of the specific form that a role transition takes, it is likely to induce a substantial amount of stress (Bush & Simmons, 1981; Eccles, Midgley, & Adler, 1984; Moreland & Levine, 1984; van de Vliert & Allen, 1984). This stress can be associated with one or more components of the transition process, which include (1) anticipating the transition, (2) scheduling the transition, and (3) producing the transition and adjusting to it afterwards (Moreland & Levine, 1984). Although a number of suggestions have been offered regarding the determinants of transition stress and the ways that role occupants manage this stress, additional research on role transitions in school settings is needed. Attention should be given, for example, to how movement from grade to grade and from school to school alters the self-concept and self-esteem of children of different ages. To what extent are transition-induced decreases in self-esteem due to perceived inadequacy in fulfilling teachers' versus classmates' expectations, and how does the relative contribution of these two factors vary as a function of the child's developmental level? Effort is also needed to develop strategies (e.g., anticipatory socialization) that teachers and school administrators can use in helping students to cope with the emotional strain associated with abandoning old, comfortable roles and accepting new, frightening ones.

Work Contexts

The work that adults do is a critical determinant of their standard of living, interpersonal relationships, and social status. Because work is often a source of stress, it can negatively affect mental health. Most work is done in group contexts of one sort or another, so an understanding of behavior in work groups is necessary for developing strategies to reduce the negative consequences of work-induced stress. Attention must be given to both how work groups generate stress and how they buffer their members against it.

Group Environment

Work groups exist in physical, social, and temporal environments, which can profoundly affect the amount of stress that group members experience. Aspects of physical environments that induce stress include crowding (Paulus & Nagar, 1989); dangerous and confining work settings, such as submarines and coal mines (Harrison & Connors, 1984; Vaught & Smith, 1980); unpleasant (e.g., poorly lit, noisy) factories and offices (Oldham & Rotchford, 1983); and the introduction of new technology (Gutek, Bikson, & Mankin, 1984). Stressful characteristics of social environments include group embeddedness within larger organizations (Alderfer & Smith, 1982; Ancona & Caldwell, 1988), overlapping group memberships (Davis & Stern, 1980), entrances by newcomers and exits by oldtimers (Moreland & Levine, 1982, 1989), and influence from outsiders (Greer, 1983; Levine & Moreland, 1985). And stress-inducing features of temporal environments include group formation and termination (Krantz, 1985; Moreland, 1987; Sutton, 1987), time limits and deadlines (Kelly & McGrath, 1985), and scheduling and synchronizing activities (McGrath & Rotchford, 1983).

Group Composition

The composition of a work group can also influence members' stress. It has been found, for example, that larger groups typically produce less member satisfaction, participation, and cooperation than do smaller groups (Kerr, 1989; Pinto & Crow, 1982). Research also indicates that member variability on such dimensions as age can increase interpersonal conflict and turnover (Pfeffer, 1983; Wagner, Pfeffer, & O'Reilly, 1984). Finally, the sex composition of work groups can affect members' behaviors and feelings. In mixed-sex groups, males tend to be more active and influential than females, more likely to engage in agentic activities and less likely to engage in communal activities, and more concerned about resolving issues concerning status and power (Anderson & Blanchard, 1982; Dion, 1985; Martin & Shanahan, 1983). There is also evidence that, under certain circumstances, "token" females in work groups experience a variety of problems, including social isolation, role entrapment, and powerlessness (Izraeli, 1983; Kanter, 1977).

Status Systems

Status systems reflect the prestige and power relations among group members. Compared to people with lower status, those with higher status have more opportunities to exert social influence, are more successful in their influence attempts, are evaluated more favorably, and have higher self-esteem (Sande, Ellard, & Ross, 1986; Skvoretz, 1988; Weisfeld & Weisfeld, 1984). Because it is generally more rewarding to have high than low status, acquiring and maintaining status are important aspects of group life. Status systems develop rapidly in groups, and recent theoretical accounts suggest that certain categories of people (e.g., women, African-Americans) are at a disadvantage in competing for status, which in turn may cause them to be more vulnerable to stress-related psychological problems.

According to "expectation states" theory (Berger, Rosenholtz, & Zelditch, 1980), group members form expectations about one another's likely contributions to group goal attainment on the basis of personal characteristics, and people who possess "valuable" characteristics elicit more positive expectations and are accorded higher status within the group. But even when the characteristics assumed to predict performance are in fact irrelevant, people who do not possess those characteristics find it difficult or impossible to convince other group members of their worth (Ridgeway, 1982).

According to "ethological" theory (Mazur, 1985), group members assess one another's strength on the basis of appearance cues, such as size and musculature, and brief dominance contests (e.g., staring). People who appear strong are assigned higher status than those who appear weak. Because females are less likely than males to manifest physical dominance cues, ethological theory (like expectation states theory) suggests that females are at a relative disadvantage in acquiring status within work groups.

Although low status often increases stress and thereby undermines mental health, the psychological costs of high status should not be overlooked. People accorded high status by their fellow group members are often held accountable for group performance. Evidence indicates, for example, that when group failure occurs, high-status members (i.e., leaders) are often the recipients of substantial hostility from lower-status members, who feel that their trust was betrayed (Levine, 1989). Leaders' anxiety about being punished for group failure and their efforts to prevent such failure can induce high stress and increase their vulnerability to psychological problems.

Roles

Roles are shared expectations about how individuals occupying particular positions within a group ought to behave. Role enactment often produces considerable stress for members of work groups. One source of stress is role ambiguity, which occurs when the behavioral requirements of a role are unclear. In this case, the role occupant does not know precisely what is expected of him or her. Another source of stress is role conflict, which occurs when a person (1) occupies two or more roles that have incompatible expectations (interrole conflict) or (2) faces contradictory expectations concerning a single role (intrarole conflict). In both cases, the role occupant is pulled in two (or more) directions. There is substantial evidence that role ambiguity and role conflict have negative effects on members of work groups. These effects include increased tension and propensity to leave the group and decreased job satisfaction and organizational commitment (Fisher & Gitelson, 1983; Jackson & Schuler, 1985; see also King & King, 1990).

Other role-related sources of stress involve role assignment, role transition, and role innovation. During role assignment, when decisions are made about who should play which role in a work group, a variety of tactics can be used to maneuver particular people into (or out of) particular roles (Moreland & Levine, 1982). The nature of these tactics, as well as their level of success, can produce conflict and stress within the group. And as we suggested earlier, role transitions within a work group or between groups are often quite stressful (Brett, 1980; Frese, 1984; Louis, 1980). Particularly difficult are transitions involving dismissals, layoffs, plant closings, and mergers, which force role occupants to give up the rewards of one group with no guarantee that they can obtain similar rewards in another group (Brockner, 1988; Dooley & Catalano, 1988; Greenhalgh, 1983; Marks & Mirvis, 1986; Sutton, 1987). Finally, efforts to change the expectations associated with a particular role (role innovation) are often difficult and frustrating, because occupants of complementary roles are reluctant to cooperate (Brett, 1984; Nicholson, 1984).

Innovation Efforts

In addition to altering the expectations for their roles, members of work groups sometimes attempt to produce other forms of innovation. Such efforts are frequently initiated by numerical minorities who believe that the group would be more effective if certain changes were made in its composition, structure, and/or process (Levine & Moreland, 1985; Moscovici, 1985; Nemeth & Staw, 1989). Although minority members can sometimes be quite influential, research on opinion deviance in small groups suggests that these individuals often have difficulty changing majority members' overt behavior. And even when they are successful, minority members often pay a stiff price in terms of liking and acceptance (Levine, 1989; Levine & Russo, 1987). A particularly interesting form of attempted innovation in organizations is "whistle blowing," when someone attempts to strengthen the organization by revealing its problems to outsiders who presumably will force a solution to these problems. Like opinion deviates in small groups, whistle blowers in organizations are frequently punished for their attempted innovation (Graham, 1986; Near & Miceli, 1986). Why do majority members of both small and large groups frequently ignore the advice of innovators, attempt to alter their opinions, and/or expel them from the group? Perhaps because majority members validate their opinions through social comparison and the presence of a dissenting minority threatens their confidence in these opinions (Festinger, 1950).

Social Comparison of Outcomes

In addition to using social comparison to evaluate their opinions, members of work groups also use comparison to evaluate their job characteristics and outcomes (Goodman, 1977; Salancik & Pfeffer, 1978). For example, workers seeking to assess the fairness of their compensation compare their own job-related inputs and outcomes to those of coworkers (Crosby, 1984; Greenberg, 1982; Martin, 1981). In some cases, these comparisons yield negative information, which can produce maladaptive responses (e.g., feelings of inadequacy and helplessness, anger, and aggression). A recent analysis of outcome evaluation in group contexts reveals the complexity of this social comparison process. Levine and Moreland (1986, 1987) suggest that comparisons can differ regarding (1) the identities of the source and target of comparison (self/self, self/other, group/group), (2) the group identifications of the source and target (intragroup, intergroup), and (3) the time period(s) during which the outcomes under consideration occur (intratemporal, intertemporal). Each of these comparisons, in turn, can yield information indicating that the source's ratio of outcomes to inputs is higher, equal, or lower than the target's ratio. Finally, the source's affective, cognitive, and behavioral reactions to comparison information can vary as a function of several factors. These factors include the source's motive in initiating the comparison (e.g., equity or self-enhancement) and the type of comparison that he or she makes (e.g., collective action is more likely if negative information is obtained from a group/group than a self/other comparison).

Directions for Future Research

Although participation in work groups often induces stress, more research is needed on the potential benefits of such participation. These include tangible rewards, such as money, as well as intangible rewards, such as friendship, the opportunity to display task-relevant ability, and the status and self-esteem derived from group membership (Crocker & Luhtanen, 1990; Tajfel & Turner, 1979). In addition, more research is needed on the potential benefits of playing multiple roles and attempting innovation.

In contrast to much of the work on multiple roles, there is evidence that enacting several roles is sometimes beneficial rather than harmful. Sieber (1974), for example, has argued that the disadvantages of multiple roles are exaggerated and that "role accumulation" has distinct advantages, including increased status security and enhanced self-concept. The impact of role playing on self-concept also has been emphasized by Stryker and Serpe (1982), and Thoits (1983) has presented data indicating that multiple identities (based on multiple roles) act as a buffer against certain types of psychological distress (see also Linville, 1987). The benefits of playing multiple roles may stem, at least in part, from the need to make transitions between them. Role transitions force individuals to learn new skills, to interact with different people (or at least to interact differently with the same people), and to adopt new self-definitions. Thus, both Brett (1984) and Nicholson (1984) suggest that job transitions can enhance personal development as well as produce role innovation.

The risks of attempted innovation may also be exaggerated. For one thing, people who actively seek to change a group's composition, structure, and/or process often have strong ideological reasons for their behavior, which may insulate them against rejection from those who disagree (Moscovici, 1976). Moreover, such people are frequently not alone but instead have allies within the group. Evidence indicates that the presence of even one social supporter provides substantial reassurance to a dissenter (Allen, 1975). Finally, rather than always desiring opinion agreement from others, people sometimes assert their uniqueness, or individuality, through disagreement (Codol, 1984; Lemaine, 1974; Snyder & Fromkin, 1980). In these cases, negative reaction from others may be taken as a sign of success rather than failure. Thus, ideology, social support, and the desire to feel unique may mitigate the costs of deviance and perhaps even transform them into benefits.

Helping Contexts

Individuals often use groups to help them solve personal and social problems, or at least reduce the stress associated with these problems. Some of these groups are formed for the explicit purpose of providing help (e.g., psychotherapy groups, human potential groups, self-help groups). Other groups are not formed to provide help, but nevertheless are called on to do so from time to time (e.g., informal groups of friends who provide social support). To the extent that various kinds of groups are used to solve problems and reduce stress, it is important to understand the factors that underlie their effectiveness.

Psychotherapy Groups

Professionally led groups designed to enhance members' psychological functioning have been used for many years (Bion, 1961). These groups differ in theoretical orientation (e.g., psychoanalytic or behavioral), but all seek to alleviate psychological problems through leader-managed group interaction (Kutash & Wolf, 1990; Long, 1988; Yalom, 1985). Psychoanalytic group therapy, for example, assumes that repressed feelings from the past underlie personal and social difficulties in the present. Practitioners of this form of therapy use group discussion to help individuals recognize and deal with the unconscious residue of their early experience. In contrast, behavioral group therapy emphasizes the need to change problematic behavior itself rather than merely understand its origin. Practitioners of this form of therapy use group activities based on learning theory (e.g., behavior rehearsal, feedback, and modeling) to reduce the frequency and intensity of problematic behavior. Several possible determinants of the effectiveness of group therapy have been identified, including pregroup training, group composition, level of group development, therapist leadership style, and group cohesiveness (Forsyth, 1990; Klein, 1983; Yalom, 1985). With the possible exception of pregroup training, the critical mediators of therapy effectiveness are not well understood.

Members of psychotherapy groups often are unacquainted before treatment and do not expect to interact afterwards. In cases of this kind, the group is created at the first therapy session and serves only one function for its members—allowing discussion of problems that arose and continue to cause difficulty *outside* the group. There are other cases, however, in which members of psychotherapy groups are intimately acquainted before treatment and expect to interact closely afterwards. The most obvious example is family therapy (Alexander & Malouf, 1983; Jacobson & Bussod, 1983; Nichols, 1984). Here, the group was created before (often long before) the first therapy session and serves multiple functions for its members—allowing discussion of problems that arose and continue to cause difficulty *within* the group, providing food and shelter, satisfying affectional needs, and so on. Although there are several varieties of family psychotherapy (e.g., structural, strategic, and behavioral), they all focus on changing the behavior patterns among family members. A recent meta-analytic review indicates that family therapy has positive effects on family interactions and behavior ratings, as compared to no-treatment and alternative treatment controls (Hazelrigg, Cooper, & Borduin,

1987). Nevertheless, conceptual and methodological problems remain in evaluating the effectiveness of family therapy techniques, particularly those based on systems theory, and in clarifying the processes that underlie therapeutic success (Bednar, Burlingame, & Masters, 1988; Wynne, 1988).

Human Potential Groups

Beginning in the 1960s, many people who did not view themselves as psychologically impaired, but who nonetheless wished to undergo psychological change (e.g., personal growth and self-actualization), began to join human potential groups. In most such groups, the leader is seen as more knowledgeable and "advanced" than other members but behaves much as they do. Two types of human potential groups are often distinguished, although mixed cases are common (Back, 1973; Johnson, 1988; Yalom, 1985). One is the T-group, which is designed to help members learn about group dynamics and improve their group-related skills. The other is the sensitivity-training or "encounter" group, which seeks to enhance members' spontaneity, personal awareness, and interpersonal sensitivity. Debate has long raged about the benefits and risks of participation in human potential groups. The available evidence is mixed. For example, although some enduring positive changes are produced by encounter groups, these changes occur primarily in self-reports rather than behaviors (Berman & Zimpfer, 1980). In addition, encounter-group participants sometimes suffer significant harm as a result of their experience (Hartley, Roback, & Abramowitz, 1976).

Self-Help Groups

The interest in human potential groups during the last quarter century has been paralleled by a dramatic rise in the number of self-help groups (Cole, 1983; Katz, 1981). These groups are formed by individuals who share a troubling condition or life experience and who believe that they will benefit from interaction with similar others, typically without professional leadership. Self-help groups can be categorized into several types, depending on their goals. These goals include changing addictive behaviors (e.g., Alcoholics Anonymous), providing social support and coping strategies for stressful life events (e.g., Parents without Partners), enhancing primary care or rehabilitation for medical problems (e.g., the Lupus Foundation and the Stroke Club), and achieving social rights (e.g., Gay Activists' Alliance). In spite of their differences, self-help groups share certain common characteristics, including (1) inspirational testimonials about members' experiences with the shared problem, (2) mutual assistance that benefits both helpers and helpees, (3) discussions of similarities in the problems that members face, and (4) collective praise when members experience improvement and social support when they do not (Forsyth, 1990). A general statement about the effectiveness of self-help groups in assisting members to overcome, or at least adapt to, their problems cannot be made, due to the wide variability in the composition, structure, and processes of such groups and the paucity of methodologically sound studies. Nevertheless, there is evidence that such groups are sometimes quite useful to their members (Hinrichsen, Revenson, & Shinn, 1985).

Social Support Networks

So far, our discussion has emphasized the consequences of participating in small groups that are designed to provide psychological help to their members. However, people who have problems can also benefit from their social relationships outside psychotherapy, human potential, and self-help groups. A good deal of recent attention has been given to how memberships in informal social networks can buffer individuals against the negative effects of stress (Brownell & Shumaker, 1984; Cohen & Syme, 1985; Cohen & Wills, 1985; Gottlieb, 1988; Sarason, Sarason, & Pierce, 1990). The impact of social support on coping has been studied for a variety of problems, including bereavement, unemployment, chronic illness, and marital conflict. Although there is substantial evidence that network memberships can benefit people who are under stress, the psychological mechanisms that produce these positive effects are not clear. In seeking to provide a theoretical basis for the effectiveness of social support, Wills (1985) discussed several social psychological theories that are relevant to support relationships (social exchange, social comparison, self-esteem, personal control) and suggested several functions that these relationships may serve (esteem support, informational support, instrumental support, social companionship, motivational support). In addition, Fisher, Goff, Nadler, and Chinsky (1988) offered a social psychological analysis of the factors that dispose individuals to avoid using social support or to seek support either within or outside their social networks.

Directions for Future Research

Three lines of work concerning helping groups seem particularly promising. One involves efforts to apply theoretical ideas from social psychology to psychotherapy settings. As Klein (1983) notes, there has been little, if any, intellectual exchange between social psychologists who study small groups and therapists who use such groups to improve members' psychological functioning. It seems likely that social psychological research on a number of topics, including status formation, power, leadership, coalition behavior, and social influence, would be applicable to group therapy settings.

A second promising line of work involves the creation, functioning, and demise of self-help groups. How are such groups formed? How are new members recruited and socialized? How do groups deal with old members who violate norms of appropriate conduct? What causes self-help groups to decline, and how do members react to their demise? At least partial answers to these questions might be found in research conducted on other types of groups (Greenhalgh, 1983; Levine, 1989; Levine & Moreland, 1985; Moreland, 1987; Moreland & Levine, 1982, 1989; Sutton, 1987).

Finally, a number of interesting issues concerning how social networks buffer their members against stress remain to be explored. These include the kinds of network members who are most and least likely to seek and offer assistance (e.g., newcomers or oldtimers), the dimensions of support that network members provide (e.g., assistance in identifying and defining problems or provision of intragroup and/or extragroup help), and the degree to which "mere membership" in the network is a form of social support (e.g., because association with the network increases members' self-esteem). Several lines of social psychological work bear on these issues (e.g., Crocker & Luhtanen, 1990; Fisher et al., 1988; Moreland & Levine, 1989).

CONCLUSION

Our goal in writing this chapter was to shed light on how membership in small groups influences mental health. We examined relevant research dealing with family, school, work, and helping contexts. This review indicated that group membership is a powerful determinant of mental health in both children and adults and suggested that any serious effort to understand mental health must consider the psychological benefits and risks associated with group membership.

Several social psychological processes play a role in mediating the impact of group variables on mental health outcomes. These processes include social influence, social comparison, attribution, expectancy confirmation, observational learning, self-perception and identity formation, attachment/cohesion, and role enactment. Given the wide range of human needs (survival, psychological, informational, identity) that group membership either satisfies or frustrates and the complex ways in which groups influence their members, it seems premature to identify one or two social psychological processes as the "core" mechanisms that explain how group variables influence mental health. Instead, it is probably wiser to adopt a more eclectic (if less elegant) explanatory goal, which explicitly recognizes that different processes may mediate different mental health outcomes in different group contexts.

Although much is already known about the impact of group processes on mental health, many exciting research questions remain to be answered. Given the current interdisciplinary interest in small groups and the availability of powerful new tools for analyzing the process and outcome of group interaction (Dabbs & Ruback, 1987; Futoran, Kelly, & McGrath, 1989; Gottman, 1987; Ickes & Tooke, 1988; Kenny & LaVoie, 1984), the stage is set for a strong research initiative on groups and mental health. The only missing ingredient is a greater awareness by both researchers and funding agencies of the tremendous research opportunities in this area

Acknowledgment

Preparation of this chapter was supported by a grant from the Office of Educational Research and Improvement, Department of Education, to the Center for the Study of Learning, Learning Research and Development Center, University of Pittsburgh.

REFERENCES

Alderfer, C. P., & Smith, K. K. (1982). Studying intergroup relations embedded in organizations. *Administrative Science Quarterly, 27*, 35–65.

Alexander, J. F., & Malouf, R. E. (1983). Intervention with children experiencing problems in personality and social development. In P. H. Mussen (Ed.), *Handbook of child psychology* (4th ed.) (Vol. 4, pp. 913–981). New York: Wiley.

Allen, V. L. (1965). Situational factors in conformity. In L. Berkowitz (Ed.), *Advances in experimental social psychology* (Vol. 2, pp. 133–175). New York: Academic Press.

Allen, V. L. (1975). Social support for nonconformity. In L. Berkowitz (Ed.), *Advances in experimental social psychology* (Vol. 8, pp. 1–43). New York: Academic Press.

Allen, V. L. (Ed.). (1976). *Children as teachers: Theory and research on tutoring.* New York: Academic Press.

Allen, V. L. (1983). Impact of the role of tutor on behavior and self-perceptions. In J. M. Levine & M. C. Wang (Eds.), *Teacher and student learning: Implications for learning* (pp. 367–389). Hillsdale, NJ: Erlbaum.

Ames, C. (1984). Competitive, cooperative, and individualistic goal structures: A cognitive-motivational analysis. In R. Ames & C. Ames (Eds.), *Research on motivation in education* (Vol. 1, pp. 177–207). Orlando, FL: Academic Press.

Ancona, D. G., & Caldwell, D. F. (1988). Beyond task and maintenance: Defining external functions in groups. *Group and Organization Studies, 13,* 468–494.

Anderson, L. R., & Blanchard, P. N. (1982). Sex differences in task and social–emotional behavior. *Basic and Applied Social Psychology, 3,* 109–138.

Back, K. W. (1973). *Beyond words: The story of sensitivity training and the encounter movement.* Baltimore, MD: Penguin.

Beckman, P. J. (1984). A transactional view of stress in families of handicapped children. In M. Lewis (Ed.), *Beyond the dyad* (pp. 281–298). New York: Plenum Press.

Bednar, R. L., Burlingame, G. M., & Masters, K. S. (1988). Systems of family treatment: Substance or semantics? *Annual Review of Psychology, 39,* 401–434.

Belsky, J., Gilstrap, B., & Rovine, M. (1984). The Pennsylvania Infant and Family Development Project, I: Stability and change in mother–infant and father–infant interaction in a family setting at one, three, and nine months. *Child Development, 55,* 692–705.

Berger, J., Rosenholtz, S. J., & Zelditch, M. (1980). Status organizing processes. *Annual Review of Sociology, 6,* 479–508.

Berman, J. J., & Zimpfer, D. G. (1980). Growth groups: Do the outcomes really last? *Review of Educational Research, 50,* 505–524.

Bion, W. R. (1961). *Experiences in groups.* London: Tavistock.

Bossert, S. T. (1988). Cooperative activities in the classroom. In E. Z. Rothkopf (Ed.), *Review of research in education* (Vol. 15, pp. 225–250). Washington, DC: American Educational Research Association.

Brett, J. M. (1980). The effect of job transfer on employees and their families. In C. L. Cooper & R. Payne (Eds.), *Current concerns in occupational stress* (pp. 99–136). Chichester, England: Wiley.

Brett, J. M. (1984). Job transitions and personal and role development. In K. M. Rowland & G. R. Ferris (Eds.), *Research in personnel and human resources management* (Vol. 2, pp. 155–185). Greenwich, CT: JAI Press.

Brockner, J. (1988). The effects of work layoffs on survivors: Research, theory, and practice. In B. M. Staw & L. L. Cummings (Eds.), *Research in organizational behavior* (Vol. 10, pp. 213–255). Greenwich, CT: JAI Press.

Bronfenbrenner, U. (1986). Ecology of the family as a context for human development: Research perspectives. *Developmental Psychology, 22,* 723–742.

Bronfenbrenner, U., Moen, P., & Garbarino, J. (1984). Child, family, and community. In R. D. Parke (Ed.), *Review of child development research* (Vol. 7, pp. 283–328). Chicago: University of Chicago Press.

Brownell, A., & Shumaker, S. A. (Eds.). (1984). Social support: New perspectives in theory, research, and intervention. Part 1. Theory and Research. *Journal of Social Issues, 40* (Whole No. 4).

Bush, D. M., & Simmons, R. G. (1981). Socialization processes over the life course. In M. Rosenberg & R. H. Turner (Eds.), *Social psychology: Sociological perspectives* (pp. 133–164). New York: Basic Books.

Carter, E. A., & McGoldrick, M. (Eds.). (1980). *The family life cycle: A framework for family therapy.* New York: Gardner Press.

Codol, J. P. (1984). Social differentiation and non-differentiation. In H. Tajfel (Ed.), *The social dimension: European developments in social psychology* (Vol. 1, pp. 314–337). Cambridge, England: Cambridge University Press.

Cohen, P. A., Kulik, J. A., & Kulik, C. C. (1982). Educational outcomes of tutoring: A meta-analysis of findings. *American Educational Research Journal, 19,* 237–248.

Cohen, S., & Syme, S. L. (Eds.). (1985). *Social support and health.* New York: Academic Press.

Cohen, S., & Wills, T. A. (1985). Stress, social support, and the buffering hypothesis. *Psychological Bulletin, 98,* 310–357.

Cole, S. A. (1983). Self-help groups. In H. I. Kaplan & B. J. Sadock (Eds.), *Comprehensive group psychotherapy* (2nd ed.) (pp. 144–150). Baltimore, MD: Williams & Wilkins.

Cooper, H. M. (1983). Communication of teacher expectations to students. In J. M. Levine & M. C. Wang (Eds.), *Teacher and student perceptions: Implications for learning* (pp. 193–211). Hillsdale, NJ: Erlbaum.

Crocker, J., & Luhtanen, R. (1990). Collective self-esteem and ingroup bias. *Journal of Personality and Social Psychology, 58,* 60–67.

Crosby, F. (1984). Relative deprivation in organizational settings. In B. M. Staw (Ed.), *Research in organizational behavior* (Vol. 6, pp. 51–93). Greenwich, CT: JAI Press.

Dabbs, J. M., & Ruback, R. B. (1987). Dimensions of group process:

Amount and structure of vocal interaction. In L. Berkowitz (Ed.), *Advances in experimental social psychology* (Vol. 20, pp. 123–169). Orlando, FL: Academic Press.

Dar, Y., & Resh, N. (1986). Classroom intellectual composition and academic achievement. *American Educational Research Journal, 23,* 357–374.

Davis, P., & Stern, D. (1980). Adaptation, survival, and growth of the family business: An integrated systems perspective. *Human Relations, 34,* 207–224.

Dion, K. L. (1985). Sex, gender, and groups: Selected issues. In V. E. O'Leary, R. K. Unger, & B. S. Wallston (Eds.), *Women, gender, and social psychology* (pp. 293–347). Hillsdale, NJ: Erlbaum.

Dodge, K. A. (1990). Developmental psychopathology in children of depressed mothers. *Developmental Psychology, 26,* 3–6.

Doise, W., & Mugny, G. (1984). *The social development of the intellect.* New York: Pergamon Press.

Dooley, D., & Catalano, R. (Eds.). (1988). Psychological effects of unemployment. *Journal of Social Issues, 44*(Whole No. 4).

Downey, G., & Coyne, J. C. (1990). Children of depressed parents: An integrative review. *Psychological Bulletin, 108,* 50–76.

Dunn, J. (1988). Connections between relationships: Implications of research on mothers and siblings. In R. A. Hinde & J. Stevenson-Hinde (Eds.), *Relationships within families: Mutual influences* (pp. 168–180). Oxford: Clarendon Press.

Duvall, E. M., & Miller, B. C. (1984). *Marriage and family development* (6th ed.). New York: Harper & Row.

Easterbrooks, M. A., & Emde, R. N. (1988). Marital and parent–child relationships: The role of affect in the family system. In R. A. Hinde & J. Stevenson-Hinde (Eds.), *Relationships within families: Mutual influences* (pp. 83–103). Oxford: Clarendon Press.

Eccles, J., Midgley, C., & Adler, T. F. (1984). Grade-related changes in the school environment: Effects on achievement motivation. In J. G. Nicholls (Ed.), *Advances in motivation and achievement* (Vol. 3, pp. 283–331). Greenwich, CT: JAI Press.

Eckenrode, J., & Gore, S. (Eds.). (1990). *Stress between work and family.* New York: Plenum Press.

Elder, G. H., Jr. (1984). Families, kin, and the life course: A sociological perspective. In R. D. Parke (Ed.), *Review of child development research* (Vol. 7, pp. 80–136). Chicago: University of Chicago Press.

Elder, G. H., Jr., Caspi, A., & Downey, G. (1986). Problem behavior and family relationships: Life course and intergenerational themes. In A. B. Sorensen, F. E. Weinert, & L. R. Sherrod (Eds.), *Human development and the life course: Multidisciplinary perspectives* (pp. 293–340). Hillsdale, NJ: Erlbaum.

Epstein, J. L. (1983). Selection of friends in differently organized schools and classrooms. In J. L. Epstein & N. Karweit (Eds.), *Friends in school: Patterns of selection and influence in secondary schools* (pp. 73–92). New York: Academic Press.

Fantuzzo, J. W., Riggio, R. E., Connelly, S., & Dimeff, L. A. (1989). Effects of reciprocal peer tutoring on academic achievement and psychological adjustment: A component analysis. *Journal of Educational Psychology, 81,* 173–177.

Feinman, S., & Lewis, M. (1984). Is there social life beyond the dyad? A social-psychological view of social connections in infancy. In M. Lewis (Ed.), *Beyond the dyad* (pp. 13–41). New York: Plenum Press.

Feiring, C., & Lewis, M. (1984). Changing characteristics of the U. S. family: Implications for family networks, relationships, and child development. In M. Lewis (Ed.), *Beyond the dyad* (pp. 59–89). New York: Plenum Press.

Festinger, L. (1950). Informal social communication. *Psychological Review, 57,* 271–282.

Field, T. (1987). Affective and interactive disturbances. In J. D. Osofsky (Ed.), *Handbook of infant development* (2nd ed.) (pp. 972–1005). New York: Wiley.

Fisher, C. D., & Gitelson, R. (1983). A meta-analysis of the correlates of role conflict and ambiguity. *Journal of Applied Psychology, 68,* 320–333.

Fisher, J. D., Goff, B. A., Nadler, A., & Chinsky, J. M. (1988). Social psychological influences on help seeking and support from peers. In B. H. Gottlieb (Ed.), *Marshaling social support: Formats, processes, and effects* (pp. 267–304). Newbury Park, CA: Sage.

Forsyth, D. R. (1990). *Group dynamics* (2nd ed.). Pacific Grove, CA: Brooks/Cole.

Frese, M. (1984). Transitions in jobs, occupational socialization and strain. In V. L. Allen & E. van de Vliert (Eds.), *Role transitions: Explorations and explanations* (pp. 239–252). New York: Plenum Press.

Futoran, G. C., Kelly, J. R., & McGrath, J. E. (1989). TEMPO: A time-based system for analysis of group interaction process. *Basic and Applied Social Psychology, 10,* 211–232.

Gecas, V. (1981). Contexts of socialization. In M. Rosenberg & R. H. Turner (Eds.), *Social psychology: Sociological perspectives* (pp. 165–199). New York: Basic Books.

Goldstein, M. J. (1988). The family and psychopathology. *Annual Review of Psychology, 39,* 283–299.

Goodman, P. S. (1977). Social comparison processes in organizations. In B. M. Staw & G. R. Salancik (Eds.), *New directions in organizational behavior* (pp. 97–132). Chicago: St. Clair.

Gottlieb, B. H. (Ed.). (1988). *Marshaling social support: Formats, processes, and effects.* Newbury Park, CA: Sage.

Gottman, J. M. (1987). The sequential analysis of family interaction. In T. Jacob (Ed.), *Family interaction and psychopathology: Theories, methods, and findings* (pp. 453–478). New York: Plenum Press.

Gottman, J. M. (1990). How marriages change. In G. R. Patterson (Ed.),

Depression and aggression in family interaction (pp. 75–101). Hillsdale, NJ: Erlbaum.

Graham, J. W. (1986). Principled organizational dissent: A theoretical essay. In B. M. Staw & L. L. Cummings (Eds.), *Research in organizational behavior* (Vol. 8, pp. 1–52). Greenwich, CT: JAI Press.

Greenberg, J. (1982). Approaching equity and avoiding inequity in groups and organizations. In J. Greenberg & R. L. Cohen (Eds.), *Equity and justice in social behavior* (pp. 389–435). New York: Academic Press.

Greenhalgh, L. (1983). Organizational decline. In S. B. Bacharach (Ed.), *Research in the sociology of organizations* (Vol. 2, pp. 231–276). Greenwich, CT: JAI Press.

Greer, D. L. (1983). Spectator booing and the home advantage: A study of social influence in the basketball arena. *Social Psychology Quarterly, 46,* 252–261.

Griffin, W. A., & Gottman, J. M. (1990). Statistical methods for analyzing family interaction. In G. R. Patterson (Ed.), *Depression and aggression in family interaction* (pp. 131–168). Hillsdale, NJ: Erlbaum.

Grych, J. H., & Fincham, F. D. (1990). Marital conflict and children's adjustment: A cognitive-contextual framework. *Psychological Bulletin, 108,* 267–290.

Gutek, B. A., Bikson, T. K., & Mankin, D. (1984). Individual and organizational consequences of computer-based office information technology. In S. Oskamp (Ed.), *Applied social psychology annual* (Vol. 5, pp. 231–254). Beverly Hills, CA: Sage.

Hagestad, G. O. (1981). Problems and promises in the social psychology of intergenerational relations. In R. W. Fogel, E. Hatfield, S. B. Kiesler, & E. Shanas (Eds.), *Aging: Stability and change in the family* (pp. 11–46). New York: Academic Press.

Hallinan, M. T., & Williams, R. A. (1990). Students' characteristics and the peer-influence process. *Sociology of Education, 63,* 122–132.

Hare, A. P. (1976). *Handbook of small group research* (2nd ed.). New York: Free Press.

Harris, M. J., & Rosenthal, R. (1986). Four factors in the mediation of teacher expectancy effects. In R. S. Feldman (Ed.), *The social psychology of education: Current research and theory* (pp. 91–114). Cambridge: Cambridge University Press.

Harrison, A., & Connors, M. M. (1984). Groups in exotic environments. In L. Berkowitz (Ed.), *Advances in experimental social psychology* (Vol. 18, pp. 49–87). New York: Academic Press.

Harrison, A., Serafica, F., & McAdoo, H. (1984). Ethnic families of color. In R. D. Parke (Ed.), *Review of child development research* (Vol. 7, pp. 329–371). Chicago: University of Chicago Press.

Harter, S. (1983). Developmental perspectives on the self-system. In P. H. Mussen (Ed.), *Handbook of child psychology* (4th ed.) (Vol. 4, pp. 275–385). New York: Wiley.

Hartley, D., Roback, H. B., & Abramowitz, S. I. (1976). Deterioration effects in encounter groups. *American Psychologist, 31,* 247–255.

Hartup, W. (1983). Peer relations. In P. H. Mussen (Ed.), *Handbook of child psychology* (4th ed.) (Vol. 4, pp. 103–196). New York: Wiley.

Hazelrigg, M. D., Cooper, H. M., & Borduin, C. M. (1987). Evaluating the effectiveness of family therapies: An integrative review and analysis. *Psychological Bulletin, 101*, 428–442.

Henderson, R. W. (1981). Home environment and intellectual performance. In R. W. Henderson (Ed.), *Parent–child interaction: Theory, research, and prospects* (pp. 3–32). New York: Academic Press.

Hess, R. D., & Holloway, S. D. (1984). Family and school as educational institutions. In R. D. Parke (Ed.), *Review of child development research* (Vol. 7, pp. 179–222). Chicago: University of Chicago Press.

Hetherington, E. M. (1988). Parents, children, and siblings: Six years after divorce. In R. A. Hinde & J. Stevenson-Hinde (Eds.), *Relationships within families: Mutual influences* (pp. 311–331). Oxford: Clarendon Press.

Hetherington, E. M., & Camara, K. A. (1984). Families in transition: The processes of dissolution and reconstitution. In R. D. Parke (Ed.), *Review of child development research* (Vol. 7, pp. 398–439). Chicago: University of Chicago Press.

Hinrichsen, G. A., Revenson, T. A., & Shinn, M. (1985). Does self-help help? An empirical investigation of scoliosis peer support groups. *Journal of Social Issues, 41*, 65–87.

Hoffman, L. W. (1984). Work, family, and the socialization of the child. In R. D. Parke (Ed.), *Review of child development research* (Vol. 7, pp. 223–282). Chicago: University of Chicago Press.

Hoge, D. R., Smit, E. K., & Hanson, S. L. (1990). School experiences predicting changes in self-esteem of sixth- and seventh-grade students. *Journal of Educational Psychology, 82*, 117–127.

Hops, H., Sherman, L., & Biglan, A. (1990). Maternal depression, marital discord, and children's behavior: A developmental perspective. In G. R. Patterson (Ed.), *Depression and aggression in family interaction* (pp. 185–208). Hillsdale, NJ: Erlbaum.

Humphrey, R. H., O'Malley, P. M., Johnston, L. D., & Bachman, J. G. (1988). Bases of power, facilitation effects, and attitudes and behavior: Direct, indirect, and interactive determinants of drug use. *Social Psychology Quarterly, 51*, 329–345.

Huston, A. C. (1983). Sex-typing. In P. H. Mussen (Ed.), *Handbook of child psychology* (4th ed.) (Vol. 4, pp. 387–467). New York: Wiley.

Ickes, W., & Tooke, W. (1988). The observational method: Studying the interaction of minds and bodies. In S. Duck (Ed.), *The handbook of personal relationships: Theory, research, and interventions* (pp. 79–97). Chichester: Wiley.

Izraeli, D. N. (1983). Sex effects or structural effects? An empirical test of Kanter's theory of proportions. *Social Forces, 62*, 153–165.

Jackson, S. E., & Schuler, R. S. (1985). A meta-analysis and conceptual critique of research on role ambiguity and role conflict in work settings. *Organizational Behavior and Human Decision Processes, 36,* 16–78.

Jacob, T. (Ed.). (1987). *Family interaction and psychopathology: Theories, methods, and findings.* New York: Plenum Press.

Jacobson, N. S., & Bussod, N. (1983). Marital and family therapy. In M. Hersen, A. E. Kazdin, & A. S. Bellack (Eds.), *The clinical psychology handbook* (pp. 611–630). New York: Pergamon Press.

Johnson, D. W., & Johnson, R. T. (1983). The socialization and achievement crises: Are cooperative learning experiences the solution? In L. Bickman (Ed.), *Applied social psychology annual* (Vol. 4, pp. 119–164). Beverly Hills, CA: Sage.

Johnson, D. W., Johnson, R. T., & Maruyama, G. (1983). Interdependence and interpersonal attraction among heterogeneous and homogeneous individuals: A theoretical formulation and a meta-analysis of the research. *Review of Educational Research, 53,* 5–54.

Johnson, D. W., Johnson, R. T., & Smith, K. A. (1986). Academic conflict among students: Controversy and learning. In R. S. Feldman (Ed.), *The social psychology of education: Current research and theory* (pp. 199–231). Cambridge: Cambridge University Press.

Johnson, F. (1988). Encounter group therapy. In S. Long (Ed.), *Six group therapies* (pp. 115–158). New York: Plenum Press.

Jussim, L., & Osgood, D. W. (1989). Influence and similarity among friends: An integrative model applied to incarcerated adolescents. *Social Psychology Quarterly, 52,* 98–112.

Kanter, R. M. (1977). Some effects of proportions of group life: Skewed sex ratios and responses to token women. *American Journal of Sociology, 82,* 965–990.

Karweit, N., & Hansell, S. (1983). School organization and friendship selection. In J. L. Epstein & N. Karweit (Eds.), *Friends in school: Patterns of selection and influence in secondary schools* (pp. 29–38). New York: Academic Press.

Katz, A. H. (1981). Self-help and mutual aid: An emerging social movement? *Annual Review of Sociology, 7,* 129–155.

Kellam, S. G. (1990). Developmental epidemiological framework for family research on depression and aggression. In G. R. Patterson (Ed.), *Depression and aggression in family interaction* (pp. 11–48). Hillsdale, NJ: Erlbaum.

Kelly, J., & McGrath, J. E. (1985). Effects of time limits and task types on task performance and interaction of four-person groups. *Journal of Personality and Social Psychology, 49,* 395–407.

Kenny, D. A., & LaVoie, L. (1984). The social relations model. In L. Berkowitz (Ed.), *Advances in experimental social psychology* (Vol. 18, pp. 141–182). Orlando, FL: Academic Press.

Kerr, N. L. (1989). Illusions of efficacy: The effects of group size on perceived efficacy in social dilemmas. *Journal of Experimental Social Psychology, 25,* 287–313.

King, L. A., & King, D. W. (1990). Role conflict and role ambiguity: A critical assessment of construct validity. *Psychological Bulletin, 107,* 48–64.

Klein, R. H. (1983). Group treatment approaches. In M. Hersen, A. E. Kazdin, & A. S. Bellack (Eds.), *The clinical psychology handbook* (pp. 593–610). New York: Pergamon Press.

Krantz, J. (1985). Group process under conditions of organizational decline. *Journal of Applied Behavioral Sciences, 21,* 1–17.

Kreppner, K. (1988). Changes in dyadic relationships within a family after the arrival of a second child. In R. A. Hinde & J. Stevenson-Hinde (Eds.), *Relationships within families: Mutual influences* (pp. 143–167). Oxford: Clarendon Press.

Krohn, M. D., Massey, J. L., & Zielinski, M. (1988). Role overlap, network multiplicity, and adolescent deviant behavior. *Social Psychology Quarterly, 51,* 346–356.

Kulik, C. C., & Kulik, J. A. (1982). Effects of ability grouping on secondary school students: A meta-analysis of evaluation findings. *American Educational Research Journal, 19,* 415–428.

Kutash, I. L., & Wolf, A. (Eds.). (1990). *The group psychotherapist's handbook.* New York: Columbia University Press.

Laosa, L. M. (1981). Maternal behavior: Sociocultural diversity in modes of family interaction. In R. W. Henderson (Ed.), *Parent–child interaction: Theory, research, and prospects* (pp. 125–167). New York: Academic Press.

Lemaine, G. (1974). Social differentiation and social originality. *European Journal of Social Psychology, 4,* 17–52.

Levine, J. M. (1983). Social comparison and education. In J. M. Levine & M. C. Wang (Eds.), *Teacher and student perceptions: Implications for learning* (pp. 29–55). Hillsdale, NJ: Erlbaum.

Levine, J. M. (1989). Reaction to opinion deviance in small groups. In P. Paulus (Ed.), *Psychology of group influence* (2nd ed.) (pp. 187–231). Hillsdale, NJ: Erlbaum.

Levine, J. M., & Moreland, R. L. (1985). Innovation and socialization in small groups. In S. Moscovici, G. Mugny, & E. Van Avermaet (Eds.), *Perspectives on minority influence* (pp. 143–169). Cambridge: Cambridge University Press.

Levine, J. M., & Moreland, R. L. (1986). Outcome comparisons in group contexts: Consequences for the self and others. In R. Schwarzer (Ed.), *Self-related cognitions in anxiety and motivation* (pp. 285–303). Hillsdale, NJ: Erlbaum.

Levine, J. M., & Moreland, R. L. (1987). Social comparison and outcome evaluation in group contexts. In J. C. Masters & W. P. Smith (Eds.), *Social comparison, social justice, and relative deprivation: Theoretical, empirical, and policy perspectives* (pp. 105–127). Hillsdale, NJ: Erlbaum.

Levine, J. M., & Moreland, R. L. (1990). Progress in small group research. *Annual Review of Psychology, 41,* 585–634.

Levine, J. M., & Russo, E. M. (1987). Majority and minority influence. In C. Hendrick (Ed.), *Review of personality and social psychology: Group processes* (Vol. 8, pp. 13–54). Newbury Park, CA: Sage.

Lewis, M. (1987). Social development in infancy and early childhood. In J. D. Osofsky (Ed.), *Handbook of infant development* (2nd ed.) (pp. 419–493). New York: Wiley.

Linville, P. W. (1987). Self-complexity as a cognitive buffer against stress-related illness and depression. *Journal of Personality and Social Psychology, 52,* 663–676.

Long, S. (Ed.). (1988). *Six group therapies.* New York: Plenum Press.

Louis, M. R. (1980). Surprise and sense making: What newcomers experience in entering unfamiliar organizational settings. *Administrative Science Quarterly, 25,* 226–251.

Maccoby, E. E., & Martin, J. A. (1983). Socialization in the context of the family: Parent–child interaction. In P. H. Mussen (Ed.), *Handbook of child psychology* (4th ed.) (Vol. 4, pp. 1–101). New York: Wiley.

Mackie, D. M., & Goethals, G. R. (1987). Individual and group goals. In C. Hendrick (Ed.), *Group processes* (Vol. 8, pp. 144–166). Newbury Park, CA: Sage.

Madden, N. A., & Slavin, R. E. (1983). Mainstreaming students with mild handicaps: Academic and social outcomes. *Review of Educational Research, 53,* 519–569.

Marks, M. L., & Mirvis, P. H. (October, 1986). The merger syndrome. *Psychology Today,* pp. 36–42.

Marshall, H. H., & Weinstein, R. S. (1984). Classroom factors affecting students' self-evaluations: An interactional model. *Review of Educational Research, 54,* 301–325.

Martin, B. (1987). Developmental perspectives on family theory and psychopathology. In T. Jacob (Ed.), *Family interaction and psychopathology: Theories, methods, and findings* (pp. 163–202). New York: Plenum Press.

Martin, J. (1981). Relative deprivation: A theory of distributive injustice for an era of shrinking resources. In L. L. Cummings & B. M. Staw (Eds.), *Research in organizational behavior* (Vol. 3, pp. 53–107). Greenwich, CT: JAI Press.

Martin, P. Y., & Shanahan, K. A. (1983). Transcending the effects of sex composition in small groups. *Social Work with Groups, 6,* 19–32.

Mazur, A. (1985). A biosocial model of status in face-to-face groups. *Social Forces, 64,* 377–402.

McGrath, J. E. (1984). *Groups: Interaction and performance.* Englewood Cliffs, NJ: Prentice-Hall.

McGrath, J. E., & Rotchford, N. (1983). Time and behavior in organizations. In L. L. Cummings & B. M. Staw (Eds.), *Research in organizational behavior* (Vol. 5, pp. 57–101). Greenwich, CT: JAI Press.

Messick, D. M., & Mackie, D. M. (1989). Intergroup relations. *Annual Review of Psychology, 40,* 45–81.

Miller, N., & Brewer, M. B. (1986). Social categorization theory and team learning procedures. In R. S. Feldman (Ed.), *The social psychology of education: Current research and theory* (pp. 172–198). Cambridge: Cambridge University Press.

Minuchin, P. (1988). Relationships within the family: A systems perspective on development. In R. A. Hinde & J. Stevenson-Hinde (Eds.), *Relationships within families: Mutual influences* (pp. 7–26). Oxford: Clarendon Press.

Minuchin, P. P., & Shapiro, E. K. (1983). The school as a context for social development. In P. H. Mussen (Ed.), *Handbook of child psychology* (4th ed.) (Vol. 4, pp. 197–274). New York: Wiley.

Moreland, R. L. (1987). The formation of small groups. In C. Hendrick (Ed.), *Review of personality and social psychology* (Vol. 8, pp. 80–110). Beverly Hills, CA: Sage.

Moreland, R. L., & Levine, J. M. (1982). Socialization in small groups: Temporal changes in individual–group relations. In L. Berkowitz (Ed.), *Advances in experimental social psychology* (Vol. 15, pp. 137–192). New York: Academic Press.

Moreland, R. L., & Levine, J. M. (1984). Role transitions in small groups. In V. L. Allen & E. van de Vliert (Eds.), *Role transitions: Explorations and explanations* (pp. 181–195). New York: Plenum Press.

Moreland, R. L., & Levine, J. M. (1988). Group dynamics over time: Development and socialization in small groups. In J. E. McGrath (Ed.), *The social psychology of time: New perspectives* (pp. 151–181). Newbury Park, CA: Sage.

Moreland, R. L., & Levine, J. M. (1989). Newcomers and oldtimers in small groups. In P. B. Paulus (Ed.), *Psychology of group influence* (2nd ed.) (pp. 143–186). Hillsdale, NJ: Erlbaum.

Moscovici, S. (1976). *Social influence and social change.* New York: Academic Press.

Moscovici, S. (1985). Social influence and conformity. In G. Lindzey & E. Aronson (Eds.), *The handbook of social psychology* (3rd ed.) (Vol. 2, pp. 347–412). New York: Random House.

Murphy, M. R. (1980). Analysis of 84 commercial aviation accidents: Implications for a resource management approach to crew training. *Proceedings of the Annual Reliability and Maintainability Symposium, 163,* 298–306.

Near, J. P., & Miceli, M. P. (1986). Retaliation against whistle-blowers: Predictors and effects. *Journal of Applied Psychology, 71,* 137–145.

Nemeth, C. J., & Staw, B. M. (1989). The tradeoffs of social control and innovation in groups and organizations. In L. Berkowitz (Ed.), *Advances in experimental social psychology* (Vol. 22, pp. 175–210). Orlando, FL: Academic Press.

Nichols, M. P. (1984). *Family therapy: Concepts and methods.* New York: Gardner.

Nicholson, N. (1984). A theory of work role transitions. *Administrative Science Quarterly, 29,* 172–191.

Oldham, G., & Rotchford, N. L. (1983). Relationships between office characteristics and employee reactions: A study of the physical environment. *Administrative Science Quarterly, 29,* 542–556.

Osofsky, J. D., & Osofsky, H. J. (1984). Psychological and developmental perspectives on expectant and new parenthood. In R. D. Parke (Ed.), *Review of child development research* (Vol. 7, pp. 372–397). Chicago: University of Chicago Press.

Parke, R. D., & Lewis, N. G. (1981). The family in context: A multilevel interactional analysis of child abuse. In R. W. Henderson (Ed.), *Parent–child interaction: Theory, research, and prospects* (pp. 169–204). New York: Academic Press.

Parke, R. D., Power, T. G., & Gottman, J. M. (1979). Conceptualizing and quantifying influence patterns in the family triad. In M. E. Lamb, S. J. Suomi, & G. R. Stephenson (Eds.), *Social interaction analysis: Methodological issues* (pp. 231–252). Madison, WI: University of Wisconsin Press.

Parke, R. D., & Slaby, R. G. (1983). The development of aggression. In P. H. Mussen (Ed.), *Handbook of child psychology* (4th ed.) (Vol. 4, pp. 547–641). New York: Wiley.

Parke, R. D., & Tinsley, B. J. (1987). Family interaction in infancy. In J. D. Osofsky (Ed.), *Handbook of infant development* (2nd ed.) (pp. 579–641). New York: Wiley.

Parker, J. G., & Asher, S. R. (1987). Peer relations and later personal adjustment: Are low-accepted children at risk? *Psychological Bulletin, 102,* 357–389.

Patterson, G. R. (1982). *Coercive family process.* Eugene, OR: Castalia Publishing.

Patterson, G. R. (Ed.). (1990). *Depression and aggression in family interaction.* Hillsdale, NJ: Erlbaum.

Patterson, G. R., & Forgatch, M. S. (1990). Initiation and maintenance of process disrupting single-mother families. In G. R. Patterson (Ed.), *Depression and aggression in family interaction* (pp. 209–245). Hillsdale, NJ: Erlbaum.

Paulus, P. B., & Nagar, D. (1989). Environmental influences on groups. In P. B. Paulus (Ed.), *Psychology of group influence* (2nd ed.) (pp. 111–140). Hillsdale, NJ: Erlbaum.

Perret-Clermont, A. (1980). *Social interaction and cognitive development in children.* London: Academic Press.

Peterson, P. L., Wilkinson, L. C., & Hallinan, M. (Eds.). (1984). *The social context of instruction: Group organization and group processes.* Orlando, FL: Academic Press.

Peterson, P. L., Wilkinson, L. C., Spinelli, F., & Swing, S. R. (1984). Merging the process-product and the sociolinguistic paradigms: Research on small-group processes. In P. L. Peterson, L. C. Wilkinson, & M. Hallinan (Eds.), *The social context of instruction: Group organization and group processes* (pp. 125–152). Orlando, FL: Academic Press.

Pfeffer, J. (1983). Organizational demography. In L. L. Cummings & B. M.

Staw (Eds.), *Research in organizational behavior* (Vol. 5, pp. 299–357). Greenwich, CT: JAI Press.

Pinto, L. J., & Crow, K. E. (1982). The effect of size on other structural attributes of congregations within the same denomination. *Journal for the Scientific Study of Religion, 21,* 304–316.

Reuman, D. A. (1989). How social comparison mediates the relation between ability-grouping practices and students' achievement expectancies in mathematics. *Journal of Educational Psychology, 81,* 178–189.

Richer, S. (1976). Reference-group theory and ability grouping: A convergence of sociological theory and educational research. *Sociology of Education, 49,* 65–71.

Ridgeway, C. L. (1982). Status in groups: The importance of motivation. *American Sociological Review, 47,* 76–88.

Rohrkemper, M. M., & Brophy, J. E. (1983). Teachers' thinking about problem students. In J. M. Levine & M. C. Wang (Eds.), *Teacher and student perceptions: Implications for learning* (pp. 75–103). Hillsdale, NJ: Erlbaum.

Rosenholtz, S. J., & Simpson, C. (1984). The formation of ability conceptions: Developmental trend or social construction? *Review of Educational Research, 54,* 31–63.

Rubin, Z., & Sloman, J. (1984). How parents influence their children's friendships. In M. Lewis (Ed.), *Beyond the dyad* (pp. 223–250). New York: Plenum Press.

Ruble, D. N., & Frey, K. S. (1987). Social comparison and self evaluation in the classroom: Developmental changes in knowledge and function. In J. C. Masters & W. P. Smith (Eds.), *Social comparison, social justice, and relative deprivation: Theoretical, empirical, and policy perspectives* (pp. 81–104). Hillsdale, NJ: Erlbaum.

Rutter, M., & Garmezy, N. (1983). Developmental psychopathology. In P. H. Mussen (Ed.), *Handbook of child psychology* (4th ed.) (Vol. 4, pp. 775–911). New York: Wiley.

Salancik, G. R., & Pfeffer, J. (1978). A social information processing approach to job attitudes and task design. *Administrative Science Quarterly, 23,* 224–253.

Sande, G. N., Ellard, J. H., & Ross, M. (1986). Effect of arbitrarily assigned status labels on self-perceptions and social perceptions: The mere position effect. *Journal of Personality and Social Psychology, 50,* 684–689.

Sarason, B. R., Sarason, I. G., & Pierce, G. R. (Eds.). (1990). *Social support: An interactional view.* New York: Wiley.

Schofield, J. W. (1981). Complementary and conflicting identities: Images and interaction in an interracial school. In S. R. Asher & J. M. Gottman (Eds.), *The development of children's friendship* (pp. 53–90). New York: Cambridge University Press.

Schofield, J. W. (1989). *Black and white in school: Trust, tension, or toler-*

ance? New York: Teachers College Press. (Original work published 1982)

Schunk, D. H. (1987). Peer models and children's behavioral change. *Review of Educational Research, 57,* 149–174.

Shaver, P., & Buhrmester, D. (1983). Loneliness, sex-role orientation and group life: A social needs perspective. In P. B. Paulus (Ed.), *Basic group processes* (pp. 259–288). New York: Springer-Verlag.

Sieber, S. D. (1974). Toward a theory of role accumulation. *American Sociological Review, 39,* 567–578.

Sigel, I. E., Dreyer, A. S., & McGillicuddy-DeLisi, A. V. (1984). Psychological perspectives on the family. In R. D. Parke (Ed.), *Review of child development research* (Vol. 7, pp. 42–79). Chicago: University of Chicago Press.

Singer, E. (1981). Reference groups and social evaluations. In M. Rosenberg & R. H. Turner (Eds.), *Social psychology: Sociological perspectives* (pp. 66–93). New York: Basic Books.

Skvoretz, R. (1988). Models of participation in status-differentiated groups. *Social Psychology Quarterly, 51,* 43–57.

Slavin, R. E. (1983). When does cooperative learning increase student achievement? *Psychological Bulletin, 94,* 429–445.

Slavin, R. E. (1987). Ability grouping and student achievement in elementary schools: A best-evidence synthesis. *Review of Educational Research, 57,* 293–336.

Snyder, C. R., & Fromkin, H. L. (1980). *Uniqueness: The human pursuit of difference.* New York: Plenum Press.

Sorensen, A. B., & Hallinan, M. T. (1986). Effects of ability grouping on growth in academic achievement. *American Educational Research Journal, 23,* 519–542.

Steiner, I. D. (1974). Whatever happened to the group in social psychology? *Journal of Experimental Social Psychology, 10,* 93–108.

Steiner, I. D. (1986). Paradigms and groups. In L. Berkowitz (Ed.), *Advances in experimental social psychology* (Vol. 19, 251–289). Orlando, FL: Academic Press.

Steinglass, P. (1987). A systems view of family interaction and psychopathology. In T. Jacob (Ed.), *Family interaction and psychopathology: Theories, methods, and findings* (pp. 25–65). New York: Plenum Press.

Steinhauer, P. D. (1987). The family as a small group: The process model of family functioning. In T. Jacob (Ed.), *Family interaction and psychopathology: Theories, methods, and findings* (pp. 67–115). New York: Plenum Press.

Stephan, W. G. (1985). Intergroup relations. In G. Lindzey & E. Aronson (Eds.), *The handbook of social psychology* (3rd ed.) (Vol. 2, pp. 599–658). New York: Random House.

Stryker, S., & Serpe, R. T. (1982). Commitment, identity salience, and role behavior: Theory and research example. In W. Ickes & E. S.

Knowles (Eds.), *Personality, roles, and social behavior* (pp. 199–218). New York: Springer-Verlag.

Sutker, P. B. (1982). Adolescent drug and alcohol behaviors. In T. M. Field, A. Huston, H. C. Quay, L. Troll, & G. E. Finley (Eds.), *Review of human development* (pp. 356–380). New York: Wiley.

Sutton, R. I. (1987). The process of organizational death: Disbanding and reconnecting. *Administrative Science Quarterly, 32,* 542–569.

Tajfel, H., & Turner, J. C. (1979). An integrative theory of intergroup conflict. In W. G. Austin & S. Worchel (Eds.), *The social psychology of intergroup relations* (pp. 33–47). Monterey, CA: Brooks Cole.

Thoits, P. A. (1983). Multiple identities and psychological well-being: A reformulation and test of the social isolation hypothesis. *American Sociological Review, 48,* 174–187.

Tinsley, B. R., & Parke, R. D. (1984). Grandparents as support and socialization agents. In M. Lewis (Ed.), *Beyond the dyad* (pp. 161–194). New York: Plenum Press.

van de Vliert, E., & Allen, V. L. (1984). Managing transitional strain: Strategies and intervention techniques. In V. L. Allen & E. van de Vliert (Eds.), *Role transitions: Explorations and explanations* (pp. 345–355). New York: Plenum Press.

Vaught, C., & Smith, D. L. (1980). Incorporation and mechanical solidarity in an underground coal mine. *Sociology of Work and Occupations, 7,* 159–187.

Wagner, W. G., Pfeffer, J., & O'Reilly, C. C. (1984). Organizational demography and turnover in top management groups. *Administrative Science Quarterly, 29,* 74–92.

Walsh, F. (1982). Conceptualizations of normal family functioning. In F. Walsh (Ed.), *Normal family processes* (pp. 3–42). New York: Guilford Press.

Waxler, N. E., & Mishler, E. G. (1970). Experimental studies of families. In L. Berkowitz (Ed.), *Advances in experimental social psychology* (Vol. 5, pp. 249–304). New York: Academic Press.

Webb, N. M. (1982). Student interaction and learning in small groups. *Review of Educational Research, 52,* 421–445.

Webb, N. M., & Kenderski, C. M. (1984). Student interaction and learning in small-group and whole-class settings. In P. L. Peterson, L. C. Wilkinson, & M. Hallinan (Eds.), *The social context of instruction; Group organization and group processes* (pp. 153–170). Orlando, FL: Academic Press.

Weick, K. (1971). Group processes, family processes, and problem solving. In J. Aldous, T. Condon, R. Hill, M. Straus, & I. Tallman (Eds.), *Family problem solving: A symposium on theoretical, methodological, and substantive concerns* (pp. 3–32). Hinsdale, IL: Dryden Press.

Weisfeld, G. E., & Weisfeld, C. C. (1984). An observational study of social evaluation: An application of the dominance hierarchy model. *Journal of Genetic Psychology, 145,* 89–99.

Weisner, T. S. (1984). The social ecology of childhood: A cross-cultural view. In M. Lewis (Ed.), *Beyond the dyad* (pp. 43–58). New York: Plenum Press.

Wilder, D. A. (1986). Social categorization: Implications for creation and reduction of intergroup bias. In L. Berkowitz (Ed.), *Advances in experimental social psychology* (Vol. 19, pp. 291–355). Orlando, FL: Academic Press.

Wills, T. A. (1985). Supportive functions of interpersonal relationships. In S. Cohen & S. L. Syme (Eds.), *Social support and health* (pp. 61–82). New York: Academic Press.

Wynne, L. C. (Ed.). (1988). *The state of the art in family therapy research: Controversies and recommendations.* New York: Family Process Press.

Yalom, I. D. (1985). *The theory and practice of group psychotherapy* (3rd ed.). New York: Basic Books.

Research on Relationships:
Implications for Mental Health

MARGARET S. CLARK and
M. ELIZABETH BENNETT

Work on interpersonal relationships and particularly work on intimate interpersonal relationships has burgeoned over the last 10 to 15 years. Twenty years ago if one sought out psychological research on relationships, one would have found a manageable body of research documenting determinants of initial attraction between strangers meeting for the first time and little else. Today the story is different. Social psychologists have been very actively studying interpersonal processes in relationships, including intimate relationships (Clark & Reis, 1988). Simultaneously, clinical psychologists have been documenting many differences between distressed and nondistressed relationships.

From our perspective, these findings are of obvious relevance to understanding mental health. As Holmes and Boon (1990) have recently pointed out, "[T]he knowledge acquired through basic research on close relationships has achieved a critical mass that now provides a reasonable foundation for shaping applications as diverse as preventative public education, newlywed counseling, and therapeutic interventions for those experiencing marital distress."

To fairly and comprehensively review this now large and complicated literature and/or to show all or even a substantial number of the possible links to mental health is simply impossible in a brief chapter. Rather we take the following approach. First, we briefly describe and comment on some of the recent contributions to relationship research by clinical psychologists. This category of research includes studies documenting differences between distressed and nondistressed relationships. It has generated an impressive list of such differences. Work in this area can be described as having started out at least primarily as descriptive in nature and as having then, in some cases, generated theoretical explanations for observed phenomena.

Then we turn to a second type of research, basic social psychological research on interpersonal processes. This section constitutes the heart of our chapter. We select three theoretically driven programs of research on three different sorts of processes operating in relationships. While on the surface these programs are less linked to mental health outcomes than is the other type of research (i.e., they tend not to use measures of mental health or of marital distress as outcome measures), we suspect they have tremendous relevance to mental health primarily because their focus on understanding relationship phenomena at a process level is particularly amenable to developing practical applications aimed at promoting mental health.[1]

WORK IDENTIFYING SYMPTOMS OF DISTRESS IN CLOSE RELATIONSHIPS

Given the demand for family and marital counseling, it is not surprising that clinically oriented researchers have been quite interested is what distinguishes distressed relationships from nondistressed ones. What sorts of findings have emerged from their work?

As Gottman (1982) has pointed out, early surveys in this tradition found no optimal profile of the happy marriage in terms of demographics (e.g., income or number of children). However, such surveys did detect that certain perceptions regarding the relationships were related to husbands' and wives' dissatisfaction with their relationships. For example, both dissatisfied husbands and dissatisfied wives frequently mentioned not having enough income, their spouse being too critical or nervous, and problems with in-laws. In addition, dissatisfied husbands often reported that their wife's feelings were too easily hurt and that their wife was too emotional; dissatisfied wives often mentioned their husband's poor management of income as problematical.

More recently, researchers have moved beyond identifying subjective perceptions related to concurrent dissatisfaction to identifying more objective correlates of concurrent dissatisfaction. Gottman and his colleagues, for instance, have focused on how patterns of communication may differentiate satisfied from dissatisfied marital relationships. In one study, Gottman (1979) found that expression of negative affect was more characteristic of dissatisfied than satisfied couples. Moreover, the *patterning* of couples' conversations over time was a good indicator of whether couples were happy. Specifically, dissatisfied couples are more likely than satisfied ones to reciprocate communications that have negative impact. Surprisingly, however, Gottman found that the reciprocity of communications that had positive impact did not discriminate satisfied from dissatisfied couples. Levenson and Gottman (1983) have also shown that dissatisfied couples display a pattern of "physiological linkage" that does not characterize satisfied relationships. That is, in dissatisfied relationships couples tend to get emotionally involved, excited, and distressed simultaneously, while in more satisfied relationships distressed spouses do not necessarily elicit distress in their partner. Instead, the other is more likely to make efforts to calm the spouse down. Three years later, Levenson and Gottman (1985) conducted a follow-up study with the same subjects. The more aroused during discussions a couple had been at the earlier time, the more marital satisfaction had declined. Both dissatisfaction at the time of the original study and declines in satisfaction 3 years later were predicted by males' emotional withdrawal and females' emotional involvement. The latter included both negative emotion (presumably used to express dissatisfaction) and positive emotion (presumably used to draw the husband back into the relationship).

Gottman and his colleagues have also pinpointed differences in the ways distressed versus nondistressed couples attempt to resolve disagreements. Happy couples, in an agenda-building phase enter into "validation loops." Each recognizes and tries to understand the other's concerns. Next they discuss and argue about specific issues and finally arrive at a solution. In contrast, unhappy couples start out with each spouse presenting his or her own complaints, without much responsiveness from the other. Next, irrelevant issues are brought into the discussion and the conflict increases. Later, proposals for resolution may be made, but because the couple tends to have a win–lose orientation, there may be an endless cycle of counterproposals with no real resolution resulting (Gottman, 1979).

To give a final example of Gottman's work, he and Krokoff (1989) recently made an attempt to identify concurrent predictors of *future* relationship distress and of the intensity of emotional suffering upon the breakup of a relationship. They began by observing married couples attempt to resolve a self-described high-conflict issue. At the same time, these couples filled out a well-validated measure of marital satisfaction. Three years later, the researchers recontacted most of the original participants and once again had them fill out the same measures of marital satisfaction. Measures of defensiveness, stubbornness, and withdrawal from interaction, particularly on the husbands' parts, predicted dissatisfaction at both points in time. Surprisingly, while expressing disagreement and anger (or what these authors called conflict engagement) related to unhappiness and dissatisfaction concurrently, they were predictive of significant *improvement* in marital satisfaction longitudinally. Also, for wives, while positive interaction strongly predicted concurrent marital satisfaction, it actually predicted deterioration of marital satisfaction over time. Moreover, compliance by the wife as well as her expression of sadness or fear also predicted deterioration in marital satisfaction over time. Unfortunately, the intriguing longitudinal results of this particular study may be due to statistical artifacts as pointed out by Woody and Costanzo (1990), and it must remain to future research to verify them.

Still other researchers in this tradition have examined whether the individual differences in personality traits that people bring with them to relationships can distinguish distressed from nondistressed relationships. Consider, for example, a study reported by Zammichieli, Gilroy, and Sherman (1988). These researchers had each member of a large number of suburban couples of various socioeconomic statuses fill out both Bem's Sex-Role Inventory (Bem, 1974) and the Locke-Wallace Marital Adjustment Test (Locke & Wallace, 1959). Couples made up of two androgynous individuals (i.e., two people each possessing both masculine traits, such as the ability to be aggressive and competitive, *and* feminine traits, such as the ability to be gentle and nurturing), exhibited significantly higher marital satisfaction than did 'incongruent' couples made up of one androgynous member and one sex-typed member. They *also* exhibited significantly higher marital satisfaction than did couples who fit a traditional, "complementary" model with the male high on masculinity and low on femininity and the female high on femininity and low on masculinity. Interestingly, and contrary to the authors' own predictions, the latter two groups did not differ from one another. That is, the "complementary" couples were not more satisfied than were the "incongruent" couples.

As a third example of research in this tradition, Fincham and his colleagues have completed extensive work on the differences in attributional style between distressed and nondistressed couples (see Bradbury & Fincham, 1990, for a review). They find that the sorts of attributions spouses make to explain each other's behavior distinguish satisfied from dissatisfied couples. Dissatisfied couples are more likely to see *positive* partner behaviors as caused by specific, unstable, and uncontrollable factors rather than by global, stable, and controllable factors (Fincham, Beach, & Baucom, 1987; Fincham, Beach, & Nelson, 1987; Fincham & O'Leary, 1983). In other words, dissatisfied spouses are likely to see positive marital events as being caused by factors that operate only in one particular situation rather than in all situations, factors that affect few areas of their marriage, and factors that cannot be controlled. In addition, dissatisfied couples tend to see positive partner behavior as intended to be negative, less worthy of praise, and selfishly motivated (Fincham, Beach, & Nelson, 1987; Fincham & O'Leary, 1983).

To illustrate, a woman in a dissatisfied marriage should be more likely than one in a satisfied marriage to explain her husband's gift of roses as relating to an unstable, uncontrollable, and specific cause, ("He doesn't care about me, he's just happy because he got a promotion") or to intentionally negative, selfish causes ("He just wants me to be nice while his mother is visiting," or, "He's trying to make me feel guilty"). In other words, she tends either to be suspicious of her husband's motivation or to feel that his positive behavior is a result of factors outside the relationship, not the result of stable, positive feelings for her.

To make matters worse, dissatisfied couples also tend to see *negative* relationship events as having causes that are global (i.e., affecting all areas of the relationship), stable (likely to occur again in the relationship), and directly related to the spouse's negative feelings toward the respondent (Fincham, 1985a; Fincham & Beach, 1988; Fincham, Beach, & Baucom, 1987; Fincham, Beach, & Nelson, 1987; Fincham & O'Leary, 1983). In addition, dissatisfied spouses tend to see negative spouse behavior as motivated by selfish and destructive intent, and as worthy of blame (Fincham & Beach, 1988; Fincham, Beach, & Baucom, 1987; Fincham, Beach, & Nelson, 1987).

To illustrate, a husband who reports being dissatisfied with his marriage is more likely to see his wife's being late for dinner as being his wife's fault ("She's forgetful.") as opposed to an outside circumstance, as likely to occur again ("She's *always* late."), as affecting many areas of their marriage ("She doesn't care about having a good marriage." "She doesn't care about being a good mother."), and as occurring as a result of his wife's selfishness and/or desire to hurt him ("She only cares about her own schedule." or, "She's really trying to get me back for forgetting our anniversary."). Also, couples in unhappy marriages tend to blame their spouse (or relationship in general) more than they blame themselves for negative relationship events (Fincham, 1985b; Fincham, Beach, & Baucom, 1987).

Finally, as a fourth example of research in this tradition, consider some work by Markman (1979, 1981) aimed at identifying predictors of future relationship-related distress. Markman had couples who were planning to marry interact on five tasks. Then they rated how positive or negative the interactions were from their own perspective and also filled out a measure of marital satisfaction. Couples were recontacted 1, 3, and 5½ years later (Markman, 1979, 1981). The perceived positivity of the initial interactions did not predict concurrent satisfaction or satisfaction 1 year later. However, the less positively the *initial* interaction was perceived to be, the lower the marital satisfaction was both 3 and 5½ years later.

Can research of the type we have just described be usefully applied to mental health practice? We think the answer is yes, but with limitations. One sort of application consists of identifying couples *at risk* for experiencing distress either concurrently or in the future. For instance, the Zammichieli et al. (1988) study certainly suggests that couples with *either* incongruent or complementarity sex role orientations may be at increased risk for distress relative to androgynous couples, and the Markman (1979, 1981) work suggests that negativity of interactions may also be a good predictor of future relationship distress. Interestingly, since the Zammichieli et al. work contradicts commonsense intuition about the likely effects of complementarity and since Markman (1979, 1981) found no *concurrent* effect of how negatively interactions were perceived to be on satisfaction, these predictors might be especially useful to therapists because they probably do not fit with most couples' (and therapists') *a priori* intuitions and thus may be especially likely to have been ignored in the absence of such research.

Moreover, all this research provides at least hints that the factors that differentiate distressed from nondistressed relationships *may* be sources of distress and, if eliminated, *may* alleviate the distress. So, for example, Gottman's work on communication styles might be taken to suggest that if couples can break patterns of negative reciprocity in communications, and if members of the relationship, particularly husbands, can reduce defensiveness, stubborness, and withdrawal from interaction, marital satisfaction might increase. Or, to take another example, Fincham's and Bradbury's work suggests that if we can stop distressed couples from making negative, global attributions for a spouse's bad behavior and get them to give their spouse credit for good behavior, we may be able to improve marital satisfaction.

Still, despite what appears to be the obvious applicability of these findings at a superficial level, there is good reason for considerable caution in jumping from such findings to designing mental health applications. Most of the work documents differences between distressed and nondistressed relationships. Although it is reasonable to guess that whatever factors differentiate these relationships *caused* those differences (for instance, *maybe* expressing negative emotion or reciprocating it causes marital distress), we cannot be sure of such causal links. If they are not causal factors and we attempt to change them, our interventions may have no impact at all. Moreover, as Gottman and Krokoff's (1989) work makes salient (even given methodological concerns), indicators of concurrent distress may not predict future distress. Indeed, it is possible that they will predict future improvements in satisfaction. (For instance, the Gottman and Krokoff findings at least suggest that expressing negative emotion may get members of a couple to focus on their problems, to attempt to solve them, and, perhaps, actually to solve them.) Thus if we attempt to change factors associated with distress, we may even harm a relationship.

To take our argument for caution in designing applications even further, we note that even if markers of distressed marriages really do point to behaviors that are truly harmful to relationships both concurrently and prospectively, these studies do not tell us what factors led to the behaviors in the first place. Given that, practitioners attempting to apply such findings may find themselves in a position of trying to change a behavior without understanding what motivates it. Such applications may be futile either in that it will be impossible to change the behavior and/or in that whatever superficial changes are made may be short-lived.

What do we need to enable us to design preventive and ameliorative relationship interventions in which we can have some confidence? It seems clear that we need information about the nature of the underlying and ongoing interpersonal *processes* in both distressed and nondistressed relationships. As stated earlier, due to its focus on just such interpersonal processes, social psychological work may provide some of the most useful applications coming out of relationship work even though social psychologists, unlike clinical researchers, tend not to measure such clinically relevant variables as marital distress or depression as their outcome variables. We turn now to three examples of theoretically driven, programmatic social psychological work on relationship processes. Each, we believe, has many implications for mental health practice.

THREE PROGRAMS OF BASIC SOCIAL PSYCHOLOGICAL RESEARCH ON INTERPERSONAL RELATIONSHIPS WITH SOME IMPLICATIONS FOR MENTAL HEALTH PRACTICE

Since it is impossible to review all relevant work done by social psychologists in this area, we have chosen three that, we believe, illustrate well the potential for social psychological research contributing to understanding mental health and, potentially, to mental health practice. The three theories (and associated research) we have chosen are: (1) Ellen Berscheid's theory of emotion in interpersonal relationships, (2) Abraham Tesser's self-evaluation maintenance theory, and (3) the first author's (Margaret Clark) and Judson Mills' work on communal and exchange relationships.

A Theory of Emotion in Relationships

Ellen Berscheid has described a theory of emotion in relationships that is clearly an interpersonal process theory (Berscheid, 1982; Kelley et al., 1983, Chapter 4). This theory concerns certain conditions likely to elicit emotion within the context of relationships.

To understand the theory, one first has to understand Berscheid's conception of a relationship as well as her definition of "closeness" in relationships. Berscheid, along with several others (Kelley et al., 1983), views relationships as existing when changes in the cognitive, physiological, or behavioral state of one person influence the analogous states in another person, and vice versa. In other words, for a relationship to exist, members must have mutual impact on one another. Relationships are close, in her terms, to the extent that members have frequent, strong, and diverse impact on each other over a long period. That is, if people often influence each other, influence each other in a diversity of

ways such as influencing the other's social activities, work activities, athletic activities, and sexual life (as opposed to influencing,
say, just the other's productivity at work), have strong influences
on one another as, for instance, if the other's advice makes one
think about issues for a long time, which, in turn, influences how
one behaves in many situations (as opposed to influencing the
other's behavior once in a minor way), and if this goes on for a long
time, then the relationship clearly is close.

Berscheid argues that behavior is typically organized into
action sequences that are well practiced and often emitted as a
unit. These tend to run off in an "automatic" or relatively "unconscious" fashion, and they are very difficult to change once the
sequence has been triggered. In the case of close (or highly meshed)
relationships, it is likely that many of a person's organized, automatic action sequences are intimately intertwined with the other's
automatic action sequences.

For instance, imagine a family of three—two parents and a
daughter—getting up and out of the house in the morning. Each
member may have a different organized, well-practiced pattern of
behavior and each person's routine of getting up, using the bathroom, getting dressed, eating breakfast, and traveling to work may
be either quite dependent on the other two persons' actions or
quite independent of those other actions. As an example, the
child's routines may be very dependent on those of both of her
parents. She may rely on the mother having laid out some clothes
for her routine of getting dressed to take place smoothly, on the
father's cooking her breakfast for her eating routine to run off
smoothly and on one or the other parent's calling her to get into
the car and driving her to school for her getting-to-school routine
to run off smoothly. The parents' routines may be similarly dependent on the child. For instance, the parents may be dependent
on the child's putting on her clothes and eating without a fuss in
order to get to work on time. Alternatively, two members of this
group, say the father and the daughter, may have very separate
routines. This might occur, for instance, if the mother tends to all
child care in the morning and the father simply goes about his own
morning business and leaves for work.

Now, what does all this have to do with emotion? Relying in
part on Mandler's (1975) theory of emotion, Berscheid proposes
that interruptions in a person's organized behavior sequences will
elicit heightened autonomic system arousal. The arousal, in turn,
will cause attention to be focused on the interrupting stimulus or
will elicit a search for the cause of the interruption. The arousal

itself forms the basis of emotional responding. If the interruption interferes with completing a desired plan, it will be labeled negatively and will result in negative emotion (e.g., the mother is just about ready to load up her car and drive to work and finds that the child has spilled a drink on her clothes and must change them). If, however, the interruption unexpectedly removes the presence of a stimulus that has previously interrupted a behavioral plan (e.g., the mother turns around in preparation to climb the stairs and get a new outfit but is met by the father coming down with the new outfit in hand and an offer to quickly change the child as the mother loads the car) or permits the unexpected and quick completion of organized sequences that have not finished running off (e.g., the mother goes into the child's room to help her get dressed and finds the child has efficiently and appropriately dressed herself), then the emotion will be positive. Emotion may also be positive if the person feels he or she has control over the interruptions (e.g., a person has chosen to ride a roller coaster with its unexpected and interrupting drops and knows the interruptions will end soon). In any case, arousal will presumably diminish when the original goal has been met, the old plan can be reinstated, or a new plan can be substituted.

Berscheid argues that the theory can predict a great deal about the likelihood of emotion occurring within a relationship as well as upon its demise. How can it help to predict emotion? First one must examine the degree and nature of interdependence within the relationship. If two people's organized behavioral plans are not very enmeshed (i.e., if the two people are not close), neither has much power to interrupt the other. As a result, there should be few interruptions, little resulting arousal, and little emotion in that relationship. This applies both during the course of the relationship and should it break up.

In contrast, relationships in which the behavioral plans of the members are highly enmeshed (i.e., are close) have great potential for emotional responding. Berscheid calls these relationships "emotionally invested" because each member has the capability of causing many interruptions in the other's planned behavioral plans. For example, if a husband has always successfully relied on his wife to pick him up at work, she can elicit negative emotion by being late or not showing up at all. On the other hand, if he always drives himself home, that ability does not exist. Moreover, it seems clear that if such highly enmeshed relationships break (e.g., one member dies), the other is very likely to experience a great deal of emotion. But will much emotion actually be experienced during

the course of the highly enmeshed relationship? Perhaps, but perhaps not. If the participants do not interrupt one another, little
emotion will be experienced. However, emotion will be experienced to the extent they do interrupt one another.

Clearly, this theory has implications for understanding distress in marriages and in parent–child relationships and therefore
has implications for designing preventive and ameliorative measures. Consider having the ability to predict who is going to experience most distress upon the termination of a relationship and,
therefore, who will be most in need of support. This theory
straightforwardly suggests that couples with very enmeshed
relationships are most likely to become distressed upon the
termination of their relationship and will be most in need of
support.

Of course, to put this suggestion to practical use one needs to
be able to measure enmeshment. Fortunately for the potential
mental health practitioner, Berscheid and her colleagues have
done considerable empirical work to devise such a measure and it
is now generally available (Berscheid, Snyder, & Omoto, 1989).
This measure assesses the frequency with which a person is influenced by the other as well as the diversity and strength of the
influences that occur. Further, and important for the present
point, high scores on this scale have been found to predict distress
upon relationship breakup. In particular, Simpson (1987) had students who were dating another but who were not engaged or
married participate in a longitudinal survey. During an initial
session, they filled out the closeness inventory along with other
measures including measures of satisfaction with their relationship, of the best alternative partner available, and of the best
imagined alternative partner. Three months later, the investigators were able to recontact most of their participants and
found that fewer than half of those recontacted had broken up.
These subjects were asked several questions regarding their distress at breakup. Interestingly, the only variables to reliably predict the intensity and duration of distress were the closeness
measure, the length of relationship, and the ease of finding an
alternative partner. These findings were clearly predicted on the
basis of the theory. According to the theory, closeness and length
should be related to the amount of behavioral disruption and
arousal that should occur after breakup. This arousal seems likely to be attributed to the break and labeled negatively. The
theory also suggests that the ease of finding an alternative partner
should be related to distress. Specifically, it should determine

how quickly organized plans of behavior to reach specific goals can be reinstated and consequently how quickly arousal should drop.

Very interestingly, and as predicted, another factor one would intuitively expect to predict distress upon breakup—that is, satisfaction with one's current partner—did not predict distress. Berscheid's theory explains this as well. Why? First there ought to be some relationships in which there is little enmeshment but in which participants are very satisfied. Yet, despite the perhaps high satisfaction in these relationships, there should be very little disruption of ongoing plans on the other's part when the relationship breaks and consequently little arousal and little negative emotion. Second, there may well be many relationships in which enmeshment is high and in which there are many well-organized intertwined behavioral sequences yet little emotion—positive or negative. Given the low level of positive emotion, members of such relationships may not think of themselves as highly satisfied, yet on breakup the great disruptions of their activity may cause much distress. Interestingly it is also the case that members of relationships in which well-practiced arguments and conflict regularly take place may actually experience little emotion. Yet, because of their conflicts, members of such couples may describe themselves as dissatisfied. Much to their surprise perhaps, upon breakup they may still be quite distressed (rather than relieved) because their well-practiced low-arousal conflicts have now been disrupted.

Not only does Berscheid's work strongly suggest using the Berscheid et al. (1989) measure of closeness as a predictor of potential distress upon breakup, it also suggests some potentially useful techniques for helping individuals who are experiencing distress following breakup. In particular, it suggests they ought to go back and map out the ways in which they were interdependent with the other. Then they ought to focus on either finding other people to substitute for their former partners in those routines or substituting entirely new routines for the ones that have been disrupted. To the extent to which they are successful at doing this, their distress ought to drop.

Still another potentially useful application of the Berscheid work, this time an application for couples whose relationships are still intact, has been suggested by Holmes and Boon (1989). Based on her theory, Holmes and Boon have suggested that "therapists may often need to counter the general notion that a loss of passion or emotion in marriage is necessarily indicative of deeper issues in the relationship or of future problems. They need to assure couples that an apparent decline in emotion is often a reflection of the closeness achieved in their marriages and not a cause for panic" (p. 38). We would agree and add that if, during the course of therapy, such an issue did arise, the theory suggests a positive way of handling it. Specifically, a therapist could administer the closeness inventory to the couple. If it provides evidence of closeness, the therapist could reassure the couple that there is evidence of strength in their relationship regardless of their lack of passion (and whatever other problems they have). Then the therapist could go further and suggest that if they want to establish more passion, they should start to interrupt those routines in unexpected and positive ways. Alternatively, if the inventory reveals a lack of closeness, the therapist could suggest that steps toward establishing closeness should be taken first if any hope of passion is to be restored.

A Theory of Self-Evaluation Maintenance

A second social psychological theory that not only contributes a great deal toward understanding interpersonal relationships but also has considerable potential for understanding links between relationships and mental health is Tesser's self-evaluation maintenance (SEM) theory. First, let us briefly describe the theory and some of the research that supports it.

Tesser begins with the assumption that people strive to behave in such a way as to maintain or improve their self-esteem. He also assumes that one's relationships with others can influence one's own self-esteem in important ways. In particular, he identifies two processes through which this may occur—a "reflection" process and a "comparison" process. Each can raise or lower one's self-esteem, but they do so in very different ways.

The "reflection" process can raise self-esteem by allowing one to bask in the other's glory. Thus, the relatives of a scientist who has just won a Nobel prize may find their self-esteem raised simply by virtue of being associated with the prize winner. The closer the relationship, the greater the effect. The spouse of the scientist presumably will experience a greater jump in self-esteem than will the third cousin of the scientist. On the other hand, the reflection process can also cause a person's self-esteem to deteriorate if that person has the misfortune of being associated with someone with negative attributes or behavior. For instance, the relatives of a person who commits a crime and is sentenced to prison may find that their self-esteem drops. This effect, too, should be exaggerated the closer the relationship. A parent would presumably suffer more than a cousin.

The comparison process operates in quite a different, indeed opposite, way. This process suggests that one's self-esteem may be raised by another person's poor performance by virtue of the fact that poor performance can make one's own performance look better. Thus, a student who has applied to three colleges and has been accepted to two may find her self-esteem raised when she compares her performance to that of a friend who has applied to the same three schools and has been turned down by all three. Tesser predicts this positive effect should be exaggerated the closer the relationship. Of course, comparison can have just the opposite effect on self-esteem if one discovers that one has done more poorly than another. And again, this effect should be exaggerated the closer the relationship between the two people.

Since these two processes lead to diametrically opposed predictions regarding the effects of another's good performance on one's own self-esteem and of another's bad performance on one's self-esteem, it is important to specify when each sort of effect will occur. According to Tesser, the key determinant of which process will apply is the relevance of the performance domain to the person in question. If the domain is not central to a person's identity, then the reflection process will predominate. If the domain is central to one's self-definition, the comparison process will dominate. For example, if ability at tennis is absolutely irrelevant to me, then I may experience great pride and jumps in my own self-esteem when my twin sister consistently wins championships in tennis even though I personally can't get the ball over the net. However, if I've always aspired and worked hard to be an outstanding tennis player myself and if she beats me, her good performance will presumably cause my own self-esteem to drop.

The theory is intriguing, and Tesser and his colleagues have accumulated an impressive array of studies providing clear support for the theory. For example, the theory predicts when people will be particularly helpful to friends relative to strangers and vice versa. Specifically, Tesser and Smith (1980) examined the effects of the closeness of another person and the relevance of that other person's performance to subjects on those subjects' willingness to help the other. They predicted that when relevance was low, the reflection process would predominate and, the closer the other, the more subjects ought to help the other. However, when relevance is high, the comparison process should predominate and the closer the other, the more reluctant subjects ought to be to help because comparison would make them look bad and lower their self-esteem. Subjects performed a task high in relevance to them (it was said to relate to their verbal skills and leadership) or low in relevance (it was said to relate to very little about them). Then they received feedback that indicated they performed poorly on the task. Later, they had a chance to give easy or difficult clues to a friend who had come to the study with them or to a stranger. As predicted, when relevance was high, subjects gave more difficult clues to friends than to strangers. In contrast, when relevance was low, subjects gave more difficult clues to strangers than to friends.

Another study supporting the model was reported by Tesser and Campbell (1982). As in the Tesser and Smith study, subjects participated in this study with a friend or with a stranger. All subjects took a test of both social sensitivity and esthetic judgment (and also rated the relevance of both skills to their own self-definitions). Then each subject received feedback that he or she was right on half the items and wrong on half. Next they guessed how many right their friend and a stranger got on each test. As predicted by the theory, when the task was low in self-relevance subjects were more charitable toward friends than toward strangers (i.e., they were more likely to guess that their friend had answered the question correctly.). In contrast when the task was relevant, just the reverse occurred. Subjects were more charitable toward strangers than toward friends (i.e., they were more likely to guess the stranger had answered the question correctly than they were to guess that their friend had done so.)

In still another study, Pleban and Tesser (1981) showed how the theory could predict how much closeness a person will seek with another when another performs better than the person. Male subjects first indicated how important various domains of activity were to their self-definition. Then they and another subject, previously unknown to them, answered questions on a topic high in relevance to the subject or low in relevance to the subject. The other did slightly better, considerably better, slightly worse, or much worse than the subject. Later, how close the subject chose to be to that other was measured. If the domain was high in relevance, the greater the margin was by which the other outperformed the subject, the less close the subjects chose to sit to that other, the less desire to work with that other was expressed, and the less subjects said the other was "like" them. In contrast, if the domain was low in relevance, the greater the margin was by which the other outperformed the subject, the closer subjects sat to that other, the more desire to work with that other was expressed, and the more subjects said the other was "like" them.[2]

Quite a number of other studies have also supported Tesser's model. For instance, Tesser and his colleagues have shown that it can be used to predict what performance dimensions people will consider relevant to them given the performance of others on those dimensions (Tesser & Campbell, 1980; Tesser & Paulis, 1983). It has also proved useful in understanding some aspects of family dynamics such as siblings' identification with one another and friction between siblings (Tesser, 1980) and in understanding the occurrence of emotion in relationships (Tesser, Millar, & Moore, 1988; Tesser & Collins, 1988; Tesser, Pilkington, & McIntosh, 1989).

What are the mental health implications of Tesser's and his colleagues' work? We think there are many. As with some of the work already described, it is certainly the case that the theory can predict some risk factors of distress in relationships. That is, members of couples, friendships, or sibling pairs who are close and who are pursuing very similar goals ought to be at greater risk for distress than should members of relationships who are not pursuing similar goals. Moreover, the theory suggests some strategies to prevent such distress. For instance, parents might be well advised to encourage their various children to develop different interests, particularly if those children are close in age and of the same sex. Similarly, adults whose careers are important to them might be well advised to date other adults who are pursuing quite a different career.

Of course, other forces will work against such strategies. After all, often children become interested an activity by virtue of seeing an older sibling participate in that activity. Also, because proximity is a powerful determinant of attraction, it will often be the case that people pursuing a particular career path will become romantically involved with others pursuing the same career training or in work settings. Thus, it is important to think of other strategies to reduce or to ameliorate the distress that having close relationships with others who may perform well in relevant domains may bring about. Fortunately, again the theory readily generates some possibilities. For instance, members of a couple who are in the same career might be well advised to pursue different domains *within* that career. For instance, one member of a couple composed of two lawyers might choose to pursue tax law, the other family law. Alternatively, if they are already in a certain specialty, they might be helped to draw finer distinctions between their work. For instance two lawyers working in the area of family law might differentiate themselves by emphasizing the fact that one is expert in divorce work while the other is expert in child abuse work. Alternatively, if one seems to feel career is central to his or her identity and the other does not, this probably should be encouraged. Still another, less obvious but perhaps quite effective technique, might be for two people who are pursuing very similar work to work *completely* together. For example, two professors in the same field and of the same seniority might decide to coauthor all their papers (perhaps alternating order of authorship). They might also make an agreement with their department chair to have identical salaries. Doing so will probably insulate both partners from possible negative outcomes of social comparison.

Of course, other obvious therapeutic techniques that the social comparison part of the theory suggests are decreasing closeness when comparisons become too painful (e.g., developing some new friendships when one only has friends who consistently outperform one in an important domain) and changing the relevance of an activity when comparison becomes too painful (e.g., decreasing one's emphasis on tennis and possibly taking up a new sport when one's twin consistently beats one at tennis).

The implications of the reflection process should not be neglected either. For instance, people might be encouraged to make the most of the positive outcomes of reflection. If one's sister is a wonderful artist, placing her work in one's office with her signature prominently displayed might produce some happiness. On the other hand, should reflection become too painful, a person may need to be reassured that he or she is not responsible for the other's negative behavior. He or she might also be well-advised to distance him- or herself from the other in whatever ways are most practical and/or least painful.

Finally, some recent work by Tesser and Cornell (1991) suggests that bolstering one's self-esteem in ways completely separate from the SEM processes Tesser discusses may decrease the importance of these processes for self-esteem. Thus, if SEM processes seem to be creating problems in a person's life, and especially if relevance, closeness, or behavior cannot be easily changed, perhaps therapists might be well advised to focus on other possible means to bolster self-esteem.

Works on Discovering the Norms behind the Giving and Receiving of Benefits in Relationships

A final example of basic social psychological work on relationships that we believe has potential for understanding mental health is some work on the rules governing the giving and receiving of benefits in relationships, both businesslike relationships and the sorts of relationships participants commonly call close relationships. This is work that has been done by Margaret Clark and Judson Mills.

This research centers around a distinction between communal relationships and exchange relationships. Communal relationships are characterized by mutual feelings of responsibility for the other's well-being. In these relationships, benefits are given in response to the other's needs or simply to please the other with no expectations of specific repayment. These relationships are often typified by family relationships, romantic relationships, and friendships. In exchange relationships, in contrast, members do not feel a special responsibility for each other's needs. Rather, benefits are given to repay debts created by benefits previously received or in anticipation of receiving specific repayment in the future. Exchange relationships are often typified by interactions between strangers, casual acquaintances, and business associates. Both types of relationships can vary in terms of how certain people are that they have that sort of relationship. For instance, although one may be certain about the type of relationship one wants with another, one may be quite uncertain regarding whether the other desires and/or believes he or she has the same sort of relationship. In addition communal relationships can vary in strength. That is, people feel greater obligations to meet some people's needs (e.g., the needs of their children) than other people's needs (e.g., the needs of their friend) even though they do feel a special obligation to both others.

Approximately 10 years ago, Clark and Mills (1979; Mills & Clark, 1982) began a program of research designed to demonstrate the validity of the distinction between these two types of relationships. Many of the studies have been experimental in nature. In these studies, desired relationship type has been manipulated by, in the communal conditions, having new college students interact with a physically attractive, friendly other who has expressed an interest in getting to know new people or, in the exchange conditions, having the students interact with the same other who has clearly established ties in the community, is married, and has expressed no particular interest in meeting new others.[3] Other studies have been concerned with showing that findings discovered in the laboratory studies generalize to ongoing communal and exchange relationships.

What has been discovered in this research? When subjects have been led to expect exchange relationships, they appear to follow strict exchange principles. That is, they (1) react positively to receiving immediate compensation for favors and to requests for repayment of accepted favors (Clark & Mills, 1979), (2) keep track of individual inputs into jointly rewarded tasks (Clark, 1984), and (3) feel exploited when their help is not reciprocated (Clark & Waddell, 1985). In contrast, when communal relationships are anticipated, subjects (1) react negatively to immediate compensation for favors (Clark & Mills, 1979), (2) do not keep track of individual inputs into joint tasks (Clark, 1984), and (3) do not feel exploited by unrequited help (Clark & Waddell, 1985). Instead, they are more likely to keep track of the other's needs, even when there is no opportunity for repayment (Clark, Mills, & Powell, 1986), and help others more (Clark, Ouellette, Powell, & Milberg, 1987). They also respond more favorably to the other's expressions of emotions, both in terms of how much they like the other (Clark & Taraban, 1991) and in terms of helping (Clark et al., 1987), and they tend to feel good about having helped the other (Williamson & Clark, 1989, 1992). Indeed, there is some evidence that people led to expect exchange relationships actually experience drops in mood after having chosen to help the other (Williamson & Clark, 1992). Moreover, the differences in behavior in communal and exchange relationships that have been observed in the laboratory appear to generalize to comparisons of interactions between ongoing friends and strangers (see Clark, 1984, studies 2 & 3; Clark, Mills, & Corcoran, 1989a).

In addition to the work distinguishing communal from exchange relationships, some complementary work has been done on individual differences in orientations toward relationships. In particular, Clark et al. (1987) have reported a scale designed to measure chronic individual differences in communal orientation toward relationships that predict the amount of help one person will give to another. And, Clark, Taraban, Ho, and Wesner (1989b) have developed an exchange orientation scale which has been shown to predict keeping track of individual inputs into joint tasks, dividing rewards according to who has contributed what, and reacting negatively to receiving aid that cannot be repaid.

What are some mental health implications of this work? We have categorized the implications we have thought of into four groups: (1) implications of research that shows exchange behaviors apply to exchange but not to communal relationships, (2) implications of research that shows that communal behaviors are more appropriate in communal than in exchange relationships, (3) implications of the work on individual differences in communal and exchange orientation, and (4) use of the communal–exchange distinction in understanding the therapist–client relationship.

First, what are implications of the evidence on the applicability of exchange norms to communal and exchange relationships? We start to answer this question by pointing out that we assume the cultural ideal for family relationships is that communal rather than exchange norms should be followed. As Aldous (1977) has noted, "Family members may benefit one another, but they do not usually expect reciprocation, nor do they require reciprocation necessarily from that person." Instead, "Families are generally groups whose members trust that their needs will be met eventually by someone" (p. 109). Thus we suggest that following exchange rules will generally not contribute to harmony in family relationships. Rather, doing so may often cause dissatisfaction and a sense that one is not being treated correctly. For example, a husband or wife whose spouse keeps careful track of each partner's earnings in order to determine how much money each one can spend may feel terribly distressed even though, in some sense, it seems like a "fair" thing to do and thus the distressed party may feel hard pressed to justify his or her negative feelings.

Or, consider how such exchange behaviors as formulating marriage contracts and/or offering children specific rewards for performing certain chores may affect family harmony and functioning. Marriage contracts that specify in advance exactly who will do what for whom (and thus do not allow flexibility for meeting changing needs) might well put marriages on an exchange basis, undermine use of communal norms, and create dissatisfaction. Similarly, whereas offering children specific rewards for performing specific chores or behaving in specific ways may be effective in the short run, this too may undermine use of communal norms in the long run and create disharmony. The results of research on the communal–exchange distinction suggest that it would be better to simply teach children that all family members have an obligation to contribute to the good of the household.

Next, consider implications of the findings regarding the use of exchange norms for clinical treatment of families in distress. We suspect that marriages with high levels of satisfaction may typically be those in which both members adhere to communal norms (i.e., both respond to the other's needs as those needs arise.) These relationships may deteriorate if members begin to violate communal norms by neglecting each other's needs. When this happens, couples presumably feel distress and may switch to exchange rules for giving and receiving benefits in an effort to save the marriage. However, exchange rules are not in line with what most people see as ideal for marriages and cannot provide the same sense of security as communal norms can. Consequently, members may still feel dissatisfied and the relationship may deteriorate further.

These ideas have clear implications for a commonly advocated marital therapy. Specifically, training members of couples to give specific rewards to their partner when their partner meets one of their specific needs (as several therapists have advocated—see, for instance, Liberman [1970], Stuart [1969], or the "behavior exchange" component of the "behavioral marital therapy" advocated by Jacobsen and Margolin [1979]) may have short-term benefits but fail to produce long-term improvements. Why? Couples may initially perceive improvements in their relationship just because they are now at least interacting more than before and have a "fair" rule for doing so. However, such techniques may contribute little to long-term improvement because little has been done to move the couple toward use of communal norms (and, indeed, the techniques may even interfere with that goal).

Interestingly, Jacobson (1984) has reported some results that support this reasoning. His study involved randomly assigning couples seeking therapy to either a control (no treatment), behavior exchange, communication/problem-solving, or behavior exchange plus communication/problem-solving treatment condition (only the first two conditions are relevant to the present point). Couples participated in 12–16 therapy sessions and completed measures of marital satisfaction right before and after therapy as well as 6 months later. Both the exchange and the communication/problem-solving components improved satisfaction from before to right after therapy (relative to no treatment). However, the results were quite different 6 months later. As we would have expected (but not as predicted by Jacobson), after 6 months, behavior exchange couples were not more satisfied than control couples while communication/problem-solving couples continued to show improvement and were more satisfied than control couples.

Finally we would note that explicit knowledge of exchange norms suggests what sorts of communications are likely to be seen as exploitative in exchange relationships and should therefore be avoided. Specifically, minimizing what one has received from another, exaggerating what one has given to the other, exaggerating one's costs in helping the other, minimizing (or ignoring) their costs in helping you, or minimizing one's own ability to help the other should all be perceived as inappropriate and exploitative in an exchange relationship. So, too, should acting as if an exchange relationship is really a communal one be seen as exploitative, for it suggests that the other should have to take one's needs into account even if doing so is costly or unjustified (Mills & Clark, 1986). Indeed, the first author recently received a letter from a colleague describing an exploitative communication of this last type. The colleague wrote, "The beach house I just stayed in was in many ways a disaster. There were workers hammering on the screen porch, there were no lights in the living room or bedroom, the faucet nearest the bed dripped. When I complained to the realtor, he said the carpenter wasn't done because his daughter had died recently. Hearing this put me in a uncomfortable position. If I persisted, I would seem incredibly callous. At the same time, I was very angry he brought that up. I think it is because he tried to inject aspects of a communal relationship into one that was purely exchange, and he did so in an exploitative way." (This same colleague suggested that perhaps she should have retorted that if she had to put up with a less desirable house because of the carpenter's daughter's death that perhaps the realtor should give *her* a lower price on the house due to her own three surgeries during the past year and her father's recent heart attack.)

Next consider the implications of our findings on communal behaviors—that is, that they occur more often and are more appropriate and expected in communal than in exchange relationships. At the broadest level, and again based on the assumption that our cultural ideal is for family relationships to be communal ones, to feel justly treated in family relations one must be treated communally. That is, one should feel the other attends to one's needs and meets them when necessary. Moreover, the others should seem willing to convey their own needs and to accept help. If these things do not occur, distress will occur. Less obviously, being emotionally expressive may also be important to members' perceptions that the relationship is a healthy one. This may be evidenced in several ways. People should feel good (rather than grumbling) about helping and should feel bad when they cannot help. Moreover, they should welcome expressions of emotion and be willing to express their own emotions. Interestingly, failure to

do these things should not be detrimental in exchange relationships. Indeed, if they are done in exchange relationships that
may be a sign of maladjustment on the performer's part and create
stress in the exchange relationship.

Communal norms also imply that certain types of communication between family members are likely to be perceived as
exploitative (Mills & Clark, 1986). Most straightforwardly, family
members who exaggerate their own needs or minimize the extent
to which another has already met their needs should be seen as
behaving unfairly. Both behaviors imply one person should benefit
another more than is necessary. Also, family members who are
able to help but who minimize the other's needs, exaggerate the
extent to which they have already met the other's needs and/or
minimize their own ability to meet the other's needs may be
perceived as behaving unfairly. These actions unjustly reduce
one's apparent obligation to the other. Also, exaggerating the
strength of the communal relationship to obtain greater benefits
than are justified and/or pretending that benefits given in the past
now obligate the other to repay may also be seen as exploitative in
communal relationships.

Finally, the communal work also suggests that feelings of
distress will result from members of communal relationships dis-
agreeing on the legitimacy of one another's needs and or from one
person being unable to meet the other's needs and the other not
recognizing that inability. Also, the fact that communal relationships vary in strength suggests another potential source of
discontent in communal relationships—that is discontent due to
members of close relationships having differences in their implicit
hierarchies of communal relationships. One spouse may put her
child's needs first, her husband's second, and her parents' third.
The other may put his parents' needs first, his child's second, and
his wife's third. It is easy to see how distress may then result.

Any of these implications of exchange and or communal
norms might be used by therapists treating distressed relationships. Perhaps just pointing these things out to a distressed
couple may help the members to pinpoint some specific violations
of expectations in their relationship. Or perhaps a therapist might
ask people to make explicit their implicit hierarchies of communal
relationships. Mismatches could then be pinpointed and perhaps
some intentional reorganization of hierarches on both members'
parts so that they match would prove useful. Most generally, the
work suggests that any therapy that increases family members'
attentiveness to one another's needs, knowledge about one an-

other's needs, and responsiveness to those needs should be effective. Fitting with this idea is Jacobson's (1984) finding that improving communication skills increased couple satisfaction not only immediately after therapy but also 6 months later.

Now let us turn to some clinical implications of the individual difference work on relationship orientations. First, measures of these orientations might be used in applied settings to assess just what individuals' expectations for their relationships are. Of most interest, perhaps, are the subsequent implications of the particular *match or mismatch* in orientations between members of any particular relationship type. Just as combinations of tendencies toward closeness/distance, control/dependency, and sex-role orientations have been shown to have important implications for satisfaction during courtship and marriage (see, for instance, Antill, 1983; Robinson & Jacobson, 1987; Zammichieli et al., 1988), so too may matches or mismatches in communal and exchange orientation be important. For example, if spouses match in communal and in exchange orientation, one might expect them to get along well. Best off may be couples in which both members are high in communal and simultaneously low in exchange orientation. Not only are they in agreement with one another regarding the appropriate norms, they are also in agreement with cultural dictates. To the extent to which they are able to ignore cultural dictates, spouses who are both high in exchange orientation (and low in communal orientation) may also function well.[4]

What about mismatches? Clearly, they ought to lead to dissatisfaction. Thus, for instance, in couples in which a person high in communal orientation is paired with one low in communal orientation, both may be miserable. The person high in communal orientation may feel his or her own needs are not met with sufficient regularity and/or enthusiasm and that his or her own attentiveness to the other's needs is not sufficiently appreciated. In contrast, the person low in communal orientation may feel a bit "smothered" by the other. Such relationships may be destined for trouble. Also when one person is high in exchange orientation and the other is low, both members may be unhappy. The high person may feel exploited when the other does not pay back benefits given, does not contribute enough to the relationship, and so forth. The low person may not feel trusted and may feel the other is overly concerned about record keeping. The worst combination may occur when one partner is high in communal orientation and simultaneously low in exchange orientation while the other is high in exchange orientation and simultaneously low in communal orientation. Such couples may suffer from *both* sets of problems just described.

We would also add that there may be some interesting *interactive* effects of cultural norms and individual differences in relationship orientation. For instance, because cultural norms dictate that communal norms should be followed in family relationships, family members may help each other regardless of their personal relationship orientation. However, individual differences in communal orientation may mediate how they *feel* about having to help the other. Williamson and Schulz (1990), for instance, located people both high and low in communal orientation who were willing to care for family members with Alzheimer disease. However, individual differences in communal orientation appeared to mediate emotional reactions to providing such care. Those high in communal orientation were less depressed after giving the help than were those low in communal orientation.

Still another implication of the individual difference work has to do with tendencies to form family relationships and friendships in the first place. As Snyder and Ickes (1985) point out, personality may influence the situations in which people place themselves. Given that our culture (and probably many others) seems to dictate that family relationships should be communal in nature, people low in communal orientation may be more reluctant to marry, have children, and/or form friendships than others (unless, perhaps, the spouse or friend is willing to carry most of the "caring" responsibilities in the relationship). Moreover, they may spend relatively less time interacting with their family of origin and/or with their own spouse and children if they do form the latter types of relationships (again, unless the others are willing to carry the greatest responsibility for nurturance and caring).

Finally, we note that as a theory of human relationships, the communal–exchange distinction may also serve as a means for understanding the most basic of relationships in the psychotherapy literature: the therapist–client relationship. While behavioral and cognitive–behavioral therapies place relatively little emphasis on the therapist–client relationship, psychodynamic, analytic, and eclectic therapies generally place a high degree of importance on the therapist–client relationship. In fact, some of the most promising work in the psychotherapy outcome literature emphasizes the quality of this relationship as an important factor in determining whether psychotherapy will effect a desired change in the client. The communal–exchange distinction may be useful in understanding many of the problems and strengths inherent in this relationship.

For example, many clients are initially uncomfortable with the "unequal" nature of the therapeutic relationship. The client is expected to focus on his or her problems and is explicitly or implicitly discouraged from having any concern or interest in the therapist except in cases where concern for the therapist has some bearing on the client's issue. Questions about the therapist are usually deflected back to the client as the therapist searches for the meaning and significance of the questions to the client's particular issues (e.g., I'd be glad to tell you about my children later, but I think it is interesting that you would ask about my family a week after you described to me your intense ambivalence regarding childbearing").

While the working through of issues using methods illustrated in the example chosen may be useful, it may also be useful to consider, especially in the early stages of therapy, that the client's questions may have dual meaning. True, the client in the above example may well need to discuss her feelings about motherhood in considerable depth. But, viewed from a communal–exchange perspective, she may also be reacting to the conflicting sets of norms which are inherent in the therapist–client relationship. On one hand, the therapist–client relationship has aspects that are communal in nature. The client engages in intense self-disclosure and the therapist often engages in unconditional empathy. However, in the psychotherapeutic relationship, the client never hears about the therapist' problems, so he or she cannot show concern in return. Also, the relationship is exchange in that therapist is paid a fee and contact is limited to a specific number of hours per week.

Thus, while questions of a personal nature directed toward the therapist, questions about money, and even problems concerning sexual contact in the therapist–client relationship may be understood in terms of traditional concepts of transference, countertransference, or more recent concepts of maladaptive cognitions or cognitive distortions, they may also reflect the client's and therapist's discomfort in a relationship that is neither purely exchange nor purely communal.

CONCLUSION

By now, we hope we have convinced the reader that basic research by both clinical and social psychological researchers on interpersonal relationships is of great potential utility to understanding mental health and, potentially, to mental health practice. We further hope we have convinced readers that the relevance of social psychological research in particular is due in large part to its emphasis on interpersonal processes. This emphasis, we believe, is especially likely to suggest useful mental health applications. That is, while other types of relationship research are certainly also relevant to mental health, it is social psychologists' emphasis on process at a level of analysis that produces results that can potentially be translated to preventive and ameliorative tactics.

Of course, social psychological work also has some drawbacks when it comes to thinking about applications. Most notably, unlike much clinical work, this work has almost exclusively been carried out with nonclinical populations. One important step to take is to establish the generalizability of our work to clinical populations. Here, it might be very fruitful for social psychologists to begin collaborating with clinicians who are likely to have an interest in such work and who are also likely to have easier access to the relevant populations. We would also note that social psychologists' outcome measures are often not directly relevant to mental health. Thus, not only should the generalizability of the work to clinical populations be demonstrated, social psychologists should also begin adding mental health outcome measures to their studies.

Despite the fact that much work remains to be done, we personally, one social psychologist and one clinician, are enthusiastic about the potential of social psychology fruitfully contributing to mental health practice. We would urge the interested reader to consider not just the applicability of the three particular programs of research reviewed here but also that of other social psychological programs of relationship work that would have been equally appropriate for us to have discussed. For example, the interested reader might want to examine the work of Shaver and his colleagues on attachment processes (e.g., Hazan & Shaver, 1987; Shaver, Hazan, & Bradshaw, 1988), Snyder and his colleagues' work on the relationship between self-monitoring and the nature of friendships and dating relationships (e.g., Snyder & Smith, 1986; Snyder & Simpson, 1984), Rusbult and her colleagues' work on an investment model of relationships (e.g., Rusbult, 1980; Rusbult, Johnson, & Morrow, 1986), or Reis and Shaver's work on intimacy processes in relationships (e.g., Reis & Shaver, 1988). We would also refer the interested reader to a recent article by Holmes and Boon (1990) and to a recent book by Derlega, Hendrick, Winstead, and Berg (1991) for two other discussions of possible applications of social psychological work on relationships to mental health.

Acknowledgments

Preparation of this chapter was supported by NIMH grant R03MH4025-01 and NSF grant BNS-9021603. We thank the editors of this volume for their helpful comments on an earlier version of this chapter.

NOTES

1. A third, very large area of relationship research known as social support research also exists. It includes work by epidemiologists, sociologists, and social psychologists on links between having relationships, the benefits those relationships provide, and/or are perceived to provide, and both mental and physical health. Due to length restrictions and because this work is discussed by Gore (Chapter 2, this volume), such work is not discussed further here.

2. Note, however, that the other's level of performance relative to the subject's made no difference to desired closeness when the subject outperformed that other.

3. Both the communal and the exchange relationship manipulations have been shown to be effective in producing desire to follow communal or exchange norms as mentioned (Clark, 1986; Clark & Waddell, 1985). Presumably, the communal manipulation is effective because our subjects recently made the transition to college and are likely to have an interest in forming a new friendship or romantic relationship with the attractive, sociable other. The exchange manipulation is effective because the other is busy and married and thus seems relatively unavailable for a friendship or romantic relationship. Thus, for purposes of whatever interaction takes place, following exchange rules is deemed best.

4. In their case, some qualification of some of our earlier comments may be necessary. That is, in this type of pairing it may be that following exchange (and not communal) norms leads to the greatest perception of justice even in family or romantic relationships. However, we believe that while following exchange rules exclusively may lead to a sense of justice in such relationships, it cannot provide the same sense of security that following communal rules (and knowing that someone cares about one's needs no matter what) can provide. Thus, these relationships still may not be very stable.

REFERENCES

Aldous, J. (1977). Family interaction patterns. *Annual Review of Sociology, 3*, 105–135.

Antill, J. K. (1983). Sex-role complementarity versus similarity in married couples. *Journal of Personality and Social Psychology, 45*, 145–155.

Bem, S. L. (1974). The measurement of psychological androgyny. *Journal of Personality and Social Psychology, 31*, 634–643.

Berscheid, E. (1982). Affect and emotion in interpersonal relations. In M. S. Clark & S. T. Fiske (Eds.), *Affect and cognition: The seventeenth annual Carnegie Symposium on Cognition. Attraction and emotion in interpersonal relations.* Hillsdale, NJ: Erlbaum.

Berscheid, E., Snyder, M., & Omoto, A. M. (1989). The relationship closeness inventory: Assessing the closeness of impersonal relationships. *Journal of Personality and Social Psychology, 57*, 792–807.

Bradbury, R. N., & Fincham, F. D. (1990). Attributions in marriage: Review and critique. *Psychological Bulletin, 107*, 3–33.

Clark, M. S. (1984). Record keeping in two types of relationships. *Journal of Personality and Social Psychology, 47*, 549–557.

Clark, M. S. (1986). Evidence for the effectiveness of manipulations of communal and exchange relationships. *Personality and Social Psychology Bulletin, 12*, 414–425.

Clark, M. S., & Mills, J. (1979). Interpersonal attraction in exchange and communal relationships. *Journal of Personality and Social Psychology, 37*, 12–24.

Clark, M. S., Mills, J., & Corcoran, D. (1989a). Keeping track of needs and inputs of friends and strangers. *Personality and Social Psychology Bulletin, 15*, 533–542.

Clark, M. S., Mills, J., & Powell, M. C. (1986). Keeping track of needs in communal and exchange relationships. *Journal of Personality and Social Psychology, 51*, 333–338.

Clark, M. S., Ouellette, R., Powell, M. C., & Milberg, S. (1987). Recipient's mood, relationship type and helping. *Journal of Personality and Social Psychology, 53*, 94–103.

Clark, M. S., & Reis, H. (1988) Interpersonal processes in close relationships. In M. R. Rosenzweig & L. Porter (Eds.), *Interpersonal processes in close relationships.* Palo Alto, CA: Annual Review Inc.

Clark, M. S., & Taraban, C. B. (1991). Reactions to and willingness to express emotion in communal and exchange relationships. *Journal of Experimental Social Psychology, 27*, 324–336.

Clark, M. S., Taraban, C. B., Ho, J., & Wesner, K. (1989b). *Developing a measure of exchange orientation.* Unpublished manuscript, Carnegie Mellon University.

Clark, M. S., & Waddell, B. (1985). Perception of exploitation in communal and exchange relationships. *Journal of Social and Personal Relationships, 2*, 403–413.

Derlega, V. J., Hendrick, S. S., Winstead, B. A., & Berg, J. H. (1991). *Psychotherapy as a personal relationship.* New York: Guilford Press.

Fincham, F. D. (1985a). Attributions in close relationships. In J. H. Harvey & G. Weary (Eds.), *Attribution: Basic ideas and applications* (pp. 203–234). New York: Academic Press.

Fincham, F. D. (1985b). Attribution processes in distressed and nondistressed couples: 2. Responsibility for marital problems. *Journal of Abnormal Psychology, 94,* 183–190.

Fincham, F. D., Beach, S. R., & Baucom, D. H. (1987). Attribution processes in distressed and nondistressed couples: 4. Self-partner attribution differences. *Journal of Personality and Social Psychology, 52,* 739–748.

Fincham, F. D., Beach, S. R., & Nelson, G. (1987). Attribution processes in distressed and nondistressed couples: 3. Casual and responsibility attributions for spouse behavior. *Cognitive Therapy and Research, 11,* 71–86.

Fincham, F. D., & Beach, S. R. (1988). Attribution processes in distressed and nondistressed couples: 5. Real versus hypothetical events. *Cognitive Therapy and Research, 12,* 505–514.

Fincham, F. D., & O'Leary, K. D. (1983). Casual inferences for spouse behavior in maritally distressed and nondistressed couples. *Journal of Social and Clinical Psychology, 1,* 42–57.

Gottman, J. M. (1982). Emotional responsiveness in marital conversations. *Journal of Communication, 32,* 108–120.

Gottman, J. M. (1979). *Marital Interaction: Experimental investigations.* New York: Academic Press.

Gottman, J. M., & Krokoff, L. J. (1989). Marital interaction and satisfaction. *Journal of Consulting and Clinical Psychology, 57,* 47–52.

Hazan, C., & Shaver, P. R. (1987). Romantic love conceptualized as an attachment process. *Journal of Personality and Social Psychology, 52,* 511–524.

Holmes, J. G., & Boon, S. D. (1990). Developments in the field of close relationships: Creating foundations for intervention strategies. *Personality and Social Psychology Bulletin, 16,* 23–41.

Jacobson, N. S. (1984). A component analysis of behavioral marital therapy: The relative effectiveness of behavior exchange and communication/problem-solving training. *Journal of Consulting and Clinical Psychology, 52,* 295–305.

Jacobson, N. S., & Margolin, G. (1979). *Marital therapy: Strategies based on social learning and behavior exchange principles.* New York: Brunner/Mazel.

Kelley, H. H., Berscheid, E., Christensen, A., Harvey, J. H., Huston, T. L., Levinger, G., McClintock, E., Peplau, L. A., & Peterson, D. R. (1983). *Close Relationships.* New York: Freeman.

Liberman, R. (1970). Behavioral approaches to family and couple therapy. *American Journal of Orthopsychiatry, 40,* 106–118.

Levenson, R. W., & Gottman, J. M. (1983). Marital interaction: Physiological linkage and affective exchange. *Journal of Personality and Social Psychology, 45,* 587–597.

Levenson, R. W., & Gottman, J. M. (1985). Physiological and affective predictions of change in relationship satisfaction. *Journal of Personality and Social Psychology, 49,* 85–94.

Locke, H. J., & Wallace, K. M. (1959). Short marital-adjustment and prediction tests: Their reliability and validity. *Marriage and Family Living, 21,* 251–255.

Mills, J., & Clark, M. S. (1982). Exchange and communal relationships. In L. Wheeler (Ed.), *Review of Personality and Social Psychology.* Beverly Hills: Sage.

Mills, J., & Clark, M. S. (1986). Communications that should lead to perceived exploitation in communal and exchange relationships. *Journal of Social and Clinical Psychology, 4,* 225–234.

Mandler, G. (1975). *Mind and emotion.* New York: Wiley.

Markman, H. J. (1979). Application of a behavioral model of marriage in predicting relationship satisfaction of couples planning marriage. *Journal of Consulting and Clinical Psychology, 47,* 743–749.

Markman, H. J. (1981). Prediction of marital distress: A 5-year follow-up. *Journal of Consulting and Clinical Psychology, 49,* 760–762.

Pleban, R., & Tesser, A. (1981). The effects of relevance and quality of another's performance on interpersonal closeness. *Social Psychology Quarterly, 44,* 278–285.

Reis, H. T., & Shaver, P. R. (1988). Intimacy as an interpersonal process. In S. W. Duck (Ed.), *Handbook of personal relationships* (pp 367–389). New York: Wiley.

Robinson, E. A., & Jacobson, N. S. (1987). Social learning theory and family psychopathology: A Kantian model in behaviorism? In T. Jacob (Ed.), *Family interaction and psychopathology* (pp. 117–162). New York: Plenum Press.

Rusbult, C. E. (1980). Commitment and satisfaction in romantic associations: A test of the investment model. *Journal of Experimental Social Psychology, 16,* 172–186.

Rusbult, C. E., Johnson, D. J., & Morrow, G. D. (1986). Predicting satisfaction and commitment in adult romantic involvements: An assessment of the generalizability of the investment model. *Social Psychology Quarterly, 49,* 81–89.

Shaver, P., Hazan, C., & Bradshaw, D. (1988). Love and attachment: The integration of three behavioral systems. In R. J. Sternberg & M. Barnes (Eds.), *The Anatomy of Love.* (pp. 68–94). New Haven, CT: Yale University Press.

Simpson, J. A. (1987). The dissolution of romantic relationships: Factors involved in relationship stability and emotional distress. *Journal of Personality and Social Psychology, 39,* 683–692.

Snyder, M., & Ickes, W. (1985). Personality and social behavior. In G. Lindsey & E. Aronson (Eds.), *The handbook of social psychology* (3rd ed.) (pp. 883–947). New York: Random House.

Snyder, M., & Simpson, J. A. (1984). Self-monitoring and dating relationships. *Journal of Personality and Social Psychology, 45,* 210–222.

Snyder, M., & Smith, D. (1986). Personality and friendship: The friendship worlds of self-monitoring. In V. J. Derlega & B. A. Winstead (Eds.), *Friendship and social interactions* (pp. 63–80). New York: Springer-Verlag.

Stuart, R. B. (1969). Operant-interpersonal treatment for marital discord. *Journal of Consulting and Clinical Psychology, 33,* 675–682.

Tesser, A. (1980). Self-esteem maintenance in family dynamics. *Journal of Personality and Social Psychology, 39,* 77–91.

Tesser, A., & Campbell, J. (1980). Self-definition: The impact of the relative performance and similarity of others. *Social Psychology Quarterly, 43,* 341–347.

Tesser, A., & Campbell, J. (1982). Self-evaluation maintenance and the perception of friends and strangers. *Journal of Personality, 59,* 261–279.

Tesser, A., & Collins, J. E. (1988). Emotion in social reflection and comparison situations: Intuitive, systematic and exploratory approaches. *Journal of Personality and Social Psychology, 55,* 695–709.

Tesser, A., & Cornell, D. P. (1991). On the confluences of self-processes. *Journal of Experimental Social Psychology, 27,* 501–526.

Tesser, A., Millar, M., & Moore, J. (1988). Some affective consequences of social comparison and reflection processes: The pain and pleasure of being close. *Journal of Personality and Social Psychology, 54,* 49–61.

Tesser, A., & Paulis, D. (1983). The definition of self: Private and public self-evaluation management strategies. *Journal of Personality and Social Psychology, 44,* 672–682.

Tesser, A., Pilkington, C. J., & McIntosh, W. D. (1989). Self-evaluation maintenance and the mediational role of emotion: The perception of friends and strangers. *Journal of Personality and Social Psychology, 57,* 442–456.

Tesser, A., & Smith, J. (1980). Some effects of friendship and task relevance on helping: You don't always help the one you like. *Journal of Experimental Social Psychology, 16,* 582–590.

Williamson, G. M., & Clark, M. S. (1989). Providing help and desired relationship type as determinants of changes in moods and self-evaluations. *Journal of Personality and Social Psychology, 56,* 722–734.

Williamson, G. M., & Clark, M. S. (1992). Impact of desired relationship type on affective reactions to choosing and being required to help. *Personality and Social Psychology Bulletin, 18,* 10–18.

Williamson, G., & Schulz, R. (1990). Relationship orientation, quality of prior relationship, and distress among caregivers of Alzheimer's patients. *Psychology and Aging, 5,* 502–509.

Woody, E. Z., & Costanzo, P. R. (1990). Does marital agony precede marital ecstasy? A comment on Gottman's and Krokoff's "Marital interaction and satisfaction: A longitudinal view." *Journal of Consulting and Clinical Psychology, 58*, 499–501.

Zammichieli, M. E., Gilroy, F. D., & Sherman, M. F. (1988). Relation between sex-role orientation and marital satisfaction. *Personality and Social Psychology Bulletin, 14*, 747–754.

Understanding the Mental Health Consequences of Race:
Contributions of Basic Social Psychological Processes

JAMES M. JONES

Race has been a volatile issue in the United States from its earliest beginnings. It has framed in black and white, the stark contrast between the principles of freedom liberty and equality for which the revolution was fought and the realities of slavery, genocide, and systematic legal and political abrogation of rights of citizenship of millions of Americans of color.

It is important to recognize that the question of race is fundamentally important to understanding the social and cultural nature of this society. In fact, it is over the very principles on which this nation was built that the conflicts over race have been fought. As early as 1791, de Toqueville (1945) noted the contradiction between race-based slavery and equality and liberty principles of the American Revolution. He noted specifically: "The prejudice of race . . . nowhere is . . . *so intolerant as in those states where servitude has never been known. . . ."* (p. 373, emphasis added). While it is easy to focus attention on the South and on the institution of slavery in a racial analysis, de Toqueville's observation early established a more pervasive racial effect.

Race is a biological concept whose significance, however, is its social meaning (vanden Berghe, 1967). A race is an inbreeding, geographically isolated population, distinguishable by its physical features (Zuckerman, 1990). However, about 85% of all human genetic variation in enzymes and other proteins occurs *within* members of a so-called racial group. If *homo sapiens* is the species

to which all humans belong, then race can be considered a sub-
species capable of inbreeding but rarely doing so. The geographical isolation characterizing races in earlier times has been
replaced by political, cultural, and religious factors. The meanings, expectations, and behaviors associated with race are fundamentally social psychological and have been important to the
development of social psychology for over 70 years.

What makes racism an important concept for social psychology is the multiple levels at which it can operate. In my book,
Prejudice and Racism (1972), I proposed a three-part approach as
follows:

> *Individual racism* is based on a belief in the biological inferior-
> ity of another group that is socially defined on the basis of
> physical criteria;
> *Institutional racism* is the intentional or unintentional manip-
> ulation or acceptance of institutional practices that unfairly
> restrict the opportunities of a racial group;
> *Cultural racism* is the expression of superiority of one's own
> cultural forms, values, styles and beliefs over those of an-
> other racial group.

In this society, symbolic interactions (Mead, 1934; Cooley, 1902;
Tesser, 1988) play a major role in self-definition and its behavioral
consequences. Furthermore, political, economic, and social power
congeal in one racial group. Racism, therefore, specifies a broad
pattern of actions and reactions of individuals based on their
group identification and its meaning and consequences in the
society at large.

In this chapter I express the view that race, in this society, is a
social status with psychological effects that have consequences for
actual and presumed mental health. Those consequences range
from subtle forms of self-doubt to feelings of superiority to anger at
privileged others; from hatred of others to compassion for them.
Race problems disrupt the daily opportunity to enjoy mental
health by presenting the nightmare of bias that undermines well
being. It fosters mistrust in blacks and a range of reactions in
whites from hostility to guilt.

These mental health consequences accrue to whites and blacks
alike. The racial paradigm is characterized by recursive conflict
and ambivalence (Katz, 1981). Racial conflict arises, in part, from
white feelings of superiority over blacks (based often on realistic
appraisals of relative disparaties in achievement and possesssion

of the valued rewards our culture offers) and black rejection of this premise. Psychological and behavioral attempts to overturn or reinforce this racial dominance concept provide fuel for continued conflict. Ambivalence or ambiguity can be found in the cooccurrence of the traditional American value of individual freedom and the reality of truncated opportunities for individuals based on their group membership. Understanding the mental health consequences of race will, in part, require us to learn how whites and blacks alike respond to the conflicts, contradictions, and ambiguity of racial dynamics in the United States.

Race is linked closely to culture and society in evaluative terms. It is believed, in accordance with a Darwinian analysis, that groups differ in human capabilities, that those differences can be arrayed along some continuum of competence, and the continuum has its basis in biological attributes (cf. Herrnstein, 1971). So, race has mental health significance in part because it implies biological differences to which are attached basic valuations that matter in this society. Those who belong to the dominant group in this analysis enjoy feelings of superiority, while those assigned to the subordinate groups are subject to abuse, discrimination, and devaluation.

It is perhaps, then, not surprising that social psychological analysis has found issues of race so central to an understanding of the dynamics of human interaction. William McDougall, author of one of the first textbooks in social psychology in 1907, focused early attention on race when he linked racial differences to cultural superiority in his *Is America Safe for Democracy?* (McDougall, 1921). He identified the characteristics of "race" that conferred that superiority, namely, curiosity, introversion, providence,[1] self-assertiveness, and mental ability. Research on social distance (Bogardus, 1925), socialization (Allport, 1924), stereotyping (Katz & Braly, 1933), prejudice (Allport, 1954), personal and group identity (Clark & Clark, 1939; 1947), intelligence (Klineberg, 1935), attitude and behavior relationships (Deutsch & Collins, 1951), and race relations (Myrdal, 1944) early on established a range of concerns among social psychologists with the important topic of race. Race issues have been significant problems in society, and social psychological research paradigms have been adapted to address this significant social problem. As a result, much of our understanding of race effects and what to do about them have been derived from basic and applied social psychological research. The purposes of this chapter are to illustrate the significant role social psychology has played in understanding race effects, to identify the basic mechanisms that underlie the operation of these race effects, and to suggest the most promising avenues for future research and applications.

BASIC ISSUES IN UNDERSTANDING
THE EFFECTS OF RACE

The following pages organize this work into the main themes into which the basic social psychological processes involved with race can be placed. The subject is so vast and the body of work so large that this analysis will necessarily be selective. Most of the research on race has involved the dynamics of black–white race relations. This work has emanated from the white superiority–black inferiority paradigm and sought largely to explain how, why, and to what effect white racial biases operate.

Most social psychological analyses of race effects can be categorized in one of two ways: (1) the processes by which racial bias originates, is perpetuated, and ultimately can be reduced (the focus of this work has largely emanated from studies of whites and their perceptions of, and attitudes and behaviors toward, black Americans); and (2) the processes by which victims of racial bias adapt and seek to develop positive means of psychological development and personal identity. (Again, responses of black Americans will be the focal point of this analysis.)

In the next section of this chapter, we look selectively at the research findings illustrative of each of these perspectives. The aim of this review is to demonstrate the ways in which social psychological research has illuminated our understanding of the basic mechanisms that underlie psychological responses linked to race. Five specific domains will be considered: (1) studies of stereotyping; (2) the discontinuity between racial attitudes and racial behaviors; (3) the effects of interracial interaction on racial attitudes and behavior; (4) the effects of racial bias on identity and self-esteem of blacks; and (5) positive identity consequences of group-based stigmatization. The first two domains fit clearly under the white bias perspective. The fourth and fifth domain fit under the black reaction perspective. The third domain straddles the two perspectives.

The final section tries to summarize the implications of this review and accompanying analyses for an understanding of mental health consequences of race. It further comments on what might be the most useful avenues for future research.

SOCIAL PSYCHOLOGICAL PROCESSES IN THE ANALYSIS OF EFFECTS OF RACE

Ruble, Costanzo, and Higgins (Chapter 1, this volume) describe a model by which social psychological mechanisms intervene between antecedent forces and mental health outcomes. Antecedent conditions are associated with race, culture, gender, socioeconomic status, family structure, and so on. All of these variables are intimately linked to the paradigm of race spelled out earlier. In the Ruble model, they lead to basic social psychological mechanisms, which in turn lead directly to mental health outcomes or directly to immediate precursors of these outcomes.

Mental health outcomes are conceived in terms of the major "problems" of concern to the National Institute of Mental Health (NIMH), namely, depression, anxiety, AIDS, childhood disorders, homelessness, and the like. Although the concept of mental health is commonly associated with various illness conditions, it is possible for mental health to be conceived in terms of positive self-esteem, feelings of productivity, accomplishment, meaningfulness, and inclusion in positive social groups. Thus, one of the goals for understanding racial effects is to determine how such positive mental states and social behaviors can be achieved across racial groups and interactions.

The work on cooperative learning paradigms in intergrated classroom settings reflects this approach (Aronson et al., 1978; Aronson & Thibodeau, in press; Slavin, 1980).

The basic social psychological mechanisms are grouped under the general labels of comparison with standards, consistency processes, information seeking and processing, social influence processes, and attachment/cohesion processes. These can, as noted, give rise immediately to positive or negative mental health outcomes or to direct precursors such as self-esteem, services utilization and social support, risky behaviors, affective responses, attitudes, and stress reactions. With this model as a guide, I will briefly review the development of the basic race-related dynamics and their mental health implications.

ORIGINS AND BASIC DYNAMICS OF RACIAL BIAS IN WHITES

In social psychology, concern with white biases toward blacks has fallen under the general concept of prejudice (Allport, 1954; Jones,

1972). The negative mental health consequences of prejudice for blacks has been discussed within a psychic stress model of depression (Kardiner & Ovesy, 1951), lowered esteem (Clark & Clark, 1947), and identification with the aggressor (Pettigrew, 1964). Generally missing in this analysis of white bias has been an assessment of how bias affects whites (Bowser & Hunt, 1981, provide an exception to this general trend). More recent attention has been paid to this missing link (e.g., Devine, 1989), so that the relevance of social psychological analysis has been broadened.

What has been central in the social psychological literature is the specific mechanisms of bias that describe the phenomenon of racial prejudice. The basic mechanisms, drawing upon the Ruble model, have typically involved expectancy effects and comparison to standards, attitude formation, and change. In a short chapter like this, it is not possible to review these vast literatures completely. Rather, what I try to do is trace the lines of argument and their empirical or theoretical standing.

Stereotyping

Lippmann (1922) made a distinction between the world outside and the pictures of that world we hold in our heads. That picture we hold in our heads is often defined for us by the culture in which we live. Lippman called that preformed picture a stereotype. Its importance rested principally on the degree to which it deviated from the "real world" outside our heads. Thus, a stereotype has the capacity to guide behavior based on socially constructed meanings as if the meanings were real. A stereotype "may be so consistently and authoritatively transmitted in each generation from parent to child that it seems almost like a biological fact" (p. 61).

Stereotypes, then, define an expectancy that precedes and shapes experience. When stereotypes are negative, a target of stereotypes is prejudged and his or her interactions are affected not by actual qualities or behavior but by pictures of "someone else" in the perceiver's head. Social psychological theory and research have acknowledged this important process for about 60 years. The attempt to understand the formation, maintenance, and consequences of stereotyping is one of the most consistent undertakings in social psychology over the years.

In the first classic study of stereotyping, Katz and Braly (1933) had Princeton undergraduates rate several ethnic–racial groups in terms of the traits they felt best described them. They found that these Princeton men felt "Negroes" were considered to be, in order, superstitious (84%), lazy (75%), ignorant (38%), happy-go-lucky (38%), and musical (26%). "Americans" (presumably *white* Americans) were regarded as industrious (48%), intelligent (47%), materialistic (33%), ambitious (33%), and progressive (27%). The authors had the men rate the desirability of each trait on a scale of 1 to 10. The average rating of the stereotypical traits for "Negroes" was 3.55, while for "Americans" it was 6.77. The pictures of "Negroes" in the heads of these men were more negative than the pictures of Americans. Moreover, they were surer of these pictures.

Gilbert (1951) found the content had changed little in 18 years. Karlins, Coffman, and Walters (1969) replicated the Katz and Braly study with Princeton men and found that some 35 years later, the content of the racial stereotypes had changed relatively little, but over the years, the evaluation of the traits had become less negative for blacks.

The question of stereotypes is important in racial effects because a stereotype represents a judgment of average characteristics of a social category. Apart from the accuracy and values assigned to the attributes, the applicability of the categorical trait to an individual case becomes problematic. In an interpersonal situation, a stereotype provides an *expectation* for behavior based on assumptions untested by the individual case. Thus stereotyping, demonstrably inaccurate and negative, forms the basis for expectancy effects and their negative consequences where race is concerned.

One of the most compelling examples of expectancy effects is the self-fulfilling prophesy. Word, Zanna, and Cooper (1974) studied the possibility that a person's expectation for behavior could increase the likelihood that the behavior would occur. They were able to show that when white Princeton male undergraduates were treated in an interview situation as if they were black (as determined empirically by a prior study, in a manner that suggested a variety of negative nonverbal behaviors), the interviewees were judged by an independent panel of raters to be less qualified for the position they sought. What is significant here is that through experimental methodology, Word, Zanna, and Cooper (1974) were able to disentangle the demographics of race from the effects it is theorized to have. The expectancy effect of the self-fulfilling prophesy was demonstrated in a situation that was operationally similar to one in which a white interviewer with presumed racial prejudices is interviewing a black job candidate. The final judgment can be made "objectively" because the expectancy effect creates the behavioral confirmation for that decision.

The operation of such biases is further illustrated in a study by Henderson (1979) with black policeman in Cleveland, Ohio. Personality ratings from the Cattell 16PF, and the Edwards Personality Preference Scale were correlated with peer and supervisor performance evaluations of black and white policemen. Although the two groups did not differ at all in the personality profile, the pattern of associations of the personality and performance variables differed. The performance of blacks was rated higher when they scored *lower* on personality measures of aggression, dominance, heterosexuality, and extroversion, and *higher* on deference, order, affiliation and endurance.

Combining the Word, Zanna, and Cooper and Henderson studies, the implications are significant. If the pictures of black policemen in the heads of the white police supervisors consist of a set of attributes and behaviors as profiled above, and if their behaviors (e.g., ratings of performance) reflect those pictures instead of the social reality (blacks and whites do not differ in personality profiles), then either unfair evaluations will take place or the types of blacks who will be hired will begin to reflect this personality profile. The experience of black policemen, as with others in this society, is significantly affected by the way race influences the social, perceptual, and behavioral processes of whites.

Given that stereotypes are so powerful in their ability to affect interracial interactions, it is important to understand something about how they are formed and how they can be changed. Again, social psychologists have developed increasingly sophisticated theories and empirical demonstrations of these processes.

Hamilton and Gifford (1976) showed that the phenomenon of illusory correlation offered a compelling way to explain the formation of stereotypes. Illusory correlation "is a cognitive bias in information processing that leads the perceiver to believe that two events are correlated to a greater extent than they actually are" (Acorn, Hamilton, & Sherman, 1988, p. 345).

In their classic demonstration of this process, Hamilton and Gifford (1976) had subjects read vignettes of interactions designed to pair members of two groups, A and B, with certain traits that were positive and negative. Group A had more members than group B by a 2-to-1 margin, and positive traits outnumbered negative traits by a 2-to-1 margin. When subjects were asked to recall specific actions taken by members of the two groups, they remembered a disproportionate number of negative actions of group B members more than any other category. Since negative traits and members of group B shared relative infrequency in this protocol, the authors concluded that the illusory correlation effect could be linked directly to the distinctiveness consequence of shared infrequency. One of the implications of this analysis is that selective elements of basic social cognition processes can account for the content as well as the prevalence of stereotypes; that is, the heightened association of negative attributes with minority group members.

Hamilton and Rose (1980) showed that illusory correlation processes could serve to maintain stereotypes. They found that when subjects were presented with information about different occupational groups, in spite of the fact that the different kinds of information were paired equally with each group, stereotypically consistent information was perceived to be more frequently associated with the groups than either stereotype-irrelevant or disconfirming information. The tendency to see associations that are not there, *when the association fits a picture in the head*, illustrates the difficulty of changing stereotypes by presenting reality-based, disconfirming information.

Moreover, research has demonstrated that illusory correlation effects generalize to other relevant social domains in either an evaluative way (as when being good in the intellectual domain generalizes to being good in the social domain) or a descriptive way (as when a group has a high standing on one of two linked traits, say intelligence and attractiveness, the standing will be transferred to the second linked trait (Acorn et al., 1988).

It is speculative whether stereotypes are actually formed via illusory correlation processes. If the process works as proposed, would it similarly predict illusory correlation associations for blacks or other minority groups? Would black stereotypes of whites themselves be affected by these processes? Would a black frame of reference make whites a minority, thus subjecting them to the biasing effects of illusory correlation? Would positive or negative attributes be presumed to be infrequent? Would illusory correlation predict negative in-group judgments for blacks? These questions suggest some of the additional empirical and theoretical work that will help determine the broadest impact of illusory correlation processes.

Fiske and her colleagues (Fiske, Neuberg, Beattie, & Milberg, 1987; Fiske & Neuberg, 1990) have analyzed stereotyping within the context of impression formation processes. The conventional view of stereotypes proposes a top-down process by which categorical information forms the basis of an individual judgment. An alternative view, offered by Fiske, is that data-driven processes can and do occur. Such processes are linked to specific attributes and thus lead to a more individuated judgment of a person. In both cases, affective labels are attached to the organizing information, either the category or the specific attributes. Since category-based judgments tend to perpetuate stereotyping processes, it is important to know conditions under which this dynamic is likely to be attenuated. Fiske and colleagues have shown that when the categorization is difficult, attribute-based judgments are more likely to occur. Moreover, when categorizations are difficult, affective responses will be derived from attributes rather than categories.

This clearly suggests that conditions in which categorical labels are unclear or attributes that conflict with each other or with the category label are specified, will attenuate stereotypical perceptions and their corresponding affective responses. Efforts to systematically create such conditions should have the net effect of reducing stereotyping behavior.

Rothbart and Lewis (1988) offer another means by which stereotyping effects, or categorical judgments of individuals, can be attenuated. They cite Allport's notion of "refencing" to describe the process by which individual members of a social category who violate expectations about the category are fenced out of the category, thus leaving the principle on which the category rests intact. If this process is widespread, how can one ever change a social stereotype? They argue that category membership cannot necessarily be inferred from characteristics of individual members. For example, although Clarence Thomas is black, he may be refenced into a "political conservative" and removed from the African-American category. As the attributes of a particular member become less congruent with the typical attributes of the category, the member is less likely to be associated with the category. This reasoning leads Rothbart and Lewis to suggest that rather than focusing on category members who deviate most from the stereotype as a means of changing stereotype content (say drawing attention to a black astrophysicist at Cal Tech to change the "unintelligent" content of a black stereotype), the category can be modified more effectively when an exemplar of the category is shown to possess nonstereotypical attributes. By this reasoning, a poor black urban child from a single-parent home who scores 1400 on the SATs might have more impact on prevailing categorical judgments than the black astrophysicist.

Summary

The above review has been selective but highlights the basic principles of stereotyping processes. Stereotyping has been a core aspect of racial prejudice because of its pivotal role in the organization of social information and its guiding influence on behavior directed at individual members of stereotyped social categories. Basic social psychological mechanisms such as illusory correlation and distinctiveness or salience effects illustrate how stereotypes are formed and maintained. Behavioral consequences of stereotyping are revealed by general expectancy effects, particularly self-fulfilling prophesies. Changing stereotypes is very difficult, but we have some evidence to suggest that data-driven information processing, when invoked, lessens the likelihood of category-based judgments or stereotyping effects. Moreover, research suggests that exemplar-mediated efforts to change stereotypes may be more successful than traditional category-exception approaches have been in changing the content of stereotypes.

Americans believe in fairness. Demonstrating the ways in which basic social judgment mechanisms introduce systematically biased perceptions of other people provides a starting point for changing the way white Americans understand how fairness may be compromised on the basis of race.

DISCONTINUITY BETWEEN RACIAL ATTITUDES AND RACIAL BEHAVIORS

Social psychology early on developed the notion that attitudes could be measured (Thurstone, 1927). It soon became one of the most central concepts in social psychology, even to the point of figuring prominently in Allport's (1935) definition of social psychology as "the scientific study of attitudes." One of the significant reasons for the importance of the attitude concept in social psychology was its presumed dynamic relationship to behaviors. If attitudes cause behaviors and if attitudes can be measured, understanding and ultimately influencing behavior can be developed from the attitude concept. It is also the case that such cognitively mediated effects may not capture some of the more dynamic affectively driven determinants of prejudice (cf., Stangor, Sullivan, & Ford, 1991). Understanding the dynamic interplay between cognitive and affective processes remains an important research need in the study of prejudice.

The importance of attitudes is critical to our consideration of racial effects. If discriminatory behavior is guided by racial attitudes, then changing those attitudes from negative to positive or ignorant to informed ought to be reflected in a reduction in racial discrimination.

Early on, it was the study of racial relations that cast some doubt on the attitude–behavior link. LaPiere (1934) showed that owners of hotels stated in writing that they would *not* accommodate an Asian couple if one should arrive, even after LaPiere had visited the hotels with such a couple only a few weeks earlier. Kutner, Wilkins, and Yarrow (1952) had similar results with a black couple in New York City restaurants. While this discontinuity has been thoroughly analyzed by social psychologists because of its implication for the theoretical aspects of the attitude–behavior link (Wicker, 1969), it has a different significance for racial relations.

Specifically, the question arises as to whether we can detect "true" attitudes of whites on the basis of their verbal behaviors. In the 1930s, it was not unacceptable to express antiblack attitudes publically. However, over time, as the attitudes on race have changed and public sentiments have been altered, it is less acceptable to make such an attitude statement publicly. Thus, we have the question of the extent to which racial attitudes have in fact changed in a positive direction.

Survey data clearly suggest they have but a series of experimental studies raises questions as to the extent to which these survey data capture the true feelings of whites. For example, Sigall and Page (1971) developed the "bogus pipeline" to get at racial attitudes. Under the premise that a complicated procedure was able to detect "true" feelings, whites expressed systematically more negative attitudes toward blacks when they thought they were being monitored by the bogus pipeline than when they were not. Reviewing a series of studies using unobtrusive measuring techniques (e.g., helping a stranded motorist, picking up a dropped bag of groceries, or showing a student around campus), Crosby, Bromley, and Saxe (1980) illustrated that whites showed systematic behavioral preferences for other whites over blacks in a variety of everyday social situations (see also work on aversive racism by Gaertner & Dovidio, 1986).

More recently, more refined measures of attitude have been derived from reaction times. For example, Gaertner and McLaughlin (1983) showed that white subjects gave quicker responses in a lexical decision task when the word "white" was paired with positive traits, than when the word "black" was paired with positive traits. No differences were obtained when "white" and "black" were paired with negative words. In a similar vein, Dovidio, Evans, and Tyler (1986) found that white subjects performed lexical decision tasks most quickly when primed by the word "white" and judging positive traits stereotypic of whites (e.g., ambitious). They responded most slowly when a white prime was associated with a negative black stereotype (e.g., lazy). When the word "black" was primed white subjects responded fastest to positive black stereotypes (e.g., sensitive). These findings suggest that whites do carry a stereotype of both blacks and whites, that the positive content of white stereotypes is more salient, and that for both groups, the content of the stereotype affects the processing of relevant social information.

More recently, Devine and her colleagues (Devine, 1989; Devine, Monteith, Zuwerink, & Elliot, 1991) have studied the role of automatic processes in expressions of prejudice. It is often argued that racial prejudice is inevitable because social categorization on the basis of race is such a natural human phenomenon and stereotyping seems to automatically follow this categorization process. The loop is closed when stereotyping is linked inexorably to expressions of prejudice. Devine challenges this view by suggesting that a person can exert personal control over the conscious expression of prejudicial beliefs or reactions, *even when they are aware of the negative content of stereotypes*. Devine argues that stereotypes and personal beliefs are conceptually distinct cognitive structures, and while the first may come under the influence of relatively automatic processes conditioned by cultural socialization, the latter are subject to personal cognitive and evaluative control. That is, people can *decide* that they do not want to and will not allow themselves to be prejudiced. This personal belief characterizes a low-prejudice person and is contrasted by a continuing commitment to racially biased social judgments.

This model leads Devine to predict and find empirical support showing that high- and low-prejudiced persons are equally knowledgeable about culturally based racial stereotypes and are both likely to produce stereotypical evaluations of an ambiguous behavior when the stereotypes are primed at an automatic level. However, when features of a racial stereotype are made salient, a nonprejudiced person, unlike a prejudiced person, will reject the stereotype and express his or her nonprejudiced personal belief.

This study separates out the knowledge and operation of cultural racial stereotypes and the ability of some people to develop personal beliefs that counteract their negative effects.

A second study by Devine et al. (1991) demonstrates the real active mental dynamic of confronting racial prejudice when she introduces the notion of "compunction" to her analysis. It is argued that people distinguish between what they *should* do and what they *would* do in certain interracial situations. In such racial situations, when a should–would discrepancy exists, people feel compunction about their behavior. Devine and colleagues found that when the should–would discrepancy was large for subjects who scored *low* on a measure of modern racism (McConahay, Hardee, & Batts, 1981), feelings of self-criticism and guilt were high. No such psychological reaction was obtained from high scorers on the racism scale who were exposed to such should–would discrepancies. The emotional conflict arises for these people who reject racism when they embrace values of fairness but, nevertheless, find themselves behaving in ways that seem to contradict these well-placed intentions.

Devine urges that although people may genuinely reject race-prejudicial ideology, nevertheless, they may respond automatically in prejudicial ways because of preadult socialization to stereotypical beliefs. The fact that one experiences emotional reactions when a desired positive course of action is thwarted by highly socialized negative responses leads Devine to propose that the pessimistic inevitability of racial prejudice, and the suggestion that it has changed far less than popular belief maintains, (cf. Gaertner & Dovidio, 1986) may well be overstated. According to Devine, these pessimistic views of racial relations fail to consider the real struggles that are being undertaken by many white Americans to overcome the habit of prejudice.

Greenwald (1990) makes similar points about the automatic components of prejudice and offers three propositions that describe their consequences:

Proposition 1: Unconscious prejudices may be much more uniformly shared in most human populations than are conscious prejudices. The work reviewed above would support this conclusion.

Proposition 2: The effects of prejudice can be reduced by focusing an evaluator's conscious attention on the prejudice-eliciting attribute. That is, by focusing attention on racial attributes of target persons, unconscious processes are made conscious and automatic biases can be defended against.

Proposition 3: Economically, socially, and politically significant manifestations of prejudices are expected to occur in the behavior of persons who, at a conscious level, disavow prejudice. One of the most intriguing implications of this proposition, according to Greenwald, is that explicit regulations associated with affirmative action are necessary because unconscious processes will perpetuate discrimination by those in hiring positions.

Finally, McConahay, Kinder, Sears, and colleagues have looked at another form of subtle bias as expressed by the concept of "symbolic racism" (McConahay & Hough, 1976; Kinder & Sears, 1981; Sears, 1988). Symbolic racism is contrasted with "old-fashioned racism" by the symbolic nature of the content of racial attitudes or beliefs. It is a blend of antiblack sentiment and pro-American values reflected in the principles of individualism and the work ethic canons of the Protestant ethic. It is further represented symbolically by "the expression in terms of abstract, ideological symbols and symbolic behaviors of the feeling that blacks are violating cherished values or making illegitimate demands for changes in the status quo" (McConahay & Hough, 1976, p. 38). Like Devine's analysis, symbolic racism is rooted in preadult socialization to cultural values that include antipathy toward black Americans. The crux of the symbolic racism analysis, though, is its negative behavioral consequences (e.g., opposition to busing [Sears & Allen, 1984], to black political candidates [Kinder & Sears, 1981], to bilingual education [Sears & Hoddy, in press]), which are not directly traceable to *real* racial threats and subsequent self-interested reactions. Rather, generalized and moralistic resentments toward blacks offer a more powerful explanation for racial prejudice.[2]

Recent tests of symbolic racism theory (Sears & Kosterman, 1991) offer strong support for the specific *additive* combination of antiblack sentiment and attitudes of *inegalitarianism*. The antiblack sentiment surfaces in automatic negative affect and attaches to inegalitarian values. Although Sears and Kosterman do not say this directly, it is likely that the obverse of inegalitarianism is equity, defined as the proportionality of outcomes to inputs. Thus antiblack sentiment is based on the notion that black inputs are less than white inputs and, *therefore*, provide a legitimate basis for lower outcomes. Sociopolitical efforts to equalize outcomes as a function of race, then, violate the equity principle.

Sears and Kosterman (1991) find that when measures of symbolic racism combine antiblack sentiment with inegalitarian beliefs (e.g., "whites are better at running things than blacks are and should be allowed to do so"), maximum race–bias effects are obtained. Moreover, antiblack affect, *not* pro-white affect, was a key component of opposition to race-based policies and programs.

Katz (1981) has similarly offered a values-conflict model of racial behavior. He suggests that a conflict may exist within a person between traditional values embodied in the Protestant ethic and more liberal, well-meaning values of humanitarianism and egalitarianism. Katz and Hass (1988) showed that antiblack sentiment could be manipulated by priming the salience of either Protestant-ethic values (increasing the negative sentiment) or humanitarian values (decreasing negative sentiment). This confirms the value ambivalence proposed by Katz and the predicted variability of white responses in certain racial contexts.

Summary

Whether attitudes accurately predict behaviors is a subject of theoretical and empirical importance for social psychology. It is additionally of practical importance when racial effects are considered. Evidence for the discontinuity of attitudes and behaviors raises serious questions about the level of racial bias in this society. Social psychological research has become increasingly sophisticated in its ability to detect subtle forms of bias through unobtrusive observations (Crosby, Bromley, & Saxe, 1980), reaction times to cognitive tasks (Gaertner & McLaughlin, 1983; Dovidio, Evans, & Tyler, 1986; Devine, 1989), and political behaviors (Kinder & Sears, 1981; Sears & Hoddy, in press).

The importance of accurately detecting "true" racial feelings and demonstrating their relationship to social behavior has implications for the mental health of whites as shown by the guilt and self-critical judgments made by whites when confronted by the contradiction between their feelings of what they should and would do in interracial situations. Moreover, for blacks and other victims of bias, the evidence for continued forms of subtle racial bias confirms strongly held feelings and experiences with race-based disadvantage. The demonstrated discontinuity of attitudes and behaviors provides a legitimate basis for mistrust of whites. The linkage of many of these biased perceptions and behaviors to fundamental societal values (e.g., McConahay, & Hough, 1976; Katz, 1981) even further complicates the problem because it embeds the conflict in values about which it is more difficult to argue the culpability of individual perceptions.

EFFECTS OF INTERRACIAL INTERACTION
ON BEHAVIOR

In considering ways to ameliorate racial antipathies, Allport (1954) noted that "[t]he assumption underlying various participation and action programs is that contact and acquaintance make for friendliness. . . . [W]e know that this is not always the case. Contact in a hierarchical social system, or between people who equally lack status . . . or contacts between individuals who perceive one another as threats, are harmful rather than helpful" (p. 488). Specifying the conditions under which racial contact could be expected to produce an improvement in racial relations was outlined in what has become known as "the contact hypothesis." The basic premises of this hypothesis are as follows:

1. Contact should be of equal status groups.
2. Attributes of the disliked groups must disconfirm the prevailing stereotyped beliefs about them.
3. Contact must create or encourage an interdependence among groups.
4. Contact must promote individual acquaintance as opposed to group-based perceptions.
5. Social norms must favor group equality.

Much research has been conducted over the past 40 years to determine whether, when the conditions for equal status, interracial contact are met, amelioration of interracial attitudes and behaviors takes place. The evidence is generally positive when such conditions are met. However, the most difficult aspect of this research is obtaining real-world situations in which this is the case (Amir, 1969; Miller & Brewer, 1984).

Interracial interaction takes place at two levels—individual and group. At the individual level, the interacting parties are influenced by personal characteristics, styles, values, and goals and any history of interaction between them. At the group level, their interaction is influenced primarily by their conception of the other's group status as well as their own. The attitudes, beliefs, understandings, and identifications each has with his or her own group, and perceptions of the similar aspects of the other group, may enter the situation such that an interpersonal interaction may actually be, at a symbolic level, an intergroup interaction.

Research in this area has tended to emphasize two basic mechanisms: social identity and social comparison (Miller & Brewer, 1984). The main lines of reasoning suggest that intergroup conflict is part of a general process of social categorization in which there is a tendency (1) to categorize people into groups; (2) to accentuate the differences between members of one's own group and those of another; (3) to accentuate the similarities among members of one's own group; (4) to evaluate the characteristics of members of one's group more positively; and (5) to derive positive social identities from group membership (Tajfel, 1982; Turner, 1985; Abrams & Hogg, 1990).

When racial conflict exists at the group level, all of the perceptual dynamics described earlier (e.g., stereotyping, illusory correlation, automatic processing of socialized antipathies) become operative at the individual interaction level. When one's social identity is salient, it affects one's responses, leading him or her to react to others on the basis of their corresponding group membership and not their personal characteristics. As a result, we know that social identity is linked to in- and outgroup distinctions, that outgroup members are undifferentiated in their social characteristics relative to ingroup members (Park & Rothbart, 1982), and the relative lack of complexity with which outgroup members are perceived leads to more extreme judgments of them (Linville & Jones, 1980). Since race is a heavily evaluated social category, it would be expected that social identity processes would increase the use of category-based judgments in interpersonal interactions. The warning by Allport noted above is given empirical credence in numerous studies (Crosby et al., 1980; Jones, 1991b).

The critical task for social identity theorists is to find a way to reduce the utilization of category-based information in contexts where group identities are characterized by convergent boundaries (those in which multiple cues—racial, political, economic—determine group identities) (Brewer & Campbell, 1976). Under these circumstances, the multiple cues that elicit group identification magnify the likelihood that group-based categorical information will be invoked. Miller and Brewer (1984) suggest that this decategorization process involves moving from a pure category-based interaction, in which interactants are completely circumscribed by their respective social categorical groupings, to differentiation, where the self is distinguished somewhat from other members of the ingroup and the other is distinguished from other members of the outgroup, to personalization, in which interactants ignore group boundaries and employ only personal information that is category independent. Miller and Brewer go on to suggest that the decategorization processes will be most successful when (1) an interpersonal rather than task orientation is promoted; and (2) roles, assignments, subgroup composition, and social functions are assigned in a category-independent way. Programmatic research supports these strategies for reducing the operation of category-based judgments in interracial settings (e.g., Miller, Brewer, & Edwards, 1985).

While most theorists propose differentiation processes as a means of blurring group boundaries and thus reducing the utilization of categorical information, Gaertner et al. (Gaertner, Mann, Murrell, & Dovidio, 1989; Gaertner, Mann, Dovido, Murrell, & Pomare, 1990) offer a re-categorization strategy instead of the generally used de-categorization processes. The aim of the re-categorization strategy is to eliminate the former group boundaries and replace them either with a single inclusive boundary (i.e., a single superordinate group identity to which formerly separate group members now adhere—for example, two school districts are forced to merge into one with a corresponding merger of formerly separate parent–teacher's associations) or no group boundary at all (i.e., a simple collection of n individuals.) Intergroup bias is expected to be reduced by either of these re-categorization processes.

Gaertner et al. (1989) found strong empirical support for the effects of both of these re-categorization mechanisms. Specifically, superordinate re-categorization reduced bias by making former outgroup members more attractive. Re-categorized individuation reduced bias by making former ingroup members less attractive. Consistent with the work of Sherif (1966), the superordinate re-categorization had a stronger overall bias-reduction effect. The finding for the increased attractiveness of former outgroup members was given further support in a follow-up study (Gaertner et al., 1990). This re-categorization approach offers a potentially effective strategy by which interracial contact can, under the right conditions, reduce racial conflict and promote racial harmony. Of course, as with the contact hypothesis, creating conditions in which two groups can come together in this intuitively favorable way requires specifying the conditions under which it will happen. As of now, that has not been done, but continuing research development will be very important to follow.

The contact hypothesis has been given its greatest test in the context of school desegregation. The presumed linkage of racially integrated schooling, academic achievement, and interpersonal relationships has found mixed results. One of the strongest findings is the relationship of cooperative, interdependent learning structures on relationships and performance. Aronson and colleagues (Aronson et al., 1978; Aronson & Thibodeau, in press) label one such approach the "jigsaw classroom." In this setting, individual members of six-person groups learn some of the facts necessary to solve a problem. They then come together with other group members and teach them their knowledge so that the overall group performance is maximized. Aronson and colleagues propose three mechanisms that mediate the positive effects of such interdependent learning environments; empathic role taking, attributions for success and failure, and a closer link between self-esteem and academic performance. An impressive amount of data has been accumulating to support the idea that when cooperative rather than competitive learning strategies are adopted and valued, performance is high, self-esteem is high, and intergroup relationships are more positive.

Summary

For many theorists, prejudice is linked to racial antipathies based on ignorance. Racial segregation has long been viewed as the primary culprit for such ignorance. However, the empirical literature is mixed on the effects of desegregation. The caveats contained in the contact hypothesis continue to be instructive. As long as ours is a hierarchical social structure defined in part by race, and/or as long as racial competition continues to be a salient dimension of interracial interaction, it is likely that the effects of interracial interaction will vary from positive to negative. What the approaches reviewed above all suggest is that reducing the category-based (racially motivated) perception of individuals is one way to reduce the hierarchial and competitive judgments that undergird the conflict we seek to reduce.

The de-categorization approach emphasizes individualism and seeks to systematically remove all vestiges of group-based identifying information. As we have implied, when group identities are based on convergent boundaries, this task is difficult indeed. Alternative re-categorization approaches continue to recognize group boundaries and only attempt an *inclusive* instead of an *exclusive* strategy for promoting boundary salience. There may be something more practical in accepting the inevitability of group categorization, but the benign way in which laboratory studies produce positive reframing of social judgments may not withstand the deeper-seated animosities of real-life group conflict.

Perhaps the bottom line here is that the approaches described above seem to follow from the majority as perpetrator perspective. That is, the aim of these strategies is to reduce group boundaries because they have been symptomatic of the bias we seek to eliminate. However, from the vantage of the stigmatized, group boundaries define a layer of protection if not entitlement that is not easily shed. When considering the perspective of blacks, then, strategies for reducing white bias may run directly counter to those employed by blacks as adaptations to stigmatization. We turn next to consideration of these possibilities.

PSYCHOLOGICAL ADAPTATIONS TO RACIAL BIAS IN BLACKS

The preceding discussion has focused on sources of bias in the perceptions and behaviors of whites toward blacks. The problem of race has largely been pursued both theoretically and empirically in these terms. However, there is a connectedness between the races with regard to the perceptual and behavioral mechanisms described. The characteristics, behaviors, and intentions of blacks provide the "data" for the social psychological processes described above. Just as important, the perceptions, behaviors, and intentions of whites provide the data for black reactions.

The reactions of blacks to prejudice and racism have also held an important place in social psychological research. The psychological consequences of racial bias was the focus of the research of the Clarks (Clark & Clark, 1947). This and other work helped drive the legal policy of racial integration enunciated in *Brown v. Board of Education* (1954) and its social policy enactment, busing.

While there are many different aspects to black reactions to racial bias, the question of how an individual black child could develop positive self-regard and wholesome self-esteem in the face of societal denigration became the dominant issue for social psychological analysis. Kardiner and Ovesy (1951) painted a bleak picture:

> The Negro, in contrast to the white, is a more unhappy person; he has a harder environment to live in, and the internal stress is greater. By "unhappy" we mean he enjoys less, he suffers more. There is not one

personality trait of the Negro the source of which cannot be traced to his difficult living conditions. *There are no exceptions to this rule.* The final result is a wretched internal life. (p. 81, emphasis added)

The approaches to understanding the psychological consequences of race-based discrimination have had two foci: first is an attempt to understand the dynamics of racial identity and self-esteem; the second is an effort to demonstrate the psychological mechanisms that confer positive identity and esteem in the face of group-based stigmatization. We will consider the work in each of these areas in turn.

Effects of Racial Bias on Identity and Self-Esteem of Blacks

Racial identity is socially constructed in a societal context of race-based discrimination, bias, and stigmatization. How children psychologically construct positive personal identities that include aspects of the stigmatized racial identities has been a focus of several decades of research (Clark & Clark, 1947; Kardiner & Ovesy, 1951; Banks, 1976; Cross, 1991; Burlew & Smith, 1991). The mechanisms by which racial identity is constructed include choice of characteristic labels and transitions through stages of identity, each of which is characterized by the content of self and group labels and their behavioral consequences. Understanding how choices of evaluative and identifying labels occur and what motivates movement through identity stages has been a major research focus.

Clark and Clark's (1947) classic study raised the question of how soon a black child develops awareness of his or her racial identity, and once developed, whether interpersonal preferences followed racial in- or outgroup patterns. Using the doll-choice technique modified from procedures developed by Hartley and Hartley in 1939 (cf. Cross, 1991), the Clarks found that black children had accurate identification by age 5 (85% selected the colored doll in response to the question, "Show me the doll that looks like you"). However, their racial preference suggested less than positive racial acceptance (45% selected the colored doll in response to the question, "Show me the doll that is nice"; 34% chose the colored doll in response to the question, "Show me the doll you want to play with"). This negative relationship between racial identity and preference was extended to suggest a negative relationship between self-esteem and racial identification.

This proposed self-esteem, racial identification relationship has been interpreted to suggest that societal stigmatization of the racial group is internalized as "self-hatred" in black children, leading to lowered personal esteem. While the doll technique continues to be used (Powell-Hopson & Hopson, 1988), significant critiques of this methodology suggest not only that the paradigm may be flawed, but that the conceptual link between group identification and negative personal esteem has neither empirical nor conceptual foundation (Banks, 1976; Cross, 1991).

The research question has focused on the mechanisms by which racial identity is formed in a confusing and conflict-filled racial environment. The bulk of the work has sought to measure the content of identity, based on sociopolitical assumptions of intergroup conflict (Baldwin & Bell, 1985; Cross, 1979; Thomas, 1971; Taylor, 1973; Millones, 1980). For example, Cross (1979) proposed a four-stage model in which a negative racial identity is "shocked" by an encounter that drives the person to see the racial aspects of self differently. The preencounter self gives way to a new immersion in racial experience, unconditionally positive and uplifting. Over time, conditions are established that moderate the racial immersion and lead to a more balanced identity that integrates the pre- and postencounter attitudes into an internalized bicultural identity. Several researchers have elaborated this model by developing measurement instruments with good psychometric properties and validating them against behavioral and other conceptually relevant constructs (Helms, 1990; Parham, 1989; Ponteretto & Wise, 1987).

There has been a broad-based attempt to measure the content of racial identity in blacks, but less attention has been paid to basic mechanisms by which alternative paths to identity are followed and different stages of development are achieved. Burlew and Smith (1991) propose a multidimensional approach to measuring racial identity, which includes measures of (1) developmental processes; (2) Afrocentric characteristics; (3) group-based preferences and identifications; and (4) internalization of racial stereotypes. It is clear that the dynamic of racial bias introduces complicated psychological demands on the emergent sense of self of black children. The behavioral consequences of these processes become increasingly important as these children get older. We will return to some of the dynamics of these processes when we consider stigmatization effects on positive identity development.

The central question of racial identity takes on a sociopolitical meaning for the individual (Jones, 1991a). Black identity and cultural involvement often conflict with a global, nonracial identity and mainstream inclusion.[3] The assimilationist perspective of the melting-pot approach seems to force one to choose the inclusionary option against the distinctiveness option (cf. Brewer, 1991). This "choice" becomes political when the group well-being is framed in terms of black and white, and the assimilationist choice is viewed as part of the problem, *not* part of the solution (cf. Cleaver, 1968).

The goal of an identity that is balanced between individual and group aspects, assimilation, and distinctiveness needs across time defines the bicultural identity model (Cross, 1991; Jones, 1991a). The mechanisms by which one achieves this balance, the behavioral consequences, and the social contexts that affect its developmental course remain to be determined.

Positive Identity Consequences of Group-Based Stigmatization

One of the ongoing assumptions about the relationship of self-esteem to racial stigmatization is the negative association between them. Racial stigma carries, in this view, a tendency toward self-deprecation or lowered self-esteem (Kardiner & Ovesy, 1951; Clark & Clark, 1947; Pettigrew, 1964). However, the data do not consistently support this linkage of self-esteem and racial stigma (cf. Cross, 1991). How do members of stigmatized social groups develop and maintain positive self-esteem? Crocker and Major (1989) propose three specific ways that the esteem of members of a stigmatized group can be "protected" from the undermining influences of racial stigma:

Attribute negative feedback to prejudices against their group. The causes of negative feedback in the form of poor performance, denial of an opportunity, or hostile behavior can be attributed to internal (ability, qualifications, character, specific behaviors) or external (situational factors or aspects of an evaluative or behaving other) factors. Opting for external attributions for negative feedback that is category based, removes all logical implication of the feedback for personal attributes. Empirical support for this idea is found in Crocker, Voelkl, Cornwell, and Major (1989), who found that negative feedback lowered the self-esteem of black subjects when they thought the evaluator was not aware of their race. When they thought the evaluator was aware of their race, self-esteem measures were unaffected by the negative evaluations.

Crocker et al. offer a *discounting* explanation for such effects (cf. Major & Crocker, in press), suggesting that perceptions of prejudice and racism in whites allow blacks to discount the validity of negative feedback from them, thus minimizing the impact of that unfavorable evaluation.

Compare their outcomes with those of the ingroup instead of those of the outgroup. Major and Crocker propose that ingroup social comparison reduces the likelihood of unfavorable social comparisons with more advantaged outgroup members. They specifically suggest three reasons for this tendency: (1) a proximity effect (blacks compare with others with whom they share social environments); (2) a similarity effect (comparisons with similar others increases accuracy of self-evaluations); and (3) a self-protective effect (avoidance of painful or unpleasant social comparisons). While these ingroup comparison tendencies are not peculiar to any specific group, they may be more compelling for racially stigmatized groups because of the high probability of unfavorable outgroup comparisons.

Selectively devalue those dimensions on which the group fares poorly while valuing those on which the group fares well. The impact of a given evaluative judgment on self-esteem will depend in large measure on the degree of centrality it holds in the structure of the self-concept. This proposition suggests that one can maintain positive self-regard by selectively valuing (making central to the self) those attributes or abilities about which relatively favorable feedback is anticipated. Whereas the previous two mechanisms may be seen as self-esteem protective, selective valuation could be seen as a more proactive esteem-enhancing mechanism. Centralizing favorable domains of evaluation will necessarily increase the likelihood of positive evaluative feedback.

One of the core features of social identity theory (SIT) is the postulate that ingroup preference or positive social identity occurs as a result of favorable in- versus outgroup comparisons (Tajfel & Turner, 1979). Explaining how this operates with members of stigmatized groups poses problems similar to those addressed by Crocker and Major (1989). In Tajfel and Turner's analysis, there are also three ways in which positive value can be derived.

Social Mobility

Members of the stigmatized group can move to the dominant group. This option is clearly limited in its ability to provide broad-based esteem to members of stigmatized groups when the basis of their group membership, race, cannot be altered.

Social Competition

Another option is to mount a direct attack on the social position of the outgroup. Again, certain reality principles may make such an option of limited utility, but in individual cases, strategies of physical attack, boycotts, and the like can serve to enhance the relative status of stigmatized ingroups.

Social Creativity

The most complex and perhaps effective means of maintaining a positive social identity involves social perceptual processes similar to those proposed by Crocker and Major. These involve:

1. *Adopting new comparison dimensions on which the ingroup is superior to the outgroup.* This is similar to the "selective valuation" strategy proposed by Crocker and Major and offers an increased likelihood of favorable social comparison with outgroup members.

2. *Changing the values of existing dimensions.* This strategy would follow from a heightened sense of ethnic or cultural identity in which one could place positive value on attributes that have commonly held lower value. For example, internal locus of control is generally associated with positive characteristics and external locus of control with less favorable ones. Redefining the value of locus of control would serve to create positive identity where a negative characteristic once stood.

3. *Adopting a new lower-status comparison group.* This downward comparison strategy has been shown to have very effective self-esteem protection capacities when dealing with a variety of unfavorable circumstances including health, threatening events such as earthquakes (Taylor, 1983), and other esteem-threatening circumstances (Wills, 1981).

It is fairly clear that the Tajfel and Turner analysis shares similar features with the Crocker and Major account. This is particularly true with the social creativity mechanism. However, the Tajfel and Turner model seems to provide more active, aggressive, and broad-based mechanisms for cognitive reappraisal designed to promote positive social identity and self-esteem. Whereas the Crocker and major analysis emphasizes the protective aspects of esteem maintenance that minimize psychological damage, the Turner analysis focuses more on the creation of positive esteem. A related approach proposed by Deaux (Chapter 10) in this volume suggests that redefining the self is an option that ultimately serves a self-protective function.

Another approach has been proposed by Steele based on his self-affirmation theory (1988, 1992). According to self-affirmation theory, when an important self-concept is threatened, an individual's primary self-defensive goal is to affirm the integrity of the self, not necessarily to resolve the particular threat. As a result, adaptation to a specific self-threat is subsumed by more general motivations to either affirm a broader self-concept or a different but equally important aspect of the self-concept.

Steele applies this reasoning to an analysis of persistent academic underachievement of blacks on predominantly white college campuses (Steele, 1992). Steele argues that when faced with persistent and expected devaluation in the academic arena, the resultant expected self-concept vulnerability leads blacks to "disidentify" with the academic domain of self, substituting either more global self-referents or equally important alternative domains (say, sports, social activism, etc.). By disidentifying with academic performance domains, one can avoid the self-concept implications of underperformance by self in other arenas. These self-affirming alternatives allow one to maintain positive identity in the face of expected vulnerabilities in an important self domain. Disidentification insulates one from the ego threat of racial bias in academic life.

There is good news and bad news from these analyses. The good news is that in spite of continued widespread racial bias in our society, as detailed earlier in this chapter, victims of stigmatizing bias can and do maintain positive identities and self-esteem. The bad news is that the result of these social–cognitive strategies may often be underperformance in important domains in which such bias takes place. If this is true, the pernicious effect of psychological adaptation to discriminatory circumstances is a self-fulfilling perpetuation of the attitudes and beliefs of the majority population that "justify" bias (for those who accept the bias) and automate biased reactions in those who seek more egalitarian personal beliefs.

Summary

These dynamics are profoundly important as we continue to try to understand the mental health consequences of race. Since race is a

social category that is relatively immutable but socially significant, some of the options may not be available. Moreover, the
cultural and political context surrounding race may well over-
determine the options that are likely to be used. Racial or group
identities, long defined as a part of the problem of intergroup
conflict, are now, for minority group members, playing an important role in their efforts to achieve political parity. In a time when
many people feel that finding common ground is crucial to the
amelioration of intergroup conflict, there is a growing body of
evidence that social identities are acquiring political currency (cf.
S. Steele, 1990) that makes such efforts increasingly difficult. In
the balance hangs the daily mental health prospects of members of
all groups. Physical and psychological conflict, aggression, and
hatred compromise the mental health of all parties involved. The
basic social psychological knowledge that we bring to bear on
these important processes is one of the most important tools we
have to combat the perpetuation of racial animosity and ill will.

CONCLUSION

Race is a complex phenomenon in our society. Its complexity is
based on numerous factors, including (1) its historical meaning
and circumstances; (2) its uncertain biological basis; (3) its somewhat confusing link to culture; (4) its sociopolitical significance;
and (5) its far-ranging psychological meaning. Against this backdrop of complexity, social psychology has woven an empirical,
theoretical, and applied approach to this important subject that
necessarily has simplified the issues of race and helped to better
understand its manifestations. This heuristic strategy has paid off
well in many respects, as I hope the foregoing review and analysis
support. However, as we look ahead to continuing contributions of
social psychology, we must look at new possibilities, some of
which will necessarily confront the complexities alluded to above.

Conceptualizing Models and Focus of Analysis of Effects of Race

I believe racial research is importantly influenced by guiding
assumptions about the target or goal of the analysis and the appropriate level at which the analysis should take place. In reviewing
research on race in social psychology, one of the most striking
features of the work is its declining significance in the last decade

(cf. Jones, 1983; Graham, 1992). In attempting to account for this waning interest, I offered four possible explanations (Jones, 1983):

Race is a second class variable in social psychology. That is, employing race (biologically defined) as a variable (except as a stimulus property of other persons) generally fails to accommodate either of the twin canons of laboratory experimentation: random assignment of subjects to experimental conditions, and manipulation of the independent variables.

Race is perceived to be less of a social problem than it was. This may be less true now than it was perceived to be in the early 1980s. However, one of the reasons for this claim is not only the lowered importance of race as a social problem, but the heightened importance and focus on other social issues.

Race is confounded with ethnicity, culture, and social class. Although fundamentally biological in its basic meaning, race has *practical* importance because of its association with cultural and socioeconomic factors. However, failing to ascertain the specific elements of culture and class in the operation of racial effects, it is difficult to operate with precision.

Shift in analysis from a group to an individual focus. While the individual level of analysis enables racial research in social psychology to take on the best features of our empirical, scientific paradigm, it creates lacunae in our ability to understand the complexities of a sociocultural phenomenon that has core elements that are historical, geographical, and sociopolitical.

I have developed a simple organizing model that, I believe, may help us to understand where race research fits and which directions future research might profitably take. Table 7.1 offers a schematic view of the implications of these distinctions.

Target of Analysis

By target of analysis, I mean what drives social psychology's concern with race—why is race an important variable for analysis? I propose two motivating reasons: race is a social problem and understanding differences associated with race aids in forming a broader picture of human diversity.

Race as a Social Problem. This has been the dominant focus as is clearly suggested by the preceding review. Racial bigotry and

TABLE 7.1 Levels and Targets of Analysis of Racial Effects on Behavior

Level of analysis	Target of analysis	
	Social problem	Human diversity
Reactionary model	1. Prejudice 2. Negative reactions to bias 3. Culture of poverty	1. Coping/resilience 2. Biculturalism 3. Models of triumphant person
Evolutionary model	1. Cultural disadvantage	1. Racial/ethnic versions of human capability 2. Cultural achievement 3. TRIOS

hostility are certainly issues for this society that can be framed in social problem terms: whites are biased, discriminatory, and stigmatizing; blacks and other stigmatized groups suffer from the bias. The social-problem approach to race typically focuses on the agents of stigma, seeking to understand the source of racial antipathies, to illustrate ways in which it is manifested in the psychological or behavioral character and ways in which racial bias can be ameliorated. The foregoing review shows how successfully social psychology has identified the mechanisms that seem to foster this sort of perception and concomitant behavior.

The other side of the coin concerns the consequences of stigma for the stigmatized. Generally, lowered self-esteem, heightened hostility, distrust, and behavioral and psychological problems are associated with racial stigma. This too is a social problem in that significant segments of society are not equal in the pursuit of life, liberty, and happiness. It is important to note, however, that whether one is concerned with the agents or the objects of bias, the outcome of the analysis will be a focus on deficiency of character, capability, or compassion. That is, the social-problem approach is, by and large, a focus on the deficiencies of human character and capability.

Race Research Can Broaden Knowledge of Human Diversity. Race, from this perspective, presents an opportunity to broaden horizons, not simply a social problem to be solved. Much of the critique of racial research is its largely comparative nature, which seems always to be conducted against a normative backdrop of Anglo-European male standards. While this dominance is easily understandable from a sociology-of-knowledge perspective, questions are raised by the relative absence of cultural, ethnic, and racial analyses that, when they do occur, usually only serve as counterpoint to the dominant themes. If the aim or goal of our research is to form a comprehensive understanding of human behavior, then learning how people who are culturally different develop meaningful standards of conduct, overcome deprivation and resist discrimination, hone survival skills, and achieve psychological well-being would be significant to the broadest understandings. The social-problem approach limits the extent to which such human outcomes can be framed in positive terms. The human-diversity approach makes this enterprise its *raison d'être.*

Levels of Analysis

The level of our analysis is determined by where we look for psychological and behavioral processes or mechanisms that explain racial effects. I have proposed two levels at which social psychological analysis of race effects take place. At the reactionary level, racial effects are triggered by whites' reactions to blacks; and blacks reactions to oppression, hostility, and so forth. At the evolutionary level, racial effects are triggered by the evolutionary character and nature of the race group in question.

Reactionary Analyses of Race. Reactionary analyses start from the premise that what is important to know about racial groups is their reaction (1) to members of other racial groups and/or (2) to conditions of bias and deprivation in everyday life that follow from racial group membership. The study of racial prejudice, for example, has assumed that the sources of bias linked to intergroup conflict result largely from childhood socialization and the corresponding mental representations of racial groups implied by that socialization. This level of analysis, in the case of Afro-Americans, typically begins with the notion that what is important about black behavior can be derived from reactions and adaptations to circumstances associated with slavery, segregation, racism, stigmatization, and poverty. To fully understand the reactionary elements of racial effects, one must fully understand the stimulus properties from which they derive and the adaptations and responses to which they give rise. To some extent, the analysis becomes circular when the terms for understanding the reactions are defined by the properties of the stimulus to which the person is reacting. The psychological, behavioral, and cultural template through which adaptations are interpreted require another level of consideration, the evolutionary framework.

Evolutionary Analysis of Race. This level of analysis assumes that each racial group not only has developed its characteristic reaction and adaptation to bias, but utilizes its own unique cultural history in forming the characteristic patterns of reaction and social development. Evolutionary or developmental models seek to understand the unfolding of cultural patterns as an interplay of cultural tendencies and preferences and the demands of particular circumstances over time. The questions posed by an evolutionary analysis are necessarily more complex and difficult to answer than those framed by a simple reactionary analysis.

The research on race reviewed here can be placed predominantly in one cell—the reactionary–social problem cell. Some of the most successful analytical and practical outcomes of social psychological research on race come from understanding bases of prejudice and ways to ameliorate some of its most pernicious effects. As a further illustration, the culture-of-poverty approach is considered in this cell because it is predicated on the notion that being poor leads to certain characteristic forms of adaptation that undermine the ability of people to take advantage of real opportunities.

By contrast, the "cultural disadvantage" argument can be seen as a variant of the culture-of-poverty reasoning, or as a reflection of the belief that basic cultural styles are ill-suited to success in a modern industrial, information-age society. If one can show that certain patterns of social organization, cognitive processing, social perception, decision-making strategies follow from an evolution of cultural patterns and those patterns are negatively linked to social success, then those who have been socialized to them will be at a "cultural disadvantage." This thinking leads one to posit cultural disadvantage as an evolutionary–social Problem.

Moving around the table, one can also see that distinctive (i.e., evolutionary) cultural forms can also be linked to social success. Most salient in this regard is the observation that Asian-Americans seem to excel in academic endeavors due to motivating features of their cultural socialization. More difficult to understand, but no less significant, are the boundary conditions for certain individual manifestations of social tendencies. For example, although future time orientation and competitiveness are usually linked to success, cooperative, present-time orientations are in some instances associated with higher levels of adaptation and achievement. Rather than focusing on the social-problem consequences of failing to maintain a future time perspective, the evolutionary–human diversity approach offers the challenge of discerning how each basic orientation can have positive *and* negative manifestations. The analytical task is to determine the boundary conditions for positive or negative consequences of each.

Finally, we can see that reactions to adversity in the form of stigma and bias are not necessarily a "mark of oppression," as Kardiner and Ovesy (1951) postulated. Rather, adaptations to adversity can be defeating or triumphant. Although social psychological analysis has tended to focus on the reactionary–social Problem approach, there is encouraging evidence that this analysis is expanding to include more of the reactionary–human diversity perspective. The work of Steele and Major and Crocker employs basic social psychological mechanisms of self-affirmation and attributional styles to explain how persistent negative bias may not inevitably lead to self-devaluation. Devine, too, argues that the pessimism of the social-problem approach should be moderated to acknowledge that people can and do adopt personal beliefs that are not prejudiced, even if their fundamental socialization in a racist society makes it extremely difficult for them to overcome automatic reactions to racial stimuli.

It is also encouraging to see how research by members of stigmatized groups are forging a conception of personal identity and development that is not limited to a melting-pot, central-tendency approach to self. Rather, the emergence of "biculturalism" to explain how one adapts to the duality of individualism and group identity promises to broaden our understanding of how similarities and differences can both have positive motivational characteristics (cf. Cross, 1991; Helms, 1990; LaFromboise & Rowe, 1983; Ramirez, 1983; Suinn et al., 1987). Brewer's (1991) optimal distinctiveness theory is an explicit step toward severing the conceptual exclusivity of self and group motivational dynamics. Resilience, hardiness, and coping are increasingly analyzed in the literature on stresses of varying kinds, including those precipitated by racial bias.

To sum up, we have successfully employed a social problem-driven analysis of reactions to racial factors over the past decades of research in social psychology. Our basic mechanisms have been employed effectively and practical interventions have proven successful. There is growing evidence that this reactionary approach is being successfully expanded to look more broadly at human diversity as a primary analytical goal. Lagging behind is recognition of the contributions of defining cultural characteristics that have evolved over time and thus have basic influences on the modes of performance, perception, and behavior that our analysis of racial effects must understand.

In the decade ahead, it is my personal belief that the evolutionary–human diversity cell should attract the most new attention. I have placed the TRIOS model in this cell as one representative of this approach. TRIOS is an acronym standing for five dimensions of human experience: time, rhythm, improvisation, oral expression, and spirituality. The concepts emerged from an analysis of racial differences in sports performance (Jones & Hochner, 1973), African religion and philosophy (Jones, 1972; Mbiti, 1970), Trinidadian culture (Jones & Liverpool, 1976), and psychotherapy with black clients (Jones & Block, 1984).

These five dimensions reflect basic ways in which individuals and cultures orient themselves to living. They refer to how we experience and organize life, make decisions, arrive at beliefs, and derive meaning. TRIOS is important because on these dimensions of human experience, we will find divergences between the Euro-American and African-American perspective. The culture in which we live has evolved from the Euro-American perspective, but both have interacted and necessarily share in the fabric of contemporary culture. The matter is in part one of emphasis and preference.

Central Processes, Applications, and Future Directions

Social psychological mechanisms have proven quite effective in accounting for basic linkages between antecedent conditions and mental health outcomes. The social-problem focus of these analyses is consistent with the disease approach to mental health. As a society, we seem to better understand solving social problems and eradicating disease than capitalizing on human diversity and promoting health. A basic question remains: Will the basic mechanisms of comparison to standards, consistency, information seeking and processing, social influence, and attachment/cohesion that work so well in explaining prejudice, stereotyping, threats to esteem, and identity also work well in a somewhat different framework?

One manifestation of a different framework comes from

observing how prejudice and discrimination work when race is not the most salient stigmatizing status. A black newspaper columnist recently wrote about his experiences with discrimination in Japan (Williams, 1992). What was significant about his account was that race seemed to matter in some ways but not in others. Being "foreign" mattered more in most respects, and while white and black Americans differed on race, they did not on their "American-ness." Many white Americans learned a great deal about "stigma" and vowed that it changed their perspective on racial relations in the United States. They professed to greater empathy with blacks in America.

It should not be necessary to go to Japan to discover similarities that transcend race. We will be able to identify those social psychological mechanisms that motivate perceptions of similarities across racial boundaries but also accept differences across those same boundaries as an expansion of human capacities. The social utility of the values of tolerance and compassion, the positive implications of diversity and distinctiveness, and the best way to conceive of cooperative versus competitive processes in interpersonal and/or intergroup dynamics all remain challenges for social psychological analysis. We have briefly surveyed the accomplishments of social psychology in understanding some of the major social problems associated with race in this country. The coming decades will challenge us further to show the unique blend of theory, methodology, levels of analysis, and social applications of social psychology and to continue to provide leadership in addressing issues of race in America.

NOTES

1. McDougall (1921) defines providence as one who is "so constituted as to find some satisfaction in possession; that is to say, there must be in him an impulse to save or hoard which finds satisfaction in the act of hoarding, an impulse which prompts him to postpone enjoyment of the pleasure of immediate use to the satisfaction of possession" (pp. 121–122).

2. However, Bobo (1983; 1988) challenges the symbolic racism view that opposition to race-based programs is not reflective of self-interested defense. He argues that the values themselves are the basis of white well-being, so even when there is not a locally identifiable self-interest (e.g., a symbolic racist who opposes busing but has no children in the school system), whites gain from upholding the values that confer racial privilege. Andrew Hacker (1982) has gone even further in delineating the "white privilege" argument.

3. This conflict was illustrated in the 1984 presidential primary election when NBC's Marvin Kalb questioned Jesse Jackson on *Meet the Press:* "[A]re you a black man who happens to be an American running for the presidency, or are you an American who happens to be a black man running for the presidency?" (Jones, 1991a, p. 307). Kalb later clarified his question to be one of priorities. The implication of this line of thinking was that black and American priorities were inherently conflicted.

REFERENCES

Abrams, D., & Hogg, M. A. (Eds). (1990). *Social identity theory: Constructive and critical advances.* New York: Springer-Verlag.

Acorn, D. A., Hamilton, D. L., & Sherman, S. J. (1988). Generalization of biased perception of groups based on illusory correlations. *Social Cognition, 6,* 345–372.

Allport, G. W. (1935). Attitudes. In C. M. Murchison (Ed.), *Handbook of social psychology* (pp. 798–844). Worcester, MA: Clark University Press.

Allport, G. W. (1954). *The nature of prejudice.* Reading, MA: Addison Wesley.

Allport, F. H. (1924). *Social psychology.* Boston: Houghton Mifflin.

Amir, Y. (1969). Contact hypothesis in ethnic relations. *Psychological Bulletin, 71,* 319–342.

Aronson, E., Stephan, C., Sikes, J., Blaney, N., & Snapp, M. (1978). *The jigsaw classroom.* Beverly Hills, CA: Sage.

Aronson, E., & Thibodeau, E. (in press). The jigsaw classroom: A cooperative strategy for reducing prejudice. In Lynch, Modgil & Modgil (Eds.), *Cultural diversity in the schools.* London: Falmer Press.

Baldwin, J. A., & Bell, Y. R. (1985). The African self-consciousness scale: An Africentric personality questionnaire. *Western Journal of Black Studies, 9,* 61–68.

Banks, W. C. (1976). White preference in Blacks: A paradigm in search of a phenomenon. *Psychological Bulletin, 83,* 1179–1186.

Bobo, L. (1983). White's opposition to busing: Symbolic racism or realistic group conflict? *Journal of Personality and Social Psychology, 45,* 1196–1210.

Bobo, L. (1988). Group conflict, prejudice, and the paradox of contemporary racial attitudes. In P. A. Katz and D. A. Taylor (Eds.), *Eliminating racism: Profiles in controversy* (pp. 85–116). New York: Plenum Press.

Bogardus, E. (1925). Measuring social distances. *Journal of Applied Sociology, 9,* 299–308.

Bowser, B. P., & Hunt, R. G. (Eds.) (1981). *Impacts of racism on White Americans.* Beverly Hills, CA: Sage.

Brewer, M. B. (1991). The social self: On being the same and different at the same time. *Personality and Social Psychology Bulletin, 17,* 475–482.

Brewer, M. B., & Campbell, D. T. (1976). *Ethnocentrism and intergroup attitudes: East African evidence.* New York: Halstead Press.

Burlew, A. K., & Smith, L. R. (1991). Measures of racial identity: An overview and a proposed framework. *Journal of Black Psychology, 17,* 53–71.

Clark, K. B., & Clark, M. P. (1939). The development of consciousness of self and the emergence of racial identification in Negro pre-school children. *Journal of Social Psychology, 10,* 591–599.

Clark, K. B., & Clark, M. P. (1947). Racial identification and preference in Negro children. In T. M. Newcomb & E. L. Hartley (Eds.), *Readings in social psychology* (1st ed.). New York: Holt.

Cleaver, E. (1968). *Soul on ice.* New York: McGraw Hill.

Cooley, C. H. (1902). *Human nature and the social order.* New York: Scribner.

Crocker, J., & Major, B. (1989). Social stigma and self-esteem: The self-perspective properties of stigma. *Psychological Review, 96,* 608–630.

Crocker, J., Voelkl, K., Cornwell, B., & Major, B. (1989). *Effects on self-esteem of attributing interpersonal feedback to prejudice.* Unpublished manuscript, State University of New York at Buffalo.

Crosby, F., Bromley, S., & Saxe, L. (1980). Recent unobtrusive studies of black and white discrimination and prejudice: A literature review. *Psychological Bulletin, 87,* 546–563.

Cross, W. E. (1979). The Negro-to-Black conversion experience: An empirical analysis. In A. W. Boykin, A. J. Anderson, & J. F. Yates (Eds.), *Research directions of Black psychologists* (pp. 107–130). New York: Russell Sage Foundation.

Cross, W. E. (1991). *Shades of Black: Diversity in African-American identity.* Philadelphia: Temple University Press.

de Toqueville, A. (1945). *Democracy in America.* New York: Vintage Books.

Deutsch, M., & Collins, M. E. (1951). *Interracial housing.* Minneapolis: University of Minnesota Press.

Devine, P. G. (1989). Stereotypes and prejudice: Their automatic and controlled components. *Journal of Personality and Social Psychology, 56,* 5–18.

Devine, P. G., Monteith, M. J., Zuwerink, J. R., & Elliot, A. J. (1991). Prejudice with and without compunction. *Journal of Personality and Social Psychology, 60,* 817–830.

Dovidio, J. F., Evans, N. E., & Tyler, R. B. (1986). Racial stereotypes: The contents of their cognitive representations. *Journal of Experimental Social Psychology, 22,* 22–37.

Fiske, S. T., Neuberg, S. L., Beattie, A. E., & Milberg, S. J. (1987). Category-based and attribute-based reactions to others: Some informational conditions of stereotyping and individuating processes. *Journal of Experimental Social Psychology, 23,* 399–427.

Fiske, S. T., & Neuberg, S. L. (1990). A continuum of impression formation, from category-based reactions to individuating processes: Influences of information and motivation on attention and interpretation. In M. P. Zanna (Ed.), *Advances in Experimental Social Psychology, 23,* 1–74.

Gaertner, S. L., & Dovidio, J. F. (1986). The aversive form of racism. In J. F. Dovidio & S. L. Gaertner (Eds.), *Prejudice, discrimination and racism* (pp. 61–90). Orlando, FL: Academic Press.

Gaertner, S. L., Mann, J. A., Dovidio, J. F., Murrell, A. J., & Pomare, M. (1990). How does cooperation reduce intergroup bias? *Journal of Personality and Social Psychology, 59,* 692–704.

Gaertner, S. L., & McLaughlin, J. P. (1983). Racial stereotypes: Associations and ascriptions of positive and negative characteristics. *Social Psychology Quarterly, 46,* 23–30.

Gaertner, S. L., Mann, J. A., Murrell, A. J., & Dovidio, J. F. (1989). Reducing intergroup bias: The benefits of recategorization. *Journal of Personality and Social Psychology, 57,* 239–249.

Gilbert, G. M. (1951). Stereotype persistence and change among college students. *Journal of Abnormal and Social Psychology, 46,* 23–30.

Graham, S. (1992). Most of the subjects were White and Middle-Class . . .: Trends in published research on African-Americans in selected APA journals, 1970–1989. *American Psychologist, 47,* 629–639.

Greenwald, A. J. (1990). *What cognitive representations underlie prejudice?* Invited address, Annual Convention of then American Psychological Association. Boston, MA.

Hacker, A. (1992). *Two nations.* New York: Scribner.

Hamilton, D., & Gifford, R. E. (1976). Illusory correlation in interpersonal perception: A cognitive basis of stereotypic judgments. *Journal of Experimental Social Psychology, 12,* 392–407.

Hamilton, D. L., & Rose, T. L. (1980). Illusory correlation and the maintenance of stereotypic beliefs. *Journal of Personality and Social Psychology, 39,* 832–845.

Helms, J. (Ed.). (1990). *Black and white racial identity: Theory, research, and practice.* New York: Greenwood Press.

Henderson, N. D. (1979). Criterion-related validity of personality and aptitude scales: A comparison of validation results under voluntary and actual test conditions. In C. Spielberger (Ed.), *Police selection and evaluation: Issues and techniques* (pp. 179–195). Westport, CT: Greenwood.

Herrnstein, R. (1971). I.Q. *Atlantic Monthly, 3*(228), 43–64.

Jones, J. M. (1972). *Prejudice and racism.* Reading, MA: Addison Wesley.

Jones, J. M., & Hochner, A. R. (1973). Racial differences in sports activities: A look at the self-paced versus reactive hypothesis. *Journal of Personality and Social Psychology, 27,* 86–95.

Jones, J. M. (1991a). The politics of personality: Being Black in America. In R. L. Jones (Ed.), *Black psychology* (3rd ed., pp. 305–318). Berkeley, CA: Cobbs & Henry.

Jones, J. M. (1991b). Psychological models of race: What have they been and what should they be? In J. D. Goodchilds (Ed.), *Psychological perspectives on human diversity in America* (pp. 3–46). Washington, DC: American Psychological Association.

Jones, J. M., & Block, C. B. (1984). Black cultural perspectives. *The Clinical Psychologist, 37,* 58–62.

Jones, J. M. (1983). The concept of race in social psychology: From color to culture. In L. Wheeler & P. Shaver (Eds.), *Review of personality and social psychology* (Vol. IV, pp. 117–150). Beverly Hills, CA: Sage.

Jones, J. M., & Liverpool, H. (1976). Calypso humour in Trinidad. In A. Chapman & H. Foot (Eds.), *Humour: Theory and research* (pp. 259–286). London: Wiley.

Kardiner, A., & Ovesy, L. (1951). *The mark of oppression.* New York: Norton.

Karlins, M., Coffman, T. L., & Walters, G. (1969). On the fading of social stereotypes: Studies in three generations of college students. *Journal of Personality and Social Psychology, 13,* 1–16.

Katz, D., & Braly, K. (1933). Racial stereotypes in one hundred college students. *Journal of Abnormal and Social Psychology, 28,* 280–290.

Katz, I. (1981). *Stigma: A social psychological analysis.* Hillsdale, NJ: Erlbaum.

Katz, I., & Hass, R. G. (1988). Racial ambivalence and American value conflict: Correlational and priming studies of dual cognitive structures. *Journal of Personality and Social Psychology, 55,* 893–905.

Kinder, D. R., & Sears, D. O. (1981). Prejudice and politics: Symbolic racism versus racial threats to the good life. *Journal of Personality and Social Psychology, 40,* 414–431.

Klineberg, O. (1935). *Negro intelligence and selective migration.* New York: Columbia University Press.

Kutner, B., Wilkins, C., & Yarrow, P. R. (1952). Verbal attitudes and overt behavior. *Journal of Abnormal and Social Psychology, 47,* 549–562.

LaFromboise, T., & Rowe, W. (1983). Skills training for bicultural competence: Rationale and application. *Journal of Counseling Psychology, 30,* 589–595.

LaPiere, R. E. (1934). Attitudes vs. actions. *Social Forces, 13,* 230–237.

Linville, P., & Jones, E. E. (1980). Polarized appraisals of out-group members. *Journal of Personality and Social Psychology, 38,* 689–703.

Lippman, W. (1922). *Public opinion.* New York: Macmillan.

Major, B., & Crocker, J. (in press). Social stigma: The consequences of attributional ambiguity. In D. M. Mackie & D. L. Hamilton (Eds.), *Affect, cognition, and stereotyping: Interactive processes in group perception.* Orlando, FL: Academic Press.

Mbiti, J. (1970). *African philosophy and religions.* New York: Anchor Books.

McConahay, J. G., Hardee, B. B., & Batts, V. (1981). Has racism declined? It depends on who's asking and what is asked. *Journal of Conflict Resolution, 25,* 563–579.

McConahay, J. B., & Hough, J. C. (1976). Symbolic racism. *Journal of Social Issues, 32*, 23–45.

McDougall, W. (1921). *Is America safe for democracy?* New York: Scribner.

Mead, G. H. (1934). *Mind, self and society.* Chicago: University of Chicago Press.

Miller, N., & Brewer, M. B. (1984). Beyond the contact hypothesis: Theoretical perspectives on desegregation. In N. Miller & M. B. Brewer (Eds.), *Groups in contact: The psychology of desegregation* (pp. 281–302). Orlando, FL: Academic Press.

Miller, N., Brewer, M. B., & Edwards, K. (1985). Cooperative interaction in desegregated settings: A laboratory analog. *Journal of Social Issues, 41*, 63–75.

Millones, J. (1980). Construction of a Black consciousness measure: Psychotherapeutic implications. *Psychotherapy: Theory, Research, and Practice, 17*, 175–182.

Myrdal, G. (1944). *An American dilemma: The Negro problem and modern democracy.* New York: Harper.

Parham, T. (1989). Cycles of psychological Nigrescence. *The Counseling Psychologist, 17*, 187–226.

Park, B., & Rothbart, M. (1982). Perception of out-group homogeneity and levels of social categorization: Memory for the subordinate attributes of in-group and out-group members. *Journal of Personality and Social Psychology, 42*, 1051–1068.

Pettigrew, T. E. (1964). *Profile of the Negro American.* New York: Van Nostrand Reinhold.

Ponteretto, J. G., & Wise, S. C. (1987). A construct validity study of the racial identity attitude scale. *Journal of Counseling Psychology, 33*, 57–61.

Powell-Hopson, D., & Hopson, D. F. (1988). Implications of doll color preferences among Black pre-school children and White pre-school children. *Journal of Black Psychology, 14*, 57–63.

Ramirez, M. (1983). *Psychology of the Americas: Mestizo perspectives on personality and mental health.* New York: Pergamon Press.

Rothbart, M., & Lewis, S. (1988). Inferring category attributes from exemplar attributes: Geometric shapes and social categories. *Journal of Personality and Social Psychology, 55*, 861–872.

Sears, D. O. (1988). Symbolic racism. In P. A. Katz and D. A. Taylor (Eds.), *Eliminating racism: Profiles in controversy* (pp. 53–84). New York: Plenum Press.

Sears, D. O., & Allen, H. M. (1984). The trajectory of local desegregation controversies and White's opposition to busing. In N. Miller & M. B. Brewer (Eds.), *Groups in contact: The psychology of desegregation* (pp. 123–151). Orlando, FL: Academic Press.

Sears, D. O., & Kosterman, R. (1991, October 11). *Is it really racism? The origins and dynamics of symbolic racism.* Paper presented at the annual meetings of the Society for Experimental Social Psychology, Columbus, OH.

Sears, D., & Hoddy, L. (in press). The symbolic politics of opposition to bilingual education. In J. Simpson & S. Worchel (Eds.), *Conflict between and among people*. Chicago: Nelson-Hall.

Sherif, M. (1966). *Group conflict and cooperation: Their social psychology*. London: Routledge & Kegan Paul.

Sigall, H., & Page, R. (1971). Current stereotypes: A little fading a little faking. *Journal of Personality and Social Psychology, 18*, 247–255.

Slavin, R. (1980). Effects of biracial learning teams on cross-racial friendships. *Journal of Educational Psychology, 71*, 381–387.

Stangor, C., Sullivan, L. A., & Ford, T. E. (1991). Affective and cognitive determinants of prejudice. *Social Cognition, 9*, 359–380.

Steele, S. (1990). *The content of our character: A new vision of race in America*. New York: St. Martin's Press.

Steele, C. M. (1988). The psychology of self-affirmation: Sustaining the integrity of the self. In L. Berkowitz (Ed.), *Advances in experimental social psychology* (Vol. 21, pp. 261–346). San Diego, CA: Academic Press.

Steele, C. M. (1992). Minds wasted, minds saved: Crisis and hope in the schooling of Black Americans. *Atlantic Monthly, 269*(4), 68–78.

Suinn, R., Ricard-Figueroa, K., Lew, S., & Gigil, P. (1987). Suinn-Lew Asian Self-Identity Acculturation Scale: An initial report. *Educational and Psychological Measurements, 47*, 402–407.

Tajfel, H., & Turner, J. C. (1979). An integrative theory of intergroup conflict. In S. Worchel & W. G. Austin (Eds.), *The social psychology of intergroup relations*. Monterey, CA: Brooks-Cole.

Tajfel, H. (1982). The social psychology of intergroup relations. *Annual Review of Psychology, 33*, 1–39.

Taylor, J. (1973). The phenomena of acting in, out, through, up and without: Implications for treatment. *Psychotherapy: Theory, Research, and Practice, 10*, 78–82.

Taylor, S. E. (1983). Adjustment to threatening events: A theory of cognitive adaptation. *American Psychologist, 38*, 1161–1173.

Tesser, A. (1988). Toward a self-evaluation maintenance model of social behavior. In L. Berkowitz (Ed.), *Advances in experimental social psychology* (Vol. 21, pp. 181–228). New York: Academic Press.

Thomas, C. (1971). *Boys no more*. Beverly Hills, CA: Glencore Press.

Thurstone, L. L. (1927). Attitudes can be measured. *American Journal of Sociology, 33*, 529–554.

Turner, J. C. (1985). Social categorization and the self-concept: A social cognitive theory of group behavior. In E. J. Lawler (Ed.), *Advances in group processes* (Vol. 2, pp. 77–122). Greenwich, CT: JAI Press.

vanden Berghe, P. (1967). *Race and racism: A comparative perspective*. New York: Wiley.

Wicker, A. W. (1969). Attitudes versus actions: The relationship of verbal and overt behavioral responses to attitude objects. *Journal of Social Issues, 25,* 41–78.

Williams, J. (1992, January 5). West meets East: A cross-cultural journey. *Washington Post Magazine,* pp. 13–29.

Wills, T. A. (1981). Downward comparison principles in social psychology. *Psychological Bulletin, 90,* 245–271.

Word, C., Zanna, M. P., & Cooper, J. (1974). The nonverbal mediation of self-fulfilling prophesies in interracial interaction. *Journal of Experimental Social Psychology, 10,* 109–120.

Zuckerman, M. (1990). Some dubious premises in research and theory on racial differences. *American Psychologist, 45,* 1297–1303.

Social Cognition as a Social Science:
How Social Action Creates Meaning

E. TORY HIGGINS

Although "social cognition" only became a recognized and rapidly expanding area about 10 years ago, social psychology as a field has always been both social and cognitive. Indeed, one might argue that during the '40s and '50s, social psychology was one of the few bastions of the cognitive perspective against the forces of radical behaviorism (see, e.g., Zajonc, 1980). What was "new" about the new area of social cognition that developed in the late '70s was the consideration of information-processing variables as an alternative to traditional motivational variables for explaining classic social phenomena—the "information processlytizing" of social psychology (see Higgins & Bargh, 1987).

The recent social–cognitive movement in social psychology has been criticized for simply being cognitive psychology with social objects and for not being "social" enough. Such criticisms fail to appreciate the unique contributions of social cognition in two respects—*unique both as a cognitive science and as a social science*. To appreciate these contributions of social cognition, one must distinguish between the cognition of social psychology, how cognitive variables underlie social phenomena, and the social psychology of cognition, how social variables impact on cognition. From a levels-of-analysis perspective, the former involves a cognitive science perspective while the latter involves a social science perspective.

The implicit message in the criticism that social cognition is

simply cognitive psychology with social objects is that this kind of
social cognition simply takes current models in cognitive psychology that were developed for nonsocial objects and tests their
generalizability to social objects. Although some social–cognitive
research has performed this useful generalizability function, most
research in the cognition of social psychology has developed original cognitive models to apply to social phenomena. The largest set
of such models are the attribution models developed by Bem,
Heider, Jones, Kelley, Schachter, Weiner, and others that are now
used by psychologists in general (for a recent review of these
models, see Ross & Fletcher, 1985). Other models of cognitive
processes that were developed or extensively elaborated in social
psychology include models of salience (for reviews, see McArthur,
1981; Nisbett & Ross, 1980; Taylor & Fiske, 1978), knowledge
accessibility (for reviews, see Higgins, 1989a; Smith, 1990; Wyer &
Srull, 1986), and human inference and decision making (for reviews, see Hastie, Penrod, & Pennington, 1983; Nisbett & Ross,
1980; Sherman & Corty, 1985). In addition, various models of the
motivation–cognition interface have been developed by social
psychologists over the years: in the '50s and '60s, cognitive–consistency approaches to motivation and information–transmission
approaches to attitudes (see Abelson, 1968; McGuire, 1969); in the
'70s, models of social learning (e.g., Bandura, 1977; Mischel, 1973)
and of intrinsic/extrinsic motivation (e.g., Deci, 1975; Kruglanski,
1975; Lepper & Greene, 1978; Ross, 1975); in the '80s, theories of
affect and goals, assessment and evaluation, and action and control (see Higgins & Sorrentino, 1990; Sorrentino & Higgins, 1986).
These cognitive models developed by social psychologists have
general applicability in cognitive science.

   Even when existing models in cognitive psychology have been
applied to social objects, the purpose typically has been to use the
models to discover new factors underlying important social phenomena rather than to test the generalizability of the models.
Social psychology has been more concerned than cognitive psychology with understanding the underpinnings of social problems,
such as aggression, group conflict, discrimination, and biased
evaluations, and thus has studied variables that can produce such
problems, such as social pressure, attitude formation, social beliefs, and person perception. Not all cognitive mechanisms and
processes are equally relevant to understanding social problems. It
is the social psychological perspective that guides selection of
those cognitive variables most likely to shed light on social problems. By providing a basis for determining which existing models

in cognitive psychology to elaborate and extend to social problems, social psychology enhances the contribution of cognitive
science to society.

Thus, the criticism of social cognition that it is simply cognitive psychology with social objects ignores the basic and original
contributions that the "cognition of social psychology" has made
to cognitive science. This criticism also fails to consider the contributions of the other kind of social cognition—the "social psychology of cognition." This is not surprising given that most of what is
reviewed under the "social cognition" label represents the cognition of social psychology rather than the social psychology of
cognition (see, e.g., the recent annual reviews of social cognition by
Higgins & Bargh [1987], Sherman, Judd, & Park [1989], and
Schneider [1991]). What, then, is the "*social* psychology of cognition"? What makes something "social"? One answer to these questions, and an answer I especially like, was provided almost a
century ago by the eminent social scientist, Max Weber (1967):

> In "action" is included all human behavior when and in so far as the
> acting individual attaches a subjective meaning to it. . . . Action is
> social in so far as, by virtue of the subjective meaning attached to it by
> the acting individual (or individuals), it takes account of the behavior
> of others and is thereby oriented in its course. (pp. 156–157)

Thus, action is "social" when its meaning and orientation
takes account of other people (see also Thomas & Znaniecki, 1918).
This definition of "social" applies not only to social cognition but
to social psychology in general. Within social psychology, social
cognition is specifically concerned with how "social" factors relate
to "cognition." In regard to "cognition," Weber (1967) also pointed
out that people assign meaning to the events in their lives and then
respond to those meanings. The social psychology of cognition,
then, is concerned with how the meaning that people assign to the
events in their lives (e.g., their representation, interpretation, and
evaluation of life events) is transformed because their actions take
others into account. Examples of the social psychology of cognition, to be discussed more fully later, include representing events
differently depending on whose perspective on the event one takes
or to whom one plans to describe the event.

Distinguishing between the cognition of social psychology and
the social psychology of cognition is especially important given the
objective of the present volume to relate social psychology and
mental health. Since the early '70s, the cognition of social psychol-

ogy, especially social–cognitive work on attributional styles, self-schemata, automaticity, and construct accessibility, has had an increasing impact on clinical approaches to affective disorders, particularly depression (see, e.g., Dykman & Abramson, 1990; Moretti & Shaw, 1989; Segal, 1988). In contrast, the social psychology of cognition has had little direct impact on theories and research in mental health. Given that clinical psychologists have increasingly considered "cognitive" factors to have a central role in mental health, one might expect that they would be particularly interested in how the meaning that people assign to the events in their lives is transformed because their actions take others into account. After all, this social science perspective on social cognition permits, indeed promotes, an integration of the two dominant approaches in clinical theory and practice—the "cognitive" and "interpersonal" approaches. Perhaps, the social psychology of cognition has not had the impact one might expect simply because it has not been clearly distinguished from the cognition of social psychology. If social–cognitive social psychologists themselves have not provided an overview of this distinct perspective, it would not be surprising if clinical psychologists are not aware of its special utility. The major purpose of this chapter is to provide such an overview.

Like the cognitive science perspective on social cognition, the social science perspective on social cognition has a long history of contributions in social psychology. The purpose of this chapter is not to provide an exhaustive review of these contributions but simply to illustrate some of them, and especially those that could have implications for mental health and personal adjustment. As the reader will certainly note, some of the research areas covered have traditionally been associated with divisions in social psychology other than social cognition, such as the "ingroup/outgroup" and "conformity" areas. This simply underscores the fact that the social psychology of cognition has received insufficient recognition as an aspect of social cognition.

ROLE ENACTMENT AND ROLE TAKING

Role enactment is a quintessential example of "social" action. In the traditional view, role enactment relates to conduct that adheres to certain positions in the social structure rather than to individuals per se. Role expectations are the conceptual link between social structure and role enactment. As defined by Sarbin and Allen (1968), role expectations "are comprised of the rights and privileges, the duties and obligations, of any occupant of a social position in relation to persons occupying other positions in the social structure" (p. 497). Role enactment in terms of role expectations, then, is social action. Sarbin and Allen (1968) also point out that role expectations operate as imperatives concerning a person's cognitions as well as his or her conduct during role enactment. Thus, role enactment is social action that can influence meaning.

Despite its promise as a window on the social psychology of cognition, relatively little attention has been paid by social psychologists to the effects of role enactment on cognition. One of the earliest studies on this issue was conducted by Jones and de-Charms (1958). They used instructions to establish different perceiver roles for the same target person. Naval Air Cadets heard a tape-recorded interview between a psychologist and an ex-prisoner of war who had signed communistic propaganda statements. One group of subjects was assigned the (imaginary) role of members of a judicial board of inquiry who were to decide what the formal charges should be, another group was assigned the role of members of a medical–psychological board of review empowered to determine why the prisoner did what he did; a third group of subjects was assigned the role of potential friend of the prisoner. The subjects' attributions of personality characteristics to the target on the basis of the same target person information varied markedly depending on the role that they were assigned.

Anderson and Pichert (1978) manipulated subjects' role expectations by assigning them either to the role of home buyer or to the role of burglar before they read a story containing information about the properties of a house. The subjects' memory for the features of the house was strongly influenced by their role assignment. Thus, role enactment can influence memory. But beyond that, memory itself can constitute a role. Wegner (1986) describes how established groups, such as social organizations or couples, assign members to different memory roles in which each member has the responsibility to remember events and facts in particular life domains (e.g., "financial," "family").

In a study that demonstrated the influence of role enactment on both performance and the interpretation of it, Ross, Amabile, and Steinmetz (1977) assigned one member of each pair of subjects to play the role of "questioner" and the other member of the pair to play the role of "contestant" in a "question and answer" game. Each role was made explicit to both members of the pair. The "questioner" role permitted the actor to ask challenging questions that displayed esoteric knowledge, whereas the "contestant" role caused most actors to display a lack of such knowledge. Thus, the role assignments influenced the ability of subjects to demonstrate their general knowledge. But more important, the subjects in the different roles evaluated their own knowledge and their partner's knowledge differently despite being exposed to the same target behavior, with the "contestant" subjects evaluating themselves most negatively.

Role enactment can also influence reasoning. In a study on Kahneman and Tversky's (1973) "base rate fallacy," for example, Zukier and Pepitone (1984) assigned subjects either to the role of "scientist" or to the role of "clinical counselor" before reading about the target person information and receiving the base rate information. The subjects in the role of scientist were much more likely to use the base rate information appropriately than were the subjects in the role of clinical counselor.

Even preparation for role enactment can influence how information is processed. In an early classic study, Zajonc (1960) showed that subjects assigned the role of "transmitter" of information represent the information in a more unified and organized way than subjects assigned the role of "recipient" even prior to the communication's taking place. The results of several subsequent studies suggest that because the role of "speaker" involves expectations to produce clear, concise messages, speakers tend to polarize and distort stimulus information in preparation for message production (see Higgins, 1981a).

The effect of role enactment on meaning can have important implications for mental health. Such effects were vividly described by Goffman (1961) in his book, *Asylums*. Goffman (1961) describes how the social roles of "staff" and "inmates" within the total institution of the asylum contribute to the patients' feelings of inferiority, weakness, guilt, and blameworthiness. Similarly, Shrauger (1982) suggests that some therapists believe that it is their role to highlight and draw attention to the client's problems, conflicts, and nonnormative motives, and it is the client's role to accept the negative feedback they receive during the session. In such cases, role enactment in therapy sessions could further lower client's self-confidence and self-esteem.

Role enactment can also be used as a positive intervention strategy. Janis, for example, has shown how "role playing," such as a heavy smoker enacting the role of a medical patient who had just been informed by her physician (played by the experimenter) that she had lung cancer requiring immediate surgery, can produce more change than simply receiving the same information (e.g., Janis & Mann, 1965). Role playing has also been shown to be effective in reducing racial prejudice (see Stephan, 1985).

Successful role enactment requires taking into account the expectations and standards of others. In short, it requires role taking. More generally, role taking involves responding as a function of inferences concerning how others will or would respond. Thus, role taking is social action. There are two basic kinds of role taking: (1) "putting oneself in someone else's shoes," or situational role taking, which involves infering how you would respond if you were in the situation of another person; and (2) "seeing the world through another person's eyes," or individual role taking, which involves infering how another person would respond if he or she were in your situation (see Higgins, 1981b).

Role taking is a fundamental process underlying all social interaction (Mead, 1934). A basic rule of interpersonal communication, for example, is that the communicator should take the recipient's characteristics into account; that is, the communicator should role-take (see Higgins, 1981a). Higgins, McCann, and Fondacaro (1982) examined the impact of such social action on meaning. Communicators had to perform situational role taking when producing a message about a target person for recipients who had either the same or different information about the target person. They did so by "sticking to the facts" more when communicating to the recipient who had different target information. This role taking was found to influence the communicators' own subsequent memory for the target information.

Perhaps, the most striking evidence of the importance of role taking in constructing meaning is found in the social–developmental literature which reports qualitative shifts in children's role taking ability (for a review, see Higgins, 1981b). There is a developmental increase in children's ability to shift perspective when they are asked to process the same input from different points of view, which results in older children's representing events differently depending on which role or perspective they are asked to take (see, e.g., Feffer, 1970). Developmental and individual differences in role taking have also been found to underlie differences in social maturity, interpersonal sensitivity, and prosocial behavior (see, e.g., Moore & Underwood, 1981; Selman, 1980). In addition, interventions that increase role taking skills have been found to improve social behavior (e.g., Chandler, 1973; Spivak & Shure, 1974).

Empathy is related to role taking but involves feeling how another feels and not just inferring another's cognitive point of view. There is some evidence that people instructed to empathize with a target person remember more about that person than those not so instructed (e.g., Harvey, Yarkin, Lightner, & Town, 1980). There is also recent evidence that individuals who are vulnerable to one kind of distress or another because their self-concept is discrepant from a particular type of desired self (e.g., the self they would like to be vs. the self they believe they ought to be) (see Higgins, 1987) empathize better with others who are suffering from the same kind of distress (e.g., feeling sad vs. worrying, respectively). These differences in empathy, in turn, produce differences in how others' distress is interpreted and evaluated (Houston, 1990). To the extent that therapists both empathize with and interpret the reactions of their clients, therapeutic outcomes might be enhanced by considering the above set of interrelations.

SOCIAL POSITIONS AND IDENTITIES

For symbolic interactionism, the branch of social psychology that has always taken a social science perspective on meaning, another concept of fundamental importance is social "position." A social position is any socially recognized category of actor and serves as a cue to or predictor of the attributes (traits, appearance, behaviors) of those to whom the category is attached. When others attach a positional category to a person, they expect particular attributes of that person and tend to behave toward that person on the basis of these expectations (see Stryker & Statham, 1985). Some social positions, such as social roles, involve normative expectations (i.e., beliefs about duties and obligations) and carry sanctions, whereas other social positions involve probabilistic expectancies and carry no sanctions; that is, it is not that social category members ought to or must behave in certain ways but simply that they typically do behave in certain ways. The former kind of social position has already been considered. Let us turn now to some social–cognitive phenomena concerning the latter kind of social position.

Often there are attributes that people are expected to possess simply because they are members of some social category (see also Jones, Chapter 7, this volume). Even when the persons do *not* in fact possess the attributes, they are responded to as if they did possess them, and the constraints of being thus responded to can ultimately cause the persons to behave in a manner consistent with the attribute expectancies. This "self-fulfilling prophecy" (see Merton, 1957) exemplifies another relation between social action and meaning. Merton (1957) described how the self-fulfilling prophecy could account for some of the dynamics of intergroup conflict in America. Jones (Chapter 7, this volume) discusses mental health consequences of such attribute expectancies for race as a social category.

A classic experimental test of the dynamics of self-fulfilling prophecies was conducted by Word, Zanna, and Cooper (1974). They performed a pair of studies. In the first, the nonverbal behavior of whites interviewing black and white job applicants was examined to determine whether the white interviewers' expectancies about "whites" versus "blacks" would cause them to respond differently to the same target information. (The "job applicants" were all confederates trained to behave in the same way during the interview.) Indeed, different interviewing styles were used for the white and black targets (less personal and friendly for the black target). In the second study, white job applicants (who were now the subjects) were interviewed by confederates using either the "black target" interview style or the "white target" interview style identified in the first study. Those subjects who received the "black target" style performed worse in the interview than did subjects who received the "white target" style. Thus, these job applicants' behaviors would have confirmed the original expectancies about "blacks" and "whites" if the persons receiving the "black target" style had been black and the persons receiving the "white target" style had been white, as would normally be the case. In a study of expectancies regarding the "attractive female" and "unattractive female" categories, Snyder, Tanke, and Berscheid (1977) found similar experimental evidence of people responding to others as function of their (false) expectancies for social category members and thereby shaping the others' behaviors to become more consistent with the expectancies (see also Deaux & Major, 1987; Zanna & Pack, 1975).

A classic demonstration that this social action–meaning relation exists outside the laboratory was conducted by Rosenthal and Jacobson (1968). At the beginning of the school year, teachers were led to categorize some of their students as "potential late bloomers," thus producing the expectation that these students would excel if given the appropriate support and guidance. These students, in fact, were randomly selected and did not differ from their fellow students. Nevertheless, the school performance of these students improved over time more than that of the other students.

The importance of social factors in these kinds of effects is indicated by the fact that self-fulfilling prophecies are more likely to occur when the perceiver has power over the target than the reverse (see Darley & Fazio, 1980). Of course, therapists have greater power than do clients in therapy sessions, and thus there is a danger that therapists' categorizations of clients (e.g., "paranoid," "dependent," "passive–aggressive") could influence their actions toward clients so as to bias and distort their conclusions. There is also the risk that targets will incorporate into their own self-concepts the negative attributes they have instantiated in the constrained social interaction (see, e.g., Fazio, Effrein, & Falender, 1981; Snyder & Swann, 1978).

Dispositional inferences, such as "industrious," "aggressive," "paranoid," or "generous," can also be considered social positions to the extent that people use these terms to identify types of individuals who share similar properties that distinguish them from people in general. The use of dispositional terms can lead to social expectancies that influence social action and meaning. And the effects of such expectancies can themselves vary as a function of other social-action variables. Davis (1962), for example, selected all female dyads in which the members were equal in dominance. One member of each dyad was led to believe that the other member was quite dominant. The interaction was set up to be either cooperative or competitive. When the social context was cooperative, the dyad member who believed that her partner was dominant behaved quite submissively. When the social context was competitive, the dyad member who believed that her partner was dominant tended to dominate the interaction.

Assignment of individuals to socially recognized dispositional categories serves various societal functions (see Wicklund, 1986). The dispositional categories can be relatively narrow, as in the case of traits, or relatively broad, as in the case of personality types. Dispositional inferences, in turn, have a major impact on subsequent information processing (for reviews, see Higgins & Stangor, 1988; Wyer & Srull, 1986, 1989). This impact can be problematic. For example, people often use their prior dispositional judgment of a person as the basis for their subsequent responses to the person without taking into account sufficiently how some irrelevant contextual variable may have contributed to the initial judgment (e.g., mood, set, salience of alternatives, temporary knowledge, accessibility). Problematic responses to group members can also occur, as when information-processing variables involved in social identification contribute to stereotyping (see Hamilton, 1981).

When people are assigned social positions by others, they sometimes appropriate the terms of the placement for themselves (see Stryker & Statham, 1985). Such internalized positional designations are called "social identities." Although social roles often become social identities, these two types of social positions are distinct. An individual can enact a particular role but not identify with it, or an individual can identify with a social position that involves no role responsibilities (e.g., being "short"). Activation of social identities can also influence people's actions and subjective meanings. In a classic study by Charters and Newcomb (1952), for example, Catholic students' social identity as Catholics was made salient by emphasizing the common religious affiliation of everyone in the room. Activation of the social identity was found to shift the students' personal opinions toward orthodox Catholic beliefs (see also Gerard, 1954).

Assignment to social identities is itself a social process (see Becker, 1963). Such assignment can influence how information is processed. Frable, Blackstone, and Scherbaum (1990), for example, have found that individuals with (invisible) social identities that are statistically unusual and centrally defining (e.g., bisexual, wealthy) will process a dyadic interaction differently than will their "normal" partner, tending to role-take more often and to remember spontaneously more detailed information about the surroundings of the interaction. It is remarkable how easily social identities can be formed. Providing even a minimally meaningful basis for social categorization, such as the picture preferences of anonymous strangers, can be sufficient for social identities to be formed. And these social categorizations can influence subsequent responses to members versus nonmembers of the social category despite having minimal relation to personal identities (for a review, see Stephan, 1985).

An especially fascinating phenomenon is the ad hoc division of people into different groups that creates ingroup/outgroup identities, which in turn produce biased responses in favor of other members of one's social identity and against members of the alternative social identity (see Tajfel & Turner, 1979). For example, in their classic camp studies, Sherif and Sherif (1969) found that even before there was contact with outgroup members, a strong sense of social identity (i.e., a strong "we feeling") was associated with the perception that members of one's own social identity were superior to members of the alternative social identity. Even in the absence of prior stereotypes, social categorization can increase perceptions of differences between members of different social identities. And increasing the salience of alternative social identities increases the perception of similarity within social identities (see Stephan, 1985). Such findings have major significance for mental health outcomes related to intergroup relations (see Jones, Chapter 7, this volume; Levine & Moreland, Chapter 5, this volume). The establishment of social identities, even when based on minimal group differences, can increase perceptions that members of "other" social identities are dissimilar to fellow members of one's own social identities, and perceived dissimilarity in turn can promote disliking (see Hensley & Duval, 1976).

Social Selves

Social identities constitute one part of the self-concept. Personal identities, which refer to people's individual characteristics, the type of individual they believe they are, constitute another part. As Tajfel and Turner (1979) point out, both social and personal identities carry emotional and value significance (see also Deaux, Chapter 10, this volume). People are motivated to have social and personal identities that match their values. This in turn produces positive self-evaluation and positive affect. To the extent that people's *personal* identities are not providing positive self-evaluation, they will be motivated to achieve positive self-evaluation by possessing positive *social* identities. This can be accomplished both by perceiving fellow identity members positively and by promoting positive outcomes for fellow identity members. Thus, social action in the form of ingroup/outgroup bias can be in the service of enhancing the meaning of self (see Tajfel & Turner, 1979).

The distinction between social and personal identities is useful. It is important to note, however, that both types of self-identities are social. The self-concept as a whole is social to the extent that it is formed on the basis of social interaction and interpersonal relations (for reviews, see Deaux, Chapter 10, this volume; Higgins, 1989b; Markus & Cross, 1990; Rosenberg, 1979; Stryker & Statham, 1985). Moreover, the self-concept constitutes just one part of the self-system, the part that represents a person's current self-state. The self-system also consists of standards or self-guides that represent a person's valued end states. Self-guides are acquired from a socialization history of social interaction involving self-other contingencies (see, e.g., Higgins, 1989b; Markus & Cross, 1990). Children learn that significant others respond differently to different self-features and that these different responses make them feel good or bad in different ways. Thus, the self-guide part of the self-system is also social.

People are motivated to reach a condition in which their self-concept or current state matches their self-guides or valued end states. Thus, self-guides are used both for self-regulation and self-evaluation (see Carver & Scheier, 1981; Duval & Wicklund, 1972; Higgins, 1991; James, 1948; Rogers, 1961). Given that self-guides are social, then self-regulation and self-evaluation are inherently social actions. How do these forms of social action affect meaning?

First and foremost, self-regulation and self-evaluation in relation to self-guides are a major determinant of how people feel about themselves and their lives. People who possess discrepancies between their actual selves and their self-guides, for example, are vulnerable to various kinds of emotional problems (see Carver & Scheier, 1981; Duval & Wicklund, 1972; Higgins, 1991; James, 1948; Rogers, 1961). Self-discrepancy theory (see Higgins, 1991) hypothesizes that the motivational significance of possessing a self-discrepancy is different depending on which type of self-guide is involved in the discrepancy. The theory proposes that a discrepancy of the actual self from an ideal self guide (i.e., someone's hopes and wishes for you) holistically represents the "absence of positive outcomes," whereas a discrepancy of the actual self from an ought self-guide (i.e., someone's beliefs about your duties and obligations) holisitically represents the "(expected) presence of negative outcomes." Consistent with this proposal, my colleagues and I (for a review, see Higgins, 1991) have found that people who possess actual:ideal discrepancies are vulnerable to suffering dejection-related problems (e.g., feeling sad, disappointed, discouraged), whereas people who possess actual:ought discrepancies are vulnerable to suffering agitation-related problems (e.g., feeling nervous, worried, tense).

Second, regulating one's behaviors and activities in order to meet self-guides can change the meaning of the behaviors and activities. Deci and Ryan (1985), for example, suggest that people will internalize interpersonal contingencies and then use these internal standards or self-guides to monitor their activities. They suggest that when an activity is regulated in terms of these internal standards, the activity becomes extrinsically, rather than intrinsically, motivated. Deci and Ryan also state that when people engage in activities in terms of internal standards, they experience pressure and tension, with shame and guilt being common affective consequences. In addition, both current enjoyment of the activity and future interest in engaging in the activity are undermined.

Third, individuals' self-concepts, self-guides, and the relationships among them can influence how they process information about others. People tend to judge others on self-relevant dimensions and will use the self as a reference point when the self is salient or accessible and they know little about the target other (for a review, see Markus & Wurf, 1987). People, for instance, will use their own preferences as a basis for inferring the preferences of people in general (Ross, Greene, & House, 1977). In a recent study, Higgins and Tykocinski (in press) tested whether the psychological situations represented by different self-discrepancies produce differential sensitivity to events, even events that happened to others. As predicted, individuals with predominant actual:ideal discrepancies remembered better events reflecting either the presence of positive outcomes (e.g., someone finding a $20 bill on the pavement) or the absence of positive outcomes (e.g., someone arriving too late to see a movie) than events reflecting either the absence of negative outcomes (e.g., someone missing his or her worst school day because it is election day and classes have been canceled) or the presence of negative outcomes (e.g., someone travelling in a crowded subway). The reverse was true for individuals with predominant actual:ought discrepancies. These results suggest that people who regulate themselves in terms of a particular type of self-guide become sensitive to events that reflect the same psychological situations experienced when that self-guide is or is not fulfilled.

Understanding the nature of the social self-system and its impact on meaning is considered critical by many psychologists concerned with psychological adjustment and mental health. The self-system, moreover, has been implicated in the development and maintenance of many types of psychopathology (for a review, see Moretti, Higgins, & Feldman, 1990). Psychotherapists generally believe that changes in the self-system are central to therapeutic improvement. Seward (1962), for example, found that insight into self-dynamics was a common goal of all therapeutic schools. In particular, several contemporary theories suggest that reducing discrepancies between the self-concept and valued self states or self-guides will reduce psychological distress. Moretti et al. (1990) propose a set of possible therapeutic interventions for depression aimed at several targets within the self-system that could reduce self-discrepancies.

Social Audiences

Self-guides are valued end states for a person that are associated with some significant other, such as the representation of your mother's hopes and wishes for you. When planning or performing some action, people take into account the standpoint of their significant others on their action. This "other" standpoint, then, becomes a basis for self-regulation (see, e.g., Higgins, 1989b). In this sense, "other" self-guides can be thought of as internal audiences (see Horney, 1946). And, more generally, the beliefs, opinions, preferences, and values of significant others can become a basis for self-regulation in regard to issues or targets other than just the self. Thus, a person's significant others can function as internal audiences influencing his or her responses to a wide variety of issues.

Internal Audiences

The influence of significant others as internal audiences can be quite broad (see, e.g., Schlenker, 1985). In some cases, the significant others may be the members of a social category. Such reference groups can function to provide a person with a set of norms or values that he or she believes is shared by members of the reference group (see Kelley, 1952; Merton & Kitt, 1952; Newcomb, 1952; Sherif, 1948). A social identity group is a reference group in which one is an accepted member. There are other reference groups to which a person does not belong that nevertheless provide the person with norms or values. People may be motivated to meet these standards (positive reference groups) or to avoid meeting these standards (negative reference groups). An early study by Siegel and Siegel (1957) distinguished between the influence of membership groups and the influence of reference groups on attitudes. All first-year female students wanted to be in a particular residence in their second year. By chance (a lottery), some got into this residence (membership group) and the rest did not (nonmembership group). Among those who did not get in, some wanted to get into the residence in their third year (reference group) and the rest did not (nonreference group). Siegel and Siegel found that both membership group and reference group in the second year influenced attitude change from the first to the second year (as compared to the nonmembership/nonreference group). In a more recent study, Carver & Humphries (1981) found that when Cuban-American students were told that a supposed representative of the Cuban government (a negative reference group for the students) favored the liberalization of relations between Cuba and the United States, they were more opposed to such liberalization than when the Cuban government was not mentioned.

Internal or imaginary audiences can also be individuals, such as your parents, best friends, spouse, or boss (see, e.g., Elkind, 1967). For example, in a study supposedly on "visualizing scenes and people," Baldwin and Holmes (1987) tested whether activating alternative internal audiences would influence people's subsequent responses to a sexually permissive essay. Undergraduate female subjects visualized either two campus associates or two older members of their family, with the former being more sexually permissive than the latter. The subjects liked the sexually permissive essay more when the internal audience was their campus associates, and they were not aware of being influenced by previously visualizing this audience. In a direct test of how representations of significant others influence memory for novel persons, Andersen and Cole (1990) tested undergraduates' recognition memory for features of four fictional characters they read about. False recognition of features not possessed by these novel persons was much more likely for features possessed by a subject's significant other than for features possessed by a subject's nonsignificant other. "Transference" in therapy involves a similar phenomenon in which a client responds to the therapist as if the therapist possessed characteristics, including orientations toward the client, that the therapist does not actually possess but are possessed by a significant other of the client.

Internal audiences are audiences that need not be present in the immediate context to impact on subjective meaning because their viewpoint has been internalized. There are also noninternalized social audiences that can influence meaning without being present in the immediate context. Such audiences have been referred to as "anticipated audiences." It has long been recognized that anticipation of performance before an audience influences people's current responses and information processing. In an early study, Burri (1931) found that memory of stimulus words was poorer when subjects anticipated recalling the words in front of an audience than when no audience was anticipated. Grace (1951) found that anticipating the sex of the audience to whom a list of male-related and female-related objects would later be reported influenced the order in which subjects recalled the objects. In the classic Zimmerman and Bauer (1956) study, communicators who anticipated summarizing information on an issue for an audience with a particular opinion on the issue distorted the information in recall toward their audience's opinion. The literature on anticipatory attitude change (for a review, see Cialdini & Petty, 1981) has also shown that polarizing attitudes in anticipation of an audience can produce a persistent change in meaning (see Cialdini, Levy, Herman, Kozlowski, & Petty, 1976; see also McFarland, Ross, & Conway, 1984).

Social audiences, then, can influence social action and meaning even when they are not present in the immediate context; that is, meaning can be created by taking an internal audience into account. But, of course, social audiences also directly influence people by forming part of their immediate situation that is taken into account. Let us now consider the impact on meaning of such external audiences.

External Audiences

External or concurrent social audiences can impact on subjective meaning even in the absence of actual social interaction. One example of this are "observer" effects on people's responses. The presence of an observer in the same room increases self-focused responses (see Carver & Scheier, 1978). It also increases motivation to compare one's current performance to a relevant standard, such as a greater preference for working on problems for which norms on other students' performance are available than on problems for which no norms are available (Scheier & Carver, 1983). In a study by Diener and Srull (1979), subjects worked on a series of task trials under self-aware and non–self-aware conditions. When the subjects believed that they had surpassed a social standard (the average performance of other students on the task trial), they felt more satisfied and rewarded themselves more when they were self-aware than when they were not self-aware.

Simply the composition of a group, independent of social interaction, can influence social information processing. In a study by Higgins and Petty, for example, subjects' recall of the behaviors (stereotypically male and stereotypically female) of a target person (ostensibly male or female) was less stereotypical when their sex was in the minority of the group than when it was in the majority (see Higgins & King, 1981, Study 1). Apparently, for this sample of "modern" undergraduates, increasing the distinctiveness of gender increased the accessibility of the modern view of sex-linked attributes, which in turn influenced their processing of the stimulus information. Group composition has also been shown to influence self-perception (see, e.g., McGuire & Padawer-Singer, 1976).

When there is actual social interaction, the responses of social audiences directly influence people's actions and judgments. To consider just one example, taking into account the aversive behavior of one's marriage partner during interaction increases the likelihood that negative interpersonal attributions will be made (e.g., "For him to have done that proves he doesn't love me anymore"). These attributions in turn cause reactions that produce further negative attributions (e.g., "For me to have done *that* proves that I don't love *him* anymore"). Such a series of "social action-meaning" relations could eventually lead to the social action of divorce (for a discussion of such processes, see Holmes & Boon, 1990).

One important determinant of people's self-concept is how other people take them into account. Individuals infer their own attributes and states by considering how others respond to them. That is, people's meaning of themselves as target is influenced by their perception of others' social actions toward them. Cooley (1964) characterized this process as the "looking-glass self." Such reflected appraisals need not be accurate. Felson (1989), for example, reports that preadolescents' self-perceptions were influenced by the reflected appraisals of their parents, but these reflected appraisals were not accurate representations of the parents' actual appraisals. Reflecting the social interaction nature of these reflected appraisals, there is a shift in adolescence in the relative importance of parents versus peers as sources of reflected appraisal (see Rosenberg, 1979).

The phenomena of "ingratiation," "self-presentation," and "impression management" also involve people taking into account others' responses to them during social interaction. These phenomena are all concerned with one important goal of social interaction—the "face" goal of regulating one's actions in order to be perceived favorably by one's audience (see, e.g., Goffman, 1959; Jones, 1964; Schlenker, 1980; Tedeschi, 1981). Individuals for whom "face" goals are especially important, such as high self-monitors (see Snyder, 1979), are highly motivated to modify their behavior in front of an audience in order to make a good impression. McCann and Hancock (1983) found, for example, that high self-monitors were especially likely to tune their description of a target person to suit their audience's attitude toward that person. Moreover, the high self-monitors' own personal impressions of the target became increasingly consistent over time with their audience-tailored description. Thus, the high self-monitors' social action created meaning over time. There is also evidence that spontaneously presenting a favorable image of oneself can produce a positive change in self-esteem (see, e.g., Jones, Rhodewalt, Berglas, & Skelton, 1981).

"Face" goals are not the only reason that people take their audience into account during social interaction. There are a variety of other social goals as well. Communicators take their audience into account in order to maximize dyadic outcomes or "task" goals, such as referential accuracy (see Fussell & Krauss, 1989). In a classic study by Krauss, Vivekanathan, and Weinheimer (1968), for example, female undergraduates named color chips either with themselves in mind as the future audience for the names (self-as-audience) or with some other female undergraduate in mind as the future audience for the names (other-as-audience). In a subsequent referential task in which the subjects had to select the correct color chip referent for each name they were given, referential accuracy was better for names encoded with other-as-audience than names encoded with self-as-audience unless subjects were given the names they themselves had encoded earlier. Thus, the "meaning" of the color chip varied depending on which audience the encoders took into account (self or other), and the informativeness of each "meaning" was different for different decoders.

One especially important goal of communication and social interaction is to form and maintain positive interpersonal relationships. And once again there are individual and situational variables that moderate how this social goal impacts on social action and meaning. In a study by Higgins and McCann (1984), for example, high- and low-authoritarian subjects described a target person's behaviors to an audience whose status was supposedly either equal to or higher than theirs. From the perspective of social relationship goals, it was expected that high authoritarians interacting with a higher-status audience would be especially likely to tailor their descriptions of the target person to suit the audience's purported attitude toward the target person. This was the case. In addition, for the high-authoritarian subjects especially, subjects' memories of the original stimulus information were evaluatively distorted in the direction of their audience-tailored descriptions. It should also be noted that the audience-tuning effect found in this and previous studies only occurs when subjects actually produce a description for the audience (see Higgins & McCann, 1984); that is, the social action must be taken.

These kinds of audience-tailored "saying is believing" effects may, in fact, constitute one of the processes that contribute to successful therapy. When a therapist functions as an audience with a positive attitude toward the client, as in client-centered therapy (Rogers, 1959), the client's self-descriptions should be tuned in a positive direction to match the therapist's attitude. This in turn should produce changes in the client's self-beliefs and auto-biographical memory that support a more positive self-esteem. Indeed, one might even predict that this positive outcome is especially likely when the client is a high authoritarian interacting with the high-status therapist.

Social Reality

Much, if not all, of the preceding discussion of social action and meaning could have been covered under the heading of "social reality." Indeed, the concept of "social reality" captures the essence of the social science of cognition better than any other single concept. As described by Festinger (1950), beliefs, attitudes, and opinions vary in the extent to which there is physical evidence for them. It is extremely rare for a belief or opinion to be supported by hard facts of incontrovertible physical reality. The basis for holding most beliefs and opinions is social reality, the fact that others share the belief or opinion:

> [W]here the dependence upon physical reality is low, the dependence upon social reality is correspondingly high. An opinion, a belief, an attitude is 'correct,' 'valid,' and 'proper' to the extent that it is anchored in a group of people with similar beliefs, opinions, and attitudes. (p. 272)

Thus, the very nature of most of our reality is social. The reality of our subjective meanings is anchored in the fact that others share the reality. Indeed, most of our educational system consists of students accepting as reality what they are told is the belief or opinion of others (typically "expert" others). And this social reality changes over time.

One may conceptualize social reality more broadly as not only beliefs, attitudes, and opinions anchored in others sharing the reality, but also as *any knowledge or feeling that is formed or trans-formed by taking others into account.* By this somewhat broader definition, the subjective meanings that have been discussed thus far in the chapter are all examples of social reality. Most of our examples of social reality have involved social stimuli. Interestingly, some of the classic demonstrations of social reality involve physical stimuli.

In a still fascinating study, Sherif (1935, 1936) had subjects in a completely dark room estimate the movement of a point of light that, although actually stationary, appears objectively to move in different directions and amounts by different perceivers (the autokinetic effect). Sherif found that when subjects gave their estimates in a group, they slowly abandoned their initially disparate judgments and converged on a mutually shared estimate of the light's apparent direction and amount of movement. Moreover, this "social norm" influenced subjects' judgments even when they later made judgments alone. And Jacobs and Campbell (1961) found that this arbitrary social norm was maintained even when the original members of a group were replaced, one at a time, by new subjects who were themselves later replaced. Thus, subjects' social action of making judgments that took other subjects' estimates into account produced a meaning, a social reality about the light's movement, that lasted over several "generations."

In another classic study, Asch (1952, 1956) had confederates in a group give the same incorrect judgment about which of a set of comparison lines was the same length as a standard line after earlier trials in which they gave the correct answer. In each group there was only one true subject whose turn came after most of the confederates had given their judgment. Asch found that when the discrepancy between the target and incorrect judgment was small, most subjects agreed with the group's incorrect judgment at least once, whereas incorrect judgments were rare for a control group of subjects who made their judgments privately in writing. Moreover, Asch points out that at least some of the subjects gave the incorrect judgment of the group as their answer because they began to doubt the accuracy of their perception and believed that it was unlikely that they alone could be right and so many other people wrong. Thus, their social action represented social reality taking precedence over physical reality (i.e., informational conformity) (see Deutsch & Gerard, 1955) and produced a change in meaning.

Bovard (1951) had subjects judge the length (in inches) of a green rectangle of paper pasted on a larger rectangle of greyish-white cardboard. Each subject made an initial judgment and then they were all told the mean of the classroom's judgments. Later, each subject made another judgment. On the first day of the semester, there was already evidence of convergence toward the classroom mean. When the same convergence measure was taken at the end of the semester, however, there was a decrease in convergence for subjects in leader-centered classrooms (where teacher–student interaction was emphasized) but an increase in convergence for subjects in group-centered classrooms (where student–student interaction was emphasized).

In another well-known study involving social stimuli, Back (1951) had subjects first interpret a set of pictures alone, then meet in either high-cohesive or low-cohesive dyads to discuss and compare each subject's narrative interpretation, and then interpret the pictures a second time alone. The subjects in high-cohesive dyads attempted to influence each other more *and* overtly resisted influence attempts more than the subjects in low-cohesive dyads. This pattern suggests that the subjects in the high-cohesive dyads were seeking (informational) social reality by their social actions rather than simply being polite or avoiding conflict. In addition, the subjects in the high-cohesive dyads changed their final private interpretations more toward their partner's interpretation than did subjects in the low-cohesive dyads. A similar kind of group influence on narrative consensus has also been found in jury decision making (see Hastie, Penrod, & Pennington, 1983).

Studies of group influences on judgments have remained a major area of social psychology since the '50s (see Moscovici, 1985, for a recent review). These studies always involve social action, but, unfortunately, they seldom measure the subsequent influence of that action on meaning. There is evidence that individuals who conform in social influence studies generally continue to conform, at least to some extent, when they are alone and anonymous; rarely is there mere compliance (see Moscovici, 1985). Nevertheless, it would be useful if delayed measures of subjects' memory for the stimuli were collected as a standard practice. A memory measure could address interesting social–cognitive questions such as whether the impact of social action on meaning differs for informational conformity versus normative conformity. The social-audience literature reviewed earlier suggests that the impact may, in fact, be the same over time.

There are some studies that did measure meaning. A particularly intriguing study has been reported by Moscovici and Personnaz (1980). The subjects were shown a set of blue slides that had some slightly green components and were confronted with a confederate who publicly described them as "green." The confederate was apparently either in the majority or the minority. Although subjects in the minority–confederate condition rarely labeled the slides publicly as "green," they were significantly more likely than subjects in the majority–confederate condition to judge privately that the negative afterimage of the blue slides was reddish, the complementary color for green (for blue slides, the complementary color is actually yellow). Apparently, a private perceptual effect was found only for subjects who did not publicly yield to the confederate's opinion (but see Sorrentino, King, & Leo, 1980). If so, then this study suggests that resisting social influence, which is yet another kind of social action, can also influence meaning. And once again this has very interesting implications for the process of therapy given that therapy often involves clients overtly resisting the influence attempts of therapists.

An alternative way of conceptualizing some group-influence effects is that when people take others' responses into account in planning their own action, it can change the meaning of the target of action. One of Asch's great contributions to social cognition was his suggestion that the evaluation of a target can change when the context changes, not because there is a change in the evaluation of the same target but because the (referential) meaning of the target itself changes (see Asch, 1948, 1952). From this perspective, when people change their judgment of a stimulus after learning about the different judgments of others, the change in judgment may arise from a change in the meaning of the stimulus even prior to public action. Taking others' judgments into account while planning the action may be sufficient to produce the change in judgment.

Allen and Wilder (1980) examined the possibility that social influence may produce a change in meaning by having subjects simply give their interpretation of a key word or phrase in different opinion statements that they learned had elicited responses either by a unanimous group or not. The subjects did not have to give their own evaluations of the opinion statement. Subjects who learned about a unanimous group response to the statements interpreted them in more extreme ways (in a direction making the group's response more reasonable) than did the subjects in the other conditions; that is, taking into account the perspective of the unanimous group produced a change in meaning. A subsequent study demonstrated that changing the meaning of the opinion statements also produced a change in subjects' responses to them.

As Allen and Wilder (1980) suggest, taking others' responses into account when planning social action may produce changes in meaning in other cases as well. For example, people may interpret the underlying nature of someone's problem by considering how others' respond to it (e.g., Latane & Darley, 1969). Thus, someone's "problem," including physical pain, becomes a social reality and not just a physical reality. And people may infer social consensus on some issue, interpret the consensus as indicating the value of some position on the issue, and then respond in line with the supposed value. Such social influences may underlie the "bandwagon" effect. In a related phenomenon, Chassin, Presson, Sherman, Corty, and Olshavsky (1984) found that nonsmokers who overestimated the prevalence of smoking were most at risk to begin smoking later.

People also take others into account in the process of social comparison. People will use other people's responses and beliefs as a basis for judging themselves and others. Earlier we described how people take others' values or norm prescriptions into account in their self-judgments (i.e., people's use of "guides" as evaluative standards). People also take information about others' "actual" performance, abilities, or attributes into account in their self-judgments (i.e., people's use of "factual" standards) (see Higgins, 1990). Festinger (1954), for example, described how people compare their performance to others' performance in order to assess their ability (see also Hyman's, 1942, discussion of the use of reference groups as factual standards). Schachter (1959) suggested that people are motivated to be with other people in order to use their affective responses to a shared event as a basis for evaluating their own feelings. Schachter and Singer (1962) proposed, moreover, that people will use the behavior of others in the immediate situation even to identify which emotion they are experiencing. And the notion that people use information about others to make judgments is included in most attribution theories (e.g., Heider, 1958; Jones & Davis, 1965; Kelley, 1967; Weiner & Kukla, 1970).

Judgments of a target based on social comparisons can have a major impact on meaning. Research on the "change-of-standard" effect by Higgins and his colleagues, for example, has found that judgments of a target person in relation to an immediate context of other people can produce major distortions in recall over time because people do not adjust sufficiently for the social context when they subsequently use the judgment in reconstructive memory (for a review of these and other "social context" effects, see Higgins & Stangor, 1988). Developmental research has found an age-related increase in children's use of social comparison processes for self-evaluation. Moreover, the increase is associated with a decrease in self-esteem (see Ruble, 1983). There is also evidence that people with problems will often choose to compare them-

selves with people worse off than them (i.e., "downward" comparison) (see Wills, 1981; Wood, Taylor, & Lichtman, 1985). And people
will choose to associate with others depending on whether social
comparison processes will raise or lower their self-esteem (see
Tesser, 1986). When the goal is self-improvement, individuals may
compare themselves with someone who is better off than them
("upward" comparison) in order to provide a positive possibility
(see Taylor, Buunk, & Aspinwall, 1990).

CONCLUSIONS

This chapter has discussed how "social" action, which is action
that takes other people into account, produces meaning. Such
meaning, whether it involves information processing of social or
nonsocial stimuli, is social cognition. And the variables underlying
the relation between social action and meaning—social roles, social positions, social selves, social audiences, group influence,
social comparison—are part of the social psychology of cognition
or social cognition as a social science.

When one considers the factors that mediate the phenomena
described in this chapter, it is striking how often one kind of factor
is involved—the influence of *social standards*. There are many
different kinds of social standards (for a review, see Higgins, 1990),
including *guides* (representations of attributes that are valued or
preferred for some person or category of persons by some social
appraiser) and *factuals* (beliefs about the actual attributes of a
person or category of persons). Social comparison processes involve the use of factuals as standards. Reference groups can be
used either as guides (the normative function) or as factuals (the
comparison function) (see Kelley, 1952). Group judgments that
influence other individuals can also be used either as guides
(normative conformity) or as factuals (informational conformity)
(see Deutsch & Gerard, 1955).

Responses to others that lead to "self-fulfilling prophecies" are
regulated by factuals (often false) concerning social category
members. Social roles consist of duties and obligations, and the
role of communicator in particular includes rules such as "take the
audience's characteristics into account" and "produce clear and
concise messages." Thus, ought guides underlie these phenomena.
The goal of self-presentation and impression management is to
produce responses in others that match one's desired personal
identity. The goal of ingroup preferential treatment is to produce

outcomes for ingroup members that match one's desired social identity. In these phenomena, then, ideal guides, especially, are involved. And, as discussed earlier, guides underlie social selves and constitute internal audiences, and standards are activated by the presence of observers.

Factuals and guides are also central in the socialization process that underlies the social action–meaning relation. The social models involved in observational learning (see Bandura, 1977) provide factual standards of actual performance and performance outcomes in different situations. Children's inferences about their caretakers' demands and desires for them and their representations of the consequences of matching or mismatching these demands and desires constitute the ought and ideal self-guides used in self-regulation and self-evaluation (see Higgins, 1989b). The larger community also provides information about performance and outcome distributions (factual baserate norms; categorical information) and about preferred and valued behaviors in culturally defined roles and situations (normative guides). Because of socialization processes, people enter momentary contexts with particular standards already available to them. But momentary contexts themselves also provide standards, such as source effects in persuasion or group consensus effects in conformity. Momentary context standards can function as factuals (e.g., expert source, informational conformity) or as guides (power source, normative conformity).

The role of social standards in social action and meaning construction goes beyond even their impact as individual standards. Many social psychological phenomena involve not just particular types of standards but specific patterns of interrelations among standards (see Higgins, 1990). Consistent with Cooper and Fazio's (1984) characterization of dissonance as feeling responsible for an aversive event, the psychological situation of experiencing "dissonance" in the classic insufficient justification paradigm (see Aronson, 1969; Festinger, 1957) could be described as a pattern of normative guide matches (the subjects perform the role of "good experimental subject"), self-guide mismatches (the subjects behave in a manner that is discrepant from their personal values, such as lying), and social context guide nonmatches (the subjects are made to believe that it is their choice, not pressure from the experimenter, to produce the self-discrepant behavior). In comparison, the psychological situation of "obedience to authority" in Milgram's (1974) classic paradigm could be described as a pattern of normative guide matches (the subjects are assigned the role of "teacher" and in that role are expected to deliver punishment to a learner), self-guide mismatches (by hurting the learner, the subjects behave in a manner that is discrepant from their personal values), *and* social context guide matches (the subjects are pressured by the experimenter to continue to punish the learner).

According to this analysis (see Higgins, 1990), changing the dissonant pattern from a social context guide nonmatch to a social context guide match (the "no choice" control condition of dissonance studies) should transform the psychological situation from dissonance to obedience to authority. And changing the obedience to authority pattern from a social context guide match to a social context guide nonmatch (the illusion of free choice) should transform the psychological situation from obedience to authority to dissonance. The literature supports these predictions. But what is important from the perspective of the present chapter is that these two classic phenomena both involve, first, people responding in relation to multiple and conflicting social standards and, second, people experiencing a particular type of psychological situation because of the specific pattern of matches, mismatches, and nonmatches that their response produces in relation to these multiple standards. Given that the former constitutes social action and the latter constitutes meaning, both of these phenemena involve the social psychology of cognition. Indeed, various phenomena that have been assigned traditionally to different areas of social psychology (e.g., person perception, intergroup relations, attitudes, conformity, and social communication) may involve standards as a basic mediating factor. Focusing more directly on this basic factor will both increase our understanding of social psychological phenomena and strengthen our ability to address mental health and other social problems.

Consider, for example, the potential utility of focusing on standards with respect to reducing the problem of affective disorders in our society. At the diagnostic stage, a focus on types of self-guides could permit useful distinctions between those suffering from dejection-related problems (e.g., discouragement, despair) and those suffering from agitation-related problems (e.g., nervousness, dread) as a function of whether ideal self-guides versus ought self-guides predominate, respectively. At the intervention stage, it would be useful to take into account the socialization processes that produce self-guides because it is the interpersonal relations associated with self-guides, and not just the content of self-guides per se, that result in commitment to them and resistance to changing them. Regardless of whether a self-guide is rational or reasonable, a person may believe that their relationship to some significant other would be impaired by changing the self-guide.

Standards are also involved in the therapeutic process itself, with the therapist providing both new factual standards and new guides. The facilitative effect of introducing these new standards could be maximized by understanding the impact of standards on (the client's) social action and meaning construction as well as by considering the psychological situations created by the inter-relations among the old and new standards. Finally, by under-standing the etiology of standards and their role in vulnerability to depression, it is possible to develop prevention programs. To the extent that social standards underlie basic self-regulatory and self-evaluative processes, programs supporting the acquisition of adaptive standards could have far-reaching positive consequences for society. Thus, a fuller understanding of social standards in particular, and the social psychology of cognition more generally, could provide major new tools for diagnosis, intervention, and prevention of mental health and other social problems.

On a final note, when modifying social standards, or any other major social psychological variable, to improve mental health it is necessary to appreciate the complexity of the underlying regula-tory system. Rarely do these systems produce simple main effects. Rather, these systems interact with current situational forces to produce both costs and benefits for the individual—regulatory "trade-offs." Self-guides, for example, function both as goals and as standards. Thus, socialization variables that strengthen self-guides increase both the likelihood of attaining goals by increasing motivation and the likelihood of distress by increasing negative self-evaluation when standards are not met. When motivation is sufficient to attain goals, then strong self-guides are an advantage. When motivation is not sufficient, then strong self-guides are a disadvantage. Higgins (1991) suggests that this trade-off may un-derlie the general phenomenon of girls being better off emotionally than boys in early elementary school but being worse off in high school, because girls generally have stronger self-guides than boys and nonmotivational variables become more important in high school. Evidence of this regulatory trade-off was also found in a recent study by Newman, Higgins, and Vookles (in press). Fir-stborns have stronger self-guides than later-borns. As predicted, Newman et al. found that firstborns had smaller self-discrepancies than later borns (because of their stronger goal to reduce dis-crepancies) but suffered more from any self-discrepancy that they did possess (because of their more intense negative self-evaluation when a standard is not met).

The trade-offs of the regulatory systems derive in large part because of complex interactions between self-regulatory variables and social regulatory variables. And both types of regulatory variables take other people into account. Thus, mental health prevention and intervention programs need to include "social"–cognitive factors to capture the full complexity of the functioning system. To overlook this level of analysis is both inefficient and risky.

REFERENCES

Abelson, R. P. (1968). Psychological implication. In R. P. Abelson, E. Aronson, W. J. McGuire, T. M. Newcomb, M. J. Rosenberg, & P. H. Tannenbaum (Eds.), *Theories of cognitive consistency: A source book.* Chicago: Rand McNally.

Allen, V. L., & Wilder, D. A. (1980). Impact of group consensus and social support on stimulus meaning: Mediation of conformity by cognitive restructuring. *Journal of Personality and Social Psychology, 39,* 1116–1124.

Andersen, S. M., & Cole, S. W. (1990). "Do I know you?": The role of significant others in general social perception. *Journal of Personality and Social Psychology, 59,* 384–399.

Anderson, R. C., & Pichert, J. W. (1978). Recall of previously unrecallable information following a shift in perspective. *Journal of Verbal Learning and Verbal Behavior, 17,* 1–12.

Aronson, E. (1969). The theory of cognitive dissonance: A current perspective. In L. Berkowitz (Ed.), *Advances in Experimental Social Psychology* (Vol. 4, pp. 1–34). New York: Academic Press.

Asch, S. E. (1948). The doctrine of suggestion, prestige, and imitation in social psychology. *Psychological Review, 55,* 250–276.

Asch, S. E. (1952). *Social psychology.* Englewood Cliffs, NJ: Prentice-Hall.

Asch, S. E. (1956). Studies of independence and conformity: A minority of one against a unanimous majority. *Psychology Monographs, 70* (No. 9, Whole No. 416).

Back, K. W. (1951). Influence through social communication. *Journal of Abnormal and Social Psychology, 46,* 9–23.

Bandura, A. (1977). *Social learning theory.* Englewood Cliffs, NJ:Prentice-Hall.

Baldwin, M. W., & Holmes, J. G. (1987). Salient private audiences and awareness of the self. *Journal of Personality and Social Psychology, 52,* 1087–1098.

Becker, H. S. (1963). *Outsiders: Studies in the sociology of deviance.* New York: Free Press.

Bovard, E. W., Jr. (1951). Group structure and perception. *Journal of Abnormal and Social Psychology, 46,* 398–405.

Burri, C. (1931). The influence of an audience upon recall. *Journal of Educational Psychology, 22,* 683–690.

Carver, C. S., & Humphries, C. (1981). Havana daydreaming: A study of self-consciousness and the negative reference group among Cuban Americans. *Journal of Personality and Social Psychology, 40,* 545–552.

Carver, C. S., & Scheier, M. F. (1978). Self-focusing effects of dispositional self-consciousness, mirror presence, and audience presence. *Journal of Personality and Social Psychology, 36,* 324–332.

Carver, C. S., & Scheier, M. F. (1981). *Attention and self-regulation: A control-theory approach to human behavior.* New York: Springer-Verlag.

Chandler, M. J. (1973). Egocentrism and antisocial behavior: The assessment and training of social perspective taking skills. *Developmental Psychology, 9,* 326–332.

Charters, W. W., & Newcomb, T. M. (1952). Some attitudinal effects of experimentally increased salience of a membership group. In G. E. Swanson, T. M. Newcomb, and E. L. Hartley (Eds.), *Readings in social psychology* (2nd ed.) (pp. 415–420). New York: Holt, Rinehart & Winston, 2nd ed.

Chassin, L., Presson, C. C., Sherman, S. J., Corty, E., & Olshavsky, R. W. (1984). Predicting the onset of cigarette smoking in adolescents: A longitudinal study. *Journal of Applied Social Psychology, 14,* 224–243.

Cialdini, R. B., Levy, A., Herman, P., Kozlowski, L., & Petty, R. E. (1976). Elastic shifts of opinion: Determinants of direction and durability. *Journal of Personality and Social Psychology, 34,* 663–672.

Cialdini, R. B., & Petty, R. E. (1981). Anticipatory opinion effects. In R. E. Petty, T. M. Ostrom, & T. C. Brock (Eds.), *Cognitive responses in persuasion.* Hillsdale, NJ: Erlbaum.

Cooley, C. H. (1964). *Human nature and the social order.* New York: Schock   en Books. (Original work published 1902)

Cooper, J., & Fazio, R. H. (1984). A new look at dissonance theory. In L. Berkowitz (Ed.), *Advances in Experimental Social Psychology* (Vol. 17, pp. 229–265). New York: Academic Press.

Darley, J. M., & Fazio, R. H. (1980). Expectancy confirmation processes arising in the social interaction sequence. *American Psychologist, 35,* 867–881.

Davis, K. E. (1962). Impressions of others and interaction context as determinants of social interaction in two-person discussion groups. Doctoral dissertation, Duke University. (University Microfilms No. 62-397-398)

Deaux, K., & Major, B. (1987). Putting gender into context: An interactive model of gender-related behavior. *Psychological Review, 94,* 369–389.

Deci, E. L. (1975). *Intrinsic motivation*. New York: Plenum Press.

Deci, E. L., & Ryan, R. M. (1985). *Intrinsic motivation and self-determination in human behavior*. New York: Plenum Press.

Deutsch, M., & Gerard, H. B. (1955). A study of normative and informational social influences upon individual judgment. *Journal of Abnormal and Social Psychology, 51*, 629–636.

Diener, E., & Srull, T. K. (1979). Self-awareness, psychological perspective, and self-reinforcement in relation to personal and social standards. *Journal of Personality and Social Psychology, 37*, 413–423.

Duval, S., & Wicklund, R. A. (1972). *A theory of objective self-awareness*. New York: Academic Press.

Dykman, B. M., & Abramson, L. Y. (1990). Contributions of basic research to the cognitive theories of depression. *Personality and Social Psychology Bulletin, 16*, 42–57.

Elkind, D. (1967). Egocentrism in adolescence. *Child Development, 38*, 1025–1034.

Fazio, R. H., Effrein, E. A., & Falender, V. J. (1981). Self-perceptions following social interaction. *Journal of Personality and Social Psychology, 41*, 232–242.

Feffer, M. (1970). Developmental analysis of interpersonal behavior. *Psychological Review, 77*, 197–214.

Felson, R. B. (1989). Parents and the reflected appraisal process: A longitudinal analysis. *Journal of Personality and Social Psychology, 56*, 965–971.

Festinger, L. (1950). Informal social communication. *Psychological Review, 57*, 271–282.

Festinger, L. (1954) A theory of social comparison processes. *Human Relations, 1*, 117–140.

Festinger, L. (1957). *A theory of cognitive dissonance*. Evanston, IL: Row, Peterson.

Frable, D. E. S., Blackstone, T., & Scherbaum, C. (1990). Marginal and mindful: Deviants in social interactions. *Journal of Personality and Social Psychology, 59*, 140–149.

Fussell, S. R., & Krauss, R. M. (1989). The effects of intended audience on message production and comprehension: Reference in a common ground framework. *Journal of Experimental Social Psychology, 25*, 203–219.

Gerard, H. B. (1954). The anchorage of opinions in face-to-face groups. *Human Relations, 7*, 313–326.

Goffman, E. (1959). *The presentation of self in everyday life*. Garden City, NY: Doubleday.

Goffman, E. (1961). *Asylums*. Garden City, NY: Anchor Books.

Grace, H.A. (1951). Effects of different degrees of knowledge about an audience on the content of communication. *Journal of Social Psychology, 34*, 111–124.

Hamilton, D. L. (Ed.). (1981). *Cognitive processes in stereotyping and intergroup behavior*. Hillsdale, NJ: Erlbaum.

Harvey, J. H., Yarkin, K. L., Lightner, J. M., & Town, J. P. (1980). Unsolicited interpretation and recall of interpersonal events. *Journal of Personality and Social Psychology, 38,* 551–568.

Hastie, R., Penrod, S. D., & Pennington, N. (1983). *Inside the jury.* Cambridge, MA: Harvard University Press.

Heider, F. (1958). *The psychology of interpersonal relations.* New York: Wiley.

Hensley, V., & Duval, S. (1976). Some perceptual determinants of perceived similarity, liking, and correctness. *Journal of Personality and Social Psychology, 34,* 159–168.

Higgins, E. T. (1981a). The "communication game": Implications for social cognition and persuasion. In E. T. Higgins, C. P. Herman, & M. P. Zanna (Eds.), *Social cognition: The Ontario Symposium* (Vol. 1, pp. 343–392). Hillsdale, NJ: Erlbaum.

Higgins, E. T. (1981b). Role taking and social judgment: Alternative developmental perspectives and processes. In J. H. Flavell & L. Ross (Eds.), *Social cognitive development: Frontiers and possible futures* (pp. 119–153). New York: Cambridge University Press.

Higgins, E. T. (1987). Self-discrepancy: A theory relating self and affect. *Psychological Review, 94,* 319–340.

Higgins, E. T. (1989a). Self-discrepancy theory: What patterns of self-beliefs cause people to suffer? In L. Berkowitz (Ed.), *Advances in experimental social psychology* (Vol. 22, pp. 93–136). New York: Academic Press.

Higgins, E. T. (1989b). Continuities and discontinuities in self-regulatory and self-evaluative processes: A developmental theory relating self and affect. *Journal of Personality, 57,* 407–444.

Higgins, E. T. (1990). Personality, social psychology, and person–situation relations: Standards and knowledge activation as a common language. In L. A. Pervin (Ed.), *Handbook of personality: Theory and research* (pp. 301–338). New York: Guilford Press.

Higgins, E. T. (1991). Development of self-regulatory and self-evaluative processes: Costs, benefits, and tradeoffs. In M. R. Gunnar & L. A. Sroufe (Eds.), *The Minnesota symposia on child development* (Vol. 23, pp. 125–165). Hillsdale, NJ: Erlbaum.

Higgins, E. T., & Bargh, J. A. (1987). Social cognition and social perception. *Annual Review of Psychology, 38,* 369–425.

Higgins, E. T., & King, G. (1981). Accessibility of social constructs: Information processing consequences of individual and contextual variability. In N. Cantor & J. Kihlstrom (Eds.), *Personality, cognition, and social interaction* (pp. 69–121). Hillsdale, NJ: Erlbaum.

Higgins, E. T., & McCann, C. D. (1984). Social encoding and subsequent attitudes, impressions, and memory: "Context-driven" and motivational aspects of processing. *Journal of Personality and Social Psychology, 47,* 26–39.

Higgins, E. T., McCann, C. D., & Fondacaro, R. (1982). The "communication-game": Goal-directed encoding and cognitive consequences. *Social Cognition, 1*, 21–37.

Higgins, E. T., & Sorrentino, R. M. (Eds.). (1990). *Handbook of motivation and cognition: Foundations of social behavior* (Vol. 2). New York: Guilford Press.

Higgins, E. T., & Stangor, C. (1988). Context-driven social judgment and memory: When "behavior engulfs the field" in reconstructive memory. In D. Bar-Tal & A. W. Kruglanski (Eds.), *The social psychology of knowledge* (pp. 262–298). New York: Cambridge University Press.

Higgins, E. T., & Tykocinski, O. (in press). Self-discrepancies and biographical memory: Personality and cognition at the level of psychological situation. *Personality and Social Psychology Bulletin*.

Holmes, J. G., & Boon, S. (1990). Developments in the field of close relationships: Creating foundations for intervention strategies. *Personality and Social Psychology Bulletin, 16*, 23–41.

Horney, K. (1946). *Our inner conflicts: A constructive theory of neurosis*. London: Routledge & Kegan Paul.

Houston, D. A. (1990). Empathy and the self: Cognitive and emotional influences on the evaluation of negative affect in others. *Journal of Personality and Social Psychology, 59*, 859–868.

Hyman, H. H. (1942). The psychology of status. *Archives of Psychology*, No. 269.

Jacobs, R. C., & Campbell, D. T. (1961). The perpetuation of an arbitrary tradition through several generations of a laboratory microculture. *Journal of Abnormal and Social Psychology, 62*, 649–658.

James, W. (1948). *Psychology*. New York: World Publishing. (Original work published 1890).

Janis, I. L., & Mann, L. (1965). Effectiveness of emotional role-playing in modifying smoking habits and attitudes. *Journal of Experimental Research in Personality, 1*, 84–90.

Jones, E. E. (1964). *Ingratiation: A social psychological analysis*. New York: Appelton-Century Croft.

Jones, E. E., & Davis, K. E. (1965). From acts to dispositions: The attribution process in person perception. In L. Berkowitz (Ed.), *Advances in experimental social psychology* (Vol. 2, pp. 219–266). New York: Academic Press.

Jones, E. E., & deCharms, R. (1958). The organizing function of interaction roles in person perception. *Journal of Abnormal and Social Psychology, 57*, 155–164.

Jones, E. E., Rhodewalt, F., Berglas, S., & Skelton, J. A. (1981). Effects of strategic self-presentation on subsequent self-esteem. *Journal of Personality and Social Psychology, 41*, 407–421.

Kahneman, D., & Tversky, A. (1973). On the psychology of prediction. *Psychological Review, 80*, 237–251.

Krauss, R. M., Vivekanathan, P. S., & Weinheimer (1968). "Inner speech" and "external speech": Characteristics and communicative effectiveness of socially and non-socially encoded messages. *Journal of Personality and Social Psychology, 9,* 295–300.

Kelley, H. H. (1952). Two functions of reference groups. In G. E. Swanson, T. M. Newcomb, & E.L. Hartley (Eds.), *Readings in social psychology* (2nd ed.). New York: Holt, Rinehart & Winston.

Kelley, H. H. (1967). Attribution theory in social psychology. In D. Levine (Ed.), *Nebraska symposium of motivation, 15,* 192–238.

Kruglanski, A. W. (1975). The endogenous-exogeneous partition in attribution theory. *Psychological Review, 82,* 387–406.

Latane, B., & Darley, J. M. (1969). Bystander "apathy." *American Scientist, 54,* 244–268.

Lepper, M. R., & Greene, D. (1978). *The hidden costs of rewards.* Hillsdale, NJ: Erlbaum.

Markus, H., & Cross, S. (1990). The interpersonal self. In L. A. Pervin (Ed.), *Handbook of personality: Theory and research* (pp. 576–608). New York: Guilford Press.

Markus, H., & Wurf, E. (1987). The dynamic self-concept: A social psychological perspective. *Annual Review of Psychology, 38,* 299–337.

McArthur, L. Z. (1981). What grabs you? The role of attention in impression formation and causal attribution. In E. T. Higgins, C. P. Herman, & M. P. Zanna (Eds.), *Social cognition: The Ontario symposium* (Vol. 1, pp. 201–246). Hillsdale, NJ: Erlbaum.

McCann, C. D., & Hancock, R. D. (1983). Self-monitoring in communicative interactions: Social–cognitive consequences of goal-directed message modification. *Journal of Experimental Social Psychology.*

McFarland, C., Ross, M., & Conway, M. (1984). Self-persuasion and self-presentation as mediators of anticipatory attitude change. *Journal of Personality and Social Psycholoyg, 46,* 529–540.

McGuire, W. J. (1969). The nature of attitudes and attitude change. In G. Lindzey & E. Aronson (Eds.), *The handbook of social psychology.* Reading, MA: Addison-Wesley.

McGuire, W. J., & Padawer-Singer, A. (1976). Trait salience in the spontaneous self-concept. *Journal of Personality and Social Psychology, 33,* 743–754.

Mead, G. H. (1934). *Mind, self, and society.* Chicago: University of Chicago Press.

Merton, R. K. (1957). *Social theory and social structure.* Glencoe, IL: The Free Press.

Merton, R. K., & Kitt, A. S. (1952). Contributions to the theory of reference-group behavior. In G. E. Swanson, T. M. Newcomb, & E. L. Hartley (Eds.), *Readings in social psychology* (2nd ed.) (pp. 430–444). New York: Holt, Rinehart & Winston.

Milgram, S. (1974). *Obedience to authority.* New York: Harper & Row.

Mischel, W. (1973). Toward a cognitive social learning reconceptualization of personality. *Psychological Review, 80,* 252–283.

Moore, B., & Underwood, B. (1981). The development of prosocial behavior. In S. S. Brehm, S. M. Kassin, & F. X. Gibbons (Eds.), *Developmental social psychology: Theory and research* (pp. 72–95). New York: Oxford University Press.

Moretti, M. M., Higgins, E. T., & Feldman, L. A. (1990). The self-system in depression: Conceptualization and treatment. In C. D. McCann & N. S. Endler (Eds.), *Depression: New directions in theory, research, and practice* (pp.127–156). Toronto: Wall Editions.

Moretti, M. M., & Shaw, B. F. (1989). Automatic and dysfunctional cognitive processes in depression. In J. S. Uleman & J. A. Bargh (Eds.), *Unintended thought* (pp. 383–421). New York: Guilford Press.

Moscovici, S. (1985). Social influence and conformity. In G. Lindzey & E. Aronson (Eds.), *Handbook of social psychology*, (3rd ed.) (Vol. 2, pp. 347–412). New York: Random House.

Moscovici, S., & Personnaz, B. (1980). Studies in social influence V: Minority influence and conversion behavior in a perceptual task. *Journal of Experimental Social Psychology, 16*, 270–282.

Newcomb, T. M. (1952). Attitude development as a function of reference groups: The Bennington study. In G. E. Swanson, T. M. Newcomb, & E. L. Hartley (Eds.), *Readings in social psychology* (2nd ed.) (pp. 420–430). New York: Holt, Rinehart & Winston.

Newman, L. S., Higgins, E. T., & Vookles, J. (in press). Strength of self-guides and emotional vulnerability: Birth order as a moderator. *Personality and Social Psychology Bulletin.*

Nisbett, R. E., & Ross, L. D. (1980). *Human inference: Strategies and shortcomings of informal judgment* (Century Series in Psychology). Englewood Cliffs, NJ: Prentice-Hall.

Rogers, C. R. (1959). A theory of therapy, personality, and interpersonal relationships, as developed in the client-centered framework. In S. Koch (Ed.), *Psychology: A study of a science, Volume 3, Formulations of the person and the social context* (pp. 184–256). New York: McGraw-Hill.

Rogers, C. R. (1961). *On becoming a person*. Boston: Houghton Mifflin.

Rosenberg, M. (1979). *Conceiving the self*. Malabar, FL: Robert E. Krieger.

Rosenthal, R., & Jacobson, L. (1968). *Pygmalion in the classroom: Teacher expectancies and pupils' intellectual development*. New York: Holt, Rinehart & Wilson.

Ross, L., Amabile, T. M.., & Steinmetz, J. L. (1977). Social roles, social control, and biases in socialperception processes. *Journal of Personality and Social Psychology, 35*, 485–494.

Ross, L., Greene, D., & House, P. (1977). The "false consensus effect": An egocentric bias in social perception and attribution precesses. *Journal of Experimental Social Psychology, 13*, 279–301.

Ross, M. (1975). Salience of reward and intrinsic motivation. *Journal of Personality and Social Psychology, 32*, 245–254.

Ross, M., & Fletcher, G. J. O. (1985). Attribution and social perception. In G. Lindzey & E. Aronson (Eds.), *Handbook of social psychology*, (3rd ed.) (Vol. 2, pp. 73–147).

Ruble, D. N. (1983). The development of social comparison processes and their role in achievementrelated self-socialization. In E. T. Higgins, D. N. Ruble, & W. W. Hartup (Eds.), *Social cognition and social development: A socio-cultural perspective* (pp. 134–157). New York: Cambridge University Press.

Sarbin, T. R., & Allen, V. L. (1968). Role theory. In G. Lindzey and E. Aronson (Eds.), *Handbook of social psychology* (2nd ed.) (Vol. 1, pp. 488–567). Reading, MA: Addison-Wesley.

Schachter, S. (1959). *The psychology of affiliation.* Stanford, CA: Stanford University Press.

Schachter, S., & Singer, J. E. (1962). Cognitive, social and physiological determinants of emotional state. *Psychological Review, 69,* 379–399.

Scheier, M. F., & Carver, C. S. (1983). Self-directed attention and the comparison of self with standards. *Journal of Experimental Social Psychology, 19,* 205–222.

Schlenker, B. R. (1980). *Impression management: The self-concept, social identity, and interpersonal relations.* Monterey, CA: Brooks/Cole.

Schlenker, B. R. (1985). Identity and self-identification. In B. R. Schlenker (Ed.), *The self and social life* (pp. 65–100). New York: McGraw-Hill.

Schneider, D. J. (1991). Social cognition. *Annual Review of Psychology, 42,* 527–561.

Segal, Z. V. (1988). Appraisal of the self-schema construct in cognitive models of depression. *Psychological Bulletin, 103,* 147–162.

Selman, R. L. (1980). *The growth of interpersonal understanding: Developmental and clinical analyses.* New York: Academic Press.

Seward, G. H. (1962). The relation between psychoanalytic school and value problems in therapy. *Amercial Journal of Psychoanalysis, 22,* 138–152.

Sherif, M. (1948). *An outline of social psychology.* New York: Harper.

Sherif, M. (1935). A study of some social factors in perception. *Archives Psychology,* No. 187.

Sherif, M. (1936). *The psychology of social norms.* New York: Harper & Brothers.

Sherif, M., & Sherif, C. W. (1969). *Social psychology.* New York: Harper & Row.

Sherman, S. J., & Corty, E. (1985). Cognitive heuristics. In R. S. Wyer, Jr. & T. K. Srull (Eds.), *Handbook of social cognition* (Vol. 1, pp. 189–286). Hillsdale, NJ: Erlbaum.

Sherman, S. J., Judd, C. M., & Park, B. (1989). Social cognition. *Annual Review of Psychology, 40,* 281–326.

Shrauger, J. S. (1982). Selection and processing of self-evaluative information: Experimental evidence and clinical implications. In G. Weary and H. L. Mirels (Eds.), *Integrations of clinical and social psychology* (pp. 128–153). New York: Oxford University Press.

Siegel, A., & Siegel, S. (1957). Reference groups, membership groups, and attitude change. *Journal of Abnormal and Social Psychology, 55,* 360–364.

Smith, E. R. (1990). Content and process specificity in the effects of prior experiences. In T. K. Srull & R. S. Wyer, Jr. (Eds.), *Advances in social cognition: Content and process specificity in the effects of prior experiences* (Vol. 3 pp. 1–59). Hillsdale, NJ: Erlbaum.

Snyder, M. (1979). Self-monitoring processes. In L. Berkowitz (Ed.), *Advances in experimental social psychology* (Vol. 12, pp. 85–128). New York: Academic Press.

Snyder, M., & Swann, W. B. (1978). Hypothesis-testing processes in social interaction. *Journal of Personality and Social Psychology, 36,* 1202–1212.

Snyder, M., Tanke, E. D., & Berscheid, E. (1977). Social perception and interpersonal behavior: On the self-fulfilling nature of social stereotypes. *Journal of Personality and Social Psychology, 35,* 656–666.

Sorrentino, R. M., & Higgins, E. T. (Eds.). (1986). *Handbook of motivation and cognition: Foundations of social behavior* (Vol. 2). New York: Guilford Press.

Sorrentino, R. M., King, G., & Leo, G. (1980). The influence of the minority on perception: A note and a possible alternative explanation. *Journal of Experimental Social Psychology, 16,* 293–301.

Spivak, G., & Shure, M. B. (1974). *Social adjustment of young children.* San Francisco: Jossey-Bass.

Stephan, W. G. (1985). Intergroup relations. In G. Lindzey & E. Aronson (Eds.), *Handbook of social psychology* (3rd ed.) (Vol.2, pp. 599–658). New York: Random House.

Stryker, S., & Statham, A. (1985). Symbolic interaction and role theory. In G. Lindzey & E. Aronson (Eds.), *Handbook of social psychology* (Vol. 1, pp. 311–378). New York: Random House.

Tajfel, H., & Turner, J. C. (1979). An integrative theory of intergroup conflict. In W. G. Austin & S. Worchel (Eds.), *The social psychology of intergroup relations.* Monterey, CA: Brooks/Cole.

Taylor, S. E., Buunk, B. P., & Aspinwall, L. G. (1990). Social comparison, stress, and coping. *Personality and Social Psychology Bulletin, 16,* 74–89.

Taylor, S. E., & Fiske, S. T. (1978). Salience, attention, and attribution: Top-of-the-head phenomena. In L. Berkowitz (Ed.), *Advances in experimental social psychology* (Vol. 11, pp. 249–288). New York: Academic Press.

Tedeschi, J. (1981). *Impression management theory and social psychological research.* New York: Academic Press.

Tesser, A. (1986). Some effects of self-evaluation maintenance on cognition and action. In R. M. Sorrentino & E. T. Higgins (Eds.), *Handbook of motivation and cognition: Foundations of social behavior* (Vol 1, pp. 435–464). New York: Guilford Press.

Thomas, W. I., & Znaniecki, F. (1918). *The Polish peasant in Europe and America* (Vol. 1). Boston: Badger.

Weber, M. (1967). Subjective meaning in the social situation. In G. B.

Levitas (Ed.), *Culture and consciousness: Perspectives in the social sciences* (pp. 156–169). New York: Braziller.

Wegner, D. M. (1986). Transactive memory: A contemporary analysis of the group mind. In B. Mullen & G. R. Goethals (Eds.), *Theories of group behavior* (pp. 185–208). New York: Springer-Verlag.

Weiner, B., & Kukla, A. (1970). An attributional analysis of achievement motivation. *Journal of Personality and Social Psychology, 15,* 1–20.

Wicklund, R. A. (1986). Orientation to the environment versus preoccupation with human potential. In R. M. Sorrentino & E. T. Higgins (Eds.), *Handbook of motivation and cognition: Foundations of social behavior* (Vol. 1, pp. 64–95). New York: Guilford Press.

Wills, T. A. (1981). Downward comparison principles in social psychology. *Psychological Bulletin, 90,* 245–271.

Wood, J. V., Taylor, S. E., & Lichtman, R. R. (1985). Social comparison in adjustment to breast cancer. *Journal of Personality and Social Psychology, 49,* 1169–1183.

Word, C. O., Zanna, M. P., & Cooper, J. (1974). The nonverbal mediation of self-fulfilling prophecies on interracial interaction. *Journal of Experimental Social Psychology, 10,* 109–120.

Wyer, R. S., & Srull, T. K. (1986). Human cognition in its social context. *Psychological Review, 93,* 322–359.

Wyer, R. S., & Srull, T. K. (1989). *Memory and cognition in its social context.* Hillsdale, NJ: Erlbaum.

Zajonc, R. B. (1960). The process of cognitive tuning and communication. *Journal of Abnormal and Social Psychology, 61,* 159–67.

Zajonc, R. B. (1980). Feeling and thinking: Preferences need no inferences. *American Psychologist, 35,* 151–175.

Zanna, M. P., & Pack, S. J. (1975). On the self-fulfilling nature of apparent sex differences in behavior. *Journal of Experimental Social Psychology, 11,* 583–591.

Zimmerman, C., & Bauer, R. A. (1956). The effect of an audience on what is remembered. *Public Opinion Quarterly, 20,* 238–248.

Zukier, H., & Pepitone, A. (1984). Social roles and strategies in prediction: Some determinants of the use of base rate information. *Journal of Personality and Social Psychology, 47,* 349–360.

Attitudes and Consistency Theories:
Implications for Mental Health

JOEL COOPER and JOSHUA M. ARONSON

The attitude has perhaps been the most widely studied concept in social psychology. Its measurement, function, and relationship with other cognitive structures have been the focus of thousands of experiments. Our understanding of mental health can benefit from basic research aimed at a deeper theoretical understanding of the way attitudes are formed, the way they change, and the way they interact with one another.

Because attitudes are so clearly linked to affect, thought, and behavior, the difference between mental health and mental illness can be viewed, to a certain degree, as a function of how adaptive one's attitudes are to the daily conflicts and challenges of the environment. Maladaptive attitudes can disable an individual because they make it difficult to cope with the environment. Mental health, conversely, may be characterized as a set of attitudes that are flexible and adaptive (Cooper & Cooper, 1991). For any program of research to deal completely with mental health, it must come to grips with the function of the attitude as well as the ways in which attitudes change.

In this chapter, we consider the functions that attitudes play and introduce major research themes in attitude research. In so doing, we highlight some of the research results that are particularly relevant to mental health. The concluding sections of the chapter take a set of approaches to the study of attitudes and illustrate more concretely how they can inform and elucidate the processes involved in clinical practice.

ATTITUDES: AN ORIENTATION
TO THE SOCIAL WORLD

One reason that attitudes may have been so extensively studied is the important role they play in guiding our reactions to the world.

Attitudes orient us quickly toward or away from an object or issue. To the extent we have strong attitudes, we know immediately that we are for or against, like or dislike, a particular attitude object: a given person, thing, or idea. Thus, the world becomes easier to navigate with attitudes guiding our reactions to at least some portion of the environment. Without attitudes to organize and guide our reactions to people, ideas, and objects, we would be paralyzed by confusion and uncertainty. On the other hand, attitudes that are overly rigid, that have no flexibility for change and adaptation, may lead to stress when confronted with new information that is at odds with internal views.

On the positive side, attitudes can be viewed as performing an extremely important *executive function*, a guide through the world of ambiguous and often confusing stimuli. This process has been shown to function without conscious awareness when the attitude in question is one that is strong and accessible. Such attitudes are activated quickly and lead to what Fazio and his colleagues (e.g., Fazio, 1986; Fazio, Lenn, & Effrein, 1984; Fazio, Chen, McDonel, & Sherman, 1982) have referred to as automatic processing, a process whereby strong attitudes quickly orient the individual toward particular interpretations of information patterns (e.g., Fazio, Powell, & Herr, 1983) or particular courses of action (Fazio & Zanna, 1981). Consider an individual who knows she likes other people. This attitude helps her organize events in her life. If she sees a group of people, she does not need to analyze each and every stimulus that emanates from the group of people. She does not need to create a decision about whether to approach or avoid people. Nor does she need to make her decision anew, each time she confronts others. Her strong, accessible attitude helps her respond in a positive manner toward people. She is prepared to feel positively about them and to approach them. Contrast this to the reactions of the misanthrope who knows he feels negatively about people. This person also organizes information but rapidly arrives at a different conclusion. His negative reaction may make him keenly aware of the presence of others, allow him to know that he feels negatively and wishes to avoid them. Moreover, the stronger the attitudes these two people have, the more immediate and automatic their reactions will be.

Thus, strong accessible attitudes, by helping us to interpret information and form priorities about which information to process and which behaviors to engage in, can produce an economy of the first order. It saves work and processing capacity that can be devoted to higher-order functions.

Fazio et al. (1982) provided an empirical example of the effects of attitude accessibility. They argued that attitudes are more accessible when formed through direct experience, thus facilitating rapid processing of attitude-relevant information to a greater degree than attitudes formed through indirect experience. For the purposes of research clarity, Fazio et al. created an attitude in the laboratory. Subjects in this study were introduced to a set of puzzles. One group actually worked with the puzzles whereas another group merely watched someone else work with them. Subjects were then given a reaction time task; they were shown an adjective and asked to indicate as quickly as possible if the adjective described their attitude toward the puzzles. The subjects who had actually worked with the puzzles were significantly faster to indicate the descriptiveness of each adjective. The greater accessibility of the attitudes formed through direct experience had a marked effect on the correspondence between subjects' attitudes toward the puzzles and their behavior toward them. There was greater consistency between the attitudes and behavior of the subjects whose attitudes toward the puzzles were forged through direct experience.

How else do attitudes become accessible and help to guide behavior? Research has been vigorous on this question. Krosnick (1989) takes the position that accessible attitudes are those that people find important, independent of how they were formed. Wood (1982) has taken the position that the amount of information and the depth of the belief structure that supports an attitude is indicative of the attitude's impact on our behaviors while Sivacek and Crano (1982) support the position that attitudes in which we have a "vested interest" are the ones that pervasively guide our behaviors. Identifying the criteria and the mechanisms that facilitate attitudes' impact on behavior remains an active and important area of research.

Despite the advantages to mental health provided by a system that automatically guides many of our thought processes and behaviors, there are a number of problems that can arise within this attitude system, problems leading to greater stress, and, at times, maladaptive thought and action. For example, when attitudes are inconsistent or contradictory, or imply conflicting behavioral tendencies and orientations, noxious arousal or stress typically results (Cooper & Fazio, 1984; Festinger, 1957). Moreover, attitudes formed in one context may activate behaviors that are inappropriate to new environmental contexts. Consider, for example, a person raised in a politically conservative area who moves to a new locale where such attitudes are unpopular. Or consider the racial bigot whose attitudes make it impossible for him or her to adapt to a new pluralistic community. These individuals are likely to experience stress because their deeply held, highly accessible attitudes no longer lead to socially acceptable behaviors. Often, the primary goal of the psychotherapist is to help the individual change or reevaluate attitudes learned in childhood that are fundamentally at odds with productive adult functioning. It seems reasonable to assume that the more inflexible an individual's attitudes, the more likely new situations will be to arouse stress or lead to inappropriate, maladaptive behaviors.

More research is needed on the relationship among attitudes, stress, and mental health. Existing research has merely scratched the surface. We need to know more about the kinds of attitudes that promote and impair effective transactions with the social world, the systems in which those attitudes are embedded, and the strategies one might undertake to resolve conflicts between incompatible attitudes.

FROM ATTITUDES TO BEHAVIOR

Determining and predicting the relationship between behavior and attitudes have long been a primary goal of psychologists and philosophers alike. Early on, psychologists embraced the commonsense assumption that attitudes determine behavior. However, it was not long before this view was seriously questioned. LaPiere's (1934) classic study provided the first notable challenge. On an automobile tour of the United States, LaPiere accompanied a Chinese couple to over 250 hotels and restaurants. Despite the considerable anti-Chinese prejudice of the era, the couple was served without incident in all but one of the establishments. After the trip, LaPiere wrote to each of the establishment owners asking whether they would be willing to serve an oriental couple planning a visit to their area. More than 90% of the owners said they would refuse service to nonwhite customers. Thus, the owners were stating attitudes that directly contradicted their own recent behavior.

Findings like LaPiere's have not been unusual. The literature is replete with findings that suggest that people do not always act consistently with their attitudes (Wicker, 1969). However, this establishes a psychological quandary because we also know that people prefer consistency among their cognitions (Heider, 1946). Empirical work has shown time and again both the preference for consistent cognitions and how individuals will change their attitudes when such consistency is threatened (Newcomb, 1956; 1963; Abelson et al., 1968). If people prefer consistency yet sometimes fail to act consistently with their attitudes, how may the discrepancy be explained?

One successful attempt to understand the often paradoxical relationship between attitudes and behavior is the *theory of reasoned action*, developed by Ajzen and Fishbein (1980). The model assumes that people behave in a deliberate, rational way. Behavior is the result of intentions formed through a mindful consideration of their attitudes toward a behavior and a subjective norm, that is, the individual's beliefs about how others think they should behave. Thus, attitude and assessment of the appropriateness of the behavior combine to form a behavioral intention. The model views the intention to perform the behavior as the best predictor of behavior.

When attitudes are strong (i.e., highly accessible) and specific to the behavior in question, and the norms of the situation do not discourage the behavior, the attitudes are likely to lead to congruent behavior. However, the assessment of the subjective norm can weaken or eliminate the intention to behave consistently with attitudes. Thus, it is likely that LaPiere's business owners did indeed have negative attitudes toward Chinese people; however, they failed to act on these attitudes most likely because of a subjective norm: in this case, perhaps, the desire to avoid an unpleasant confrontation with the trio.

The theory of reasoned action has proved quite useful for prediction—often in health-related domains. For example, assessments of subjective norms and attitudes have been accurate in predicting the use of birth control pills (Davidson & Jaccard, 1979), cigarette smoking (Fishbein, 1980), and weight loss (Schifter & Ajzen, 1985). Because proponents of the theory view behavioral intention as the most reliable predictor of behavior, stated intentions, in addition to measures of attitude change, are used to assess the effectiveness of educational interventions. Recent research on efforts to encourage safe sex provide a noteworthy example. Jemmott, Jemmott, and Fong (1990) gave inner-city adolescents an AIDS risk-reduction intervention and found that compared to controls, these subjects reported lowered intentions to engage in risky sexual behavior. A follow-up survey indicated that these subjects had acted on their intentions; that is, those given the risk-reducing intervention reported having engaged in less risky sexual behavior than did the control subjects. Because research of this type measures self-reports of behavior rather than behavior itself, one particularly beneficial avenue for basic research is to address the conditions under which intentions will reliably predict behavior. Nonetheless, it is clear that interventions aimed at changing unhealthy attitudes can significantly impact mental and physical health.

PERSUASION: CHANGING ATTITUDES TO CHANGE BEHAVIOR

From the theory of reasoned action, and from Fazio's automatic processing model, we have a much better understanding of the occasions on which attitudes predict or lead to behaviors consistent with those attitudes. It follows, then, that the study of attempts to influence attitudes is extremely important to changing behaviors relevant to mental health. For example, convincing someone to leave a stressful job, improve a stressful relationship, or enter into psychotherapy is a function of social influence and persuasion. Within psychotherapy, convincing people to alter their self-relevant attitudes and thus try new and productive behaviors is also be a function of influence and persuasion (Cacioppo, Petty, & Stoltenberg, 1985; Frank, 1961).

The study of persuasion has traditionally been one of the major areas of basic research in social psychology. A vast literature has addressed the factors that make some communications more effective than others. Until recently, what was known about the process of attitude change through persuasion could be gleaned from the research conducted by Carl Hovland and his colleagues at the Yale Communication and Attitude Change Program. Rooted deeply in Hullian learning tradition, their approach viewed the persuasion process as one in which the target of persuasion was induced to "learn" a new attitude. Accordingly, the focus was on the variables they thought would have the greatest impact on this learning process. Aspects of the communicator, the message, and the audience were systematically varied, resulting in an approach that became known as the "who says what to whom with what effect" paradigm (Lasswell, 1948). This work focused on the importance of such factors as the credibility of a communicator (Hovland & Weiss, 1952), the strength of the communication (Hovland, Janis, & Kelley, 1953), and the existing attitudes of the audience (Hovland, Harvey, & Sherif, 1957).

In the last few years, however, a number of communication

theorists have offered a new approach to the study of persuasion that has been able to incorporate these findings in a more comprehensive, less confusing fashion. The most widely cited of these new theorists, Petty and Cacioppo (e.g., 1986) propose that individuals can be persuaded in two different ways. When people carefully process the contents of a communication, they will be influenced by the strength of the arguments. This is referred to as the "central route" to persuasion. But when unmotivated or unable to process the contents of a communication, people will take the "peripheral route" to persuasion. That is, they are more apt to be persuaded by cues or heuristics that are incidental to the content of the communication. The model assumes, then, that recipients do not always process messages in the same way. The route that is taken depends on the amount of elaboration, or careful consideration, the person is likely to give to the message content. The model is hence referred to as the elaboration likelihood model (ELM) of persuasion.

An equally important theoretical point of view has been expressed by Chaiken and her colleagues (e.g., Chaiken, 1980; Eagly & Chaiken, 1984). The heuristic processing model conceives of people as either being motivated to systematically process the content of a persuasive message or, without such motivation, to process heuristically. Although there are some interesting conceptual differences between the ELM and the heuristic processing model, the notion of systematic processing is akin to Cacioppo and Petty's concept of central processing. Heuristic processing, in which the audience uses heuristic shortcuts to process the significance of a message, is akin to the ELM's notion of the peripheral route to persuasion.

When elaboration is high—that is, when the audience is able and motivated to carefully and systematically consider the arguments embodied in a message—the process is deliberate: People will work hard to process the message and, in most cases, attitudes will change to the extent that the arguments are strong. However, when people are not motivated to examine carefully the content of the message, the likelihood of elaboration is low. For example, if the audience is uninvolved, tired, or bored, or the speaker speaks unintelligibly, persuasion is likely to be a matter of peripheral or heuristic cues. Thus, the audience member unable or unwilling to process the content of a political debate will be more likely to be swayed by a speaker's style, perceived credibility, or physical attractiveness. It is because such cues can result in considerable persuasion that politicians frequently eschew discussion of the issues in favor of campaign slogans, that advertisers pay millions to star athletes and entertainers to endorse their products, and that defense attorneys make sure their clients are well dressed for court.

The question of when message recipients will engage in central versus peripheral processing has been the focus of considerable research. One particularly important determinant appears to be personal involvement with an issue. People tend to be less swayed by peripheral cues when they care about a particular issue or when they have reason to believe they will be required to discuss the issue at a future time. For example, Chaiken (1980) varied both the number of persuasive arguments in a communication and the likability of the source. The persuasive arguments provided the basis for systematic processing, while the likability of the source provided for the possibility of a hueristic cue. Half of the subjects participating in the study were led to believe they would be discussing the issue at a later date (high involvement); half were not (low involvement). High-involvement subjects appeared to be unaffected by the likability of the source—the peripheral cue—and quite responsive to the content of the message. Low-involvement subjects, on the other hand, were far more responsive to the likability of the communicator and rather unresponsive to the message content.

Cacioppo et al. (1985) take the position that psychotherapeutic change is more stable and enduring to the extent that persuasion occurs centrally. To the extent that counseling or psychotherapy situations involve people being persuaded to change their attitudes about themselves or others, centrally induced persuasion will be longer lasting (Cialdini, Levy, Hermann, Kozlowski, & Petty, 1976) and resistant to counterattack (Petty & Cacioppo, 1983). In addition, there is some evidence that a centrally produced attitude change also leads to more attitude-consistent behaviors than a peripherally produced attitude change (Sivacek & Crano, 1982). Nonetheless, attitude change that occurs through heuristic cues can also be useful in the mental health arena. People who seem less involved in their own mental health, or who are not as capable of understanding the messages provided to them by the counselor, are likely to be persuaded by peripheral cues. Although thought to be more temporary in duration, attitudes that change in accord with heuristic cues are "not entirely without merit" (Cacioppo et al., 1985, p. 284).

The contention that central processing is basically superior to peripheral processing as a means of achieving durable changes in attitudes and behaviors is an important one that calls out for further research. When people have their attitudes changed by nonsystematic processing, it could be argued that their attitudes are *less* susceptible to counterattack because their attitudes were not formed by logical means in the first instance. Consider subjects in a study by Zanna, Kiesler, and Pilkonis (1970). By using a pairing with the onset and offset of electric shock, they were classically conditioned to feel more positively about the word "light" than the word "dark". In a subsequent test, it was also found that the subjects had more positive attitudes toward the concept "white" than the concept "black". Could logical, systematic processing change this attitude when it was formed through contiguous pairing of the concept with an unconditioned stimulus? Classical conditioning is certainly persuasion through the peripheral route. Whether it is as temporary, fragile, and susceptible to change as Cacioppo et al. (1985) contend is a fascinating and open question.

At the very least, the ELM and the heuristic processing model can be quite useful for those interested in changing maladaptive attitudes because it can aid in tailoring the most appropriate approach given a particular issue or audience.

FROM BEHAVIORS TO ATTITUDES

Previously we considered the quandary caused by the relationship of attitudes and behaviors. We noted that attitudes do not always lead to consistent behaviors, although a consideration of such factors as attitude strength and the imputed social norm greatly increase behavioral consistency. The study of persuasion is important for understanding mental health, because of its direct relationship to important self-related attitudes and the relationship between those attitudes and behaviors.

We now come at this problem from the other direction: Numerous studies have shown that under certain circumstances, people will form attitudes consistent with experimentally induced behavior and, moreover, will change preexisting attitudes to fit those behaviors. Thus, it has been suggested that we are more inclined to be rationalizing than rational (Abelson, 1972; Aronson, 1969). Various theories have attempted to explain this phenomenon, some taking radically different views of the underlying process. For example, some theories focus on the intrapsychic, stressing the importance of internal consistency for human functioning (Abelson & Rosenberg, 1958; Festinger, 1957). Others have explained the same intrapsychic phenomenon taking the perspective borrowed from the conditioning literature (Bem, 1972). Several theories have highlighted the importance of the self-concept in producing consistency effects (e.g., Aronson, 1969; Greenwald & Ronis, 1978; Steele, 1988). Still others have viewed the phenomenon as stemming from interpersonal roots, with the motivation for consistency directly resulting from a desire to present oneself as consistent to others (Schlenker, 1982; Tedeschi, Schlenker, & Bonoma, 1971). All of the above perspectives, however, share the assumption that changes in behavior will lead to changes in attitude.

Cognitive Dissonance

Of these theories, cognitive dissonance theory (Festinger, 1957) has been the most thoroughly researched and arguably the most widely accepted statement about the relationship between people's behaviors and attitudes. For this reason, it provides the best case in point for recognizing the importance of basic social psychological research leading to a greater understanding of health and mental health issues.

In brief, Festinger's version of cognitive dissonance theory holds that the perception of inconsistency among cognitions leads to psychological tension. This tension is experienced as unpleasant and needs to be reduced. People can reduce the tension by altering one or more cognitions to bring them into harmony with one another. For example, dissonance theory predicts that if a person behaves in a manner contrary to an attitude, he or she will be likely to change a cognition to reduce the tension produced by the inconsistency. Typically, people will alter the cognition that is least resistant to change. Cognitions about underlying attitudes ("I believe x") tend to be more easily modified than cognitions about behaviors ("I just said not x"), because the behavior has been committed and is hard to deny whereas the underlying attitude is murky and not as fixed (Festinger & Carlsmith, 1959).

Theorists attempting to revise dissonance theory have downplayed the role of inconsistency per se in producing dissonance phenomena. Noting that only certain inconsistencies would result in dissonance, revisionist views focused instead on the role of unwanted consequences (Cooper & Fazio, 1984) or on violations of the self-image (Aronson, 1969; Steele, 1988; Swann, 1987) in producing dissonance arousal. But all proponents of the notion of dissonance arousal agree that tension occurs when a person with a positive self-view acts contrary to his or her attitude and brings about an unwanted consequence in the process.

Induced Compliance

Consider an individual who is induced to do or say something that is at variance with an important attitude. Suppose that a politically conservative citizen, who privately believes that the homeless in New York City should be treated as vagrant criminals, is induced to make a speech to the city council advocating an increase in physical and mental health services to the homeless. Provided he feels personally responsible for the decision to give the speech, he is likely to experience tension arising from the discrepancy between his true attitude (against increasing services to the homeless) and the position he took in the speech (in support of greater services). The tension will lead to an attempt to bring the conflicting cognitions into greater harmony with one another. Since it would be difficult for him to deny making the speech, we can be fairly confident that the tension will lead to a modification of his attitudes toward mental and physical health services for the homeless.

Numerous studies have supported the prediction that attitudes will change to become more consistent with public behavior. The earliest demonstration of the prediction was the classic Festinger and Carlsmith experiment (1959). In that study, subjects performed a very dull and tedious task for a long time. Later, the experimenter induced each subject to convince a fellow student waiting to participate in the study that the task was actually quite interesting. Subjects were paid for telling this lie. As predicted by the theory, when subjects were paid a large sum for lying to the other student, their attitudes about the dull task did not change. But when the subjects were paid only a paltry sum for misleading the other student, they reduced the dissonance by changing their attitude toward the task; they came to see the task as more interesting, thus reducing the inconsistency between their attitude and what they told the waiting student.

Subsequent research has identified many conditions necessary for counterattitudinal behavior to lead to attitude change. For attitude change to occur, the behavior must be engaged in freely, for small external rewards, and must potentially lead to an unwanted consequence for which the individual feels responsible. When these conditions are met, research has consistently shown that people change their attitudes on a wide variety of issues, including smoking marijuana (Nel, Helmreich & Aronson, 1969), presidential politics (Cooper & Mackie, 1983), and an array of local and national political issues (see, e.g., Cooper & Croyle, 1984, for a review).

PUTTING ATTITUDE RESEARCH TO WORK: CHANGING MALADAPTIVE ATTITUDES

Induced Compliance

Dissonance procedures may be a particularly useful way to change unhealthy, maladaptive attitudes. By inducing people to engage in counterattitudinal behavior, we may be able to produce changes in maladaptive attitudes, which in turn may result in more permanent changes of behavior.

Consider the problem of convincing a young, male teenager to engage in safer sexual practices as a way of reducing his risk of getting the AIDS virus. He may have negative attitudes toward condom use, believing that condoms reduce the spontaneity of sex and that "anyway, it can't happen to me." His perception of the social norm (recall Ajzen & Fishbein, 1980) is that teenagers do not use condoms. Harnessing consistency motives may offer an effective approach to changing his attitude. Research on induced compliance suggests a multistep process of changing our subject's attitude toward safe sex.

First, we must obtain a behavior that is at variance with his anticondom position. This can be done in a number of ways. The most direct method would involve inducing the subject to use a condom, perhaps offering a minimal reward, or convincing him of his freedom to engage in the behavior. We know from numerous studies that rewards need to be substantial enough to elicit agreement to perform the behavior but small enough not to be perceived as the sole reason for engaging in the behavior (Cooper & Fazio, 1984; Festinger & Carlsmith, 1959). As for free will, we know that if subjects feel coerced to perform the behavior, attitude change will be minimal at best (Linder, Cooper, & Jones, 1967).

These variables are not mere details. Uncareful manipulations of reward and choice can lead to attitude change in the direction opposite to that desired. For example, if people are *overrewarded* for engaging in a given activity, they tend to abandon the activity when no longer rewarded. The abundance of the reward causes people to attribute their motivation to the reward rather than their own positive attitude toward the behavior (Lepper, Greene, & Nisbett, 1973). Similarly, exhortations to engage in particular behaviors can often result in people reasserting their freedom to do or believe the opposite of that requested (Brehm, 1972).

Thus, inducing the target to use condoms in such a way that his attitudes will follow suit will be no easy matter. Purely from a health standpoint, obtaining a behavior is more important than inducing a procondom attitude. But unless he has a strong and accessible procontraceptive attitude to guide future behaviors, our friend will likely continue engaging in risky sexual behavior.

From a pragmatic standpoint, rather than trying to induce condom use itself, it may be more feasible to have the target behave in ways that are related to his attitudes toward condom use—behaviors that could be performed in either the laboratory, the classroom, or the clinic. For example, we might induce him to make a statement to someone else stressing the importance of practicing safe sex. This methodology is akin to any number of experimental studies of induced compliance (e.g., Cohen, 1962; Scher & Cooper, 1989).

Indeed, such a study was recently performed by Thibodeau, Aronson, Dickerson, and Miller (1990). In this study, subjects were videotaped making a speech on the importance of wearing a condom during sex. Dissonance was aroused in some of the subjects by asking them a series of loaded questions designed to make them mindful of the occasions when they themselves had practiced unsafe sex. The measure of attitude change in this study was subjects' intentions to use condoms in the future. As predicted, subjects made mindful of the inconsistency between their procondom speech and their failure to always use condoms stated the greatest intentions to use condoms in the future. Follow-up interviews, moreover, indicated greater adherence to safe sex practices among those subjects made mindful of the discrepancy between their practices and their preachings.

Coming from a slightly different theoretical position, clinical psychologists have used role rehearsals (Kelly, 1955) or covert self-verbalizations (Meichenbaum & Goodman, 1971) to produce attitude-discrepant behaviors. Spivak, Platt, and Shure (1976) had children with antisocial and aggressive attitudes rehearse alternative strategies for dealing with conflict. Each of these approaches has been successful in producing both overt and covert behaviors inconsistent with maladaptive prior attitudes. Each should provide the first behavioral step toward attitude change via induced compliance.

One particularly maladaptive and destructive attitude is low self-esteem. Dissonance procedures have been successfully employed to raise the self-esteem of experimental subjects. In one induced compliance study (Jones, Rhodewalt, Berglas, & Skelton, 1981), subjects with low self-esteem were induced to make self-promoting statements about themselves under conditions of either high or low choice. The self-esteem of the subjects was measured after their speech. The results were clear. The high-choice subjects' self-esteem improved to a significant degree whereas that of the low-choice subjects remained stable. Such a procedure appears to be a plausible technique for improving attitudes about the self as well as attitudes in general, for as much research has shown, given the proper conditions, "saying is believing" (Higgins, 1987; Janis & King, 1954).

Attribution

Basic research on attribution has focused on how people explain their own and others' behavior. Many principles learned from the attributional approach can be effectively applied to the issue of health. Attribution is often inextricably linked to the attitude–behavior issue because the nature of our attitudes depends, in large part, on the way we explain our behavior. For example, we mentioned earlier that a necessary precondition for dissonance was that the person attribute the behavior to his or her own intentions.

Bem's (1972) self-perception theory is perhaps the clearest and simplest statement about the link between attributions for behaviors and attitudes about the self. The theory states that we often infer our attitudes from observations of our behavior. To the extent that the reward or coercion is minimal—or, at least, not terribly salient—we will draw an inference about the type of person we are. For example, if I vote democratic and am neither forced nor paid to do so, I will likely infer that I am a democrat. Such reasoning has led to powerful demonstrations of behavior and attitude change with often surprisingly minor manipulations.

The classic *foot-in-the-door* technique (Freedman & Fraser, 1966) is a demonstration of how attitudes about the self can be altered with minimal behavior. The study demonstrated that people were much more likely to comply with a large and rather bothersome request (displaying a large and unsightly "Drive Carefully" sign on their front lawn) if they had previously agreed to a much smaller one (signing a "Drive Carefully" petition). The effect owes, presumably, to a change in the self-concept of the subject who infers from the signing of the petition an attitude congruent with careful driving.

The opportunities for useful intervention are clear. Returning to our at-risk, sexually active teenager, the foot-in-the-door approach to inducing healthy attitudes may hold promise. Requests for small, difficult-to-refuse behaviors that are in line with a healthy attitude toward the AIDS problem could perhaps set the stage for a self-concept change in the direction of a more risk-averse self-image.

Self-attributions need not be made by the individual in order to be effective, however. They can be made *for* the individual, thus increasing the flexibility of attributional techniques for attitude and behavior change. For example, Miller, Brickman, and Bolen (1975) reasoned that one way to induce people to perform a desired behavior is to convince them that they are predisposed to such behavior. In their study, fifth graders were told repeatedly how neat and tidy they were. The children's littering behavior was observed for a period of 2 weeks. The attributions had a powerful effect on the children's tendency to litter and to clean up their surroundings. Those children who were told how neat they were littered significantly less and cleaned up significantly more than a group of children who were asked repeatedly to be neater or a control group who were told nothing at all.

EFFORT JUSTIFICATION AND THE PSYCHOTHERAPEUTIC PROCESS

One derivation from the consistency perspective that is particularly relevant to mental health is the prediction from dissonance theory that we come to value that for which we have suffered. Why is it that people often appear to persist in seemingly unrewarding jobs or find it hard to leave abusive relationships? Part of the answer may lie in our tendency to justify our behavior to ourselves. Because it is dissonant and therefore unpleasant to admit that we have spent time, money, and effort—or suffered—in vain, we can reduce this dissonance by embellishing the fruits of our labor. Aronson and Mills (1959) were the first to put this hypothesis to the test. In their experiment, they invited female students to join a group engaged in a series of discussions about sex. The young women were told that before entering the group they would have to pass a screening test in order to make sure they were not too squeamish to openly discuss sexual matters. The test involved the public reading of sexually explicit materials. One group received a rather severe initiation to the group. They had to read a list of obscene words and lurid passages excerpted from novels. A second group received a milder initiation, requiring them to read a list of "cleaner" sexual terms. The third group was not required to take the screening test. All subjects then were permitted to listen through earphones to the group they would later be joining in person. Actually, what they heard was a tape recording of a dreadfully boring discussion on the secondary sexual characteristics of lower animals. Aronson and Mills predicted that the dissonance produced by having chosen to suffer would be reduced by subjects elevating the attractiveness of the group that they had tried to join. The results confirmed this hypothesis, indicating that the women who underwent the severe initiation rated the group as more interesting and attractive than those in the mild or no initiation groups. By elevating the value of the goal for which they had suffered, their effort seemed less inconsistent.

Cooper and Axsom (1982) suggested that the effort-justification phenomenon may provide a way to understand the effects of psychotherapy. They argued that most psychotherapies, regardless of their theoretical basis, share some common features. Clients volunteer to engage in some form of effortful procedure. In some cases, it may be the the difficult business of recalling old, emotionally painful memories. In others, it may be the anxiety of revealing oneself to a potentially judgmental "authority". Whatever the rationale, most therapies engage clients in an effortful, time-consuming, and typically costly set of procedures. The formal features of the therapy situation bear a marked resemblance to the formal features of effort-justification research.

A study by Cooper (1980) underscored this similarity. Cooper established two types of psychotherapy for the treatment of snake phobia. One was an adaptation of implosion therapy (Stampfl & Levis, 1967). The other was an "effort therapy" in which subjects were led to believe that doing physical exercises (pushups, jumping jacks, etc.) would lead to an amelioration of their fear. The results showed that implosive therapy and effort therapy were equally effective at reducing subjects' fear of snakes.

Basic research often generates applications and insights into mental health problems because it isolates variables often overlooked in direct applications. Research in dissonance theory has shown conclusively that responsibility, usually operationalized as "choice", is a necessary factor for arousing cognitive dissonance. Thus, Cooper had two conditions within each of the two therapy conditions of his experiment—a choice condition and a no-choice condition. The results of the two no-choice conditions showed that neither therapy had any impact on subjects' fear of snakes. That is, the crucial determinant of fear reduction was not the type of therapy but rather subjects' expenditure of effort (physical or psychological) and their perception of choice to undergo therapy.

Whereas most of the theories underlying psychotherapy (psychoanalysis, learning theory, etc.) are silent about the need for choice, dissonance and other consistency theories are not. The importance of the choice variable helps us make sense sense of the virtual worthlessness of most therapies that are ordered or forced by social agencies. Clients in court-ordered treatment for drug and alcohol abuse, for example, are notorious for their high rates of recidivism. This makes sense in light of the importance of choice in bringing about the desired therapeutic results. The research indicates that perspective clients need to have at least the perception of decision freedom in order for the therapy to be effective.

Axsom and Cooper (1985) followed up the previous work by using effort-justification therapy to help participants lose weight. Subjects were community members seeking help with their weight loss. Participants were placed in either a high- or low-effort condition. High-effort subjects performed a set of demanding cognitive tasks as part of a "cognitive therapy". Low-effort subjects were given a much less demanding version of the tasks. The results showed that the high-effort subjects lost anaverage of 7½ pounds and maintained the weight loss after a year. Low-effort subjects lost no weight at all.

Finally, Axsom (1989) demonstrated that therapeutic gains were greatest under both high-effort and high-choice conditions. By varying the magnitudes of choice and effort in a factorial design, he was able to have university students overcome their fear of public speaking when they expended a high degree of effort under conditions of high-decision freedom.

The variables that were found to be of critical importance in this research were generated from dozens of studies conducted under the rubric of basic, theoretical social psychology. Their application to the betterment of mental health may have only been a glimmer of an idea at the inception of each project. However, without a full understanding of the theoretical underpinnings of this therapy, the conditions necessary for changing maladaptive attitudes and behaviors might never have been tested.

CONCLUSION

Attitude and attitude-consistency theories have had long histories of research. It is only recently that we began to see the functional importance of the attitude in alleviating stress and maintaining mental health. Also new is the illumination of the conditions under which attitudes—adaptive or maladaptive—lead to corresponding behaviors. We are just beginning to develop ways to apply our theories of consistency to the issues of maladaptive thought and action. Such application of theory to practice can prove appropriate and effective only with a full understanding of those theories. Basic research on such concepts as attitudes and attitude–behavior consistency must go hand in hand with application if behavioral science is to have a successful impact on mental health.

REFERENCES

Abelson, R. (1972). Are attitudes necessary? In B. T. King & E. McGinnis (Eds.), *Attitudes, conflicts, and social change.* New York: Academic Press.

Abelson, R., Aronson, E., McGuire, W., Newcomb, T. Rosenberg, M., & Tannerbaum, P. (1968). *Theories of cognitive consistency: A source book.* Chicago: Rand McNally.

Abelson, R., & Rosenberg, M. (1958). Symbolic psycho-logic. A Model of Attitudinal Cognition. *Behavioral Science, 3,* 1–13.

Ajzen, I., & Fishbein, M. (1980). *Understanding attitudes and predicting social behavior.* Englewood Cliffs, NJ: Prentice-Hall.

Aronson, E. (1969). The theory of cognitive dissonance: A current perspective. In L. Berkowitz (ed.), *Advances in experimental social psychology* (Vol. 4, pp. 2–32). New York: Academic Press.

Aronson, E., & Mills, J. (1959). The effect of severity of initiation on liking for a group. *Journal of Abnormal and Social Psychology, 59,* 177–181.

Axsom, D. (1989). Cognitive dissonance and behavior change in psychotherapy. *Journal of Experimental Social Psychology, 25,* 234–252.

Axsom, D., & Cooper, J. (1985). Cognitive dissonance and psychotherapy: The role of effort justification in inducing weight loss. *Journal of Experimental Social Psychology, 21,* 149–160.

Bem, D. (1972). Self-perception theory. In L. Berkowitz (ed.), *Advances in experimental social psychology* (Vol. 6, pp. 2–57). New York: Academic Press.

Brehm, J. W. (1972). *Responses to loss of freedom: A theory of psychological reactance.* Morristown, NJ: General Learning Press.

Cacioppo, J. T., Petty, R. E., & Stoltenberg, C. D. (1985). Processes of social influence: The elaboration likelihood model of persuasion. *Advances in Cognitive-Behavioral Research and Therapy, 4,* 218–274.

Chaiken, S. (1980). Heuristic versus systematic information processing and the use of source versus message cues in persuasion. *Journal of Personality and Social Psychology, 39,* 752–66.

Cialdini, R. B., Levy, A., Hermann, P., Kozlowski, L., & Petty, R. E. (1976). Elastic shifts of opinion: Determinants of direction and durability. *Journal of Personality and Social Psychology, 34,* 663–672.

Cohen, A. R. (1962). An experiment on small rewards for discrepant compliance and attitude change. In J. W. Brehm & A. R. Cohen (Eds.), *Explorations in cognitive dissonance.* New York: Wiley.

Cooper, J. (1980). Reducing fears and increasing assertiveness: The role of dissonance reduction. *Journal of Experimental Social Psychology, 16,* 199–213.

Cooper, J., & Axsom, D. (1982). Effort justification in psychotherapy. In G. Weary & H. Mirels (Eds.), *Integrations of clinical and social psychology.* New York: Oxford University Press.

Cooper, A., & Cooper, J. (1991). How people change: In and out of therapy. In R. Curtis & G. Stricker (Eds.), *How people change: Inside and outside of therapy.* New York: Plenum Press.

Cooper, J., and Croyle, R. T. (1984). Attitudes and attitude change. *Annual Review of Psychology, 35,* 395–426.

Cooper, J., & Fazio, R. H. (1984). A new look at dissonance theory. In L. Berkowitz (Ed.), *Advances in experimental social psychology* (Vol. 17, pp. 229–262). New York: Academic Press.

Cooper, J., & Mackie, D. N. (1983). Cognitive dissonance in an intergroup context. *Journal of Personality and Social Psychology, 44,* 536–544.

Davidson, A. R., & Jaccard, J. (1979). Variables that moderate the attitude-behavior relation: Results of a longitudinal survey. *Journal of Personality and Social Psychology, 37,* 1364–1376.

Eagly, A. H., & Chaiken, S. (1984). Cognitive theories of persuasion. In L. Berkowitz (Ed.), *Advances in experimental social psychology* (Vol. 17, pp. 268–344). New York: Academic Press.

Fazio, R. H. (1986). How do attitudes guide behaviors? In R. M. Sorrentino & E. T. Higgins (Eds.), *The handbook of motivation and cognition: Foundations of social behavior* (Vol. 1). New York: Guilford Press.

Fazio, R. H., Chen, J., McDonel, E. C., & Sherman, S. J. (1982). Attitude accessibility, attitude-behavior consistency, and the strength of the object-evaluation association. *Journal of Experimental Social Psychology, 18,* 339–357.

298 COOPER and ARONSON

Fazio, R. H., Lenn, T. M., & Effrein, E. A. (1984). Spontaneous attitude formation. *Social Cognition, 2,* 217–234.

Fazio, R. H., Powell, M. C., & Herr, P. M. (1983). Forward a process model of the attitude–behavior relation: Accessing one's attitude upon mere observation of the attitude object. *Journal of Personality and Social Psychology, 44,* 723–735.

Fazio, R. H., & Zanna, M. P. (1981). Direct experience and attitude behavior consistency. In L. Berkowitz (Ed.), *Advances in experimental social psychology* (Vol. 44, pp. 162–198). New York: Academic Press.

Festinger, L. (1957). *A theory of cognitive dissonance.* Stanford, CA: Stanford University Press.

Festinger, L., & Carlsmith, J. M. (1959). Cognitive consequences of forced compliance. *Journal of Abnormal and Social Psychology, 58,* 203–210.

Fishbein, M. (1979). A theory of reasoned action: some applications and implications. In H. Howe & M. Page (Eds.), *Nebraska symposium on motivation* (Vol. 27, pp. 65–116). Lincoln: University of Nebraska Press.

Frank, J. D. (1961). *Persuasion and healing.* Baltimore, MD: Johns Hopkins University Press.

Freedman, J. L., & Fraser, S. (1966). Compliance without pressure: The foot-in-the-door technique. *Journal of Personality and Social Psychology, 4,* 262–266.

Greenwald, A. G., & Ronis, D. L. (1978). Twenty years of cognitive dissonance: Case Study of the evolution of a theory. *Psychological Review, 85,* 53–57.

Heider, F. (1946). Attitudes and cognitive organization. *Journal of Psychology, 2l,* 107–112.

Higgins, E. T. (1987). *Social cognitive mediators of self-persuasion.* Paper presented at the annual meeting of the American Psychological Association, New York, NY.

Hovland, C. I., Harvey, O. J., & Sherif, M. (1957). Assimilation and contrast effects in communication and attitude change. *Journal of Abnormal and Social Psychology, 55,* 242–252.

Hovland, C.I., Janis, I.L., & Kelley, H.H. (1953). *Communication and persuasion.* New Haven, CT: Yale University Press.

Hovland, C.I., & Weiss, W. (1952). The influence of source credibility on communication effectiveness. *Public Opinion Quarterly, 14,* 635–650.

Janis, I. L., & King, B. T. (1954). The influence of role playing on opinion change. *Journal of Abnormal and Social Psychology, 49,* 211–218.

Jemmott, J. B., Jemmott, L., & Fong, G. T. (1990). *Reducing the risk of sexually transmitted HIV infection: Attitudes, knowledge, intentions, and behavior.* Unpublished manuscript, Princeton University.

Jones, E. E., Rhodewalt, F., Berglas, S., & Skelton, J. A. (1981). Effects of strategic self-presentation on subsequent self-esteem. *Journal of Personality and Social Psychology, 41,* 407–421.

Kelly, G. (1955). *The psychology of personal constructs.* New York: W. W. Norton.

Krosnick, J. A. (1989). Attitude importance and attitude accessibility. *Peronality and Social Psychology Bulletin, 15,* 297–308.

LaPiere, R. T. (1934). Attitudes vs. actions. *Social Forces, 13,* 230–237.

Lasswell, H. D. (1948). The structure and function of communication in society. In L Bryson (Ed.), *Communication of ideas.* New York: Harper & Row.

Lepper, M. R., Greene, D., & Nisbett, R. E. (1973). Undermining children's intrinsic interest with extrinsic reward: A test of the "overjustification" hypothesis. *Journal of Personality and Social Psychology, 28,* 129–137.

Linder, D. E., Cooper, J., & Jones, E. E. (1967). Decision freedom as a determinant of incentive magnitude in attitude change. *Journal of Personality and Social Psychology, 6,* 432–448.

Meichenbaum, D.H., & Goodman, J. (1971). Training impulsive children to talk to themselves: A means of developing self-control. *Journal of Abnormal Psychology, 77,* 115–126.

Miller, R. L., Brickman, P., & Bolen, D. (1975). Attribution versus persuasion as a means for modifying behavior. *Journal of Personality and Social Psychology, 31,* 430–441.

Nel, E., Helmreich, R., & Aronson, E. (1969). Opinion change in the advocate as a function of the persuasibility of his audience: A clarification of the meaning of dissonance. *Journal of Personality and Social Psychology, 12,* 117–124.

Newcomb, T. M. (1956). The prediction of interpersonal attraction. *Amercian Psychologist, 11,* 575–586.

Newcomb, T. M. (1963). Persistence and repression of changed attitudes: Long-range studies. *Journal of Social Issues, 19,* 3–14.

Petty, R. E., & Cacioppo, J. T. (1983). Central and peripheral routes to persuasion: Application to advertising. In L. Percy & A. Woodside (Eds.), *Advertising and consumer psychology* (pp. 1–23). New York: Lexington.

Petty, R. E., & Cacioppo, J. T. (1986). The elaboration likelihood model of persuasion. In L. Berkowitz (Ed.), *Advances in experimental social psychology* (Vol. 19, pp. 124–192). New York: Academic Press.

Scher, S. J., & Cooper, J. (1989). Motivational basis of dissonance: The singular role of behavioral consequences. *Journal of Personality and Social Psychology, 56,* 899–906.

Schifter, D. E., & Ajzen, I. (1985). Intention, perceived control and weight loss: An application of the theory of planned behavior. *Journal of Personality and Social Psychology, 49,* 843–851.

Schlenker, B. R. (1982). Translating action into attitudes: An identity-analytic approach to the explanation of social conduct. In L. Berkowitz (Ed.), *Advances in experimental social psychology* (Vol. 15, pp. 194–240). New York: Academic Press.

Sivacek, J. & Crano W. D. (1982). Vested interest as a moderator of attitude-behavior consistency. *Journal of Personality and Social Psychology, 43*, 210–221.

Spivack, G., Platt, J. J., & Shure, M. B. (1976). *The problem solving approach to adjustment.* San Francisco: Jossey-Bass.

Stampfl, T., & Levis, D. (1967). Essentials of implosive therapy: A learning theory based psychodynamic behavioral therapy. *Journal of Abnormal Psychology, 72*, 496.

Steele, C. M. (1988). The psychology of self-affirmation: Sustaining the integrity of the self. In L. Berkowitz (Ed.), *Advances in experimental social psychology* (Vol. 21, pp. 261–299). New York: Academic Press.

Swann, W. B. (1987). Identity negotiation: Where two roads meet. *Journal of Personality and Social Psychology, 53*, pp. 1038–1051.

Tedeschi, J. T., Schlenker, B. R., & Bonoma, T. V. (1971). Cognitive dissonance: Private rationalization or public spectacle? *American Psychologist, 26*, 685–695.

Thibodeau, R., Aronson E., Dickerson, C., & Miller, D. (1990). *Hypocrisy & the self-concept: Arousing dissonance without aversive consequences.* Unpublished manuscript, University of California, Santa Cruz.

Wicker, A. (1969). Attitudes versus action: The relationship of verbal and overt behavioral responses to attitude objects. *The Journal of Social Issues, 25*, 1–78.

Wood, W. (1982). Retrieval of attitude-relevant information from memory: Effects on susceptibility to persuasion and on intrinisic motivation. *Journal of Personality and Social Psychology, 42*, 798–810.

Zanna, M. P., Kiesler, C. A., & Pilkonis, P. (1970). Positive and negative attitudinal effect established by classical conditioning. *Journal of Personality and Social Psychology, 14*, 321–328.

Focusing on the Self:
Challenges to Self-Definition and Their Consequences for Mental Health

KAY DEAUX

Few discussions of an individual's potential for mental health or mental illness, whether at the professional or lay level, can avoid reference to some notion of self. Witness terms such as "self-control," "self-actualization," "self-deception," "self-destruction," "self-help," and literally hundreds of others that a standard dictionary provides. Reflecting and often contributing to this conceptual plenty, both the social psychological and the clinical enterprises give a central role to the concept of self. The *modus operandi* of the two disciplines are sufficiently different, however, that benefits potentially available from one discipline are often unrecognized by the other.

The social psychological perspective on self originates with William James and George Herbert Mead. James, the psychologist, emphasized internal processes of self-reflection and self-evaluation. Mead, the sociologist, constructed a self that relied on the interpersonal context. This early architecture of self, despite the insightful analyses of James and Mead, was overshadowed for many years by the tower of behaviorism. During this period, observable events and specific stimulus–response connections took precedence over analyses of internal and more diffuse concepts such as self. For the past two decades, however, consideration of self processes has been central to the social psychological discourse.

The assumptions that social psychologists and clinical psychologists use to frame their analysis of self often vary. Social psychologists have shown considerable diversity and ingenuity in developing self-relevant concepts. In the early 1970s, Bem (1967) used an operant model of self-perception to refute the claims of dissonance theory. Aronson (1969), in contrast, found the self a useful concept to characterize situations in which dissonance worked. More recently, in keeping with the *Zeitgeist*, analyses of self often use a cognitive, information-processing framework to talk of self-schemata (Markus, 1977) and mental representations of self (Kihlstrom & Cantor, 1983).

Within clinical psychology, analyses of self often emerge from psychodynamic models. Neo-Freudians such as Erikson and Klein emphasized the development of ego and the importance of interpersonal context. Object relations theory continues to evolve, with its proponents arguing for the importance of interpersonal context in the development of fundamental aspects of self, including gender (Chodorow, 1978). Dominant in contemporary clinical analyses of self is the work of Heinz Kohut (1971, 1977).

The emphases and assumptions of social and clinical approaches to the self often differ. Stability of self is typically assumed by clinicians, for example, while social psychologists appear to endorse a highly mutable self. The laboratory techniques of experimental social psychology rest on the investigator's ability to show immediate, situationally induced changes in self-concept. In contrast, the lengthy process of psychotherapy assumes a self resistant to change (Josephs, 1991). Social psychological models, particularly in recent years, emphasize the cognitive aspects of self. Clinicians, on the other hand, more often confront the emotional and affective aspects of self, represented by anxiety and unconscious fears (Stolorow, 1991; Westen, 1991).

Despite these differences, social and clinical approaches often find common ground. George Kelly (1955), a clinician, was an early advocate of cognitive approaches to self, introducing schema-like notions of construction and construal. William Swann (1983, 1990; McNulty & Swann, 1991), a social psychologist, works from an assumption of stability rather than flexibility, arguing that people seek to verify even negative views of themselves in order to maintain some stability and control. More explicit convergence between social and clinical models is evident in Tesser's (1991) analysis of the theoretical similarities between his self-evaluation maintenance model and Kohutian object relations theory. Looking more directly at clinical practice, Baumeister (1991) extends the experimental literature on topics such as self-handicapping to the problems of alcoholism, masochism, and suicide.

The ubiquity of the self for the social–clinical interface is documented by its coverage in several of the chapters in this volume: in Higgins's discussion of the impact of social variables on cognition (Chapter 8); in Jones' analysis of adaptations to racial bias (Chapter 7); in Ruble and Thompson's consideration of self-regulation, self-esteem, and self-efficacy (Chapter 4); in Gore's coverage of the impact of stress on self-esteem (Chapter 2); and elsewhere throughout the volume. This frequent reference to "self" processes suggests not only the relevance of self to present concerns, but the abundance of research available as well. Thus, for the author of a chapter entitled self, a major task is deciding which aspects of self to feature and discuss.

SELF-DEFINITION AND MENTAL HEALTH: A PRELIMINARY MODEL

I take self-definition as a starting point for the selection and organization of material on self. There are several reasons for this choice. First, self-definition seems a logical beginning point for understanding how self-relevant behaviors proceed. Second, questions of self-definition and of personal and social identity are attracting an increasing number of investigators and an interesting literature is amassing.[1] Third, because much of this research is quite recent, the implications of the theoretical work for clinical issues have not yet been addressed. And fourth, I argue that some of the most relevant events in terms of a person's mental health are those that pose a fundamental challenge to self-definition and self-understanding.

These concepts of self-definition and challenge to self are key to the working model for this chapter, as presented in Figure 10.1. Occupying the central position in Figure 10.1 is self-definition. Distal influences on self-definition include various socialization, structural, and demographic features. Sources of challenge or threat to self-definition are the major focus at the "input" side of the figure. Challenges to self-definition are categorized, for purposes of analysis, as either external or internal. These challenges are assumed to elicit some form of self-evaluation. Two consequences of the self-evaluative process are considered: (1) self-regulation and reconstruction, in which the outcome is some bolstering or change in self-definition; and (2) social regulation

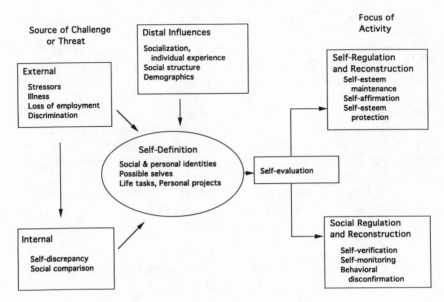

FIGURE 10.1. Self-definition and mental health.

and reconstruction, in which efforts are directed toward external audiences.

This working model assumes that changes in the self-system, or the consideration of change, have considerable relevance for mental health (see also Ruble & Thompson, Chapter 4, this volume). When an ongoing system is in some way challenged, people are most likely to express uncertainty, feel a lack of control, and show symptoms of either mental or physical illness. Prevention efforts need to be based on an understanding of the impact that challenges have on the existent self-system. At the "output" end of the sequence, understanding how individuals respond to threat can provide guidelines for treatment efforts. It is also possible for challenges to self-definition to have positive consequences. Understanding those conditions can help us foster mental *health* as well as combat mental illness.

In presenting this model in more detail, I take an admittedly sociocentric perspective, discussing current research in social and personality psychology that elaborates the model. At the same time, however, I am attempting to show, either by evidence or inference, how these principles can be useful for the clinical agenda.

THE CENTRAL ROLE OF SELF-DEFINITION

The key concept in this model is self-definition, the sense of self as it is constructed and defined by the individual. Self-definition is thus explicitly subjective, although its shape can be influenced by objective and external events.

Some of the distal influences on self-definition are listed in the upper central box of Figure 10.1. Both psychological and sociological perspectives are relevant to this process. From psychology, we learn more about the individual socialization experiences that shape the self. Psychological accounts detail the processes by which these experiences are translated into specific patterns of self-definition. Sociologists offer an important structural perspective, pointing out how status and position emerge from an existent structure and constrain the ways in which self can be meaningfully defined.

In this chapter, these distal influences are assumed rather than analyzed in any detail. However, some of the processes contributing to self-definition are described more specifically in this volume by Ruble and Thompson (internal socialization) (Chapter 4) and by Costanzo (external socialization) (Chapter 3). Other developmental treatments of self-definition include work by Harter (1983) and Higgins (1990).

Forms of Self-Definition

Definitions of self, as depicted in Figure 10.1, reflect at least three recent trends in research. First, the self is represented not as a global concept but as a series of more specifically defined domains. Thus, rather than considering a single diffuse self-concept, investigators find it advantageous to think of more specific entities such as possible selves, personal projects, and social identities. These different aspects of self find different realms of application. Thus, the personal project would emphasize individual planning whereas social identity includes a recognition of a collective, group membership. Similarly, when studying the development of self-esteem, one might want to distinguish between different domains of self-definition and self-assessed competence, such as the academic versus the social realm.

A second feature of many current conceptions of self-definition is their motivational implications. Rather than referring to a collection of static characteristics, these conceptions of self imply goals and future actions (see Pervin, 1989). Examples include the concepts of possible selves (Markus & Nurius, 1986; Markus & Ruvolo, 1989), life tasks (Cantor, Norem, Niedenthal, Langston, & Brower, 1987), and personal projects (Little, 1983). In each case, goals are an explicit part of the self-formulation, linking the present self to some future state. Markus and Nurius (1986), for example, refer to possible selves as "cognitive bridges between the present and future, specifying how individuals may change from how they are now to what they will become" (p. 961). One example of the ways in which possible selves direct action is provided in the work of Ruble and her colleagues (Deutsch, Ruble, Fleming, Brooks-Gunn, & Stangor, 1988; Ruble et al., 1990). Women who are anticipating the birth of a first child engage in a number of activities that help them construct and define themselves as mothers, including the solicitation of information from doctors, friends, and relevant publications.

Third, and perhaps most important, the self is regarded as a personal construction, individually tailored by the person to fit his or her experiences, assessments of those experiences, and anticipated future states. Common environments and common categories of membership cannot be assumed to yield equivalent self-definitions; rather, the individual's interpretations and personal meanings must be explored. This emphasis on the subjective does not deny that people's self-definitions are influenced by their position in the social structure and by demographic categories to which they belong (Stryker & Statham, 1985). Certainly, categorical memberships such as gender, ethnicity, religion, and occupation are often important components of self-definition. As constructed by society, these role positions or identities carry established meanings and often imply reciprocal role relationships with specific others. Yet even as society provides options, the individual makes choices within those possibilities. Not every categorical position is claimed as an individual identity (Deaux, 1991; Ethier & Deaux, 1990a). Members of ethnic groups, for example, do not always claim that ethnicity as an identity, nor do parents always have a salient identity as father or mother (the latter is more likely to be claimed than the former) (cf. Dion, 1989). Further, the meanings associated with the same categorical membership vary widely. Two women can be equally strong in their endorsement of mother as an identity and yet have quite different conceptions of what that identity means, either in affective value or in specific behaviors and characteristics associated with that identity.

Structure and Salience in Self-Definition

Not all aspects of a person's self-definition are equally important, leading a number of investigators to introduce notions of centrality or importance to the analysis of self-structure (e.g., McCall & Simmons, 1978; Rosenberg, 1979; Thoits, 1991). Stryker (1987), for example, hypothesizes that individuals have a hierarchical ordering of identities, with those identities that are higher on the hierarchy involving more other people and having greater implications for action. Further, he suggests that certain identities such as gender and race may serve as master statuses, influencing the definition and enactment of all other identities. Rosenberg and Gara (1985) offer an empirical approach to the determination of identity hierarchies. Using their methodology, one can determine and graphically represent individual identity patterns. In the resultant hierarchies, those identities that occupy a higher or more superordinate position are the more inclusive (and presumably more important) identities, while lower-level identities are more specific and constrained. Considerable variation is evident in these empirically derived identity patterns, again underlining the subjective character of self-definition.

Is there a relationship between an identity's position in the overall structure and mental health indicants? This question, one of obvious importance, is only beginning to be addressed. In preliminary research, Thoits (1991) hypothesized but did not find that more important identities would have a more positive impact on psychological distress and substance use. However, her results did suggest that particular combinations of identities might be related to psychological symptoms. In another exploratory project, Ouellette et al. (Ouellette, Bochnak, & McKinley, 1991) considered how the position of identities related to a particular illness (in their case, systemic lupus erythematosus) could predict depression. Two different patterns appeared to relate to depression. First, women whose predisease identity ("me before lupus") was superordinate in their identity structure were more likely to show depression than those for whom this earlier identity was less prominent. Second, women whose current identity as a "person with lupus" was integrated with other negative identities were more depressed than those for whom the patient identity was either isolated or integrated with other positive features of self. Thus, these two projects suggest that the position of an identity as well as its relationship to other identities in the structure are important indicants of psychological health.

Research on the self structure of people with specific psychopathologies has also begun (Robey, Cohen, & Gara, 1989; Rosenberg, 1989). Schizophrenics, for example, appear to have less elaborated self structures than do either "normals" or clinically depressed individuals. Interestingly, the presence of a specific patient identity seems to have different implications for the two clinical groups. Whereas patient identity is generally associated with more positive outcomes in the schizophrenic group, it is associated with greater levels of depression among the clinically depressed. Thus, the same general identity may have different implications for treatment, depending on the population being considered. Clearly, the jury is still out on the exact nature of the link between particular identity structures and mental health outcomes, but early findings suggest a number of promising leads.

Analyses of identity structure assume a relatively stable set of priorities whereby some identities are always more important than others. Yet situations can establish priorities as well, calling certain aspects of self to the fore and allowing others to recede. This view of situational saliency, variously referred to as the phenomenal self (Jones & Gerard, 1967), the working self-concept (Markus & Kunda, 1986), and the spontaneous self-concept (McGuire & McGuire, 1981), underscores the importance of context in self-definition and self-expression. If one's gender is in a minority, for example, either in the household (McGuire & McGuire, 1981) or even in a brief psychology experiment (Cota & Dion, 1986), a person is more likely to mention gender when providing a self-description. Contextual influences on self-definition need to be considered in a more time-extended sense as well. Cross and Markus (1991), for example, have shown how possible selves vary over the course of the life-span, presumably reflecting the different options available and threats presented.

Motivational states affect self-definition as well. In considering why people might claim a group-related identity and incorporate it into their self-definition, Brewer (1991) suggests that people want to maintain an optimal level of inclusion. Needs to be assimilated by a group must be balanced against needs to be distinct from other people. Thus, according to her model, social identities would become more important for the individual who was feeling too unique or different and might be rejected by the individual who felt well assimilated into his or her culture.

In summary, considerable research activity surrounds questions of self-definition, as global concepts of self have yielded to more differentiated views. Consideration of specific identities provides a promising point of entry for the clinician as well as for the psychologist. It becomes possible, for example, to look specifically at a patient or symptom-based identity and consider its development, relationship to other identities, and responsiveness to intervention and treatment. One can also focus on a particular category of interest, such as gender, age, or ethnicity, and explore how variations in the content or salience of those categories relate to specific mental health indicants. In summary, this more differentiated view of self offers several new windows of opportunity for linking theoretical and practical concerns.

SOURCES OF CHALLENGE
TO THE SELF-SYSTEM

For most people, self-definition is reasonably stable. Although certain aspects of self may be more or less salient in different situations, the constitution of self more closely resembles a slow-motion film than a high-action video segment. Self-definition is not impervious to change, however, and it is at these points of potential redefinition that mental health implications are often clearest.

Numerous circumstances, represented in the boxes at the left of Figure 10.1, can challenge a person's self-definition. Generally speaking, these challenges emerge from one of two sources. In one case, the impetus is internal, arising from some discrepancy or imbalance in the system of self-representation. (Of course, the proximal elements in this system may be traced to earlier distal causes in the socialization process.) In the other case, the challenge to self comes from some external source, such as illness, unemployment, loss of home, abuse, or stigmatization. These two types of challenges are not completely independent. Although the death of a spouse, for example, might directly affect one's ability to claim wife or husband as an identity, the effect of the loss on self-definition could also be mediated by comparisons to internal standards and goals. This mediational possibility is indicated by the path of arrows in Figure 10.1.

External Sources of Threat

Numerous external conditions can force a person to reevaluate and/or to reconstitute her or his self-definition. Many of these conditions are discussed in more detail by Gore (Chapter 2, this

volume). Events such as a serious illness, termination of employment, and the loss of a spouse or a child affect one's assessment of
the present and anticipation of the future, with obvious implications for self-evaluation and self-esteem. Dramatic events like
these often have a sudden onset. Yet, the consequences of these
events may be prolonged, both in the event itself (e.g., prolonged
illness, chronic unemployment, persistent homelessness) and in its
effects on the individual's self-definition and self-evaluation processes (Breakwell, 1986).

Events that challenge self-definition are not necessarily negative events in an objective sense. Losing one's job is an obvious
negative event that would pose questions for self-definition. Conversely, however, a promotion may create significant threats as
well. Similarly counterintuitive are Scott's (1991) observations
that people who are disabled often find the potential of a "cure"
aversive and threatening to self-definition. Even events that are
both anticipated and desired, such as marriage or the birth of a
child, often present serious challenges to self-definition. As a particular case, positive events are likely to be aversive for those who
are low in self-esteem. Consistent with a self-verification framework, Swann and his colleagues found that positive events tend to
be accompanied by negative health outcomes among low self-
esteem students (Pelham & Swann, 1990; Swann & Brown, 1990).

Not all external threats come in the form of discrete events.
Many people must contend with more continuous forms of threat
to self-definition. Stigmatization is a prime example of these sometimes subtle, sometimes not-so-subtle sources of stress. (Jones
[Chapter 7, this volume] discusses these issues more fully in relation to race.) Members of ethnic minorities, women, the elderly,
gays and lesbians, the physically disabled, and other stigmatized
groups are subject to persistent discrimination. This discrimination in turn confronts the individual with a need to reconcile often
conflicting definitions of oneself and one's group. As Steele (1990)
noted, "[P]erhaps the single most important route through which
stigma affects mental health outcomes is through its effect on
processes of self-evaluation."

A recent study by Ethier and Deaux (1990a, 1990b) provides
evidence of the ways in which a stigmatized identity can have
negative consequences. In this study, Hispanic students were interviewed at three points in time during their first year at an Ivy
League university. The Hispanic students in this primarily Anglo
environment believed that their group was devalued, and they
reported feeling that their Hispanic identity was threatened. These

perceptions of threat took their toll. Longitudinal analyses showed that stronger perceptions of threat were associated with significant decreases in self-esteem and in the endorsed importance of the Hispanic identity over the course of the first academic year. Although specific mental health outcomes were not assessed in this study, one can imagine a number of negative outcomes that might covary with self-esteem and identity importance.

Internal Sources of Threat

Internal sources of threat arise primarily from the existence and use of some set of standards (see Higgins, Chapter 8, this volume, for another discussion of social standards). Internalized standards have a variety of sources and reference points. Thibaut and Kelley's (1959) work on comparison levels, for example, assumes a standard based on the average of one's own past experiences. Higgins (1987; Higgins, Tykocinski, & Vookles, 1990) suggests a range of self-guides that serve as standards for comparison, including actual, ideal, can, and future selves. These standards can be self-generated (e.g., what I think can be, what I would like to be) or they can be provided by significant others (e.g., what my mother would like me to be, what my therapist thinks I should be). Discrepancies that exist between one's current status and some standard of comparison constitute the internal threat.

The use of other people as a standard for self-evaluation is the fundamental assumption of Festinger's (1954) social comparison theory. Research in the 35 years since Festinger's key paper has left little doubt that comparison is a widely used method of self-definition, although the patterns of comparison are far more complex than early investigators realized (Wood, 1989). Comparisons with standards can take either the individual or the group as a unit of analysis (Levine & Moreland, 1987). Thus, a person might compare the likelihood of attaining a particular possible self, for example, by using her sister as a standard, or she might estimate the likelihood of women attaining that goal as compared to men.

The extent to which a particular comparison constitutes a threat depends on a variety of factors, including the domain of the comparison, the level of performance, and the closeness of the comparison other (Tesser, 1988). As Tesser (1988) articulates in presenting his self-evaluation maintenance model, being psychologically close to a person who performs well in a domain that is relevant or important to you typically creates a threat to self-esteem. In contrast, a casual acquaintance who does well in an area that is not important to you will not pose a challenge to self-definition.

Whether the sources of threat are internal or external, they confront the individual with a challenge to the existent self-definition. Using the framework of Parkes (1971), one's "assumptive world" is questioned. The new information is in some sense anomalous and needs to be reconciled (Janoff-Bulman & Schwartzberg, 1991). Just how this is accomplished constitutes the relevant mental health agenda.

REACTING TO
SELF-DEFINITIONAL CHALLENGE

Much of the self-relevant information that people receive is consistent with their accepted self-definition. In part, as Swann (1983, 1990) suggests, this consistency results from the person's active choice to find environments in which self-conceptions can be supported. Beyond this, a person may choose to ignore inconsistent information or to deem it irrelevant or peripheral. For self-relevant information that is both relevant and inconsistent, however, the person must find some way to reconcile the information with the existent definitions of self. As Figure 10.1 depicts, self-evaluative processes are the outcome of challenges to self. Self-evaluation in turn leads to two general sets of psychological processes, one set consisting of self-regulation and self-reconstructive activities and the other oriented toward social regulation and reconstruction.

Self-Evaluation

When confronted with information inconsistent with one's definition of self, a person typically engages in some form of self-evaluation: Who am I, who do I want to be, who do I want others to think I am, and how does all of this information fit together? Often, but not necessarily always, this process is a conscious one (although more subtle and perhaps preliminary forms of threat may operate at a preconscious level as well, experienced ambiguously as a feeling that something is not quite right). Often, too, the self-evaluation process shares the stage with some kind of resistance to accepting the implications of the new information (Janoff-Bulman & Schwartzberg, 1991). At the most basic level, self-evaluation implies assigning some positive or negative value to the self or to components of the self. Thus, challenges to one's self-definition may have either positive or negative implications for self-evaluation and self-esteem. Further, depending on the nature of the threat, the self-evaluation process can focus on either personal self-esteem, associated with individual aspects of self-definition, or on collective self-esteem, associated with one's membership in recognized social groups (Crocker & Luhtanen, 1990; Luhtanen & Crocker, 1992). Moreover, group-based self-esteem can be segmented, distinguishing one's own feelings about the group in question from one's perceptions of other people's views. Sometimes these are quite discrepant. Members of ethnic groups, for example, often have positive feelings toward their ethnic group while recognizing that others view the group in a negative light (Ethier & Deaux, 1990a).

Self-evaluation often has emotional concomitants. When self-evaluation is a reaction to some perceived threat, negative emotions such as anxiety frequently are reported. Using a more differentiated model, Higgins (1987; Higgins, Tykocinski, & Vookles, 1990) predicts distinct affective reactions to different forms of discrepancy between one's current state and some alternative form of self-definition (or, in his terms, self-guide). A discrepancy between what one is (the actual self) and what one would like to be (the ideal self), for example, is associated with dejection-related suffering, such as feeling sad, discouraged, or depressed. A discrepancy between what one is and what one (or someone else) thinks one should be (the ought self), in contrast, predicts agitation-related states, such as nervousness and anxiety. Individuals differ in their tendency to use one or another standard for self-evaluation, based on different histories of socialization (Higgins, 1990). For the therapist, knowing what kinds of evaluative comparisons a client is most likely to make can help in predicting areas of difficulty and directions for treatment.

Recent work relating patterns of discrepancy to health outcomes suggests a more direct link between social psychological theory and clinical practice. Specifically, Higgins and his associates (Higgins, Vookles, & Tykocinsky, in press; Strauman, Vookles, Berenstein, Chaiken, & Higgins, 1991) considered the association between particular patterns of self-discrepancy and tendencies toward anorexia and bulimia. They found that discrepancies between the actual and ought selves were more strongly related to anorexic symptomatology, whereas persons showing bulimic symptomatology were more likely to be characterized by actual–ideal discrepancies. A variety of other physical symptoms, including migraine headaches, indigestion, and muscle cramps, also showed linkages to distinctive patterns of self-beliefs. These findings should be treated with caution, as the subjects were college students showing tendencies toward particular eating patterns rather than diagnosed clinical cases of bulimia and anorexia. Nonetheless, the potential for application is very promising.

Figure 10.1 depicts two outcomes of the self-evaluation process, one internally oriented toward the self and the other externally oriented toward the social world. These two processes are not mutually exclusive. The self-evaluative process may lead the person both to reconstruct his or her own definition and to feel a need to present that reformulated self to others. Indeed, a truly social psychological analysis cannot afford to ignore the social context as it shapes the activity of internal mechanisms.

These two processes are thought to occur whether the outcome of the self-evaluation process is positive or negative, although the implications for mental health are quite different. When the self-evaluation process yields a positive outcome, a person experiences gratifying increases in self-esteem and a general feeling of well-being. Actions taken in this context are likely to have positive implications for mental health with possible preventive benefits. In contrast, negative self-evaluations are both cause and correlate of reduced feelings of self-worth. These evaluation processes are ongoing and often cause only minor perturbations in one's general sense of well-being. In more extreme cases, however, negative self-evaluation can lead to severe depression or other conditions of mental illness.

Self-Regulation and Reconstruction

In the face of threat to self-definitions, people often engage in some form of self-regulation or self-confirmation. These efforts include processes of self-esteem maintenance, self-affirmation, and self-esteem protection. In these cases, the goal is to reestablish an image of self that both takes into account the presenting challenge and, if possible, leaves one in a positive state. Positivity is not always possible, however, and reconstruction of self-definition may result in a more negative or damaged view of self.

Several recent research programs show how resourceful people can be in their attempts to maintain self-definition and positive self-regard. Tesser's (1988) research, for example, shows that people selectively choose domains of performance and targets of comparison, calculating a balance between reflected glory and favorable comparison in order to maintain self-esteem. Perhaps most relevant to the mental health domain are the implications of this model for family dynamics and interactions among siblings (Tesser, 1984). The model predicts, for example, that children who are close in age will get along less well than those whose ages are more discrepant. Accordingly, parents might do well to develop different domains of competence in closely spaced siblings to minimize social comparison and resultant threats to self-definition.

Steele's (1988) work is useful in pointing out how individuals protect their global sense of self-adequacy by selectively choosing among various domains of self-definition. His self-affirmation model predicts that if threats are addressed to one particular domain of self, a person can choose to affirm alternative, valued aspects of the self. To demonstrate this process, Steele and his colleagues used a classical dissonance paradigm in which subjects experience conflict when they are forced to choose between two similarly valued alternatives. Conflict in this setting is interpreted as a threat to one aspect of the self. If so, then the affirmation of an alternative self should effectively reduce the threat and minimize any dissonance. To provide some subjects with the opportunity to affirm an alternative self, lab coats were provided to subjects who were either science majors or business majors. Steele assumed that this apparel would affirm the identity of the science majors but have no effect on the business majors. The results supported Steele's predictions in that the choice situation created conflict only for the business majors who had no opportunity to affirm an alternative identity.

The suggestion that making alternative forms of self-affirmation available is an effective way to cope with threats could have important mental health implications. The person who loses a job, for example, might cope better if therapy focused on alternative nonthreatened identities, for example, in addition to dealing with the lost identity per se. In a related vein, several studies have shown that people who have more identities, or a more differentiated view of self, are better able to cope and experience less stress-related illness (Linville, 1987; Thoits, 1983). Here the logic suggests that the presence of alternative identities acts as a buffer when threat is experienced in one particular domain.

Steele himself is testing the applicability of a self-affirmation model to the case of minority education. Specifically, he views the high dropout rate of African-American college students as a self-affirmation strategy in the face of challenges encountered at primarily white campuses. Thus, students who feel they cannot claim a "successful white student" identity may choose to reaffirm a nonacademic and previously established identity. If this analysis proves appropriate, it would suggest the development of intervention strategies aimed at the modification of existing identities or the development of new and more functional identities.

To the extent that one's identity is associated with other similar members of a group, additional self-protective mechanisms become available. Thus, the member of a stigmatized group may be able to cope with threats to that aspect of identity by reinterpreting the nature of the threat. Crocker and Major (1989) point to at least three such strategies: (1) attributing negative feedback to prejudice against one's group; (2) selectively comparing outcomes with members of one's own group rather than with nonstigmatized outgroup members; and (3) selectively devaluing domains in which one's own group does poorly and valuing those domains in which one's group excels. In each case, the person's group identity is both the focus of the threat and the means for dealing with it. Consequently, the stigmatized person is able to withstand the challenge to self-evaluation that discrimination presents. At the same time, it will be important to assess the consequences of using these strategies for subsequent adjustment. It is possible, for example, that short-term solutions create longer-term problems.

Not all responses to threat are positive, adaptive, or esteem-enhancing. People who experience serious traumas earlier in their life show the impact of those events on their self-concept many years later (Levesque, Deutsch, & Janoff-Bulman, 1990). Women who were sexually victimized, for example, show more traits related to maladaptive interpersonal behavior and fewer expectations of self-efficacy than do a comparable group of non-reported victims. Negative impact can also take the form of completely eliminating some aspect of the self-concept. Failure at school, for example, would generally eliminate a student identity and perhaps a possible self as a doctor; death of a spouse can remove (at least temporarily) one's identity as a wife or husband.

Breakwell (1986) suggests that people respond to threat by initiating a variety of coping strategies—some intrapsychic protectors, some interpersonal behaviors, and some intergroup actions. Undoubtedly, some of these strategies are more effective than others. Similarly, some aspects of self-definition may be more flexible or more amenable to change. With effective strategies and pliable self-definitions, challenges may be successfully handled. In contrast, the combination of pliable self-definitions with ineffective strategies for coping with challenge might characterize a particularly vulnerable situation, and thus an important area of mental health concern. Aspects of self-definition that are resistant to change could also be an important area for consideration, as indications of either ego strength or harmful rigidity.

Social Regulation and Reconstruction

A second arena in which responses to self-definitional challenge play out is the social and interactive one. In this Meadian territory, the individual can collaboratively construct (and reconstruct) the social aspects of self-definition with any number of general or specific audiences. Desired identities can be verified and undesirable ones confirmed.

Although this social activity may occur concurrently with the more internal concerns of self-regulation and reconstruction, it does not necessarily follow that the two projects are the same. One might, for example, conclude that a particular aspect of one's self-definition needs to be changed yet still want to maintain an older image in public. As an illustration, consider the middle-level sales manager who loses a job and who, after several months of unsuccessful applications, believes that a career change will be needed. At least in the short run, that manager might wish to present a public image of sales manager while attempting to develop a new set of personal projects and possibilities for self. Alternatively, he or she could cling to a personal image of sales manager while acceding to a spouse's demand to take a less prestigious but income-producing job. In the long run, however, Swann's (1983, 1990) contention that people seek to verify their personal conceptions of self to others is probably true more often than not. Predictability, control, and coherence in social life are the benefits of a self-verification strategy, even when one is verifying a negative image of self.

The evidence that people with negative self-evaluations will seek out situations in which they can verify their low images is a clear challenge for therapists. Swann and his colleagues have found, for example, that people with negative self-images seek out unfavorable feedback even when they believe that the information will make them depressed. People in these studies who were highly depressed chose negative evaluators in an experimental setting and solicited negative feedback from their roommates (Swann, Wenzlaff, Krull, & Pelham, in press). McNulty and Swann (1991)

suggest a number of theoretically derived strategies that therapists might use to deal with clients who show these patterns. Some
of these strategies focus on social regulation (e.g., making changes
in the social environment); others deal with the kind of self-
regulatory strategies discussed earlier.

Other images of self that people present to their social world
are not intrinsically negative but may nonetheless have negative
consequences for mental or physical health. Consider the interrelated topics of physical appearance, eating behavior, and gender.
From age 10 to 79, women show more concern about eating, body
weight, and physical appearance (Pliner, Chaiken, & Flett, 1990).
Appearance is a particularly important aspect of self-concept for
people who score high on measures of femininity. Given this concern with appearance, women might well choose a presentational
style that would emphasize their image of slimness. In laboratory
studies with college students, social psychologists have recently
shown that women whose femininity is threatened are more likely
to curb their eating behavior when in the presence of an attractive
male (Mori, Chaiken, & Pliner, 1987; Pliner & Chaiken, 1990). If
these experimental findings can be generalized to clinical populations, the processes of self-definition and social regulation may
find relevance in the treatment of eating disorders.

Members of stigmatized groups face particular dilemmas in
choosing how to present themselves in the social context. Often,
other people hold negative stereotypes about one's group and convey these beliefs through discriminatory actions. The potential for
self-fulfilling prophesies and behavioral confirmation are well
documented (Darley & Fazio, 1980; Deaux & Major, 1987; Miller &
Turnbull, 1986; Snyder, Tanke, & Berscheid, 1977). Early social
psychological analyses of expectancy confirmation processes suggested that the targets of expectancies were quite apt to confirm
the perceiver's initial expectations. In the case of negative
stereotypes, then, one might would predict an acceptance of these
unfavorable images by the stigmatized group.

Countervailing forces suggest a more complex picture. As
Crocker and Major (1989) suggest, the self-image of stigmatized
group members may be quite positive, bolstered by the use of
attributional and selective comparison strategies. Further, research suggests that when the attribute in question is central and
important to the target, behavioral confirmation is far less likely.
Instead, the target is prone to verify his or her self-conception.

Yet, for the member of the stigmatized group, this contrast
between external expectations and internal resolutions can still be

troublesome. The dilemma of the stigmatized group member is evidenced by the greater effort that deviants devote to monitoring their interactions with others, presumably seeking information that will help them get through the interaction (Frable, Blackstone, & Scherbaum, 1990). (This disproportionate attention to elements of the conversation is also characteristic of people whose deviation is positive in nature, such as being highly attractive or extremely successful in athletics.)

For some people, group membership is evident. Independent of how important being a woman or a Latina is personally, for example, that aspect of self will be used in the definition and reactions of others. In other cases, when a central aspect of identity is not visible, the person has choices about the degree to which that aspect of self will be presented to others. The difficulty of this choice is illustrated by data on gay identity (Frable, Wortman, Joseph, Kirscht, & Kessler, 1991). For the gay man in this sample of 820 midwesterners, being known as gay to a wide range of people was positively associated with feeling positive about a gay identity. At the same time, however, this visibility was negatively associated with general self-esteem and well-being. Thus, stigmatization continues to have negative consequences on mental health despite the empowering effects that group identity and solidarity may have.

THE SELF AND MENTAL HEALTH: LIMITS AND PROMISES

As noted in the introduction, both clinical psychologists and social-personality psychologists frequently invoke a concept of self to describe phenomena of interest. This recognition of a common territory is not news, although the implications of one field for the other still often go unrecognized. More interesting from my perspective is the increasing potential for links between the two domains.

Often, social psychologists have limited their contributions by assuming that the specific case is general law. To those in more applied domains, these specific cases sometimes seem trivial. Thus, an investigation of self that focuses on one's ability to solve anagrams or to discriminate blue and green dots, for example, is not likely to engender excitement in the clinical investigator. In contrast, recent social psychological research that considers self-structures of schizophrenics, victims of incest, or patients with diagnosed illnesses should find a responsive clinical audience. It is important for social psychological research to make clearer distinctions between central and peripheral and relevant and irrelevant aspects of self, not only recognizing the difference but also incorporating these distinctions directly into the theoretical framework. Further, it would help if clinical and social psychologists would collaborate in obtaining subject populations in order to determine, for example, the degree to which college students with self-reported bulimic tendencies are similar to clinically diagnosed bulimics.

Current research on self and identity seems a particularly fruitful domain for making genuine progress at the social psychology/mental health interface. Self-definition, as it is increasingly being conceptualized, consists of identifications that individuals make with other people and with their environment. In other words, this is a contextualized view of self that readily lends itself to a clinical analysis.

There are many potentially exciting directions for research. Issues of change, for example, so critical to the clinical process, have rarely been addressed by the social psychologist. One can ask how new identities are incorporated into the structure, and how the processes of acquisition and loss develop (Deaux, 1991). General models of adult socialization might be informed by a more focused look at self structure.

It would also be interesting to explore the degree to which different aspects of self are resistant or vulnerable to challenges. It might be the case, for example, that newly formed definitions are more susceptible to challenge than those that are held longer and are possibly better integrated into the system. Alternatively, one might predict that very "old" aspects of self would also be vulnerable to challenge, in that they have not been questioned much since their earlier adoption.[2]

Self-definition also has interesting implications for treatment, as numerous self-help groups have discovered. The beginning of treatment for the person who joins Alcoholics Anonymous, for example, is the declaration that "I am an alcoholic." This process of claiming an identity—in this case, one that was presumably rejected earlier in part because of the stigma attached to it—in turn defines an agenda for behavior. As Breakwell (1986) has noted, "action is the social expression of identity" (p. 43), and what actions are carried out depends on what identities are claimed.

Some clinicians who deal with people recovering from addiction use identity theory as a framework for understanding the changes that their clients go through. Biernacki (1986), for example, views recovery as a process of identity restructuring, and discusses several different forms of identity transition that may occur. Kellogg (1992) analyzes 12-step programs from a similar perspective.

Within the arena of health psychology, interesting questions emerge with regard to patient identities. At what point does the chronically ill person identify him or herself as a cancer "victim," a person with lupus, etc.? And to what extent does the adoption of such an identity facilitate or hinder treatment and recovery? Is the person who self-identifies as a patient more likely to comply with medical recommendations, thus suggesting positive consequences of the identity? Or is the patient identity likely to be associated with a loss of initiative and will? Research to date on mental health categories, such as schizophrenic and depressive, suggests that the answers to the questions will not be particularly simple and may well vary with the nature of the disease.

Recognizing that some aspects of the self process may be syndrome-specific does not reduce the importance of understanding basic social psychological processes. Nor does an appreciation of general patterns make one less likely to understand the specific case. Collaboration between social psychologists and clinical psychologists requires that the value of each approach be recognized and taken seriously. If this is done, the potential benefit to both the social psychological and the mental health agenda is considerable.

Acknowledgments

Numerous people read earlier versions of this chapter and made helpful comments. Among those to whom I am grateful are Shelly Chaiken, Margaret Clark, Phil Costanzo, John Levine, Paula McKinley, and Diane Ruble.

Preparation of this chapter was facilitated by a grant from the National Science Foundation (BNS-9110130).

NOTES

1. The terms "self" and "identity" have each been used in numerous ways, depending on the particular theoretical tradition represented. In this chapter, I consider "self" to be the most global concept. Other terms such as "identities," "self-identifications," and "possible selves" represent specific forms of self-definition.

2. John Levine deserves credit for this suggestion which, in the second alternative posed, draws on McGuire's inoculation model for its theoretical rationale.

REFERENCES

Aronson, E. (1969). The theory of cognitive dissonance: A current perspective. *Advances in experimental social psychology* (Vol. 4, pp. 2–32). New York: Academic Press.

Baumeister, R. F. (1991). *Escaping the self.* New York: Basic Books.

Bem, D. J. (1967). Self-perception: An alternative interpretation of cognitive dissonance phenomena. *Psychological Review, 74,* 183–200.

Biernacki, P. (1986). *Pathways from heroin addictioin: Recovery without treatment.* Philadelphia: Temple University Press.

Breakwell, G. (1986). *Coping with threatened identities.* London: Methuen.

Brewer, M. B. (1991). The social self: On being the same and different at the same time. *Personality and Social Psychology Bulletin, 17,* 475–482.

Cantor, N., Norem, J. K., Neidenthal, P. M., Langston, C. A., & Brower, A. M. (1987). Life tasks, self-concept ideals, and cognitive strategies in a life transition. *Journal of Personality and Social Psychology, 53,* 1178–1191.

Chodorow, N. (1978). *The reproduction of mothering.* Berkeley, CA: University of California Press.

Cota, A. A., & Dion, K. L. (1986). Salience of gender and sex composition of ad hoc groups: An experimental test of distinctiveness theory. *Journal of Personality and Social Psychology, 50,* 770–776.

Crocker, J., & Luhtanen, R. (1990). Collective self-esteem and ingroup bias. *Journal of Personality and Social Psychology, 58,* 60–67.

Crocker, J., & Major, B. (1989). Social stigma and self-esteem: The self-protective properties of stigma. *Psychological Review, 96,* 608–630.

Cross, S., & Markus, H. (1991). Possible selves across the life-span. *Human Development, 34,* 230–255.

Darley, J. M., & Fazio, R. H. (1980). Expectancy confirmation processes arising in the social interaction sequence. *American Psychologist, 35,* 867–881.

Deaux, K. (1991). Social identities: Thoughts on structure and change. In R. C. Curtis (Ed.), *The relational self: Theoretical convergences in psychoanalysis and social psychology* (pp. 77–93). New York: Guilford Press.

Deaux, K., & Major, B. (1987). Putting gender into context: An interactive model of gender-related behavior. *Psychological Review, 94,* 369–389.

Deutsch, F. M., Ruble, D. N., Fleming, A., Brooks-Gunn, J., & Stangor, C. S. (1988). Information-seeking and maternal self-definition during the transition to motherhood. *Journal of Personality and Social Psychology, 55,* 420–431.

Dion, K. (1989, May). [Gender differences in parental roles]. Paper presented at Nags Head conference on sex and gender, Nags Head, NC.

Ethier, K., & Deaux, K. (1990a). Hispanics in ivy: Assessing identity and perceived threat. *Sex Roles, 22,* 427–440.

Ethier, K. A., & Deaux, K. (1990b, August). *Maintaining the stability of a social identity during a life transition.* Paper presented at meeting of American Psychological Association, Boston, MA.

Festinger, L. (1954). A theory of social comparison processes. *Human Relations, 7,* 117–140.

Frable, D. E. S., Blackstone, T., & Scherbaum, C. (1990). Marginal and mindful: Deviants in social interaction. *Journal of Personality and Social Psychology, 59,* 140–149.

Frable, D. E. S., Wortman, C., Joseph, J., Kirscht, J., & Kessler, R. (1991). *Predicting self-esteem, well-being, and distress in a cohort of gay men: The importance of cultural stigma.* Unpublished manuscript.

Harter, S. (1983). Developmental perspectives on the self-system. In P. H. Mussen (Ed.), *Handbook of child psychology, Vol. 4: socialization, personality, and social development* (pp. 275–385). New York: Wiley.

Higgins, E. T. (1987). Self-discrepancy: A theory relating self and affect. *Psychological Review, 94,* 319–340.

Higgins, E. T. (1990). Development of self-regulatory and self-evaluative processes: Costs, benefits, and tradeoffs. In M. R. Gunnar & A. Sroufe (Eds.), *Minnesota symposium on child development* (pp. 125–165). Hillsdale, NJ: Erlbaum.

Higgins, E. T., Tykocinski, O., & Vookles, J. (1990). Patterns of self-beliefs: The psychological significance of relations among the actual, ideal, ought, can, and future selves. In J. M. Olson & M. P. Zanna (Eds.), *Self-inference processes: The Ontario symposium* (Vol. 6, pp. 153–190). Hillsdale, NJ: Erlbaum.

Higgins, E. T., Vookles, J., & Tykocinsky, O. (in press). Self and health: How "patterns" of self-beliefs predict types of emotional and physical problems. *Social Cognition.*

Janoff-Bulman, R., & Schwartzberg, S. S. (1991). Toward a general model of personal change: Applications to victimization and psychotherapy. In C. R. Snyder & D. R. Forsyth (Eds.), *Handbook of social and clinical psychology: The health perspective* (pp. 488–508). New York: Pergamon Press.

Jones, E. E., & Gerard, H. B. (1967). *Foundations of social psychology.* New York: Wiley.

Josephs, L. (1991). Character structure, self-esteem regulation, and the principle of identity maintenance. In R. C. Curtis (Ed.), *The relational self: Theoretical convergences in psychoanalysis and social psychology* (pp. 3–16). New York: Guilford Press.

Kellogg, S. (1992). *Identity and recovery.* Unpublished manuscript, City University of New York.

Kelly, G. A. (1955). *The psychology of personal constructs.* New York: W. W. Norton.

Kihlstrom, J., & Cantor, N. (1984). Mental representations of the self. In L. Berkowitz (Ed.), *Advances in experimental social psychology* (Vol. 17, pp. 1–47). New York: Academic Press.

Kohut, H. (1971). *The analysis of the self: A systematic approach to the treatment of narcissistic personality disorders.* New York: International Universities Press.

Kohut, H. (1977). *The restoration of the self.* New York: International Universities Press.

Levesque, D., Deutsch, F. M., & Janoff-Bulman, R. (1990, June). *The effect of trauma on self-schemas.* Paper presented at convention of the American Psychological Society, Dallas, TX.

Levine, J. M., & Moreland, R. L. (1987). Social comparison and outcome evaluation in group contexts. In J. C. Masters & W. P. Smith (Eds.), *Social comparison, social justice, and relative deprivation: Theoretical, empirical, and policy perspectives* (pp. 105–127). Hillsdale, NJ: Erlbaum.

Linville, P. (1987). Self-complexity as a cognitive buffer against stress-related illness and depression. *Journal of Personality and Social Psychology, 52,* 663–676.

Little, B. R. (1983). Personal projects: A rationale and method for investigation. *Environment and Behavior, 15,* 273–309.

Luhtanen, R. & Crocker, J. (1992). Collective self-esteem scale: Self-evaluation of one's social identity. *Personality and Social Psychology Bulletin, 18.*

Markus, H. (1977). Self-schemata and processing information about the self. *Journal of Personality and Social Psychology, 35,* 63–78.

Markus, H., & Kunda, Z. (1986). Stability and malleability of the self-concept. *Journal of Personality and Social Psychology, 51,* 858–866.

Markus, H., & Nurius, P. (1986). Possible selves. *American Psychologist, 41,* 954–969.

Markus, H., & Ruvolo, A. (1989). Possible selves: Personalized representations of goals. In L. A. Pervin (Ed.), *Goal concepts in personality and social psychology* (pp. 211–241). Hillsdale, NJ: Erlbaum.

McCall, G. J., & Simmons, J. L. (1978). *Identities and interactions* (rev. ed.). New York: Free Press.

McGuire, W. J. (1964). Inducing resistance to persuasion. *Advances in experimental social psychology, 1,* 191–229.

McGuire, W. J., & McGuire, C. V. (1981). The spontaneous self-concept as affected by personal distinctiveness. In M. D. Lynch, A. A. Norem-Hebeisen, & K. J. Gergen (Eds.), *Self-concept: Advances in theory and research.* Cambridge, MA: Ballinger.

McNulty, S. E., & Swann, W. B., Jr. (1991). Psychotherapy, self-concept change, and self-verification. In R. C. Curtis (Ed.), *The relational self:*

Theoretical convergences in psychoanalysis and social psychology (pp. 213–237). New York: Guilford Press.

Miller, D. T., & Turnbull, W. (1986). Expectancies and interpersonal processes. *Annual Review of Psychology, 37,* 233–256.

Mori, D., Chaiken, S., & Pliner, P. (1987). "Eating lightly" and the self-presentation of femininity. *Journal of Personality and Social Psychology, 53,* 693–702.

Ouellette, S. C., Bochnak, B., & McKinley, P. (1991, November). *Patient identity in women with SLE: Making a case for the usefulness of social psychological identity constructs and methods in health research.* Paper presented at the 26th annual meeting of the Arthritis Health Professions Association, Boston, MA.

Parkes, C. M. (1971). Psycho-social transitions: A field of study. *Social Science and Medicine, 5,* 101–115.

Pelham, B. W., & Swann, W. B., Jr. (1990). *Identity, investment and illness: Some unhealthy consequences of social misperception.* Unpublished manuscript.

Pervin, L. A. (Ed.). (1989). *Goal concepts in personality and social psychology.* Hillsdale, NJ: Erlbaum.

Pliner, P., & Chaiken, S. (1990). Eating, social motives, and self-presentation in women and men. *Journal of Experimental Social Psychology, 26,* 240–254.

Pliner, P., Chaiken, S., & Flett, G. L. (1990). Gender differences in concern with body weight and physical appearance over the life-span. *Personality and Social Psychology Bulletin, 16,* 263–273.

Robey, K. L., Cohen, B. D., & Gara, M. A. (1989). Self-structure in schizophrenia. *Journal of Abnormal Psychology, 98,* 436–442.

Rosenberg, M. (1979). *Conceiving the self.* New York: Basic Books.

Rosenberg, S. (1989, March). *Social self and the schizophrenic process: Theory and research.* Paper presented at Second Kansas Series in Clinical Psychology.

Rosenberg, S., & Gara, M. A. (1985). The multiplicity of personal identity. *Review of Personality and Social Psychology, 6,* 87–113.

Ruble, D. N., Brooks-Gunn, J., Fleming, A. S., Fitzmaurice, G., Stangor, C., & Deutsch, F. (1990). Transition to motherhood and the self: Measurement, stability, and change. *Journal of Personality and Social Psychology, 58,* 450–463.

Scott, R. (personal communication, November 21, 1991).

Snyder, M., Tanke, E. D., & Berscheid, E. (1977). Social perception and interpersonal behavior: On the self-fulfilling nature of stereotypes. *Journal of Personality and Social Psychology, 35,* 656–666.

Steele, C. M. (1988). The psychology of self-affirmation: Sustaining the integrity of the self. *Advances in experimental social psychology* (Vol. 21, pp. 261–302). San Diego, CA: Academic Press.

Steele, C. (1990). Draft statement to NIMH workgroup.

Stolorow, R. D. (1991). The intersubjective context of intrapsychic experience, with special reference to therapeutic impasses. In R. C.

Curtis (Ed.), *The relational self: Theoretical convergences in psycho-analysis and social psychology* (pp. 17–33). New York: Guilford Press.

Strauman, T. J., Vookles, J., Berenstein, V., Chaiken, S., & Higgins, E. T. (1991). Self-discrepancies and vulnerability to body dissatisfaction and disordered eating. *Journal of Personality and Social Psychoogy, 61,* 946–956.

Stryker, S. (1987). Identity theory: Developments and extensions. In K. Yardley & T. Honess (Eds.), *Self and identity: Psychosocial perspectives* (pp. 89–103). Chichester, England: Wiley.

Stryker, S., & Statham, A. (1985). Symbolic interaction and role theory. In G. Lindzey & E. Aronson (Eds.), *Handbook of social psychology* (Vol. 1, pp. 311–378). New York: Random House.

Swann, W. B., Jr. (1983). Self-verification: Bringing social reality into harmony with the self. In J. Suls & A. G. Greenwald (Eds.), *Psychological perspectives on the self* (Vol. 2, pp. 33–66). Hillsdale, NJ: Erlbaum.

Swann, W. B., Jr. (1990). To be adored or to be known? The interplay of self-enhancement and self-verification. In E. T. Higgins & R. M. Sorrentino (Eds.), *Handbook of motivation and cognition: Foundations of social behavior* (Vol. 2, pp. 408–448). New York: Guilford Press.

Swann, W. B., Jr., & Brown, J. D. (1990). From self to health: Self-verification and identity disruption. In B. R. Sarason, I. G. Sarason, & G. R. Pierce (Eds.), *Social support: An interactional view* (pp. 150–172). New York: Wiley.

Swann, W. B., Jr., Wenzlaff, R. M., Krull, D. S., & Pelham, B. W. (in press). The allure of negative feedback: Self-verification strivings among depressed persons. *Journal of Abnormal Psychology.*

Tesser, A. (1984). Self-evaluation maintenance processes: Implications for relationships and for development. In J. Masters & K. Yarkin (Eds.), *Boundary areas of psychology: Social and development* (pp. 271–299). New York: Academic Press.

Tesser, A. (1988). Toward a self-evaluation maintenance model of social behavior. *Advances in experimental social psychology* (Vol. 21, pp. 181–227). San Diego, CA: Academic Press.

Tesser, A. (1991). Social versus clinical approaches to self psychology: The self-evaluation maintenance model and Kohutian object relations theory. In R. C. Curtis (Ed.), *The relational self: Theoretical convergences in psychoanalysis and social psychology* (pp. 257–281). New York: Guilford Press.

Thibaut, J. W., & Kelley, H. H. (1959). *The social psychology of groups.* New York: Wiley.

Thoits, P. A. (1983). Multiple identities and psychological well-being: A reformulation and test of the social isolation hypothesis. *American Sociological Review, 48,* 174–187.

Thoits, P. A. (1991). *Identity structures and psychological well-being: Gender and marital status comparisons.* Unpublished manuscript.

Westen, D. (1991). Cultural, emotional, and unconscious aspects of self. In R. C. Curtis (Ed.), *The relational self: Theoretical convergences in psychoanalysis and social psychology* (pp. 181–210). New York: Guilford Press.

Wood, J. V. (1989). Theory and research concerning social comparisons of personal attributes. *Psychological Bulletin, 106,* 231–248.

The Principles of Multiple, Nonadditive, and Reciprocal Determinism:
Implications for Social Psychological Research and Levels of Analysis

JOHN T. CACIOPPO and GARY G. BERNTSON

The vast range of problems addressed by social psychologists is illustrated by the preceding chapters in this book. Social psychologists study the foundations, antecedents, and consequences of people's beliefs, attitudes, and behaviors, as well as how individuals and groups are influenced by social and societal factors such as mass media, government, peer and work groups, family, friends, and neighbors. Paralleling this basic research is evidence that many of the most pressing current mental, social, and economic problems (and likely problems of the next century) stem in large part from social processes such as modifiable attitudes and behavioral choices (see Lorion, 1991; McClelland, 1989; Seeman, 1989). For example, more young people in the United States die or become disabled from self-destructive behavioral choices (e.g., accidents, drug abuse, violence) than from any disease, and many of those who survive their youth have, by their own actions (e.g., teenage pregnancy, smoking, cholesterol-laden diets, dropping out of high school), laid the foundation for significant problems in later life. Given the savings that can be achieved through social interventions (e.g., Price, Cowen, Lorion, & Ramos-McKay, 1988; U.S. Department of Health, Education, and Welfare, 1979), it is surprising that the level of resources and support for basic social psychological research has remained low compared, for instance, to cardiovascular research or the neurosciences.

Among the reasons for the relative emphasis on and support for medical research are historical precedent, the apparent tractability and lawfulness of physiochemical processes within simple systems and controlled assessments contexts, and misperceptions of basic social psychological research. However, this emphasis may also stem in part from a provincialism in basic social psychological theory and research. The thesis of this chapter, therefore, is twofold: (1) social psychology is in a preeminent position to contribute to the understanding and solution of practical problems of individuals and of society; and (2) these contributions will be unnecessarily limited in theoretical scope and practical utility if a parochial level of analysis is adopted. We begin by reviewing briefly the major ways in which the term "level of analysis" has been used in psychology. We then define how we will be using the term here and outline three basic principles in which the construct of levels is fundamental. In so doing, we also illustrate how a multilevel approach to the study of social psychological phenomena can highlight the synergistic relationship between theoretical and clinically relevant research and foster the transition from microtheories in social psychology to general psychological theories.

LEVEL OF ANALYSIS

The term "level of analysis" has been used in various ways, including in reference to the levels of structural organization (e.g., Tolman, 1959; Weiss, 1941), explanation (e.g., Shaw & Turvey, 1981), and processing (e.g., Churchland & Sejnowski, 1988; Craik & Lockhart, 1972). "Level of organization" in psychology refers to the different scales on which the brain or behavior can be represented. The level of organization of psychological phenomena can vary, for instance, from the molecular (e.g., transmitters/receptors) to the cellular to the tissue to the organ to the body system to the human organism to the environmental to the sociocultural context. What constitutes a level of organization, at least at the lower levels of structure, is often guided by knowledge of anatomy or physiology, but the ultimate criterion is the usefulness of the posited organization in shedding light on some designated psychological or behavioral phenomenon.

For example, anencephalic infants display expressions and

actions reminiscent of pleasure following exposure to sweet gustatory stimuli, fear following exposure to abrupt, loud sounds or bright lights, and distress upon a needle puncture. However, the role of one's view of the self is a substantially more important determinant of emotion in the normal adult. Because the self is defined within a sociocultural context, culture can play a rather dramatic role in shaping emotional experience in the adult (Markus & Kitayama, 1991). Accordingly, organizing the data in terms of the cultural context is informative in studies of normal emotions in the adult, whereas this organization becomes superfluous when examining the emotions in the anencephalic infant (Steiner, 1979).

"Level of explanation" refers to the representation of a psychological phenomenon in terms of the classes of questions that can be asked about it—or as Marr (1982) observed, "the different levels at which an information processing device must be understood before one can be said to have understood it completely" (p. 24). The computational level encompasses questions about the main constituents of the task or phenomenon, including the goal of the computation, the representations on which the computations operate, and the logic of the strategy by which the computation can be performed. A computational analysis of decision making by highly anxious individuals, for instance, might specify a goal (e.g., to minimize failures or losses), the main components involved in the computation (e.g., efficacy expectations, outcome expectations), and the logic underlying the computation (e.g., efficacy and outcome expectations for each behavioral option are multiplied and their products compared). The level of the algorithm encompasses questions about the predetermined procedure or ordered sequence of finite instructions used to achieve the correct output from a designated input. For instance, a common computer algorithm for the computation of 1.0×10^n is to move the decimal point of the multiplicand n-digits to the right. Finally, the level of implementation refers to questions about the physical instantiation of the behavioral function and the cognitive algorithm—the manner in which the algorithm is realized physically.

The term "level of processing" has been used to refer to the number of neural units underlying a particular behavior (e.g., Churchland & Sejnowski, 1988) and to the depth of semantic analyses of words (e.g., Craik & Lockhart, 1972). Within social psychology, the term "level of processing" (or "level of analysis") has been used to mean the extent of systematic or analytic reasoning underlying a judgment or decision. Thus, whether an individual is influenced by the merits of the arguments for a recommendation or by superfluous cues associated with the recommendation has been shown to be a function of the level of message processing (see review by Petty & Cacioppo, 1986). In a general sense, therefore, the level of processing refers to the number of information-processing units separating the input and the output of interest. The level of processing in a monosynaptic reflex is quite low, relative to the level of processing underlying deliberate movements. Similarly, the level of processing in a social institution is low when inquiries are handled with pretaped phone messages and high when actions are adopted only after multiple options have been scrutinized by various groups within the organization.

When the term "level of analysis" appears in social psychology, it typically refers to the unique level of organization represented by a focus on the individual in a sociocultural context. Thus, a social psychological analysis focuses on the reciprocal impact of individuals on one another and on society; it focuses on the behavior and influence of collections of individuals (e.g., groups, institutions, governments, cultures), past, present, and future. The output of a social system is enacted by individuals whose actions are controlled by the brain and nervous system, but as Marr (1982) noted, "[A]lmost never can a complex system of any kind be understood as a simple extrapolation from the properties of its elementary components" (p. 19). Thus, to the extent that the properties of the system are not isomorphic with those of the system's elementary components, a situation that rarely obtains with biological much less social systems, a focus on elementary components contributes to an explanation only when considered in conjunction with events occurring at different levels of the system.

Consider, for instance, the phenomenon of alcoholic consumption. An understanding of osmoreceptive mechanism and volume detectors, which monitor body water balance, can offer an eloquent account of facilitated digestive reflexes and water (or alcohol) consumption. These mechanisms, however, offer only a partial account of an animal's bar pressing for alcohol, for which the principles of learning and psychopharmacology must be invoked. Moreover, they tell us little about the drinking behavior of alcoholics in bars. Conversely, even extensive studies limited to operant performance or barroom behavior would be relatively uninformative about the fundamental mechanisms of thirst if conceptualized in isolation from the physiological underpinnings. Therefore, integrative research that specifies the conditions under which each of a set of factors or processes is operative, or that specifies the relationship between empirical observations at differing levels of analysis, can be especially illuminating in efforts to understand the systems or mechanisms underlying a complex mental or social problem.

In addition, each level of organization constitutes a particular kind of representation with which to examine human mentation and behavior. Any particular representation makes certain information explicit at the expense of other information and, hence, renders some operations or insights easy and others quite difficult. The specialized utility of analyses at different levels of organization was exemplified in our earlier reference to biological versus cultural determinants of emotion in anencephalic infants and normal adults (see also Marr's, 1982, discussion of the multiplication of Arabic versus Roman numerals). The important point here is that no single level of behavioral organization is best for all psychological questions. Hence, analyzing a mental or social problem from various levels can reveal quite different insights into the mechanisms underlying the phenomenon, and, together, these insights can foster more comprehensive theories.

To the extent that explanations of mental disorders in terms of a particular level of organization have few implications for ethical forms of treatment or control (e.g., genetic engineering, psychosurgery), the explanations may have less immediate practical interest. Indeed, when genetic and neurophysiological levels of analysis have been eschewed by social psychologists, it has tended to be this feature that was objectionable (see Allport, 1947; McGuire, 1968). McGuire (1968), for instance, suggested with acknowledged trepidation that genetic factors might be a determinant of a person's attitudes:

> Any deviation from a radical environmentalism raises the specter of a laissez-faire political program which countenanced by perpetuation of the *status quo* with all its social and economic inequities. . . . The genetic doctrine is especially dismal when applied to attitude formation, because it seems to imply that "bad" attitudes like racial prejudice will be hard to change . . . it becomes understandable that even theorists who agree on little else are in complete accord on the extreme and undemonstrated notion that all attitudes are developed through experience. (p. 161)

McGuire, of course, recognized that collective denial does not change the determinants of a psychological phenomenon but only hinders accurate modeling of the phenomenon. Furthermore, analyses across levels of organization are yielding data that answer some of these earlier objections. Research in behavioral genetics, for instance, suggests that genetic and environmental factors are not as separable in their effects as was once thought. Social and environmental factors can inhibit or trigger the expression of genetic influences; conversely, genetic factors can lead individuals to seek or remain in particular social environments. Thus, monozygotic twins reared apart not only express similar levels of satisfaction with their jobs but also hold jobs that are similar in terms of complexity, motor skills, and physical demands (e.g., Arvey, Bouchard, Segal, & Abraham, 1989).

Unless explicitly stated otherwise, we use the term "levels" here to refer to levels of organization. In the following section, we review three principles that underscore the importance of multilevel integrative analyses to the study of complex mental, behavioral, and social problems. As should now be clear, a multilevel analysis refers to the study of a phenomenon from various structural scales or perspectives, ranging from the molecular ("microscopic") to the sociocultural ("macroscopic"). By integrative, we mean that observations at one level of analysis are used to inform, refine, or constrain inferences based on observations at another level of analysis.

THE PRINCIPLES OF MULTIPLE, NONADDITIVE, AND RECIPROCAL DETERMINISM

In this section, we review and elaborate on three principles that were developed in previous conferences of the Behavioral Sciences Basic Research Branch of the National Institute of Mental Health (NIMH)[1] (see also Cacioppo, Petty, & Tassinary, 1989; Cacioppo & Tassinary, 1990a). These principles were derived from a problem-oriented, in contrast to a method-oriented, approach to science (Platt, 1964). Thus, these principles reflect generalizations derived from a wide variety of inquiries of the functions of and mechanisms underlying psychological phenomena. We believe these principles and their implications for psychological theory and research are worth examining, not because they are uniquely applicable to a specific content area or to the interface between social and clinical research but rather because they can inform the design and interpretation of social psychological research, or as

Morton (1991) observed about psychological experimentation: "The correct generalizations will be at the level of mechanisms, not data. This will require thought, not observation" (p. 33).

The Principle of Multiple Determinism

This principle specifies that a target event at one level of organization (e.g., neuroeffector response, emotion) may have multiple antecedents within or across levels of organization. William James's (1894) views on emotion exemplify this point. James is well-known, and has been roundly criticized, for his assertion that emotion is the perception of the somatovisceral reactions that follow the exciting fact. Yet, by 1894, James did not regard all emotions as deriving from somatovisceral reactions but instead agreed with Baldwin (1894) that associative processes could also govern the emotions (or at least the "subtler" emotions). Thus, James suggested, there is more than one means by which an emotion could be stimulated. Similarly, aggressive behavior is multiply determined both within and across levels. Thus, aggressive behavior could result from hormonal, neurochemical, or neuropathological events at a biological level; instrumental contingencies, frustration, or paranoid delusions at a psychological level; and overcrowding, maternal defense, or territoriality at a social level.[2] Indeed, considerable evidence has amassed over the past several decades demonstrating that elements in the physiological domain and elements in the psychological domain can be influenced by a multiplicity of factors within and across levels of organization (New Frontiers in the Behavioral Sciences and Health, 1989).

The implications of this principle for theory and research are perhaps less obvious. For instance, basic social psychological research, with its emphasis on experimental control, has been criticized for yielding statistically reliable but trivial effects (e.g., Appley, 1990; Staats, 1989). Allport (1968) acknowledged that noteworthy scientific gains result from this hard-nosed approach, but he lamented the lack of generalizing power of many neat and elegant experiments: "It is for this reason that some current investigations seem to end up in elegantly polished triviality— snippets of empiricism, but nothing more" (p. 68).

However, what Allport viewed as an adversity—the generalizing problem—is transformed to an advantage and a theoretical challenge by the principle of multiple determinism. Specifically, a certain lack of generalizing power in studies of the role of single factors is a fundamental property of multiply determined phenomena. This is easy to show.

Let Ψ represent a psychological phenomenon, and let τ represent a factor (e.g., treatment) whose effect on Ψ is of some interest (Cacioppo & Tassinary, 1990b). Carefully conceived and controlled experimentation on the role of τ in producing Ψ can be denoted as $P(\Psi/\tau)$. We know the following:

$$P(\Psi/\tau) = 1 \text{ if } \tau \text{ is a sufficient cause of } \Psi. \tag{1}$$

Equation 1 specifies that if the manipulated factor or treatment (τ) is a *sufficient* cause of Ψ, then evidence of the psychological phenomenon should be observed whenever τ has occurred.

$$P(\Psi/\text{not-}\tau) = 0 \text{ if } \tau \text{ is a necessary cause of } \Psi. \tag{2}$$

Equation 2 states simply that if the manipulated factor or treatment (τ) is a necessary cause of Ψ, then evidence of the psychological phenomenon should not be found if τ has not occurred.

$$P(\Psi/\tau) = 1 \text{ and } P(\Psi/\text{not-}\tau) = 0 \text{ if } \tau \text{ is a necessary and sufficient cause of } \Psi. \tag{3}$$

Equation 3 follows directly from Equations 1 and 2. If the manipulated factor or treatment (τ) is a necessary and sufficient cause of Ψ, then evidence of the psychological phenomenon should be observed if and only if τ has occurred.

It is rare, however, for a single factor or determinant to assume a necessary and sufficient relationship with a complex psychological phenomenon, at least in a contextually generalized fashion. Rather, psychological phenomena are often subject to multiple determinants. This multiple determinism may assume one or both of two general forms. The first we term "parallel determinism," in which any of a number of factors are sufficient to evoke the psychological phenomenon. Thus,

$$P(\Psi/\tau) = 1 \text{ and } P(\Psi/\text{not-}\tau) > 0 \text{ if } \tau \text{ is a sufficient but not a necessary cause of } \Psi. \tag{4}$$

Equation 4 specifies that if the manipulated factor or treatment (τ) is a sufficient but not a necessary cause of Ψ, then evidence of the psychological phenomenon should be observed whenever τ has occurred and may be observed even when τ has not occurred.

From Equations (1), (3), and (4) and Bayes theorem, we also know that when τ is a sufficient cause:

$$P(\Psi/\tau) = P(\Psi,\tau) / [P(\Psi,\tau) + P(\text{not-}\Psi,\tau)] = 1. \qquad (5)$$

Therefore,

$$P(\Psi,\tau) = 1 \text{ and } P(\text{not-}\Psi,\tau) = 0.$$

That is, if τ is a sufficient cause for Ψ, then it should always be followed or accompanied by Ψ. Of course, Ψ may appear reliably when τ occurs, but the presence of Ψ does not necessarily imply τ.

In a second form of multiple determinism, termed "convergent determinism," the convergence of a number of factors (or one or more factors in a specific context) is required to evoke the psychological phenomenon. Thus,

$$P(\Psi/\tau) < 1 \text{ and } P(\Psi/\text{not-}\tau) = 0 \text{ if } \tau \text{ is a necessary but not}$$
a sufficient cause of Ψ. $\qquad (6)$

That is, Equation 6 specifies that if the manipulated factor or treatment (τ) is a necessary but not a sufficient cause of Ψ, then evidence of the psychological phenomenon should not be observed if τ has not occurred, and Ψ may or may not be observed if τ has occurred. Equations (4) and (6) denote multiple determinism but represent complementing perspectives. Equation (4) implies that there are multiple independent causes for Ψ, whereas Equation (6) implies there are multiple synergistic variables which interact to produce Ψ.

From Equations (2), (3), and (6) and Bayes theorem, we also know that $P(\Psi,\text{not-}\tau) = 0$ if and only if τ is a necessary cause for Ψ. That is, if τ is a necessary cause for Ψ, then Ψ should always be preceded or accompanied by τ, although τ could occur in the absence of Ψ.

It follows from the preceding analysis that if τ is a sufficient cause for Ψ, then the $P(\Psi/\tau) = 1$ and the effects documented in the experimentation will be *replicable*. Moreover, if τ is *also* a necessary cause of Ψ, then the $P(\Psi,\tau) = 1$ and the $P(\Psi,\text{not-}\tau) = 0$ and the effects documented in the experimentation will be *generalizable*. If, however, τ is a sufficient but not a necessary cause for Ψ (i.e., Ψ is multiply determined by independent events), then the $P(\Psi,\text{not-}\tau)$ may equal or approach zero (and $P(\tau/\Psi)$ approaches 1) only because the other sufficient causes of Ψ have been controlled in a particular experimental paradigm or assessment context. That is, $P(\Psi, \text{not-}\tau) = 0$ in a given experimental context by virtue of experimental control: All other determinants of Ψ have been eliminated or held constant in the experimental setting. Because Ψ is multiply determined, however, the $P(\Psi, \text{not-}\tau) > 0$ in natural (e.g., clinical) settings or populations. Thus, the "generalizing problem" need not reflect a methodological quagmire but rather can represent a theoretical challenge.

To summarize thus far, the fact that effects documented in carefully controlled experimentation lack generalizing power may not reflect any dubious feature of experimentation but simply the multiply determined nature of the phenomenon of interest.[3] By this reasoning, boundary conditions for theories can be identified, and new theoretical organizations can be discovered, when a "generalizing problem" arises, for instance, from the application of a basic social psychological theory to a clinical population or problem.

The number of processing elements, transforms, and steps necessary to account for a phenomenon tends to increase rather than decrease as the level of organization decreases. Thus, reductionistic studies are probably more, not less, subject to this generalizing problem. The illusion of generality can be achieved by the study of the behavior of simple systems rather than complex phenomena, however. Thus, documenting the $P(\Psi/\tau) = 1$, where τ is a manipulation of events within a specific neurophysiological system, demonstrates lawfulness and may create the impression of generality, but it is subject to the same objection Allport (1968) raised about social psychological experimentation. Reductionistic studies demonstrating the sufficiency of τ as a cause of Ψ are immensely important, but only because they guide and constrain more general theories of Ψ. The same holds when τ is a molar treatment investigated by social psychologists within a carefully controlled experimental paradigm.

The realization that complex psychological processes and problems are multiply determined can also foster the transition from microtheories to general psychological theories. To the extent that a phenomenon is multiply determined, it is important to document and explain each of the determinants, for only in this way can a comprehensive understanding of a psychological phenomenon be achieved. Accordingly, basic research, even when conducted within contrived experimental paradigms, can provide important information about the determinants and moderating variables underlying complex psychological phenomena.

It should be recognized, however, that the cultivation of a carefully manicured experimental paradigm is valuable only as a way station en route to a comprehensive, unified, and behaviorally relevant body of scientific knowledge. Arriving at this final destination is fostered by treating generalization not as a threat to a theory or a nuisance to an investigator but as an important theoretical tool that can clarify the reasons and conditions under which specific causal factors and processes are operative. Thus, realization that a psychological phenomenon is multiply determined has important implications for psychological theory and for our understanding of mental disorders and mental health.

In an interesting Monte Carlo study, Ahadi and Diener (1989; see also Strube, 1991) investigated the magnitude of the relations among behaviors and traits when two behaviors were modeled as being determined by three traits, only one of which was a determinant of both behaviors. The average absolute value intercorrelation among the traits was nonsignificant, verifying the initial condition of the model in which each of the traits were set up as parallel determinants. Results also revealed that the upper bound for the correlation between the two behaviors was approximately 0.30, and the upper bound for the correlation between the common trait and the behaviors was about 0.50. When four rather than two traits were modeled as determinants of each of the two behaviors, with both behaviors being determined by one trait, the upper bound of the correlation between the two behaviors dropped to 0.25, and between the common trait and behaviors dipped to 0.45. Thus, the correlations between the personality traits and behaviors (i.e., τ & Ψ, respectively) in Ahadi and Diener's (1989) simulation study ranged from small to moderate even though the behaviors were modeled to be completely determined by a small number of traits. As Ahadi and Diener (1989)noted:

> Given the wealth of literature in psychology concerning temperaments, attitudes, motivations, emotions, and so on, it appears much more reasonable to assume far greater than three or four determinants of behavior. The effect of adding any number of variables to the determination of behavior results in further decreases in the upper bound correlations that one can expect both among behaviors and between the determinants of the specific behaviors. (p. 403)

In sum, the predictable yield from isolated research on discrete determinants of a multiply determined psychological or behavioral outcome are low intercorrelations among the behaviors, low intercorrelations between the determinants of the behaviors, and a portfolio of disparate microtheories. These microtheories, each of which provides a limited account for the phenomenon of interest, are at best pieces of a larger conceptual puzzle that can foster theoretical integration and at worst imperialistic accounts that can hinder theoretical insight. This holds regardless of the level of analysis. Therefore, integrative research that specifies the conditions under which each of a set of factors or processes is operative, or that specifies the relationship between empirical observations at differing levels of analysis, constitutes an especially important theoretical advance.

A corollary of the principle of multiple determinism is the *corollary of proximity,* which states that the mapping between elements across levels of organization becomes more complex (e.g., many to many) as the number of intervening levels of organization increases. This is because an event at one level of organization (e.g., depressive behavior) can have a multiplicity of determinants at an adjacent level of organization (e.g., cognitive), which in turn may have a multiplicity of implementations at the next level of organization (e.g., neurophysiological), and so forth. The implication is not to avoid venturing across the abyss separating the macroscopic and the microscopic levels of organization but to proceed incrementally across levels of analysis. Understanding a behavioral problem at multiple levels of organization can be important in optimizing the selection and application of clinical interventions. Linking physiological functions to clinical progress and outcomes via intervening psychological and social processes may improve predictions of these outcomes and, more important, differentiate similar outcomes that were achieved by different means (e.g., see Cacioppo & Petty, 1986). Adoption of this approach could therefore prove useful ultimately in answering questions about what interventions and therapist behaviors are best for what problems in which individuals.

The Principle of Nonadditive Determinism

This second principle also implies that the understanding of complex mental processes and behavior can be advanced by multilevel integrative analyses. According to this principle, properties of the collective whole are not always predictable from the properties of the parts until the properties of the whole have been clearly documented and studied across levels. Thus, the principle of non-additive determinism builds on the preceding principle in underscoring the potential interactions among the determinants.

Analyses have traditionally focused on a given level of organization (e.g., behavioral, social psychological) with generally good success. Theories of emotion within social psychology, for instance, have been derived largely from verbal analyses, and the resulting knowledge regarding people's conceptual organization of emotion has contributed to our understanding of the cognitive antecedents and consequences of emotion (e.g., priming, cognitive appraisal, mood congruence effects). Analyses of a phenomenon when restricted to a given level of organization can also mask the underlying order in data, however. That is, certain properties of, or the order underlying, a mental or behavioral phenomenon may emerge only when examined across levels of organization. In an illustrative study cited by Markus and Kitayama (1991), Bontempo, Lobel, and Triandis (1989) compared the public and private responses of individuals from a collective culture to those from an individualist culture. They asked these individuals to indicate how enjoyable it would be to engage in a time-consuming behavior (e.g., visiting a friend in the hospital). Cultural context did not affect what individuals reported in the public condition; all subjects indicated their self-sacrificial behaviors would be enjoyable. However, only individuals from the collective culture reported that these behaviors would be enjoyable in the private condition. The "failure to replicate" the results of the public conditions in the private conditions does not imply that the mechanisms underlying emotions lack generality, but rather they suggest that self-construals derived from the soicocultural context can be a powerful theoretical element (e.g., see Markus & Kitayama, 1991). Note, however, that this theoretical insight was served by thinking about the evocation of emotion across levels of organization. Indeed, as Markus and Kitayama (1991) observe, were one to have limited the analysis of emotions to a cultural level of analysis, then one might have underestimated the generality of fundamental psychological processes or erroneously concluded that "culturally divergent individuals inhabit incomparably different worlds."

A conceptually similar illustration in a different venue is provided by Haber and Barchas (1983), who found that the administration of amphetamine had no reliable effect on primate emotional behavior until the primate's position in the social hierarchy was considered. Specifically, amphetamine administration increased dominant behaviors in primates high in the social hierarchy but increased submissive behaviors in primates low in the social hierarchy. Although this result can be explained in terms of Hull-Spence drive theory, it is interesting because it demonstrates how the effects of the physiological changes on behavior can *appear* unreliable (or chaotic) until analysis is extended across multiple levels of organization. A physiological analysis, regardless of the sophistication of the measurement technology, may not have unraveled the orderly relationship that existed between the physiological manipulation and behavior. There are, of course, physiological mechanisms underlying these phenomena, but the identification and understanding of these mechanisms are often better served by systematic investigations within and across multiple levels of organization rather than by a reductionistic or a macroscopic focus alone.

Interestingly, although not cast within a formal analytic framework or psychological principle, Lorion (1991) recently summarized succinctly the implication of this (and the following) principle:

> Psychology's potential contributions to improving the nation's health will be limited . . . if its diverse fields merely combine their respective findings. Instead, the discipline must engage in heuristic challenges presented by issues related to health promotion and disease prevention with truly collaborative exchanges across its multiple fields. To do so, psychologists must develop mechanisms to share their insights with each other and, in doing so, broaden their vision of psychological processes. (pp. 518–519)

The Principle of Reciprocal Determinism

This third principle specifies that there can be a reciprocal influence between microscopic (e.g., biological) and macroscopic (e.g., social, cultural) factors in determining brain and behavioral processes. As suggested above, research in behavior genetics has revealed that there are a wide variety of genetic influences that are repressed unless or until certain environmental factors are introduced—that is, brain and behavioral processes are a function of particular genetic factors, the expression of which is governed by environmental agents (Plomin, 1989). Within social psychology, Zillmann (1984) has demonstrated that violent and erotic material influences the level of physiological arousal in males, and that the level of physiological arousal has a reciprocal influence on the perceptions of and tendencies toward sex and aggression. If the social psychological level of analysis were ignored, the mapping between physiological reactions and behavior would appear more haphazard. Were the biological level of analysis to be ignored, our understanding of the determinants of the behavior would be incomplete.

Reciprocal determinism has also contributed to the explosion of interest in the burgeoning field of psychoneuroimmunology. Immune functions were traditionally considered to reflect specific and nonspecific physiological responses to pathogens or tissue damage (Roitt, Brostoff, & Male, 1985). It is now clear, however, that immune response are heavily influenced by central nervous processes that are shaped by psychological factors (see reviews by Ader, 1981; Kennedy, Glaser, & Kiecolt-Glaser, 1990). Indeed, effects of psychological context now appear to be among the most powerful determinants of the expression of immune reactions. Thus, an understanding of immunocompetence will be inadequate in the absence of considerations of psychosocial factors. Research on these interactions were activated by studies demonstrating the direct and moderating effects of psychosocial factors (e.g., conditioned stimuli, bereavement, social support, major life events) on immune competence (e.g., see Kennedy et al., 1990). However, few would question that significant decrements in immune function also exert at least indirect (and perhaps more direct) influences on psychosocial factors such as mood and stress. Thus, a complete understanding of psychoneuroimmunological processes may be inadequate in the absence of the analysis of reciprocal influences.

SOCIAL PSYCHOLOGY AS A HUB DISCIPLINE

Thus far, we have reviewed principles of behavior that underscore the need to examine complex psychological phenomena and mental disorders from multiple levels of analysis and to work toward theoretical integrations of the empirical observations and microtheories that emerge within and across these diverse levels of analysis. Although examining the processes underlying mental health from multiple points of view may be the look of the future, it is not entirely new to social psychology. As Gordon Allport (1968) noted:

> An individual is a member of many publics, of many institutions, of many social systems. . . . It was Sapir who advised all social and

psychological scientists to form the habit of looking at their data both from the concrete individual point of view and from the abstract social point of view. It enriches research and theory to do so. (p. 55)

As we noted at the outset of this chapter, a variety of the most vexing and costly mental disorders today are social phenomena: the spread of AIDS, juvenile delinquency, child and spousal abuse, prejudice and stigmatization, family discord and divorce, worker dissatisfaction and productivity, drug abuse, and social anxieties and phobias are illustrative. Analyses of these problems across multiple levels of organization will likely contribute to the development of comprehensive theories and effective solutions. However, before one can effectively address the mechanism underlying some psychological disorder, one must have a clear description of that disorder. Because many of the problems in mental health arise from, relate to, or manifest behaviorally at a social psychological level of analysis, social psychology is in a unique position to furnish detailed descriptions of these phenomena and their sociocultural antecedents and consequences. Without carefully designed experiments on an agreed-on phenomenon, very expensive and misleading data are likely to result regardless of the level of analysis.

Second, research on a phenomenon from a different (e.g., physiological) level of analysis, particularly in the early stages, is served well by paradigms that allow the phenomenon of interest to be controlled by specific stimuli, conditions, or contexts in a temporally precise fashion. Recent advances in the neurophysiological substratums of learning and memory, for instance, owe a large debt to decades of basic research on classical conditioning because the paradigm for forming conditioned responses is so well developed (e.g., see Gormezano & Wasserman, in press). Similarly, social psychology has the potential to play a central role in the adaptation or development of paradigms within which to study disordered social processes.

Third, although social psychological theories of ordered and disordered social processes can be treated as autonomous from their structural or functional implementations, the documented relationships among variables can guide and constrain inquiries and inferences at other levels of analysis. For example, theory and research in social psychology have drawn attention to the likelihood that emotions in normal adults are not a function of actions per se but of some sort of monitoring system. Carver and Scheier

(1990) have further suggested that discrepancies between the expected and the perceived rate of progress toward goals are compared within this monitoring system, resulting in positive affect (if progress exceeds expectations) or negative affect (if expectations exceed progress) and action accommodations. The focus of theories such as Carver and Scheier's, with their emphasis on the self and expectancies, have important implications for analyses of affect and affect-disorders whether from a cross-cultural or neurophysiological perspective (e.g., see Markus & Kitayama, 1991).

Fourth, the specification of the social psychological basis of some health problems can be of immediate help in developing practical interventions. Consider the relative utility of specifying the sociocognitive versus the neurophysiological basis of patient delay following the onset of gynecological cancer. Women can now survive most gynecological cancers. Research on gynecological cancer further indicates that the prognosis for survival and for the quality of life following medical treatment is related to the stage of the cancer at diagnosis (Andersen, 1986). Women with advanced rather than early-stage disease at diagnosis, even if they survive, are more likely to suffer depression, to experience marital and family problems, and to require extended and expensive medical treatment. Hence, patient delay in seeking a diagnosis by women with cancer is a serious problem that carries large and long-term personal, family, and societal costs. The form of the representation provided, for example, by neuroscientific analyses of patient delay, while perhaps contributing to a more complete understanding of the phenomenon, is not optimal for identifying the determinants of patient delay or for developing effective interventions to minimize these delays. Substantial savings in resources and human suffering are there to be reaped, not through a specification of the brain circuits underlying patient delay but by well-conceived public health campaigns that identify the early signs of cancer and that minimize the material, emotional, and social costs of seeking diagnosis and treatment (Andersen, 1986).

Finally, support for social psychological research can be cost-effective due to the status of the field as a hub discipline. The applied areas of health, clinical, and counseling psychology rely heavily on basic theory and research developed in social psychology. Work in cognitive psychology, cognitive neuroscience, and artificial intelligence has benefited by examining the processes by which complex social decisions and choices are made. Social psychology is also a "hub" discipline in that it links to more departments in the social and behavioral sciences than any other.

Fields such as psychiatry, education, nursing, preventive medicine, communication, political science, education, family science, public policy, economics, social work, dentistry, sociology, journalism, linguistics, and cognitive science draw on basic research and theory in social psychology. As implied by the diversity of these related fields, the status of social psychology as a hub discipline derives in large part from the myriad interesting psychological phenomena that manifest (though are not entirely explicable) at a social psychological level of analysis.

If comprehensive explanations for these phenomena are also to stem from the field of social psychology, then some modifications may be required in the training of the next generation of social psychologists. To begin, social psychology training programs might attempt to overcome the tension between reductionistic and social psychological perspectives that has existed for at least the past half century (e.g., see the inaugural presidential address to the Division of Personality and Social Psychology by Allport, 1947). Reductionism has contributed to the solution of some of the most perplexing scientific problems in human history (e.g., see Boorstin, 1983) and has much to contribute to our understanding of social and psychological phenomena. However, it is counterproductive to presume that reductionism will convert the abstractions of the psychological sciences to a set of physical essentials and invariants. To do so ignores (1) the distinction between levels of explanation, (2) the scientific breakthroughs that can result from research across levels of organization, (3) the rich theoretical insights about the nature and timing of the relationships among variables that can be derived from descriptions of phenomena from multiple scales or perspectives, and (4) the economy of thought to be reaped by capitalizing on the form of representation most appropriate for the task. In addition, scientific provincialism in which any single level of analysis (e.g., neuroscientific, social psychological) is thought to be the most appropriate for understanding complex mental and social problems undermines multilevel, integrative analyses, alienates scientists working at "unchosen" levels of organization who might otherwise contribute relevant data and theory, and renders it acceptable to ignore relevant theory and data on a phenomenon of interest simply because they were not born from one's own level of analysis.

Social psychology training curricula might also be designed to equip its graduates with the background and expertise required to deal conceptually and experimentally with the complexities of multiply determined phenomena. For instance, Ahadi and Diener's (1989) simulation studies of the determination of behaviors by multiple traits demonstrate that the theoretical magnitude of an empirical result cannot be judged by effect sizes alone. Thus, training in methods, experimental design, and statistical analysis, which furnish important tools for the social psychologist, might be augmented by considering the implications of the principles of multiple, nonadditive, and reciprocal determinism.

Perhaps more important, however, is a bridling of the emphasis on academic specialization and publication counts to allow students to secure a broader background in psychology. It is conceivable that social psychological research might be facilitated, for instance, by (1) requiring predoctoral students to complete two minors in addition to the required work in social psychology; (2) including "affiliated" (e.g., clinical, counseling) faculty in social psychological training programs to expose students to the complexities and theoretical richness of mental and social problems; (3) promoting student participation in interdisciplinary programs; and, possibly, (4) increasing student exposure to courses such as history and systems, philosophy of science, research ethics, and theory construction.

Students perhaps learn best, however, by observing models and by observing the consequences of their own actions in research. Thus, a multilevel integrative analysis could be a particularly powerful research training component if it represented the approach taken successfully by the training faculty. Bootstrapping is not the only means of achieving this feature in a social psychology training program. For example, a training faculty may have active research programs on affect, attitudes, and social cognition or interests in personality processes and individual differences. The complementing perspectives that can be brought to bear on these elemental social processes can range, of course, from the biological and developmental to the sociological and political, from the theoretical to the applied, and from the cognitive/experimental to the clinical. While few social psychology programs have the number and kind of faculty required to staff such a training program themselves, most social psychology programs exist within a larger department of specialized faculty, some of whom perhaps have interests in phenomena that stem from or can be related to social psychological phenomena. Research discussions and collaborations among such faculty and their students might not only constitute a rich training environment but yield new insights into the determinants and functions of, and mechanisms underlying, social psychological phenomena and mental and social problems.

NOTES

1. The NIMH Behavioral Sciences Assessment Panel met during 1987 and 1988 to develop a conceptual framework for the advancement of research in the behavioral sciences (New Frontiers in the Behavioral Sciences and Mental Health, 1989). The panel members included Marilyn Brewer, Glen Edler, Walter Kintsch, Lewis Lipsitt, Martha McClintock, Anne Petersen (chair), Robert Plomin, David Reiss, and Arnold Sameroff.

2. Of course, phenomena such as maternal defense and territoriality can be examined at multiple levels as well, consistent with the suggestion that multilevel integrative analyses can inform a wide variety of phenomena that manifest in a sociocultural context or level of analysis.

3. Similarly, if Ψ is multiply determined by synergistic variables (see Equation 5) that coexist in the laboratory but not typically in nonlaboratory settings, then a "generalizing problem" will again be encountered. The resolution of this generalizing problem will again rest on insight into the multiply determined nature of Ψ.

REFERENCES

Ader, R. (1981). *Psychoneuroimmunology*. New York: Academic Press.

Allport, G. W. (1947). Scientific models and human morals. *Psychological Review, 54*, 182–192.

Allport, G. W. (1968). The historical background of modern social psychology. In G. Lindzey & E. Aronson (Eds.), *The handbook of social psychology* (Vol. 1, pp. 1–80). Reading, MA: Addison-Wesley. (Original work published 1954)

Andersen, B. L. (1986). *Women with cancer: Psychological perspectives*. New York: Springer-Verlag.

Appley, M. H. (1990, Winter). Time for reintegration? *Science Agenda*, pp. 12–13.

Arvey, R. D., Bouchard, T. J., Segal, N. L., & Abraham, L. M. (1989). Job satisfaction: Environmental and genetic components. *Journal of Applied Psychology, 74*, 187–192.

Baldwin, M. J. (1894). The origin of emotional expressions. *Psychological Review, 1*, 610–623.

Boorstin, D. J. (1983). The discoverers: *A history of man's search to know his world and himself*. London: J. M. Dent & Sons Ltd.

Cacioppo, J. T., & Petty, R. E. (1986). Social processes. In M. G. H. Coles, E. Donchin, & S. W. Porges (Eds.), *Psychophysiology: Systems, processes, and applications* (pp. 646–679). New York: Guilford Press.

Cacioppo, J. T., Petty, R. E., & Tassinary, L. G. (1989). Social psychophysiology: A new look. *Advances in Experimental Social Psychology, 22*, 39–91.

Cacioppo, J. T., & Tassinary, L. G. (1990a). Centenary of William James' *Principles of Psychology:* From the chaos of mental life to the science of psychology. *Personality and Social Psychology Bulletin, 16*, 601–611.

Cacioppo, J. T., & Tassinary, L. G. (1990b). Inferring psychological significance from physiological signals. *American Psychologist, 45*, 16–28.

Carver, C. S., & Scheier, M. F. (1990). Origins and functions of positive and negative affect: A control process view. *Psychological Review, 97*, 19–35.

Churchland, P. S., & Sejnowski, T. J. (1988). Perspectives on cognitive neuroscience. *Science, 242*, 741–745.

Craik, F. I. M., & Lockhart, R. S. (1972). Levels of processing: A framework for memory research. *Journal of Verbal Learning and Verbal Behavior, 11*, 671–684.

Gormezano, I., & Wasserman, E. A. (in press). *Learning and memory: The behavioral and biological substrates.* Hillsdale, NJ: Erlbaum.

Haber, S. N., & Barchas, P. R. (1983). The regulatory effect of social rank on behavior after amphetamine administration. In P. R. Barchas (Ed.), *Social hierarchies: Essays toward a sociophysiological perspective* (pp. 119–132). Westport, CT: Greenwood Press.

James, W. (1950). *Principles of psychology* (Vol. 1). New York: Dover Publications. (Original work published 1890)

James, W. (1894). The physical basis of emotion. *Psychological Review, 1*, 516–529.

Kennedy, S., Glaser, R., & Kiecolt-Glaser, J. (1990). Psychoneuroimmunology. In J. T. Cacioppo & L. G. Tassinary (Eds.), *Principles of psychophysiology: Physical, social, and inferential elements* (pp. 177–190). New York: Cambridge University Press.

Lorion, R. P. (1991). Prevention and public health: Psychology's response to the nation's health care crisis. *American Psychologist, 46*, 516–519.

Markus, H. R., & Kitayama, S. (1991). Culture and the self: Implications for cognition, emotion, and motivation. *Psychological Review, 98*, 224–253.

Marr, D. (1982). *Vision: A computational investigation into the human representation and processing of visual information.* San Francisco: Freeman.

McClelland, D. C. (1989). Motivational factors in health and disease. *American Psychologist, 44*, 675–683.

McGuire, W. J. (1968). The nature of attitudes and attitude change. In G. Lindzey & E. Aronson (Eds.), *The handbook of social psychology* (Vol. 3, pp. 136–314). Reading, MA: Addison-Wesley.

Morton, J. (1991). The bankruptcy of everyday thinking. *American Psychologist, 46*, 32–33.

National Institute of Mental Health. (1989). *New frontiers in the behavioral sciences and mental health: An assessment.* Working paper, Rockville, MD: Behavioral Sciences Research Branch, Division of Basic Sciences.

Petty, R. E., & Cacioppo, J. T. (1986). *Communication and pesuasion: Central and peripheral routes to attitude change.* New York: Springer-Verlag.

Plomin, R. (1989). Environment and genes: Determinants of behavior. *American Psychologist, 44,* 105–111.

Price, R. H., Cowen, E. L., Lorion, R. P., & Ramos-McKay, J. (Eds.). (1988). *Fourteen ounces of prevention: A casebook for practitioners.* Washington, DC: American Psychological Association.

Roitt, I., Brostoff, J., & Male, D. (1985). *Immunology.* St. Louis: Mosby.

Seeman, J. (1989). Toward a model of positive health. *American Psychologist, 44,* 1099–1109.

Shaw, R., & Turvey, M. T. (1981). Coalitions as models for ecosystems: A realist perspective on perceptual organization. In M. Kubovy & J. R. Pomerantz (Eds.), *Perceptual organization* (pp. 343–415). Hillsdale, NJ: Erlbaum.

Staats, A. W. (1989). Unificationism: Philosophy for the modern disunified science of psychology. *Philosophical Psychology, 2,* 143–164.

Steiner, J. E. (1979). Human facial expression in response to taste and smell stimulation. *Advances in Child Development and Behavior, 13,* 257–295.

Tolman, E. C. (1959). Principles of purposive behavior. In S. Koch (Ed.), *Psychology: A study of a science* (pp. 92–157). New York: McGraw-Hill.

U.S. Department of Health, Education, and Welfare. (1979). *Healthy people: The Surgeon General's report on health promotion and disease prevention* (Report No. 017-001-00416-2). Washington, DC: U.S. Government Printing Office.

Weiss, P. (1941). Self-differentiation of the basic patterns of coordination. *Comparative Psychology Monographs, 17*(4).

Zillmann, D. (1984). *Connections between sex and aggression.* Hillsdale, NJ: Erlbaum.